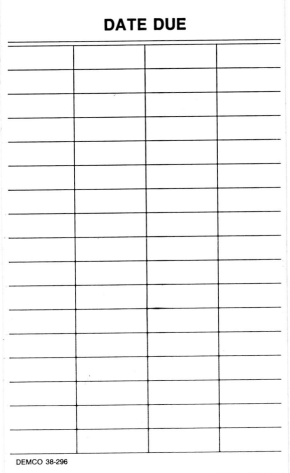

DATE DUE

DEMCO 38-296

REFUGEES IN INTER-WAR EUROPE

REFUGEES IN INTER-WAR EUROPE

The Emergence of a Regime

CLAUDENA M. SKRAN

CLARENDON PRESS · OXFORD
1995

n Street, Oxford OX2 6DP
rk
ok Bombay
Salaam Delhi
Florence Hong Kong Istanbul Karachi
Kuala Lumpur Madras Madrid Melbourne
Mexico City Nairobi Paris Singapore
Taipei Tokyo Toronto
and associated companies in
Berlin Ibadan

Oxford is a trade mark of Oxford University Press

Published in the United States
by Oxford University Press Inc., New York

British Library Cataloguing in Publication Data
Data available

Library of Congress Cataloging in Publication Data
Skran, Claudena M.
Refugees in inter-war Europe : the emergence of a regime /
Claudena M. Skran.
Includes bibliographical references.
1. Refugees—Europe—History—20th century. 2. Refugees—
Government policy—Europe—History—20th century. 3. Europe—
Emigration and immigration—History—20th century. I. Title.
HV640.4.E8S57 1994 362.87'094'0904—dc20 94-25052
ISBN 0-19-827392-4

1 3 5 7 9 10 8 6 4 2

Typeset by Graphicraft Typesetters Ltd., Hong Kong

Printed in Great Britain
on acid-free paper by
Bookcraft (Bath) Ltd.
Midsomer Norton, Avon

To D.E.D.

PREFACE

THE original idea for this book arose out of discussions I had with the late Hedley Bull, Montague Burton Professor of International Relations at Oxford. A scholar who was interested in many facets of international relations, Bull first suggested to me that I investigate the refugee issue for my M. Phil. thesis. Since then, I have benefited from the insights and assistance of many people. The late R. J. Vincent, my supervisor for my doctoral thesis, was a great inspiration to me. He first introduced me to human rights, a subject he had written on and cared deeply about. His untimely departure has been a great loss to all his students and colleagues, and to the study of international politics. I am also indebted to two others at Oxford for supervising me at earlier stages of my work: the late Professor Joseph Frankel, a political refugee from Poland himself, and J. P. D. Dunbabin of St Edmund Hall.

Barbara Harrell-Bond, co-ordinator of the Refugee Studies Programme (RSP) at Oxford, has encouraged me at all stages of my work. The RSP, which she founded, is unique in that it seeks to bring together scholars, practitioners, and refugees in the hope of improving refugee assistance world-wide. I am particularly fortunate to have had the opportunity to work with Ahmed Kardawi, Philip Ramaga, and many others associated with the RSP.

A number of scholars of international relations gave me useful advice on regimes and other theoretical aspects of this study, especially Esther Brimmer, Michael Doyle, Chong-do Hah, Gil Loescher, Adam Roberts, Michael G. Schechter, and James C. Sperling. I am grateful to historians Steven Beller, William Bremer, Michael Hittle, Peter Pulzer, and Kenneth Waltzer for their insights into the Inter-war Period. I particularly enjoyed sharing this project with others interested in the League of Nations, including Martin Dubin, Betty Sargent, and Anique van Ginneken.

I would especially like to thank Dorrit Friedlander and Rudolf Uhlman for sharing their experiences as refugees with me.

Financially, I am indebted to the Rhodes Trust for funding the initial three years of my studies at Oxford; to the Gilbert Murray

Trust for helping me to finance my research at the League of Nations in Geneva; and to Lawrence University for support while I converted my dissertation into a book manuscript.

While doing research for this book, I had the pleasure of working in libraries throughout Europe and North America. In doing so, I received the benefit of the knowledge and experience of many librarians. I would particularly like to thank the Documents Librarians at the Bodleian Library, Oxford, and Sven Wetlander of the League of Nations Archives in Geneva.

In preparing this manuscript, I owe my thanks to Barbara Toman and Gretchen Revie, for editing; to my research assistant, Susan Peter, for her valuable assistance in typing and proof-reading to Priga Udeshi, Rustom Kandawalla, and Vicki Koessl, for help in preparing the index; and to Liz Cronmiller, for keeping Natalie entertained so that her mother could type.

Finally, I would like to thank my parents, Dale L. and E. Orlean Skran, and my husband, David E. Duncombe, for their financial and moral support.

While I am indebted to many people for their help in preparing this book, the ideas and responsibility for them are entirely my own.

C.M.S.

Appleton, Wis.
February 1994

CONTENTS

LIST OF TABLES

LIST OF ABBREVIATIONS

Annals	*Annals of the American Academy of Political and Social Science*
ARC	American Red Cross
BFO	British Foreign Office
CP	Cecil Papers
GRSC	Greek Refugee Settlement Commission
ICRC	International Committee of the Red Cross
IGCR	Intergovernmental Committee for Refugees
IGO	intergovernmental organization
ILO	International Labour Organization
JDC	American Jewish Joint Distribution Committee
JGM	James G. McDonald Papers
LNA	League of Nations Archives
LNTS	*League of Nations Treaty Series*
NBKR	Noel-Baker Papers
NER	Near East Relief
NP	Nansen Papers
OAU	Organization of African Unity
PVO	private voluntary organization
RM	Reichsmark
RSP	Refugee Studies Programme, University of Oxford
UNHCR	United Nations High Commissioner for Refugees
UNTS	*United Nations Treaty Series*

Refugees: A Human Problem
in a World of States

DESPITE the end of the Cold War, the refugee issue shows no signs of disappearing. In fact, the number of refugees—people who flee their home countries because of war or persecution and seek safety in another—is actually increasing. One year after the fall of the Berlin Wall, the United Nations estimated that there were seventeen million refugees world-wide, more than double the number a decade earlier.[1] Whether they are found on crowded trains escaping Bosnia, on leaky boats in the South China Sea, or near starvation in the mountains of Iraq, refugees are living reminders of the conflict and injustice present in the world today. Taken individually, each refugee has his or her own story of personal tragedy to tell. Taken together, refugees constitute a humanitarian problem on an immense scale.

The humanitarian needs of refugees are legion. In contemporary refugee movements, it is not unusual for thousands, or even millions, of refugees to flee their homes with few possessions. Upon arrival in host countries, refugees require food, shelter, clothing, and medical care. After their emergency needs are met, permanent arrangements are required. In some instances, refugees may return to their home countries within a relatively short period of time. For the vast majority, however, their initial flight is just the beginning of a protracted period of waiting before they can begin new lives elsewhere. Eventually, this limbo may end with the refugees' return to their home countries. However, if political circumstances do not permit repatriation, alternative solutions are demanded. This necessitates either finding a country willing to accept the refugees permanently or fully integrating them into the country in which they initially found asylum.

[1] According to the UNHCR, there were approximately 8.2 million refugees in 1980, and 17 million in 1990.

2   A HUMAN PROBLEM IN A WORLD OF STATES

Refugees, however, are not only a humanitarian concern. Without exception, a major refugee flow from one country to another has important political repercussions. Within host countries, the arrival of large groups of refugees may disrupt an established pattern, such as a fragile ethnic balance or a stable economy. The financial costs of refugee relief, maintenance, and resettlement can be enormous, and resentment about spending money on foreigners may trigger outbreaks of xenophobia on the part of the native population. The presence of refugees in a host country can also complicate its relations with the refugee-producing country. Officially, accepting a refugee is a purely humanitarian response. In fact, assisting refugees is often interpreted by refugee-producing countries as a hostile act. If the influx involves armed refugees, it may embroil the host country in violent disputes with the country of origin.

In international politics, refugees can become pawns in global power struggles, and refugee assistance can be used to discredit an opponent. The strong support of the United States and Western Europe for refugees from Eastern Europe during the Cold War is a case in point. While the resolution of the East–West conflict has ended this flow and made possible the return of some refugees to their home countries, it has also generated new problems. In the former Soviet Union, Yugoslavia, and elsewhere in countries once under Communist rule, fighting between rival ethnic groups has forced millions to flee their homes. Moreover, the end of the Cold War has done little to resolve other sources of international tensions, such as those between the rich Northern states and the poor Southern ones. One manifestation of this conflict is the rejection by developed countries of asylum-seekers from developing countries on the grounds that they are merely economic migrants and not entitled to the special assistance given to refugees: the rejection of most Haitian refugees by the United States is but one example. Environmental degradation also continues and in fact is becoming more severe. In the future, famine, desertification, drought, and other disasters threaten to produce millions more refugees.[2]

[2] Jodi L. Jacobson, *Environmental Refugees: A Yardstick of Habitability*, Worldwatch Paper no. 86 (Nov. 1988).

Refugees also present a challenge to conventional ways of thinking about international politics. Since the Treaty of Westphalia in 1648, the international system has been made up of sovereign, territorially-based political units called states. Traditionally, students of international politics have focused on the role of states within this system, not on that of individuals or groups within states. Refugees do not fit neatly into the state-centric paradigm, which assumes that each individual belongs to a state. By severing their ties with their home countries, refugees can no longer depend on the diplomatic protection of their governments; yet they do not automatically and immediately become part of another state. Thus, refugees fall between the cracks of the state system: they are individuals operating internationally, without direct ties to one particular state.

This is a book about refugees, specifically about refugees in inter-war Europe and international responses to them.[3] In Part I, the causes and consequences of refugee movements throughout the twentieth century are explored. In Part II, international responses to European refugee movements from 1919 until 1939 are presented and analysed. In Part III, the impact of international efforts on government policy towards refugees is evaluated. The major argument of this book is that international assistance efforts of the inter-war era constituted an international regime, and this regime had—and continues to have—a significant impact on refugee policy.

In Chapter 1, I begin with an argument about why refugees first emerged as an international issue after the First World War, and continue in Chapter 2 with a description of the origins and dimensions of the major refugee groups of the inter-war years. In linking inter-war and contemporary refugee movements, this work challenges the popularly held notion that refugee problems have significantly changed since 1945. Contemporary refugee crises are

[3] Although there were large population movements outside Europe during the 1920s and 1930s, they are outside the scope of this work because they took place largely within one country or colony. For instance, an estimated 30 million Chinese were internally displaced by the Sino-Japanese conflict from 1937 until 1939. See Walter Adams, 'Extent and Nature of the World Refugee Problem', *Annals of the American Academy of Political and Social Science*, 203 (May 1939), 26; Cyrus H. Peake, 'Refugees in the Far East', *Annals*, 203 (May 1939), 55.

4 A HUMAN PROBLEM IN A WORLD OF STATES

said to be worse than those of the past because unprecedented numbers of refugees face long periods of exile, primarily in Third World countries. American diplomat William Smyser, for instance, contends that 'the second half of the twentieth century has witnessed an unprecedented explosion in the number and impact of refugees'.[4] In a comprehensive study of refugees and world politics, Leon Gordenker argues that recent refugee movements present 'a contrast with earlier migrations' because of unparalleled numbers of refugees, their location in the developing world, and the growth of transnational networks to assist them.[5]

It is true that in the last decade of the Cold War era the majority of people considered to be refugees were located in the developing world of Asia, Africa, and Latin America.[6] But the notion that the contemporary refugee crisis is unique lacks a historical perspective and neglects this important fact: mass refugee movements are neither new nor exclusive to specific regions. They have been an enduring and global issue throughout the twentieth century. Before the Second World War, the European continent experienced refugee flows similar to those taking place in Eastern Europe and the developing world today. Those refugee movements began in the early twentieth century, when the Balkan wars forced several hundred thousand people to flee their homes.[7] The two World Wars caused even more disruption. The Second World War alone displaced a staggering number of people—more than thirty million. Even during the relatively peaceful Inter-war Period, millions of people became refugees, including Germans, Poles, Hungarians, Russians, Greeks, Turks, Armenians, Bulgarians, Jews, Italians, and Spaniards.[8] In 1926, for instance, an estimated 9.5 million were considered refugees. While the number of refugees is

[4] Smyser also argues that refugee problems are different from those of the past because of the extended period of time they spend in exile, and because their location has moved from Europe to the Third World. W. R. Smyser, 'Refugees: A Never-Ending Story', *Foreign Affairs*, 64 (Fall 1985), 154–68.

[5] Leon Gordenker, *Refugees in International Politics* (New York: Columbia University Press, 1987), 49–59.

[6] In 1990, for instance, 0.7 per cent of the world's refugees lived in Latin America, 33 per cent in Africa, and 62.5 per cent in Asia. US Committee for Refugees, *World Refugee Survey* (Washington, DC: US Committee for Refugees, 1990).

[7] Sir John Hope Simpson, *The Refugee Problem: Report of a Survey* (London: Oxford University Press, 1939), 551.

[8] Michael R. Marrus, *The Unwanted: European Refugees in the Twentieth Century* (New York: Oxford University Press, 1985), 51 and 297.

approximately the same as that of the refugee population of 1980, it is a proportionally larger figure because the world's population doubled in the mean time.[9]

Even when pre-1945 refugee movements are considered, it is often with the stipulation that European refugees are fundamentally different from non-European ones. In particular, the typical European refugee is said to have been an individual escaping political persecution or interstate war, while his or her Third World counterpart is part of a mass movement fleeing political and economic breakdown brought on by civil war or social unrest. While it is true to say that each refugee movement—and each refugee—is distinct, the differences between European and non-European refugees have been greatly exaggerated. Certainly, Cold War refugees tend to fit the profile of an individual facing political persecution. These refugees, however, constituted only a fraction of European refugees in the twentieth century. In fact, there are remarkable similarities between the refugee movements of interwar Europe and those taking place in the developing world since 1945 and in former Communist countries since the collapse of the Soviet Union.

First, mass refugee movements of this century have been generated primarily by common historical processes which have affected the entire international system. The development of highly destructive military technology and the advent of total war have meant that international conflicts have affected entire populations, not just soldiers. As a result, modern conflicts—be they interstate wars, such as the First and Second World Wars, or internationalized civil wars, such as the Salvadorean or Nicaraguan civil wars—are very likely to produce large numbers of refugees. In addition, throughout this century, when multi-ethnic empires have been transformed into homogeneous nation-states, mass refugee movements have been an unfortunate by-product. This process often involves a combination of economic pressure and political persecution, thus prompting refugees to leave for a variety of reasons. After the First World War, attempts to create new national states forced millions to become refugees, and the Nazis' attempt to

---

[9] In 1930 the world's population was approximately 2 billion while by 1980 the population had more than doubled to 4.4 billion. *Encyclopedia Americana* (Danbury, Conn.: Grolier, 1988), 403; *Information Please Almanac* (Boston: Houghton Mifflin, 1991), 136.

achieve purity forced thousands of Jews into exile. The Serbian policy of 'ethnic cleansing' is not unlike these earlier policies, and the results have been similar: refugees. In the developing world, ethnic violence, civil war, and refugee flows have all been a part of the nation-building process after decolonization.

Though varying in time and place, refugee movements throughout this century have generated analogous types of refugee problems. Because of the erection of immigration barriers world-wide, travelling to a safe haven has become more difficult than in the nineteenth century. For some refugees, even finding a place of permanent asylum has proved nearly impossible. The Vietnamese refugees confined in closed camps in Hong Kong in the late 1980s are reminiscent of the Jewish refugees who desperately tried to find countries to accept them in the late 1930s. Even when refugees have found a country to take them, problems continue. Generally, the refugees have found shelter in relatively poor countries; even in rich countries, refugees are often perceived as being a financial burden. While repatriation is considered the preferred solution to refugee problems, it often proves impossible, at least in the short run. Thus, host countries have to cope with large groups of impoverished refugees for indefinite periods of time. As early as 1922, international refugee workers complained that Russian and Greek refugees languished in camps for as long as two years. This would be just a foreshadowing of the situation fifty years later, when Afghan refugees would remain in camps for more than five years. As a consequence of these factors, a continuing need developed for durable solutions which are group-oriented, not simply directed at individual refugees, and tailored to the economic needs of host countries.

Given the many parallels between inter-war and contemporary refugees, it should not be surprising that current international assistance programmes have their origins in inter-war Europe. Nevertheless, most studies of international assistance to refugees begin their stories with the formation of the International Refugee Organization (IRO) after the Second World War.[10] This

[10] For a history of the IRO, see Louise Holborn, *The International Refugee Organization, a Specialized Agency of the United Nations. Its History and Work: 1946–1952* (London: Oxford University Press, 1956); John G. Stoessinger, *The Refugee and the World Community* (Minneapolis: University of Minnesota Press, 1956).

approach ignores the fact that organized efforts for refugees on an international level began shortly after the First World War, when the League of Nations appointed the first High Commissioner for Refugees. From this beginning an international refugee regime developed to assist and protect refugees and continued until the outbreak of war in 1939. After a hiatus during the Second World War, refugee assistance first resumed in earnest under the direction of the International Refugee Organization (IRO) and, after 1951, under the United Nations High Commissioner for Refugees (UNHCR). Although created to deal solely with refugees from the Second World War, the UNHCR adapted its mandate to include the growing numbers of refugees arising from decolonization and civil strife in Eastern Europe, Africa, Asia, and Latin America. Today, the UNHCR is a major source of international protection and assistance for the millions of refugees scattered throughout the globe, and is at the centre of the current international refugee regime.[11]

My approach to the subject of international responses to refugee movements is inherently multidisciplinary. From the field of international relations, I make use of a theoretical concept, that of an international regime. This term refers to the formal or informal arrangements created by states to deal with a particular issue: in this case, refugees. Regimes are inspired by principles; they uphold standards and embody rules, usually in the concrete form of international law. They are often centred on formal institutions, such as a United Nations agency, and decision-making within them involves both governments and non-governmental organizations. While a regime framework precludes some of the depth possible in a study of the refugee policy of a particular state or refugee group, it provides a broader perspective than that found in more focused studies.[12] Using a regime framework allows us to

---

[11] The most comprehensive history of the UNHCR is given in Louise W. Holborn, *Refugees: A Problem of Our Time: The Work of the United Nations High Commissioner for Refugees, 1951–1972* (Metuchen, NJ: Scarecrow Press, 1975).

[12] On national responses to Jewish and other refugees from Nazi Germany, see A. J. Sherman, *Island Refuge: Britain and Refugees from the Third Reich: 1933–1939* (London: Paul Elek, 1973); Gerhard Hirschfeld (ed.), *Exile in Great Britain* (Leamington Spa: Berg Publishers, 1984); David S. Wyman, *Paper Walls: America and the Refugee Crisis, 1938–1941* (New York: Pantheon Books, 1985); Michael Blakeney, *Australia and the Jewish Refugees, 1933–1948* (Australia: Croom Helm, 1985); Timothy P. Maga, *America, France, and the European Refugee Problem,*

analyse how different governments responded to successive waves of refugees over a period of twenty years, something relatively few historical or political works do.

Another benefit of using international regime theory is that it facilitates our understanding of why international co-operative efforts begin. The long history of an international refugee regime makes the refugee issue unique in the field of human rights. Human rights did not receive widespread recognition as a legitimate international concern until after the Holocaust and the conclusion of the Second World War. Before then, a government's treatment of its citizens within its own territory was deemed to be a purely domestic affair. Although human rights are officially recognized in the United Nations Charter and the Universal Declaration of Human Rights,[13] international mechanisms designed to promote and protect them still remain embryonic.[14] In comparison, the international institutions and procedures designed to assist and protect refugees are highly developed. The reasons for the emergence of the inter-war refugee regime is a topic which will be taken up in Chapter 3.

Using regime theory also allows us to consider the degree to which regimes 'matter', a subject of great debate within the field of international relations. This is an important discussion: if regimes matter, the implication is that states are driven not simply by short-term calculations of national interest, but by international norms and rules. In this book, the impact of the international refugee regime on governmental policy towards refugees in four areas is assessed: the securing of legal protection (Chapter 4); the

1933–1947 (New York: Garland, 1985). For information on Canadian responses to Russian, German, Mennonite, and other refugees, see Gerald E. Dirks, *Canada's Refugee Policy: Indifference or Opportunism?* (Montreal: McGill-Queen's University Press, 1977). On French responses to Spanish refugees, see Louis Stein, *Beyond Death and Exile: The Spanish Republicans in France, 1939–55* (Cambridge, Mass.: Harvard University Press, 1979). On the treatment of Greek, Turkish, and Bulgarian refugees in the Near East, see Stephen P. Ladas, *The Exchange of Minorities: Bulgaria, Greece, and Turkey* (New York: Macmillan, 1932). For information specifically on Greece and Greek refugees, see Dimitri Pentzopoulus, *The Balkan Exchange of Minorities and its Impact upon Greece* (Paris: Mouton, 1962).

[13] The preamble of the UN Charter reaffirms 'faith in fundamental human rights'. Article I (3) gives 'promoting and encouraging respect for human rights and fundamental freedoms for all without distinction as to race, sex, language, or religion' as one of the purposes of the UN.

[14] Jack Donnelly, 'International Human Rights: A Regime Analysis', *International Organization*, 40 (Summer 1986), 599–642.

provision of durable solutions (Chapter 5); the breakdown of im-migration barriers (Chapter 6); and the prevention of refugee movements (Chapter 7). The position taken here is that regimes can both constrain and promote state behaviour towards refugees, but only in certain circumstances. The object of Chapter 8 is to determine those conditions under which regimes can have a sig-nificant impact on refugee policy, and those in which they do not.

Although this book deals with a topic familiar to students of European history between the two World Wars, it utilizes a less familiar approach. Much of the literature on refugees of the inter-war era concentrates on the failure of international efforts to as-sist Jewish refugees from the Third Reich in 1938 and 1939. The ill treatment of these refugees is often blamed on the League of Nations, an organization whose record on refugees has been termed 'regrettably inadequate and confused'.[15] There is no doubt that the response of the League of Nations and governments to the refugee crisis of 1938–9 could have been dramatically improved. But to base an evaluation of the League's refugee assistance in the entire Inter-war Period on the experiences of its final two years, a period when the entire organization was disintegrating, is ex-tremely short-sighted. Doing so ignores the many successful ven-tures in assistance carried out for refugees, including Russians, Greeks, Bulgarians, Turks, Armenians, and even many Jews. Moreover, it neglects to take into account the lasting legacy of refugee assistance efforts begun during the 1920s and 1930s. It is the premiss of this book that, rather than being seen as a failure, these first twenty years of international refugee assistance should be recognized as a time of great creativity and innovation, a time when much was accomplished with minimal resources, and a time when millions of refugees were helped to begin new lives. This work is, in fact, a tribute to the 'idealists', a generation of leaders who created and supported the League of Nations in those tumultuous years.

In this book, I also attempt to contribute to the field of refugee studies by adding to the understanding of contemporary refu-gee problems. As argued above, the refugees of inter-war Europe were not as different from other refugees as people have been led

---

[15] F. P. Walters, *A History of the League of Nations* (London: Oxford University Press, 1960), 189. Walters' evaluation of the League's refugee work has been ac-cepted by other authors. See, for instance, Marrus, *The Unwanted*, 90.

to believe. Moreover, the Inter-war Period is particularly important because it was during this time that an international refugee regime was first created. Much of its history, both successes and failures, has been largely forgotten or ignored, however, probably because of its association with the discredited League of Nations and because of preoccupations with more recent refugee crises. In this case, a lack of institutional memory has meant that refugee practitioners have had to reinvent the wheel.[16] For instance, in the early 1980s government and UNHCR officials began to stress the need for refugee aid to be linked to development assistance, resulting in an international conference, ICARA II, on development and African refugees.[17] While presented as a 'new' idea at the time, in fact the notion was a long-delayed revival of some of the ideas behind the League of Nations—sponsored settlement programmes for refugees in Greece and Bulgaria in the 1920s. Recent studies of international organizations have also shown that, for progress to be made over time, governments and non-governmental actors must learn from the past.[18] In part, this work is an attempt to contribute to international learning about refugee issues.

[16] This is the idea of Barbara Harrell-Bond, co-ordinator of the RSP.
[17] Robert F. Gorman, *Coping with Africa's Refugee Burden: A Time for Solutions* (Dordrecht: Martinus Nijhoff, 1987).
[18] See *International Organization*, 46 (Winter 1992). Special issue on knowledge, power, and international policy coordination.

PART I

Refugees and the Need for a Regime

1

The Emergence of Refugees as an Issue in International Politics

INTRODUCTION

PEOPLE who flee their homes to seek safety elsewhere are not new to the twentieth century: they have existed since the dawn of time. Yet the application of the term 'refugee' to people who flee their home countries for another is only as old as the international state system—about 400 years old. According to the *OED*, the term 'refugee' was first applied to the French Huguenots, victims of religious persecution who fled France after the revocation of the Edict of Nantes in 1695—only one group among the many victims of religious persecution of the early modern period. A century later the same term was applied to British loyalists after the American Revolution. In the nineteenth century political exiles from Tsarist Russia, known by the fashionable term *émigrés*, populated the cities of Europe. The forced population movements of the early twentieth century brought the word 'refugee' back into popular use, partly because it became the preferred term used by the vast array of international and national relief agencies.[1] The term has continued to be used for the millions uprooted in the post-1945 period.

Despite the long history of forced migration, twentieth-century refugee movements significantly differ from earlier ones in this important respect: they attracted the attention of political leaders and became international issues.[2] Modern-day refugees drew the attention of policy-makers because they numbered millions, not thousands. These mass movements were, in turn, the result of

---

[1] Paul Tabori, *The Anatomy of Exile* (London: Harrap, 1972), 24.
[2] Louise Holborn, *The International Refugee Organization, a Specialized Agency of the United Nations. Its History and Work: 1946–1952* (London: Oxford University Press, 1956), 4–5; and Michael R. Marrus, *The Unwanted: European Refugees in the Twentieth Century* (New York: Oxford University Press, 1985), 14.

broad political and social changes that affected the entire international state system, not simply developments within a particular country. Once in existence, refugee movements became the focus of international attention because of the problems they created. After 1919 the rapid development of immigration controls worldwide made it difficult for refugees to find new, permanent homes. Some found locating a temporary place of asylum virtually impossible. For the refugees who did find a new country, some of the same factors which forced them to flee in the first place often made it difficult for them ever to return to their home countries, or to fully integrate into the ones that offered them asylum. In addition, increased governmental support for social welfare meant that societies became reluctant to take on financial obligations to non-citizens, including refugees. For these reasons, refugees posed unique problems for policy-makers in the twentieth century.

THE ORIGINS OF MASS REFUGEE MOVEMENTS

In terms of size and scope, refugee movements in inter-war Europe dwarfed all previous ones. They were mass migrations that significantly affected both the refugee-producing countries and the refugee-receiving ones. Included in these movements were such diverse ethnic groups as Germans, Poles, Baltic peoples, Magyars, Russians, Greeks, Turks, Bulgarians, Armenians, Jews, Czechs, Italians, and Spaniards. The refugees sought safety in every country in Europe, and in many other countries around the world. Inter-war refugee movements contrasted sharply with previous European experiences with refugees. Although from the fifteenth to the seventeenth century the European continent experienced large movements of religious refugees, the nineteenth century was relatively free from such troubles.[3] During this period the typical refugee was a revolutionary exile. Exiles from Poland after 1830,

[3] The best-known refugee group of this period were the 200,000 French Huguenots who left Catholic France following the revocation of the Edict of Nantes in 1685. Other refugees left neighbouring countries. In 1492 Catholic Spain expelled approximately 120,000–150,000 unconverted Jews. Beginning in 1609, the Spanish deported approximately 275,000 Muslims to North Africa. Spain also forced out Protestants from the Spanish Low Countries (now Belgium). From 1577 until the 1630s about 115,000 people, or fourteen per cent of the entire population, emigrated to what is now the Netherlands. Similarly, in England, the Crown also

from Germany and Italy after 1848, from France after 1871, and
from Tsarist Russia throughout the century could be found in
London, Berlin, Geneva, Paris, and other major cities. These refugees numbered thousands and were relatively affluent; consequently, they did not constitute a relief problem.[4] Among the
refugees were such distinguished persons as Louis Philippe, Prince
Metternich, Victor Hugo, Karl Marx, and Lenin. Despite strong
socialist and anarchist leanings among some refugees, they had
little trouble finding new countries because the liberal states of
Western Europe welcomed them.[5]

In the nineteenth century large population movements took place
in the form of emigration to the New World. Even though some
of these migrants—particularly Eastern European Jews fleeing
pogroms, and Irish escaping the potato famine—exhibited some
of the characteristics of modern refugees, they were labelled as
immigrants. As long as the United States and other countries of
immigration accepted virtually everyone, European governments
did not have to deal with their own refugees. Large population
movements also took place during the First World War. These
flows, however, were temporary and did not create lingering problems; after the war, most refugees simply returned to their homes.
In the Inter-war Period Europe once again began to experience
mass refugee movements. In order to understand the causes of
these movements, they need to be analysed at three different but
interconnected levels: those of the individual, the state, and the
international system.[6]

At the level of the individual, there are as many reasons for
mass movements as there are refugees. A refugee leaves his or her

expelled religious minorities, including Puritans, Quakers, and Irish Catholics.
Aristide Zolberg, 'The Formation of New States as a Refugee-Generating Process',
Annals, 467 (May 1983), 31–4. On religious refugees throughout history, see
Frederick A. Norwood, *Strangers and Exiles: A History of Religious Refugees*,
i–ii (Nashville: Abingdon Press, 1969).

[4] Marrus estimates that 5,000 Polish insurgents fled to France in 1831, at least
20,000 Germans and Italians became refugees after the revolutionary upheaval
of 1848, and 45,000 fled the Paris Commune for England and Belgium. *The
Unwanted*, 15–26.

[5] On the British response, see John Slatter (ed.), *From the Other Shore: Russian
Political Emigrants in Britain, 1880–1917* (London: Frank Cass, 1984).

[6] This typology draws heavily on the analysis of the causes of war given by
Kenneth N. Waltz, *Man, the State and War: A Theoretical Analysis* (New York:
Columbia University Press, 1959).

home voluntarily, albeit under compulsion from outside forces. The decision to flee, rather than to fight or die, is a personal one. The 1951 Refugee Convention identifies a refugee as a person who is outside his or her home country because of a 'well-founded fear' of persecution based on race, religion, nationality, membership of a particular social group, or political opinion.[7] This definition identifies persecution, rather than economic breakdown or violent conflict, as the major reason why a refugee leaves his or her home country. In fact, a combination of political, economic, and personal factors actually contribute to a refugee's decision to flee. Although there are many reasons for an individual refugee's flight, our primary concern here is to determine why individuals flee certain states more than others.

Since the beginning of the modern state system in the late seventeenth century, certain types of states have produced more refugees than others. In the words of Sir John Hope Simpson, director of the comprehensive refugee survey undertaken by the Royal Institute of International Affairs in the 1930s, 'the cause of every refugee movement is tyranny of one kind or another, but the forms of tyranny differ'.[8] In the inter-war years a popular explanation for refugee movements blamed the rise of totalitarian governments, those which demand the total allegiance of people to their states. Simpson, for instance, identified the National Socialists in Germany and the Communists in the Soviet Union as two such governments.[9]

This particular explanation, however, has some significant drawbacks. In the case of the Soviet Union, most of the Russian refugees fled during the Russian Civil War, before the Bolsheviks gained full control of the country. After 1922 Soviet authorities virtually stopped emigration.[10] The major human-rights violations of the Stalinist period—including the liquidation of the kulaks, forced collectivization, and the Great Purges—resulted in the deaths of approximately twenty million but produced very few refugees,

[7] 'United Nations Convention Relating to the Status of Refugees, 28 July 1951', *UNTS* 189/2545, art. 1 (2), 152.
[8] Sir John Hope Simpson, *The Refugee Problem: Report of a Survey* (London: Oxford University Press, 1939), 5.
[9] Ibid. 5–6. Holborn, *The International Refugee Organization*, 1, supports this conclusion.
[10] Alan Dowty, *Closed Borders: The Contemporary Assault on Freedom of Movement* (New Haven, Conn.: Yale University Press, 1987), 69.

primarily because the Soviet government maintained a no-exit policy.[11] Nazi Germany's persecution of political dissidents and Jews did create a mass exodus before the outbreak of war in 1939, but the same was not true of other Fascist governments. Mussolini's Italy produced relatively few refugees and, ironically, Italy became a haven for German Jewish refugees until 1938. After Franco's rise to power in Spain, 400,000 people did leave the country, but they did so primarily as a result of their defeat in the Civil War. The actual historical record, then, contradicts the simple explanation that links totalitarianism and refugee flows.[12]

A better explanation of the above refugee flows is that revolutionary changes and major political upheavals within a country have become more likely to produce a mass exodus because a larger percentage of the country's people participate in them. In the nineteenth century autocratic governments repressed challenges to their authority, but usually forced only a small number of revolutionaries to leave the country. The development and proliferation of modern military technology has meant that 'violent clashes over the social order', as well as interstate war, have the potential for extreme destruction.[13] Military conflict itself can affect both soldiers and civilians. Numbered among the refugees from the Russian Revolution and Spanish Civil War were 'cross-fire refugees', people fleeing from two opposing sides in a conflict. Moreover, if economic breakdown takes place as a result of conflict, famine and drought victims may join the refugee flow. In this sense, the victims of the Russian and Ukrainian famines of the early 1920s are not unlike the Ethiopians who fled civil war and famine in the mid-1980s.

---

[11] Robert Conquest, *The Great Terror: A Reassessment* (New York: Oxford University Press, 1990), 485–6.

[12] This explanation, however, remained a popular one in the Cold War period. Until 1980 the United States government officially defined a refugee as a person fleeing 'from a communist dominated country or area'. This attitude was still reflected among American policy-makers even after the repeal of the law in 1980. During his tenure as Vice-President, George Bush identified 'the Soviet Union, its sympathizers, or its clients' as major causes of refugee movements world-wide. George Bush, 'Remarks on United States Refugee Policy', in Joseph M. Kitagawa (ed.), *American Refugee Policy: Ethical and Religious Reflections* (New York: Presiding Bishops Fund for World Relief, The Episcopal Church, 1984), 23.

[13] This term was coined by Zolberg *et al.* in their comprehensive study of the causes of refugee movements in the developing world. Aristide Zolberg *et al.*, *Escape from Violence: Conflict and the Refugee Crisis in the Developing World* (New York: Oxford University Press, 1989).

While the theory regarding factors internal to particular countries partly explains the resurgence of mass refugee movements, it fails to explain the largest refugee movements of the Inter-war Period—the approximately two million refugees produced between Turkey, Greece, and Bulgaria. Nor does it explain the numerous refugees created in the wake of the First World War, after the actual fighting had stopped. The most important cause of these refugee flows cannot be found solely in the internal politics of any of these countries, but rather has to do with changes in the very nature of the international system. During the twentieth century the nation-state system, begun in Western Europe more than three hundred years ago, expanded and became global. One feature of this process has been the break-up of empires into independent nation-states. After the Second World War, for instance, decolonization brought an end to the British, French, and other European empires and created numerous new states. This process of nation-state formation has not been entirely peaceful. Aristide Zolberg, a specialist in international migration, argues that 'massive refugee flows are most prominently a concomitant of the secular transformation of a world of empires and of small self-sufficient communities or tribes into a world of national states'.[14] Although Zolberg's primary concern is with explaining refugee movements in the developing world, he stresses that it would be a mistake to conclude that 'the persecution of victim groups is a peculiar by-product of the formation of nation-states in non-Western societies'.[15] Instead, he argues that Europe has experienced the same phenomenon twice previously. The first took place during the fifteenth and sixteenth centuries, when the state system first established itself in Western Europe. In this era, religion, rather than nationality, was the foundation of the state; as a result, religious minorities often became refugees. The second took place during the Inter-war Period, when the Russian, Austro-Hungarian, German, and Ottoman Empires collapsed and nation-states replaced them.

---

[14] Zolberg, 'The Formation of New States', 30. In a later work, *Escape from Violence*, Zolberg revises his thesis to add 'violent changes over the social order' as the other main cause of refugee movements. Unless otherwise noted, the ideas for this section are derived from the original article.

[15] Ibid., 31.

In explaining the refugee-producing process, Zolberg emphasizes the role of the nation-state, a legal and political unit which
incorporates a nation inside its territorial boundaries.[16] In the case
of the Russian and Austro-Hungarian Empires, it proved impossible to organize the ethnically mixed region into viable, homogeneous political units: 'The yawning gap between the formula and
social realities generated enormous tensions', out of which emerged
two groups of victims: minorities and the stateless.[17] Minorities are
people who lived in one nation-state but associated themselves
with a different nationality, usually the dominant nationality in
some other state. Some Magyars, for example, lived in Romania
but associated themselves with Hungary. Of course, minorities had
previously existed; but after the creation of nation-states they
became 'political misfits'. The stateless are people without ties to
any established nation-state. The most prominent stateless group
of the twentieth century was the Jews but there have been others,
including Armenians and gypsies. The stateless faced the greatest
risks because they had no nation-states to defend their rights or to
receive them if they fled from their countries of residence.[18]

According to Zolberg, mass refugee flows are a likely, but not
automatic, result of the creation of nation-states. In fact, governments can create homogeneous states using a variety of methods.
First, governments can attempt to assimilate minorities or to contain them. The United States, for instance, practised both policies
by encouraging the 'Americanization' of European immigrants and
sponsoring the placement of American Indians on reservations. A
government also may provide minorities with some degree of
autonomy. The minorities treaties of the League of Nations, for
instance, attempted to give special protection to minority groups.
On the other hand, governments can suppress, expel, or even
exterminate minority groups in order to achieve homogeneity

---

[16] Hugh Seton-Watson, *Nations and States* (London: Methuen, 1982), 1. See also
Alfred Cobban, *The Nation State and National Self-Determination* (New York:
Thomas Crowell, 1969).   [17] Zolberg, 'The Formation of New States', 28.
[18] Zolberg credits Hannah Arendt for inspiring much of his analysis. See Hannah
Arendt, *The Origins of Totalitarianism* (New York: Harcourt, Brace, 1951), esp.
269–90. Both Zolberg and Arendt define the term 'stateless' in a different way
from its common usage in international law. In international law, a stateless person
is one 'without nationality'. See L. Oppenheim, *International Law: A Treatise*, i
(London: Longmans, Green, 1905), 366.

quickly.[19] If a government follows one of these strategies, all too often a refugee flow will result.

Zolberg details a process by which people in victimized groups become refugees. The starting-point is usually 'triggered by a change of internal or external circumstances; the initial stage takes the form of a generalized political crisis, in the course of which victim groups are especially likely to emerge'. He also points out that the 'formation of nation-states out of the debris of empires usually also entails the abolition of the *ancien régime*, a partial or thoroughgoing revolution, in the course of which entire social strata may come to be viewed as obstacles in the same sense as cultural minorities'. Ironically, Zolberg notes, 'refugees may be the more fortunate segment of the original target, others of whom may be subjected to a worse fate, including not only immobilization but even murder'.

The nation-state formation process also has an international component. Because the process takes place within a region, 'the tensions it generates within any given country interact with those simultaneously experienced by others. The result is heightened tensions between states, often leading to international conflict, which in turn exacerbates the refugee-producing conditions in each state of the region.'[20] If the nation-state formation process leads to interstate war, this too may produce refugees.

What is particularly insightful about Zolberg's analysis is that it explains how internal and systemic forces interact in producing refugee movements. While a specific government may persecute a particular ethnic group, this persecution should be seen as part of a broader historical process affecting many countries. Nazi Germany, for instance, practised particularly brutal policies towards Jews and gypsies, ranging from discrimination to persecution and extermination. But the Nazis were not alone in their pursuit of policies aimed at ridding themselves of what they considered to be undesirable ethnic minorities. These groups comprised a large percentage of the refugees of the 1920s and 1930s.[21] This conclusion is disturbing because it means that refugee movements cannot simply be blamed on non-democratic governments. Instead, it

---

[19] Raymond Pearson, *National Minorities in Eastern Europe, 1848–1945* (London: Macmillan, 1983), 9–11.   [20] Zolberg, 'The Formation of New States', 27–31.
[21] See Joseph S. Roucek, 'Minorities: A Basis of the Refugee Problem', *Annals of the American Academy of Political and Social Science*, 203 (May 1939), 1–16.

implies that a key component of the international system—the belief that the nation-state is the ideal political unit—contributes to the creation of mass refugee movements. At the same time it indicates that the same factor which led to the creation of refugees—the desire to create ethnically homogeneous nation-states—complicates the solutions to refugee problems.

IMMIGRATION RESTRICTIONS AS AN OBSTACLE TO THE RESOLUTION OF REFUGEE PROBLEMS

Although the scale of refugee movements increased in the Inter-war Period, this alone did not generate the perception among policy-makers of a refugee crisis. Larger population movements had taken place with little fanfare in the previous two hundred years. Migration peaked between 1845 and 1924, when fifty million people, primarily Europeans, travelled to the western hemisphere, at a time when the world's population was only about one billion.[22] In the years immediately preceding 1914 over one million Europeans emigrated annually to the United States alone. For these people, migration was a relatively easy task whether they left because of violent conflict, religious persecution, or rural overpopulation: they simply travelled to the New World. If the United States and other countries of immigration had continued to absorb surplus European labour at this rate in the 1920s, the story of inter-war refugees would have been very different. In fact, people forcibly uprooted probably never would have been called refugees at all. But this was not to be the case. Instead, the development of immigration restrictions world-wide erected a new obstacle to the resolution of refugee problems. John Stoessinger sums up the problem in this way: 'What distinguishes the refugee of the twentieth century is the immense difficulty, and often impossibility of finding a new home.'[23]

The abrupt end to the relatively free immigration of the nineteenth century began in the United States and spread elsewhere.

[22] Between 1500 and 1960 the number of Africans and Asians who moved, either freely or by force, is estimated at only fifteen million. Jonas Widgren, 'International Migration and Regional Stability', *International Affairs*, 66/4 (1990), 752.

[23] John G. Stoessinger, *The Refugee and the World Community* (Minneapolis: University of Minnesota Press, 1956), 6.

As a result, migrants found themselves subject to increasing government regulation. The most visible sign of this was the requirement that all international travellers carry a passport, a device for controlling movement across frontiers. Originally introduced as a temporary measure in the First World War, the use of passports continued after the war. Other signs included border controls and the requirement that aliens register upon landing. In addition to these bureaucratic measures, many governments sharply restricted immigration, in terms both of the number and of the ethnic background of those who would be allowed to enter.

In this regard, the United States led the way with the Immigration Acts of 1921 and 1924, both of which constituted a sharp departure from past immigration policy. Although the United States had excluded Chinese immigrants as early as 1882 and Japanese immigrants after 1907, in other respects the United States maintained open borders. The laws of 1921 and 1924 changed existing policy by establishing a quota system designed to limit total immigration to the United States and to ensure a certain ethnic composition. The 1924 quota limited European immigration to only 150,000 people per year, and blatantly favoured immigrants born in northern and western European countries at the expense of those born in southern and eastern European ones: the former received 85 per cent of the quota, and the latter only 15 per cent. The new system gave Great Britain the largest quota, 77,000, while Germany garnered the next largest, 68,000. In contrast, people born in Russia had to emigrate under the Russian quota of 2,300. Greece and Turkey had even smaller quotas—100 people each.[24]

At about the same time the British Dominions enacted immigration restrictions aimed at keeping their population British. Australia restricted immigration for non-British migrants, especially Asians, and promoted emigration schemes to bring British settlers to Australia.[25] By the Undesirable Immigrants Exclusion Act of 1919, New Zealand prohibited the entry without a special permit of all persons not of British birth or parentage. In Canada, immigration policy distinguished between immigrants from 'preferred' countries (Belgium, France, Germany, Switzerland, the

[24] William S. Bernard (ed.), *American Immigration Policy: A Reappraisal* (New York: Harper & Brothers, 1950), 25–7.
[25] Michael Blakeney, *Australia and the Jewish Refugees, 1933–1948* (Australia: Croom Helm, 1985), 29–30.

Netherlands, and the Scandinavian countries) and those from 'non-preferred' countries (Austria, Czechoslovakia, Poland, Hungary, Yugoslavia, the Baltic states, and Russia). A law of 1923 specified that immigrants from non-preferred countries would only be admitted as agriculturalists with means, as farm workers, and as domestic servants.[26] Canada, however, made special provisions to accept Russian refugees with agricultural skills, primarily Mennonites who joined existing Mennonite communities in western Canada.[27]

In Latin America, countries also developed restrictive immigration policies. Brazil, Argentina, Bolivia, Paraguay, and others wanted immigrants, but only those willing to be agricultural colonists. Moreover, these countries often sought out immigrants from Italy, Spain, and Portugal, countries with similar cultural traditions.[28] At the same time Latin American governments restricted the entry of certain groups, especially Jews.[29]

For the countries of Europe, the imposition of global immigration restrictions meant that they could not easily export their surplus populations, including refugees, overseas. This majority would have to stay in Europe, even though few countries there welcomed immigrants. In Britain, for instance, the Aliens Order of 1920 required that an alien demonstrate that he could support himself and his family before he was allowed to enter.[30] This law, like its American counterpart, signalled a major departure from past practices. For most of the nineteenth century Britain maintained an extremely liberal policy. No immigrant could be prevented from landing, and before 1890 an immigrant did not even have to inform the government of his or her arrival. British law did not recognize expulsion to be legal without extradition treaties; expulsion was, in fact, very rare. Although the 1905 Aliens Act should be considered a retreat from British liberalism, the exception made in the Act for political refugees lessened its effect in practice. It is interesting to note that, at the time of the Russian Revolution, the Bolsheviks Litvinov and Chicherin lived in London,

[26] Bernard, *American Immigration Policy*, 210–13.
[27] Gerald E. Dirks, *Canada's Refugee Policy—Indifference or Opportunism?* (Montreal: McGill-Queen's University Press, 1977), 38–9.
[28] Bernard, *American Immigration Policy*, 219.
[29] Simpson, *The Refugee Problem*, 273.
[30] Sherman, *Island Refuge: Britain and Refugees from the Third Reich: 1933–1939* app. (London: Paul Elek, 1973), II: 'Immigration Regulations', 273.

while in 1929 an escaping Trotsky could not gain permission to enter Britain.[31]

In Europe, only France served as a country of immigration. The Great War had taken a heavy toll on French manpower, creating a post-war labour shortage. In the early 1920s the French government encouraged immigration to facilitate reconstruction and to supply a labour force for its growing industrial and agricultural sectors.[32] At the end of 1926 the French government reversed this policy in response to an unemployment crisis. This new policy resulted in the practical suspension of all immigration for workers, except those needed in agriculture.[33]

In the 1930s immigration controls that were already tight grew even tighter. In response to the economic conditions of the Great Depression, governments around the world moved to prevent the entry of labourers. In 1931 State Department officials announced that the United States government would begin strictly to enforce the provision in the immigration laws that prohibited the admission of persons likely to become a public charge. This policy was remarkably effective. Within five months immigration from Europe had been cut by 90 per cent. In the entire decade, the United States admitted only about 500,000 people. At a time when thousands tried desperately to leave Germany, only one-quarter of the quota for northern and western Europeans was filled.[34]

Other countries with a tradition of welcoming immigrants followed the lead of the United States. In 1931 a Canadian law limited admission to American citizens, British subjects, and agriculturalists who were unlikely to become public charges.[35] In Australia, the government restricted immigration by requiring a landing permit.[36] Brazil, Colombia, and other Latin American countries also adopted quota systems and other restrictive policies.[37] Argentina, for instance, required that entry permits be given only

[31] Bernard Porter, 'The British Government and Political Refugees, c.1880–1914', in Slatter (ed.), *From the Other Shore*, 24–5.

[32] Tom Kemp, *The French Economy 1913–39: The History of a Decline* (London: Longmans, 1972), 94.

[33] League of Nations, 'Report of the Director', *International Labour Conference, Tenth Session*, ii (Geneva: ILO, 1927), 145.

[34] Robert A. Divine, *American Immigration Policy, 1924–52* (London: Oxford University Press, 1957), 77–90.   [35] Dirks, *Canada's Refugee Policy*, 44.

[36] Blakeney, *Australia and the Jewish Refugees*, 39.

[37] Samuel Guy Inman, 'Refugee Settlement in Latin America', *Annals*, 203 (May 1939), 187–91.

to those with no irregularities in their papers including a police certificate of good conduct.[38] Taken as a whole, these immigration policies resulted in 'setting up an elaborate network of restrictions which practically froze intercontinental migration for the years from 1930 through the end of the Second World War'.[39] Although restrictions loosened somewhat after 1945, strict governmental control over both emigration and immigration remains a reality.[40]

A number of factors combined to bring about this end to the relatively free global migration of the nineteenth century. One of the most important was the development of nationalist doctrines— ideas which, as we have seen, also contributed to the creation of refugee movements in inter-war Europe. As mentioned above, the United States, Canada, and other countries adopted immigration policies reflecting racist and ethnocentric thinking that were designed to maintain a specific ethnic or racial composition. These policies can be seen as an attempt to maintain a given culture, increase ethnic homogeneity, and prevent the entry of 'undesirable' ethnic minorities. In the United States, for instance, debates about immigration quotas reflected a desire to keep out southern and eastern Europeans, including Italians, Greeks, and Jews, who, restrictionists believed, were from inferior races.[41]

Although nativism accounts for immigration policies that tried to ensure an ethnic make-up, this notion alone does not explain why governments restricted the overall level of immigration. In the case of the United States, the 1924 immigration law reduced the number of European immigrants to about 15 per cent of the pre-1914 level. Reductions in the the level of immigration were primarily due to changes in the domestic economies of particular states. In the case of the United States, the largest recipient of immigrants prior to 1914, the industrial revolution brought about the mechanization of industry and agriculture. This greatly reduced the need for manual labour, which traditionally had been provided by immigrants.[42] Newly formed trade unions used their influence to protect domestic labourers from new immigration they

[38] Olga Elaine Rojer, *Exile in Argentina, 1933–1945: A Historical and Literary Introduction* (New York: Peter Lang, 1989), 79.
[39] Bernard, *American Immigration Policy*, 228.
[40] This is the thesis of Dowty, *Closed Borders*.
[41] On the nativist tradition in American politics, see John Higham, *Strangers in the Land: Patterns of American Nativism 1860–1925* (New Brunswick, NJ: Rutgers University Press, 1955).   [42] Divine, *American Immigration Policy*, 9.

believed would drive down wages.[43] In addition, much of the 'free land' that had been available in the Americas, Australia, and New Zealand was already taken by the time of the First World War. During the 1930s unprecedented levels of unemployment spurred governments to restrict immigration of new workers even more. These policies reflected the prevailing belief among government officials, labour leaders, and the public that immigration caused unemployment and that foreign workers took jobs from natives. Despite contemporary evidence to the contrary, this belief underpinned virtually all the restrictive legislation of the 1930s.[44] In addition, this same belief influenced governments to restrict or prohibit the employment of foreigners already within the country. France, for instance, established a quota on the number of foreign workers who could work in specific industries. Such legislation hit refugees especially hard because they usually had few assets and had to rely heavily on their ability to earn money to support themselves.

Other changes in society made countries both inside and outside Europe less willing to accept newcomers. In European countries, in particular, governments increasingly accepted responsibility for the social welfare of their inhabitants. If a government agreed to admit an immigrant, it faced the prospect of financially supporting that person and perhaps his or her entire family. By the 1920s Austria, Belgium, Denmark, France, Germany, Italy, the Netherlands, Sweden, and the United Kingdom had compulsory pension schemes. These same governments also provided a variety of other programmes, including insurance against unemployment, accident, and sickness.[45] In the Great Depression this situation worsened because the needs of both the local population and refugees increased at a time when the revenues of governments decreased. Consequently, governments felt even more reluctant to allow the entry of indigent foreigners.

[43] Vernon M. Briggs, Jr., *Immigration Policy and the American Labor Force* (Baltimore: Johns Hopkins University Press, 1984), 42.

[44] For refutations of this belief, see Bernard Ostrolenk, 'The Economics of an Imprisoned World: A Brief for the Removal of Immigration Restrictions', *Annals*, 203 (May 1939), 194–201; Dorothy Frances Buxton, *The Economics of the Refugee Problem* (London: Focus Publishing, 1939).

[45] Peter Flora and Jens Alber, 'Modernization, Democratization, and the Development of Welfare States in Western Europe', in Peter Flora and Arnold J. Heidenheimer (eds.), *The Development of Welfare States in Europe and America* (New Brunswick, NJ: Transaction Books, 1981), 59.

Governments also hesitated to admit foreigners because they considered them to be potential political threats. Generally, governments viewed refugees with even greater suspicion than normal migrants because of the refugees' allegedly dubious loyalty. British restrictions on aliens, for instance, were prompted during a bout of spy-fever during the First World War.[46] After the Russian Revolution American business leaders feared that admitting immigrants from Russia would spread Bolshevism in the United States, and they abandoned their traditional support for an open immigration policy.[47] Similarly, Argentina adopted immigration restrictions specifically to keep out radicals from the Spanish Civil War beginning in 1936.[48] In 1933 a League of Nations report warned that 'the existence of many thousands of unprotected and unassisted refugees might well prove fertile soil for subversive propaganda and unrest'.[49] Even Simpson, a refugee advocate, warned that a politically uprooted refugee 'may sink into the underworld of terrorism and political crime'.[50] This intense distrust of refugees contrasted sharply with nineteenth-century attitudes towards political exiles. In that era governments generally welcomed refugees and treated them with higher regard than that extended to ordinary migrants.[51]

Clearly, governments exaggerated the danger of politically active refugees to their societies, and unjustly interned aliens during the Second World War.[52] But, in regard to the political implications of assisting refugees, policy-makers reacted to a real danger. In the Inter-war Period, refugees had become tools of foreign policy. Just as invading armies sometimes forced people from their homes in order to hinder opposing military forces, some governments did the same in a political sense. Hannah Arendt contends that early Nazi persecution of the Jews can be seen less as an attempt to get rid of the Jews than as an attempt to spread anti-Semitism in western Europe. Furthermore, she stresses that the

[46] David French, 'Spy Fever in Britain, 1900–1915', Historical Journal, 21/2 (1978), 366.   [47] Bernard, American Immigration Policy, 18.
[48] Rojer, Exile in Argentina, 78.
[49] League of Nations, 'Russian, Armenian, Assyrian, Assyro-Chaldean and Turkish Refugees: Report of the Sixth Committee to the Assembly' (1933) [A.39.1933], 1.   [50] Simpson, The Refugee Problem, 9.
[51] Marrus, The Unwanted, 15.
[52] Jacques Vernant, The Refugee in the Post-War World (London: Allen & Unwin, 1953), 18; Bernard Wasserstein, Britain and the Jews of Europe 1939–1945 (Oxford: Clarendon Press, 1979), 88–108.

ability to denationalize refugees and render them stateless was a powerful weapon of totalitarian politics.[53] Vera Dean argues that Nazi Germany hoped to use refugee expulsions as a way to extract money from western European governments.[54] Studies of refugees and foreign policy since that time indicate that the use of refugees as tools of foreign policy continued after the inter-war years.[55]

Thus, the spread of nationalist doctrines, combined with the economic, social, and political changes mentioned above, meant that refugees of the Inter-war Period faced difficult obstacles in their quest for new countries and new lives. In only a very few cases did the adoption of immigration policies which favoured specific ethnic groups make it easier for refugees to find new countries. These policies facilitated the immigration of refugees with ethnic ties to a national state: the Greek refugees who settled in Greece are a case in point. But the same policies worked strongly against refugees without direct ties to a nation-state, such as Armenians and Jews, and against those deemed to be from the 'inferior' races of southern and eastern Europe. Overall, immigration restrictions had a disproportionately negative impact on refugees. At the time, virtually no countries made a distinction between economic migrants and refugees: that is, the immigration laws of most countries treated refugees—people who had fled their home countries because of persecution or violent conflict—as being the same as other migrants, primarily people who left their home countries to improve their economic position.[56] Immigration laws in the United States, for instance, exempted refugees only from the literacy test, despite an American tradition of asylum.[57] Moreover, refugees usually faced even more obstacles than ordinary migrants. Because of the circumstances of their flight, refugees often had meagre resources. Consequently, many were rejected on the grounds that they were likely to become public charges. Many lacked valid travel documents, and some had been rendered

[53] Arendt, *Origins of Totalitarianism*, 269, 278.

[54] Vera Micheles Dean, 'European Power Politics and the Refugee Problem', *Annals*, 203 (May 1939), 24.

[55] Michael S. Teitelbaum, 'Immigration, Refugees, and Foreign Policy', *International Organization*, 38 (Summer 1984), 437–41.

[56] For a review of the refugee policies of major countries, see Simpson, *The Refugee Problem*, 262–96.

[57] Read Lewis and Marian Schibsby, 'Status of the Refugee under American Immigration Laws', *Annals*, 203 (May 1939), 74.

stateless by denationalization laws. In addition, refugees could not always choose an opportune time for departure or wait for months for admission to a particular country. For refugees, emigration was not simply an economic issue, but a personal imperative.

THE REFUGEE PROBLEM AND NEW HOPES FOR ITS SOLUTION

From the point of view of governments, refugees are a problem because they do not fit within the normal parameters of a world of nation-states. In the Inter-war Period, mass refugee movements were by-products of efforts to achieve ethnically pure nation-states and ideologically homogeneous political systems. These same causes prevented the refugees from returning home without danger of persecution. In addition, the New World no longer acted as a safety-valve for Europe's forced migrants because of the imposition of immigration restrictions there. Consequently, the refugees primarily had to be re-established in Europe. This solution, however, created its own problems. Most refugees still found themselves to be an unwanted minority in a host country, without legal protection or the means of earning a livelihood. In reflecting on their situation, Hannah Arendt describes the refugees' world in graphic terms: 'Once they had left their homeland they remained homeless; once they had left their state they became stateless; once they had been deprived of their human rights they were rightless, *the scum of the earth.*'[58]

Although new obstacles to the solution of refugee problems emerged in inter-war Europe, the international attention focused on refugees also generated new hopes. To begin with, refugees after 1914 had a much better chance of survival than those of previous eras. In the nineteenth century a few relatively affluent revolutionary exiles found their way to the capitals of western Europe, but others were not so fortunate. Michael Marrus describes the harsh realities facing pre-twentieth-century refugees: 'Thrust unexpectedly on a society usually indifferent to outsiders of any sort, many refugees would quickly succumb to hunger, disease, or exposure. Large masses of people simply could not

---

[58] Arendt, *Origins of Totalitarianism*, 266. Emphasis added.

move from place to place supported by meagre social services. Winters, generally, would finish them off.'[59] The creation of a large number of international philanthropic organizations changed this situation. During and after the First World War the number of agencies engaged in refugee assistance mushroomed. These agencies provided on-the-spot, emergency relief to refugees and others in need. For the first time, large groups of homeless people could be kept alive pending some solution to their predicament. International agencies also helped refugees to become self-supporting and to find new, permanent homes.

While the First World War accelerated the development of new methods of destruction, it also brought new demands for peaceful co-operation between countries. In 1919 forty-two governments formed the League of Nations, an international, intergovernmental organization, 'in order to promote international co-operation and to achieve international peace and security'.[60] Within a very short time governments and private organizations called on the League to deal with a variety of social and political problems: epidemics in eastern Europe, prisoner-of-war repatriation, and refugee assistance. The League took up the role of refugee advocacy and attempted to help refugees find new homes and become self-supporting, despite immigration restrictions and unfavourable economic conditions.

In addition, governments around the world began to respond to the plight of refugees. Gradually, the idea that refugees should be considered a special kind of migrant gained acceptance. Through the development of international law, many countries took on special responsibilities towards refugees. Some also modified their immigration policies to favour refugees. Writing in 1938, Sir John Hope Simpson optimistically noted these changes: 'New means of rapid communication have meant for the refugee that to a certain extent the world is his asylum and the world is concerned with his fate.'[61] What Simpson was referring to is the development of an international regime, a concept that will be explored in Chapter 3.

[59] Marrus, *The Unwanted*, 5.
[60] 'Preamble, Covenant of the League of Nations', reprinted in Inis Claude, *Swords into Plowshares* (New York: Random House, 1984), 453. For a list of members of the League of Nations see F. P. Walters, *A History of the League of Nations* (London: Oxford University Press, 1960), 64–5.
[61] Simpson, *The Refugee Problem*, 10.

2

The Origins and Dimensions of the Refugee Problem in Inter-War Europe

A SERIES of refugee movements characterized migration in inter-war Europe, leading two scholars to call the period 'the era of refugees'.[1] These refugee movements, begun after the First World War, hastened the collapse of the existing European order. In place of the Russian, German, Austro-Hungarian, and Ottoman Empires, the peacemakers of 1919 eagerly assisted the creation of states in eastern and central Europe, including Austria, Hungary, Czechoslovakia, Yugoslavia, Poland, Latvia, Lithuania, and Estonia.[2] The transformation of central and eastern Europe from multi-ethnic empires to nation-states displaced millions of people, primarily members of ethnic minorities, from the new states. Though some happily joined ethnic brethren in other states, others fled as refugees. Approximately one to two million Poles migrated to Poland[3] and one million ethnic Germans moved to Germany[4] from their previous homes in the Russian and Austro-Hungarian Empires. The new Baltic states of Latvia, Lithuania, and Estonia accepted tens of thousands of refugees.

One of the countries most seriously affected was Hungary, the new state formed from the Magyar half of the Habsburg Empire, which had the misfortune to be on the losing side in the First World War. By the punitive Treaty of Trianon, Hungary retained only 33 per cent of its former territory and 42 per cent of its

---

[1] Arieh Tartakower and Kurt R. Grossman, *The Jewish Refugee* (New York: Institute of Jewish Affairs, 1944), 1.

[2] For an account of the Paris Peace Conference, see Harold Nicolson, *Peacemaking 1919* (London: Constable, 1964).

[3] Michael R. Marrus, *The Unwanted: European Refugees in the Twentieth Century* (New York: Oxford University Press, 1985), 52. An alternative estimate of 1 million can be found in Sir John Hope Simpson, *The Refugee Problem: Report of a Survey* (London: Oxford University Press, 1939), 76.

[4] Marrus, *The Unwanted*, 71. An alternative estimate of 600,000 can be found in Walter Adams, 'Refugees in Europe', *Annals*, 203 (May 1939), 26.

population. Of the people with a Magyar mother tongue, approximately 3.2 million, or one-third of the total, lived outside Hungary.[5] The new, amputated state of Hungary soon found that, in addition to its existing economic and political troubles, it had to deal with a flood of refugees. By 1920 Hungary had received 300,000 Magyar refugees driven out by the successor states of Romania, Czechoslovakia, and Yugoslavia. In Hungary they lived in poverty, dependent on what relief the government could provide.[6] This proved to be a tremendous expense. The addition of refugees and disabled war veterans, for instance, doubled the budget for pensions.[7]

Despite the number of people involved in these early movements, by and large the new nation-states involved managed to cope with their refugees. Most new migrants were immediately naturalized by their new country and could begin a new life as full citizens. Some people, however, were not so fortunate. In theory, the treaties drawn up at the Paris Peace Conference placed all former citizens of the old empires into a new state. In practice, this could not be perfectly carried out. If no state accepted a person, they became legally stateless. The largest group of stateless people were Jews from the former Russian Empire, who were denied citizenship by the secessionist states of eastern Europe. In addition, individuals who failed to take advantage of the provisions in the peace treaties within a given time limit often found themselves stateless.[8] The problems of statelessness, however, did not compare with those brought by two large refugee movements: the arrival in Europe of more than one million Russian refugees, and the creation of approximately two million refugees in the Balkans.

THE RUSSIAN REFUGEES

The most dramatic refugee movement of the immediate postwar period was that of more than one million Russian refugees,

---

[5] Raymond Pearson, *National Minorities in Europe 1848–1945* (London: Macmillan, 1983), 172.

[6] C. A. Macartney, *Hungary: A Short History* (Edinburgh: Edinburgh University Press, 1962), 212. Marrus estimates 250,000 (*The Unwanted*, 72). An alternative estimate of 426,000 can be found in István A. Mócsy, *The Effects of World War I— The Uprooted: Hungarian Refugees and Their Impact on Hungary's Domestic Politics, 1918–1921* (New York: Columbia University Press, 1983), 12.

[7] Mócsy, *The Effects of World War I*, 187–94.

[8] Marrus, *The Unwanted*, 70–1.

a product of the breakup of the Russian Empire.[9] In this case, the process of nation-state formation coincided with a social and political revolution within Russia itself. During the revolutionary process, an entire social class became defined as an obstacle to the achievement of homogeneity. The Russian migration also resulted from the adoption of illiberal rule in the newly formed Soviet Union; this development effectively prevented many of the refugees from ever returning to their home country.

Contrary to popular stereotypes, the typical Russian refugee was not a princess or an ageing archduke. Aristocrats, former officials of the Tsarist and Provisional governments, representatives of finance, commerce, industry, and the liberal professions, and other supporters of the *ancien régime* could all be found in the Russian migration, but the defeated White armies constituted its core. Accompanying the soldiers were civilians, either their families or people simply seeking to escape the chaos and economic breakdown brought by the revolution and civil war. As a result of these factors, the overwhelming majority of refugees were single men of military age. In Yugoslavia, for instance, men constituted 70 per cent of the refugees, and 70 per cent of them were single. In addition, very few children could be found among the refugees. Although most of the soldiers and civilians came from the peasant class, which constituted 80 per cent of the Russian population at the time of the revolution, it was still underrepresented in the total migration. The Russian migration also included ethnic Russians who lived in places which had become independent states, such as Poland and the Baltic countries.[10] In addition, the refugees included Jews from the former Russian

---

[9] Estimates made during the inter-war years of the total number of Russian refugees vary a great deal. Simpson cites estimates which range from 750,000 to 3 million. In 1922 the High Commissioner for Russian Refugees estimated that there were 1.5 million Russian refugees. Walter Adams estimates 1 million Russian refugees. See Simpson, *The Refugee Problem*, 80–2; League of Nations, 'Report to the Council on March 24th, 1922 by Dr. Nansen', *Official Journal* (May 1922), annex 321, p. 385; Adams, 'Refugees in Europe', 31. Estimates made since the Inter-war Period vary as well. Heller and Nekrich give figures ranging from 860,000 to 2 million, and conclude that 'more than a million people left Russia'. Michael Marrus estimates that there were about 1 million Russian refugees at the highest point. Mawdsley lists the highest estimate, one of 3.5 million made by an unofficial Soviet source. Mikhail Heller and Aleksandr Nekrich, *Utopia in Power: The History of the Soviet Union from 1917 to the Present* (New York: Summit Books, 1986), 143; Marrus, *The Unwanted*, 60–1; Evan Mawdsley, *The Russian Civil War* (Boston: Allen & Unwin, 1987), 286.

[10] Simpson, *The Refugee Problem*, 63 and 83–92.

Empire, many of whom found themselves to be the victims of attacks by both the Red and White Russians during the Civil War.[11] Ironically, the Russian Revolution of November 1917 did not generate many refugees. Some opponents of Communism did flee the new regime for foreign soil, but most congregated on the periphery of the Russian empire to join one of the White armies, each one led by a rival general. It was not until 1919 that a full-scale war broke out between these forces and the Red Army. Although the Whites, the only anti-Bolshevik opposition with a professional army, initially did well, they never successfully co-ordinated their efforts or won the support of the peasant population. Even the assistance of British, French, American, and Japanese forces, and the support of the Czech legions, did not ensure their victory.[12] Once the White armies and their Allied supporters suffered a series of defeats at the hands of the unified Bolsheviks, mass migrations out of the former Russian Empire began.

The first major evacuation of refugees to a foreign country took place after the Red Army entered the Ukraine in the spring of 1919: an estimated 6,000 soldiers and 5,000 civilians left Odessa for Constantinople and Balkan ports. In 1919–20 the virtual collapse of the White armies in European Russia forced many more to flee from the Tsarist territory. In the north, the British provided a sea escape-route for General Miller's army when they evacuated Archangel in September 1919. In the west, civilians and soldiers fled to Poland, Finland, and the Baltic states after the defeat of General Yudenich's forces in December 1919. Fighting continued in this area throughout 1920 as the Poles and Ukrainian nationalist forces, aided by some Whites, battled the Soviets. Many Jews, who were attacked by both sides, fled into Poland and Romania to escape. After the Poles and the Soviets agreed to a truce in October 1920, the Poles dismissed their White allies, thus bringing an end to White resistance on this front. In the south, the defeat of Deniken's army led to the evacuation of Novorossiisk with British help by March 1920. Since the British had supported Deniken, they accepted some responsibility for these refugees. General Wrangel held out still longer, even after the British withdrew their support, but he soon gave in as well. In just five days in November 1920, the French helped to evacuate approximately

[11] Marrus, *The Unwanted*, 61–6.
[12] Joseph L. Wieczynski (ed.), *The Modern Encyclopedia of Russian and Soviet History* (Gulf Breeze, Fla.: Academic International Press, 1978), vii, 136–49.

135,000 of Wrangel's followers, including 70,000 soldiers, from the Crimea for Constantinople.[13] Even after the defeat of most of the White armies, refugee movements continued. The devastating famine which struck the Volga provinces, Transcaucasia, and the Ukraine in 1921 and 1922 claimed over 5 million lives and forced many from their homes. These people fled primarily to escape starvation brought on by drought and the Bolshevik policy of forced grain requisition.[14] The anti-Bolshevik struggle survived the longest in the east, where the remnants of Admiral Kolchak's army fought on after the murder of their leader. With Japanese help, they continued for two more years before being finally defeated. Afterwards, refugees streamed into Manchuria and the Treaty ports of China.[15] By 1922 the fledgeling Soviet regime had won control of the former Russian Empire, and, in the process, created a mass exodus.

The evacuation of the White armies, like their conduct of the Civil War, lacked organization. The exact number of Russian refugees at any given time is difficult to determine. Because the refugees had such a dramatic impact on their hosts, early estimates tend to be higher than later ones. By 1922 an estimated 900,000 Russian refugees found themselves in virtually every country bordering the former Russian Empire, having arrived in a piecemeal fashion.[16] In the north, Finland and the Baltic countries provided refuge for 55,000. In central Europe, Poland hosted 175,000 refugees and Germany about 240,000.[17] In western Europe, France accepted the largest number of Russian refugees,

[13] Sir John Hope Simpson, *Refugees: Preliminary Report of a Survey* (London: Royal Institute of International Affairs, 1938), 36–9; Simpson, *The Refugee Problem*, 67–9. For an account of Deniken's evacuation, see Mawdsley, *The Russian Civil War*, 223–5. Estimates of the number of refugees evacuated with Wrangel vary. Wieczynski, *The Modern Encyclopedia*, 146, and George Jackson and Robert Devlin (eds.), *Dictionary of the Russian Revolution* (New York: Greenwood Press, 1989), 638, give a figure of 150,000. Mawdsley, *The Russian Civil War*, 270, says 146,000.
[14] Heller and Nekrich, *Utopia in Power*, 120; see also Robert Conquest, *The Harvest of Sorrow: Soviet Collectivization and the Terror-Famine* (New York: Oxford University Press, 1986), 53.   [15] Simpson, *Preliminary Report of a Survey*, 39.
[16] According to Simpson, the number of Russian refugees in Europe and the Far East had dwindled to 860,000 by 1922. Unless otherwise noted, the statistics in this paragraph are based on Simpson's estimates for 1922. Simpson, *The Refugee Problem*, 561.
[17] The number of Russian refugees in Germany fluctuated dramatically from 1919 until 1923. In the autumn of 1920 it was estimated that over half a million Russians were in Germany. By the spring of 1921 this had been reduced to 300,000 and by early 1922 to fewer than 250,000. Later in 1922 the number once again approached a half-million as refugees left France for Germany to take advantage

about 70,000.[18] Britain initially offered refuge to 15,000, rescued from Archangel by its fleet, but by 1922 only 9,000 remained.[19] To the south, the Balkan countries settled almost 140,000 refugees. Constantinople, then under Allied control, contained a refugee population of 200,000 at its peak, but by 1922 only 35,000 remained. Russian refugees wound up as far away as Asia, with some 145,000 residing in China, Manchuria, and Mongolia (see Table 1). Considerable numbers of refugees also settled in Canada and the United States.[20] The exodus included approximately 200,000 Jews, the vast majority seeking refuge in Poland, Romania, and Lithuania.[21]

The number of Russian refugees peaked in 1922, the year in which the Soviet government began strictly to prohibit emigration. Although by 1924 the refugee situation had stabilized in Europe, Russian refugees continued to migrate to the Far East until 1935. Large groups passed though Siberia on the Trans-Siberian Railway from 1929 to 1932, the years of forced collectivization.[22] Despite heavy restrictions, a handful of Soviet defectors also made their way to the West, but they never became a mass movement.[23]

Initially, the Russian refugees constituted an emergency relief

of the lower cost of living. In 1923 refugees went from Germany to France, this time to escape hyperinflation. In 1925 the German census recorded fewer than 250,000 Russians and by 1930 only 100,000 remained. Robert Chadwell Williams, *Culture in Exile: Russian Emigres in Germany, 1881–1941* (Ithaca, NY: Cornell University Press, 1972), 111–12. Simpson estimates that there were 90,000 Russian refugees in Germany in 1930 (*The Refugee Problem*, 561).

[18] The exact number of Russian refugees who migrated to France is in dispute. The French government consistently reported hosting 400,000 Russian and Armenian refugees to the League of Nations in the 1920s and early 1930s. In 1936 this figure was reduced to 63,000 Armenians and 72,000 Russians.

[19] Simpson, *The Refugee Problem*, 82, 561.

[20] Estimates of the number of Russian refugees who went to the United States vary between 15,000 and 20,000 (Simpson, *The Refugee Problem*, 468–9). The number that migrated to Canada is even harder to determine. From 1921 to 1930, 130,000 people labelled as either Ukrainians, Poles, or Russians entered Canada. Presumably a good proportion of these were refugees. During this period the number of males was abnormally high, over 60 per cent, a further indication of a refugee element (Simpson, *The Refugee Problem*, 488–9).

[21] League of Nations, 'Conference on the Russian Refugee Question: Resolutions' (26 Aug. 1921) [C.277.M.203.1921.VII], 4.

[22] Simpson, *The Refugee Problem*, 84.

[23] For an account of these early defectors, see Gordon Brook-Shepherd, *The Storm Petrels: The Flight of the First Soviet Defectors* (New York: Harcourt Brace Jovanovich, 1977).

TABLE 1. *Estimated Distribution of Russian Refugees*

Country	1922	1930	1937
Turkey	35,000	1,400	1,200
The Balkans			
Greece	3,000	2,000	2,200
Romania	35,000	13,000	11,000
Yugoslavia	34,000	30,000	27,500
Bulgaria	31,000	22,000	15,700
Subtotals	138,000	68,400	57,600
Poland and the Baltic Countries			
Estonia	15,000	11,000	5,300
Finland	20,000	10,000	8,000
Latvia	16,000	16,000	13,000
Lithuania	4,000	5,000	5,000
Poland	175,000	85,000	80,000
Subtotals	230,000	127,000	111,300
Central Europe			
Austria	4,000	3,000	2,500
Hungary	3,000	5,000	4,000
Czechoslovakia	5,000	15,000	9,000
Germany	240,000	90,000	45,000
Subtotals	252,000	113,000	60,500
Other European Countries			
France	70,000	175,000	110,000
Britain	9,000	4,000	2,000
Others	19,000	16,000	15,000
Subtotals	98,000	195,000	127,000
Far East	145,000	127,000	94,000
Totals	863,000	630,400	450,400

Source: Sir John Hope Simpson, *The Refugee Problem: Report of a Survey* (London: Oxford University Press, 1939), 561.

problem. Although wealthier refugees lived comfortably in France, Germany, and England, those who remained in countries on the periphery of the former Russian Empire faced disease and starvation. The situation in Constantinople, the dumping-ground for General Wrangel's army, was particularly acute. In November 1921 the Allied Commander-in-Chief made an appeal on behalf of the refugees, saying 'we are faced with 28,000 starving Russians on the streets, mostly invalids, women, and children, faced with winter, starvation, and death'.[24]

Even after the emergency needs of the Russian refugees were met, their situation continued to pose a problem both for the refugees and for their host countries. Although most of the refugees eventually found a country of asylum, their travails did not end there. Unlike refugees joining new nation-states, the Russians were not quickly naturalized by their host governments. Instead, they lived as aliens in foreign lands, often with an insecure legal status and subject to expulsion at a moment's notice. In addition, many lacked internationally acceptable travel documents, which prevented them from travelling to other countries, even if they had friends or jobs waiting for them. Although deaths and naturalizations gradually reduced the Russian refugee population, nearly twenty years after the conclusion of the Russian Civil War approximately half of the original refugees still maintained that status (see Table 1).[25] What many refugees had thought would be only a temporary retreat had turned into permanent exile.

The Russian migration had a dramatic impact on the many countries that hosted the refugees. A distinctive feature of this exodus was the formation of 'Russia Abroad', a grouping of exiles in the cultural centres of Berlin and Paris. In these cities, refugees ran schools, published newspapers, and wrote literature, all in an attempt to perpetuate Russian culture.[26] In eastern Europe, the impact of large numbers of destitute Russian refugees was quite different: it created a social welfare burden for the host

[24] 'Starving Russians in Constantinople: General Harington's Plea to the Editor of the Times', *The Times* (4 Nov. 1921).

[25] Simpson reports that the Russian refugee population was reduced to 630,000 by 1930, and to 450,000 by 1937 (*The Refugee Problem*, 110, 561).

[26] Marc Raeff, *Russia Abroad: A Cultural History of the Russian Emigration, 1919–1939* (New York: Oxford University Press, 1990); T. F. Johnson, *International Tramps: From Chaos to Permanent World Peace* (London: Hutchinson, 1938); Williams, *Culture in Exile*.

governments. In 1926 alone, nine governments reported spending 20 million gold francs (about £800,000) on the upkeep of Russian refugees.[27] In addition, the presence of ex-soldiers among the refugees could be a destabilizing political force, especially for the newly formed regimes. In Bulgaria, for instance, the activities of armed refugees from Wrangel's army threatened to destabilize the radical Stamboliiski government.[28] Even during the emergency phase of Russian migration the refugees appeared to be a political threat. In writing of the plight of General Wrangel's army, one newspaper editorial said that 'there is nothing they can do but loaf and starve. It is no wonder if they have lost, or are losing, all hope, and all morale, all sense of being members of and co-operators in a reasonable world. Of such stuff are Bolsheviks made.'[29]

The Russian refugees also threatened the homogeneity of the newly formed nation-states of eastern Europe. Every state in the region had at least a 15 per cent minority population, while four states—Czechoslovakia, Yugoslavia, Poland, and Romania—had a minority population that comprised more than 33 per cent of the total population. Although the percentage of Russians in the total populations of Yugoslavia and Bulgaria was relatively small, both countries contained diverse ethnic groups and a history of minority problems.[30] In Estonia and Latvia, the Russian refugees joined existing Russian populations to form the largest minority group, making up 8 and 11 per cent of the total populations of these two states, respectively. In Lithuania and Czechoslovakia, Russians formed the third largest minority group, making up approximately 3 and 4 per cent of their respective populations. But, with the exception of Yugoslavia, Russian cultural centres never developed in these countries. A newly found sense of nationalism, combined with anti-Russian feeling among political leaders, meant that governments did little to encourage separate cultural activity within their borders.[31]

[27] League of Nations, 'Armenian and Russian Refugees: Report to the Seventh Assembly' (3 Sept. 1926) [A.44.1926], 2. The figures include Bulgaria, Estonia, Finland, Greece, Latvia, Poland, Yugoslavia, Switzerland, and Czechoslovakia. The data for Bulgaria, Greece, and Czechoslovakia also include the upkeep of Armenian refugees.

[28] R. J. Crampton, *A Short History of Modern Bulgaria* (Cambridge: Cambridge University Press, 1987), 95.

[29] 'The Tragedy of Wrangel's Army', *Morning Post* (5 Apr. 1921).

[30] C. A. Macartney, *National States and National Minorities* (New York: Russell and Russell, 1968), 518–42.   [31] Raeff, *Russia Abroad*, 22.

Poland constituted a slightly different case. Although the 200,000 Russian refugees in Poland made up less than 1 per cent of its total population, they joined Ruthenes, Ukrainians, and White Russians, who numbered millions and harboured separatist aspirations. The entry of Jews as part of the Russian migration caused even greater problems. In 1921 approximately 180,000 Jewish refugees joined what was already the largest Jewish community in eastern Europe, a community that made up approximately 10 per cent of the overall population.[32] In an era of anti-Semitism this relatively small influx of people provoked controversy; the Polish government openly encouraged the Jewish refugees to move elsewhere.

Jewish refugees in Romania confronted a similar situation. Romania contained the second largest Jewish community in eastern Europe, although they made up only about 4 per cent of the total population.[33] A Romanian government official reported in August 1921 that the country had received 100,000 refugees, and 95,000 of them were Jewish. Although by March 1922 this number had declined to 45,000, the Romanian government felt that their country was being flooded with Jewish refugees.[34] Thus, even this small influx was of significance and fuelled anti-Jewish feelings.

The departure of the Russian refugees also left an enduring mark on the Soviet Union itself. Although the total number of Russian expatriates made up only about 1 per cent of the total Russian population, the percentage loss among the professional classes was more dramatic.[35] This loss meant that the talents of the most educated people in pre-revolutionary Russia would not be available for the reconstruction of the Soviet Union. Moreover, the presence of the refugees in countries bordering the Soviet Union, and in the major cities of western Europe, meant that the new regime had numerous anti-Soviet lobby groups to contend with.

---

[32] Tartakower and Grossman, *The Jewish Refugee*, 24; Ezra Mendelsohn, *The Jews of East Central Europe between the World Wars* (Bloomington, Ind.: Indiana University Press, 1983), 23. According to Simpson (*The Refugee Problem*, 76–7), the Polish government reported in 1922 that it hosted 550,000 Russian refugees, including 165,000 Jews. These figures, however, also include transients and former residents of the Russian empire whose homes became part of Poland after the First World War.   [33] Mendelsohn, *The Jews of East Central Europe*, 178.
[34] Marrus, *The Unwanted*, 64. Simpson, *The Refugee Problem*, 77.
[35] Pearson, *National Minorities in Eastern Europe*, 171.

REFUGEE MOVEMENTS IN THE BALKANS

The transformation of the ethnically mixed Ottoman empire into nation-states created mass refugee movements in the region now encompassing Greece, Turkey, and Bulgaria. In the multi-ethnic Ottoman Empire, the ruling Turks developed the 'millet system' in order to deal with conquered peoples. A 'millet' was a minority corporation with ecclesiastical, scholastic, and juridical autonomy; and the system applied to religious minorities, such as Orthodox Greeks, Gregorian Armenians, Armenian Catholics, Jews, and Protestants. This practice was in keeping with the Koran, which requires respect for other keepers of the 'Great Book', the Jews and Christians. Under the 'millet system' minority groups, especially the Greeks and Armenians, led a relatively prosperous life. Although subject to heavy taxes and occasional bursts of violence, the groups enjoyed religious freedom and local self-government. Many grew to positions of importance in the Ottoman economy and administration, and Greeks and Armenians largely staffed the civil service and banking system. Greeks were well represented in shipping, manufacturing, commerce, and the free professions, as well as among traders and shopkeepers. This system of minority protection, however, broke down in the nineteenth century, when nationalism grew among the various ethnic groups.

In Greece, following its independence, the 'Great Idea' of restoring historic Greece on both sides of the Aegean blossomed.[36] In Bulgaria, nationalists propagated the idea of 'Greater Bulgaria'. At the centre of the Ottoman Empire, the Young Turks seized power in 1908 and set about trying to create a Turkish nation-state. The transformation of the Ottoman Empire into nation-states was by no means a peaceful one. From 1912 until 1922 the Balkans experienced constant warfare and at least eighteen separate refugee movements, largely composed of national minorities.[37]

The two Balkan wars had a profound effect on the politics of the region. Bulgaria, for its part, unwillingly ceded much of Macedonia to Greece and Serbia. Greece emerged as a winner from

[36] Richard Clogg, *A Short History of Modern Greece* (Cambridge: Cambridge University Press, 1979), 76–8.
[37] It is beyond the scope of this study to discuss all these movements in detail. For more information see Simpson, *The Refugee Problem*, 13–14; Stephen Ladas, *The Exchange of Minorities: Bulgaria, Greece, and Turkey* (New York: Macmillan, 1932).

the conflict, having increased its land area by 70 per cent and its population from 2.8 million to 4.8 million (although not all were Greeks).[38] In Turkey, the disastrous wars prompted a re-evaluation of policy. They had shown that national minorities, if left alone, would only evolve and break away. Assimilation, after hundreds of years of allowing separate identities, presented a difficult and slow process, so the Turks sought an alternative solution.[39] This policy was, in fact, to be applied to Greeks.

The division of spoils after the First World War created the immediate background for inter-war refugee movements. At the Paris Peace Conference, Smyrna was a key issue for Venizelos, the Greek Prime Minister and chief negotiator. Incorporating Smyrna, known as Izmir to the Turks, into Greece had long been a cherished part of the 'Great Idea'—it could not be compromised. Although Turks outnumbered Greeks in Smyrna by 950,000 to 620,000, Venizelos was confident that the higher birth-rate among the Greek population would soon secure a Greek majority. More troubling was the fact that Italy had been promised the area by the agreement of St Jean de Maurienne in April 1917.[40] Despite these hindrances, Venizelos, a persuasive diplomat, soon won support for his ideas, particularly from Lloyd George, the British prime minister. On 15 May 1919 Greek troops landed in Smyrna with the authorization of the British, French, and Americans in order to protect the local inhabitants. Within six months the Greeks and Italians had come to terms over the disputed territories and adopted a common line at the Paris Peace Conference.[41]

Almost a year after the Greek occupation of Smyrna began, on 20 May 1920, the Allies announced the terms of the proposed peace treaty for Turkey. Under its terms, Turkey was to lose eastern Thrace to within twenty miles of Constantinople. Greece would administer Smyrna and its hinterland, and a plebiscite would be held in five years to determine its fate. Turkey would also lose part of its territory for the creation of independent Armenia and

[38] Clogg, *Short History of Modern Greece*, 102.
[39] Ladas, *The Exchange of Minorities*, 13–14.
[40] Clogg, *Short History of Modern Greece*, 112.
[41] In a secret pact, the 'Tittoni–Venizelos Agreement', Italy recognized Greece's claim to Smyrna and eastern and western Thrace. In return, Greece agreed to accept Italian sovereignty over the Valona region and to support their claims in Albania. C. A. Macartney and A. W. Palmer, *Independent Eastern Europe* (London: Macmillan, 1962), 131–2.

Kurdistan.[42] The treaty prompted a mixed reaction within Turkey. Although the Sultan signed the Treaty of Sèvres on 10 August 1920, it was not popular among Turkish nationalists, and it fuelled the grievances of nationalists led by Mustafa Kemal (Atatürk).[43]

In an attempt to enforce their claim, the Greeks launched an attack towards Ankara on 21 March 1921. They scored early victories, but soon lost the military and diplomatic advantage. In 1921 Kemal reached accords with the Italians, Soviets, and French. Greece, now torn by internal political disputes and led by the pro-German King Constantine, had only the lukewarm support of officially neutral Britain. The war went badly for the Greeks and ended with the retreat of their forces towards the coast.[44] Kemal and the nationalist forces had maintained the territorial integrity of Turkey, rejecting an imposed peace plan.

After the Turkish army recaptured the city of Smyrna in September 1922, spot killing and looting erupted, followed by massacres of the Christian population. Some 30,000 Christians died, with Armenians suffering the heaviest losses. The city was set on fire and thousands fled to the waterfront to escape the inferno.[45] All in all, over one million Anatolian Greek and Armenian refugees arrived in Greece within the space of a few weeks.

After the mass exodus, it soon became apparent that a Greek minority would no longer be tolerated on Turkish soil. Both the Greek and Turkish governments formally agreed to this resolution of the situation when they signed a population exchange agreement in January 1923. The controversial agreement provided for the compulsory exchange of Turkish nationals of the Greek Orthodox religion and Greek nationals of the Muslim religion, with a few minor exceptions.[46] The agreement uprooted approximately

[42] Treaty of Sèvres in Fred L. Israel (ed.), *Major Peace Treaties of Modern History 1648–1967*, iii (New York: Chelsea House, 1967), 2055–213.

[43] Bernard Lewis, *The Emergence of Modern Turkey* (London: Oxford University Press, 1968), 241–7.

[44] Macartney and Palmer, *Independent Eastern Europe*, 135–6.

[45] Exactly who set the fire is a matter of dispute. For instance, Donald Everett Webster, *The Turkey of Atatürk: Social Process in the Turkish Reformation* (Philadelphia: American Academy of Political and Social Science, 1939), 96, blames the Armenians.

[46] The Convention made exceptions for the Muslims of western Thrace and Greeks of Constantinople. It also provided that all movable property could be taken, and made provisions for those who were to be exchanged to be financially compensated for their immovable property. For the French text and English translation of the Convention see *Parliamentary Papers* (1923), i. 817–27. The French text is reprinted in Ladas, *The Exchange of Minorities*, 787–94.

1.5 million people: Greece exchanged 380,000 Muslims for 1.1 million Christians from Turkey. In fact, most of the Greeks left Turkey before the agreement was signed; only 200,000 did so afterwards. In contrast, virtually all of the Muslim population left Greece after the conclusion of the agreement.[47]

A similar population movement took place between Greece and Bulgaria. Following the Treaty of Neuilly, the punitive peace treaty of 27 November 1919, Bulgaria lost territory to both Greece and Yugoslavia. Because the governments of Greece and Bulgaria both believed that peace between the two countries would be impossible as long as Bulgarian minorities remained, they arranged a population exchange. In theory, the exchange was voluntary, but, in practice, Greek refugees from Asia Minor pressured Bulgars to leave Macedonia and then returning Bulgars overran Greek villages inside Bulgaria. From 1923 to 1928 almost all of the Greeks inside Bulgaria left; some 46,000 took advantage of the convention. Of the 139,000 Bulgarians living in Greece in 1920, approximately 92,000 migrated under the terms of the convention. The lower emigration rate among Bulgars living in Greece was probably due to the boycott of the convention by the Macedonian Revolutionary Organization.[48]

Also during this period Armenians fled the new Turkey. Traditionally Armenians had suffered persecution at the hands of the Ottomans, but after the collapse of the empire they became what Zolberg terms a 'stateless victim group'. The Armenians occupied an especially precarious position in Turkish society became they were primarily urban, middle-class, and conspicuously engaged in the Ottoman civil service and banking system. Moreover, like other stateless peoples, no Armenian nation-state existed to defend them. In 1915 the Turks adopted a radical method of dealing with the unwanted Armenian minority: genocide. Armenians were rounded up, then either massacred or marched off into the desert. In the process, an estimated half of the 3 million Armenians in the Ottoman Empire died.[49] Survivors of the genocide went to

---

[47] Ladas, *The Exchange of Minorities*, 438–9, 705; Clogg, *Short History of Modern Greece*, 120–1. For further discussion of the agreement see Dimitri Pentzopoulus, *The Balkan Exchange of Minorities and its Impact upon Greece* (Paris: Mouton, 1962), 61–7. [48] Ladas, *The Exchange of Minorities*, 105–7, 121–3.

[49] David Marshall Lang, *Armenia: Cradle of Civilization* (London: Allen & Unwin, 1979), 287–9. Leo Kuper estimates that 800,000–1,000,000 died in the genocide (*Genocide: Its Political Use in the Twentieth Century* (New Haven, Conn.: Yale University Press, 1982), 105, 113–14).

TABLE 2. *Estimated Distribution of Armenian Refugees, 1924*

The Balkans	
Bulgaria	18,000
Greece	45,000
Romania	6,000
Subtotal	69,000
The Middle East	
Cyprus	2,000
Iraq	8,000
Palestine and Transjordan	1,800
Syria and Lebanon	65,000
Subtotal	76,800
Europe	
France	40,000
Other Countries	20,000
Subtotal	60,000
Total	205,800

Source: Sir John Hope Simpson, *The Refugee Problem: Report of a Survey* (London: Oxford University Press, 1939), 558.

Soviet Armenia and Syria. Still more fled at the end of the Greco-Turkish war. By 1924 approximately 200,000 Armenians were scattered throughout Europe and the Middle East, principally located in Syria, France, Greece, and Bulgaria (see Table 2).[50]

Following this flurry of refugee movements, Greece, Turkey, and Bulgaria all contained large refugee populations. Greece, host to almost 1.4 million refugees, equal to 20 per cent of the total population, received the largest influx and bore the greatest burden (see Table 3). The significance of this refugee movement is magnified when it is noted that the refugees arrived within a very short period of time at only one or two cities in Greece. Moreover, many arrived penniless, wearing only summer clothing and carrying icons. Some only spoke Turkish, despite the fact that they were ethnic Greeks. In contrast to the Russian refugees, the

[50] Simpson, *The Refugee Problem*, 33, 43.

TABLE 3. *Origins of Refugees in Greece, 1926*

Asia Minor	1,000,000
E. Thrace	190,000
Caucasus	70,000
Bulgaria	30,000
Constantinople	70,000
Total	1,360,000

Source: League of Nations, *Greek Refugee Settlement* (Geneva. 1926), 13.

majority were old men, women, and children—many male adults had been killed in the war. Most came from urban areas and were merchants, shipbuilders, bankers, professionals, grocers, small traders, artisans, and domestic servants. Included among the rural refugees were substantial numbers of peasants, sailors, and fishermen.[51]

Re-establishing the refugees was a mammoth task for the relatively underdeveloped and politically unstable Greek state. The government quickly moved to naturalize the refugees as full citizens, which immediately had an impact on domestic politics. The refugees contributed to the formation of a republic by voting overwhelmingly for the abolition of the monarchy in 1924. In addition, Anatolian refugees could be easily found among the leading cadres of the Greek Communist Party.[52]

Although Turkey and Bulgaria hosted fewer refugees, they also faced acute conditions. These two countries, like Greece, quickly naturalized the refugees of similar ethnic origin, but the task of resettlement could not be accomplished overnight. At the time, Bulgaria had the characteristics of an underdeveloped country, including rural underemployment and a low standard of living. Seventy-five per cent of its population depended on agriculture for a living in a country with relatively little arable land and high population growth rates.[53] The social and economic problems

[51] League of Nations, *Greek Refugee Settlement* (Geneva: League of Nations, 1926), 1–16. An estimate of 1.3 million is given by Simpson (*The Refugee Problem*, 17) and Clogg (*Short History of Modern Greece*, 121).

[52] Clogg, *Short History of Modern Greece*, 122–3.

[53] Fred S. Pisky, 'The People', in L. A. D. Dellin (ed.), *Bulgaria* (New York: Frederick Praeger for Mid-European Studies Center of the Free Europe Committee, 1957), 79–80.

TABLE 4. *Origins of Refugees in Bulgaria, 1926*

Greece	122,000
Yugoslavia	31,000
Turkey	70,000
Romania	28,000
Total	251,000

Source: Sir John Hope Simpson, *The Refugee Problem: Report of a Survey* (London: Oxford University Press, 1939), 25.

created by the arrival of 250,000 ethnic Bulgar refugees, approximately 5 per cent of the total population, complicated the agrarian reform programme begun by the struggling Stamboliiski government because the vast majority were poor peasants (see Table 4).[54] About three-quarters of the male refugees were peasants, day labourers, or rural artisans. Moreover, Bulgaria had to make provision for 50,000 Russian and Armenian refugees. Turkey hosted approximately 400,000 refugees from Greece, approximately equal to 3 per cent of the total population. These refugees occupied a position similar to that of their Bulgarian counterparts. Over 90 per cent came from peasant backgrounds, and most arrived with minimal property at a time when Turkey was struggling with the process of economic modernization.[55]

At the conclusion of the population exchanges, the Balkans had been transformed. Greece achieved a degree of homogeneity practically unknown in the area. From 1920 to 1928 the Greek ethnic element in Greece rose from 80 per cent to 94 per cent. During the same period the Turkish minority declined from 14 to 1.6 per cent.[56] Bulgaria virtually eliminated its Greek minority, making it the closest approximation to a nation-state in eastern Europe. Even so, two minority groups—Turks and gypsies—still made up 10 per cent of the population.[57] Turkey, now free of its Armenian and Greek populations, had become an essentially Muslim, Turkish state. Overall, a great 'unmixing of populations'

[54] Crampton, *Short History of Modern Bulgaria*, 87.
[55] Simpson, *The Refugee Problem*, 23–7, 558, 561. In 1926 Bulgaria had a total population of 5.5 million. In 1927 Turkey had a total population of 13.6 million. Macartney, *National States*, 538, 540.   [56] Simpson, *The Refugee Problem*, 21.
[57] Pearson, *National Minorities in Eastern Europe*, 175.

had taken place and, in the process, over 2 million people had become refugees.[58]

REFUGEES FROM THE THIRD REICH

In the 1930s a radical attempt to create a homogeneous nation-state produced the flight of 400,000 refugees, primarily Jews, from the Third Reich. In Hitler's Germany, the Nazis took the goal of creating a homogeneous nation-state to its radical extreme. From traditional anti-Semitism, the quasi-science of race prominent in the late nineteenth century, and prevailing nationalist ideas, the Nazis formulated a unique ideology.[59] The 1920 platform of the Nazi party set down its parameters: 'None but members of the nation may be citizens of the state. None but those of German blood, whatever their creed, may be members of the nation. No Jew, therefore, may be a member of the nation.'[60] Once Hitler came to power, the Nazi regime began a social revolution aimed at creating a Fascist state and a racially pure society. Under this scheme, political dissidents, especially Communists and Socialists, were viewed as enemies of the state. But the group most severely affected by the Nazi revolution was the Jews.

Like the Armenians, the Jews differed in religion and ethnicity from the dominant nationality of their home state. Although Jews made up less than 1 per cent of the German population, they occupied a prominent economic position, especially in the liberal professions and commercial classes. In addition, the Jews were a stateless people in the sense that they had no nation-state to defend their interests. The Nazi adoption of racial theories added a dangerous new twist to traditional animosities against them. Because Jews were identified as a racial group, they had no escape route within the system: religion could be changed but race could

[58] These words are generally attributed to Lord Curzon.
[59] On the development of Nazi attitudes towards the Jews see P. G. J. Pulzer, *The Rise of Political Anti-Semitism in Germany and Austria* (New York: John Wiley and Sons, 1964).
[60] Quoted in Norman Bentwich, *The Refugees from Germany, April 1933 to December 1935* (London: Allen & Unwin, 1936), 23.

not. For the German Jewish population, only the options of flight or death remained.

In contrast to the Russian and Greek refugees, who were driven from their home countries in a short period of time, refugees from the Third Reich left over a six-year period in four major waves, each spurred by an initiative of the Nazi government: (1) the rise of Hitler in 1933; (2) the creation of the Nuremberg Laws in September 1935; (3) the incorporation of Austria and the Sudetenland in 1938; and (4) *Kristallnacht* in November 1938. Tragically, these movements turned out to be just a prelude to the massive population displacements of the Second World War and to the death of 6 million Jews in the Holocaust.[61]

In Germany, the election of Adolf Hitler as Chancellor provided the international stimulus for both social revolution and mass exodus. In April 1933 the Nazi government began a national boycott of Jewish businesses, the first step in an effort to purge Jews from the German economy. The regime took other measures to exclude Jews and political opponents from the civil service, the medical and legal professions, the media, the performing arts, and education. Under a new naturalization and citizenship law, any naturalization granted between November 1918 and January 1933 could be withdrawn if the person was deemed undesirable, a measure which aimed at eastern-European Jews who became German citizens after the First World War. The same law also allowed for the denationalization of those German nationals living abroad who prejudiced German interests.[62] Several champions of liberal ideas, including Albert Einstein, Heinrich Mann, and Ernest Toller, fell victim to this law.[63]

As a consequence of these actions, a total of 80,000 left the Reich by August 1935. Of these, Jews made up 80 per cent. Twenty per cent of the refugees came from the professions, including lawyers, doctors, teachers, scientists, professors, and scholars. The majority, however, worked in commercial occupations, ranging from industrialist and financier to craftsman and clerk. Political

---

[61] Kuper, *Genocide*, 124. See also Yehuda Bauer, *A History of the Holocaust* (New York: Franklin Watts, 1982).

[62] A. J. Sherman, *Island Refuge: Britain and Refugees from the Third Reich: 1933–1939* (London: Paul Elek, 1973), 20–2. For a comprehensive survey of Nazi treatment of the Jews see Lucy Dawidowicz, *The War Against the Jews: 1933–45* (Harmondsworth: Penguin Books, 1975); Simpson, *The Refugee Problem*, 126–39.

[63] Bentwich, *The Refugees from Germany*, 33.

TABLE 5. *Estimated Distribution of Refugees from the Third Reich*

Country	Dec. 1933	June 1935	Dec. 1937	Aug. 1939[1]
Europe				
Belgium	2,500	600	600	25,000
Britain	3,000	2,500	5,500	56,000
France	25,000	10,000	9,500	40,000
Holland	5,000	4,000	7,100	23,000
Others	8,100	8,600	15,500	*
Repatriation	9,000	18,000	20,000	*
	52,600	43,700	58,200	144,000
Palestine	6,500	27,000	42,000	90,000
USA	200	6,000	26,300	100,000
Central and South America	nil	3,000	20,300	*
South Africa	nil	300	4,800	*
Others	nil	500	2,400	66,000
Totals	59,300	80,500	154,000	400,000

Source: Sir John Hope Simpson, *The Refugee Problem: Report of a Survey* (London: Oxford University Press, 1939), 663.

[1] A. J. Sherman, *Island Refuge* (London: Paul Elek, 1973), 264–5; [2] Arieh Tartakower and Kurt Grossman, *The Jewish Refugee* (New York: Institute of Jewish Affairs, 1944), 52; Malcolm J. Proudfoot, *European Refugees: 1939–52, A Study in Forced Population Movements* (London: Faber & Faber, 1957), 27, 319; and estimates by the author.
* Included in the 'Others' category.

refugees, including Communists, Socialists, Protestants, Catholics, trade-unionists, and liberal intellectuals, also escaped from the increasingly repressive Third Reich.[64]

Starting life anew for the first wave of refugees was a difficult but not impossible task. Initially, the majority of the refugees travelled to countries bordering Germany, especially France. By 1935 at least two-thirds of the refugees had been resettled. Almost 50 per cent of the total went permanently overseas, including 27,000 to Palestine and 6,000 to the United States (see Table 5).[65] Once

[64] James G. McDonald, *Letter of Resignation . . . Addressed to the Secretary-General of the League of Nations* (London, 1935), 33–4; Bentwich, *The Refugees from Germany*, 36–7. McDonald's letter contains a review of all Nazi legislation against German Jews up to and including the Nuremberg Laws.
[65] Simpson, *The Refugee Problem*, 562.

inside a host country, the Jewish refugees often found themselves to be once again the victims of anti-Semitism. In addition, all the refugees maintained a precarious legal position. Although most left Germany through normal emigration channels using a valid passport, once outside Germany they could not renew their travel documents or count on any diplomatic protection from the German government. This left them subject to exploitation and expulsion by host governments. Moreover, the refugees often struggled for economic survival. All emigrants from Germany had to pay a flight tax of up to 50 per cent of their capital, severely reducing the amount of money the refugees could take with them.[66] Finding a job in a new country was also difficult, primarily because of the deep economic depression which engulfed most of the world in the 1930s.

A relative lull in emigration came to an abrupt halt with the promulgation of the Nuremberg Laws in September 1935. This legislation represented an even more radical attempt to exclude Jews from the German nation-state. The laws precisely defined who were Jews and non-Aryans and forbade sexual relations between them and Germans. The laws also relegated Jews and non-Aryans to the status of subjects, and, as non-citizens, they lost the right to vote.[67] Along with the laws came an increase in persecution of the Jewish population. Firing of Jewish employees, boycotting of Jewish businesses, excluding Jewish producers from supply cartels, and blackmailing Jewish owners into 'Aryanizing' their firms became the order of the day.[68] In response to these new initiatives, thousands of people, primarily Jews, left the country. Although they had to pay increasing flight taxes, most refugees still managed to find a place of refuge. By the end of 1937 a total of 150,000 refugees had left Germany. During this time, however, the actual number of refugees in western Europe remained

---

[66] Sherman, *Island Refuge*, 25, estimates that refugees from 1933 until 1937 suffered a 30–50 per cent capital loss in emigrating from Germany.

[67] The Nuremberg Laws identified Jews on a racial, not a religious, basis. The laws defined a Jew as a person with 3 or 4 Jewish grandparents or 2 Jewish grandparents and either (1) belonging to the Jewish religious community, or (2) the offspring of a marriage to a Jew after 15 September 1935, or (3) married to a Jew. A *Mischlinge* of the first degree was defined as a person with 2 Jewish grandparents who did not fulfil any of the special requirements. A *Mischlinge* of the second degree was defined as a person with one Jewish grandparent. The term 'non-Aryan' referred to people of Jewish descent who were Christian—usually, Catholic—in religion.   [68] Sherman, *Island Refuge*, 60–1.

constant at about 35,000, because the number of new refugees approximated the number that settled overseas (see Table 5).[69]

Beginning with the annexation of Austria in March 1938, what had been a gradual exodus of the German Jewish population turned into a major refugee crisis. In Austria, a process that had taken several years in Germany occurred in three months. The Nazis quickly moved to eliminate Jews from all aspects of economic life and to reduce them to poverty. Vienna, a city with a large Jewish population, became a free-for-all as people tried desperately to flee the country. Under the direction of Adolf Eichmann, the Gestapo began the practice of forcibly deporting people and dumping them across the nearest border. In addition to Jews, members of the Social Democratic Party and supporters of the Schuschnigg government also fled. In contrast to the first two waves of refugees, these found it almost impossible to find a country willing to give them temporary asylum. Often they had no documents or money with them. The countries around Austria responded to the mass exodus by closing their borders to prevent the entry of refugees. Given the situation, it is not surprising that many lost hope entirely; after *Anschluss*, the suicide-rate among Jews soared.[70]

The German occupation of the Sudetenland on 1 October 1938 produced another torrent of refugees. At the time of the German occupation about five thousand refugees from Germany and Austria already lived in Czechoslovakia. Soon anti-Nazi Sudeten Germans, Czechs, and Jews from the annexed areas joined the other refugees in the rump state. The Czech government reported in November 1938 that there were over 90,000 refugees in Czechoslovakia, including 73,000 Czechs, 10,000 Germans, and 7,000 Jews, Poles, and others.[71]

A bad situation became even worse in November 1938. On 7 November a young Polish Jew shot and killed Ernest vom Rath, Third Secretary at the German Embassy in Paris, in revenge for the deportation of his parents from Germany to Poland. Two days

[69] Simpson, *The Refugee Problem*, 139–41, 562; Marrus, *The Unwanted*, 130.
[70] Sherman, *Island Refuge*, 85; Marrus, *The Unwanted*, 167–70.
[71] Sir John Hope Simpson, *Refugees: A Review of the Situation since September 1938* (London: Oxford University Press, 1939), 36. According to Simpson, the number of refugees in Czechoslovakia rose still higher by February 1939 after the flight of 186,000 Czechs from Slovakia.

later, on November 1938, the Nazis retaliated by organizing a night of terror against the remaining Jews in Germany. During *Kristallnacht*, 'the night of broken glass', 100 Jews died and 20,000 were arrested. In addition, rioters attacked Jewish property, homes, and synagogues. When the pogrom finally came to an end, enormous property damage had been done, including 3 million Reichsmarks (RM) in broken glass alone.[72]

But the horrors of *Kristallnacht* did not end with the dawn of the next morning. On 12 November Goering announced that all Jews in Germany had to pay a collective fine of 1 billion RM in compensation for vom Rath's murder. In addition, Jewish owners had to repair all property damages at their own expense. Other new laws sought totally to exclude Jews from social life, forbidding them to enter cinemas and other places of public entertainment, depriving them of the right to public assistance, and expelling them from all universities. Still more sought to bring about the complete pauperization of the Jewish population by giving the authorities the right to liquidate all Jewish enterprises and by forcing Jews to turn over their securities, jewels, and art objects.[73]

Kristallnacht and its aftermath turned a manageable refugee flow into an uncontrollable flood. For these refugees, even finding a place of temporary refuge became nearly impossible as doors around the world closed to prevent a mass influx. The most poignant symbols of the desperate flight of thousands were refugee ships like the *St Louis*.[74] These ships travelled from port to port seeking a country willing to accept their human cargo, a mission that often ended in vain. Despite the great risks of flight, by the year ending June 1939 120,000 refugees had left the Reich, a number approximately equal to that of the previous five years. The bulk of this emigration look place in the winter of 1938–9.[75] As a result, the number of German Jewish refugees in Europe and the United States more than doubled by May 1939.

The German invasion of Czechoslovakia in March 1939 forced still more refugees to flee, including Sudeten German and Czech

[72] Sherman, *Island Refuge*, 165–7.
[73] Simpson lists all the relevant legislation in *Refugees: A Review*, app. 1, pp. 111–13.
[74] Ronald Sanders, *Shores of Refuge: A Hundred Years of Jewish Emigration* (New York: Schocken Books, 1988), 459–67.
[75] Simpson, *Refugees: A Review*, 24; Sherman, *Island Refuge*, 204.

officials, Sudeten Jews, Jews from the new Protectorate, and Jews formerly from Germany and Austria. Flight from Germany and its conquests continued up until the outbreak of war in September 1939. At that time Sir Herbert Emerson, High Commissioner for Refugees, estimated that approximately 400,000 refugees had fled the Third Reich since 1933, including 225,000 Jews from Germany, 134,000 Jews from Austria and Bohemia-Moravia, and 40,000 non-Jews.[76]

By the time the Second World War started, the 1933 Jewish population of greater Germany of approximately 500,000—less than 1 per cent of the total population—had been reduced by about 50 per cent.[77] In Austria, the Jewish population also decreased dramatically after the German annexation. In 1938 about 180,000 Jews lived in Austria[78] but, by July 1939, 97,000—more than 50 per cent—had fled.[79]

The typical refugee was a young person, as emigration priority was given to young people. Over 80 per cent of Jews under 40 left Germany between 1933 and 1939. As a result, by September 1939 75 per cent of the Jews left in Germany were over 40.[80] The majority of refugees were from the middle and upper classes, although this became less true as the emigration progressed.

When the Second World War started, refugees from the Third Reich were scattered throughout the world. Palestine surpassed all European countries in its absorption of the products of this diaspora: about 90,000 Jewish refugees, or about 25 per cent of the total, settled there. Britain accepted 56,000, and the United States about 100,000. Refugees ended up as far away as Shanghai, the only port in the world where passengers could disembark without a passport; it hosted 10,000 refugees by May 1939. In Latin America, Argentina hosted the largest number of German Jews, about

---

[76] League of Nations, 'International Assistance to Refugees: Supplementary Report to the Twentieth Assembly by Sir Herbert Emerson' (20 Oct. 1939) [A.18(a).1939.XII], 2; and Sherman, *Island Refuge*, 269–70. An alternative estimate of 800,000 civilians, including 420,000 Jews, is given by Malcolm Proudfoot, *European Refugees: 1939–52. A Study in Forced Population Movement* (London: Faber & Faber, 1957), 318–19.

[77] Simpson, *Refugees: A Review*, 29; Sherman, *Island Refuge*, 170; Norwood, *Strangers and Exiles*, 284. Marrus, *The Unwanted*, 129, estimates 525,000 Jews and 600,000 non-Aryans.

[78] Marrus, *The Unwanted*, 167–8; Sherman, *Island Refuge*, 170. Simpson, *Refugees: A Review*, 29, estimates 190,000.   [79] [A.18(a).1939.XII], 2.

[80] Dawidowicz, *The War Against the Jews*, 239–40.

45,000.[81] Sadly, about one-quarter of the refugees settled in countries later occupied by the Nazis (see Table 5).

OTHER REFUGEES FROM FASCISM

The rise of Fascism in the 1920s and 1930s created refugee movements from countries other than Germany. In general, these movements produced small groups of refugees who resembled the nineteenth-century political exiles rather than the large number of refugees generated by the break-up of the Ottoman, Austro-Hungarian, and Russian Empires. In Portugal, for instance, political opponents fled the country following attempts to overthrow the dictatorship of Antonio Salazar in 1927. Other incidents in the 1930s brought the total number of exiles to somewhere around two thousand.[82] These refugees generally found places of asylum, especially in Latin America. In Italy, Mussolini's rise to power created a steady trickle of refugees. The emigration consisted primarily of political refugees, including those directly threatened by the government and those who left the country in order to oppose Fascism from abroad.

The Italian Migration

Refugees left Italy in four major waves. The first began after the March on Rome in October 1922 and continued until 1926. During this period political opposition was difficult but not impossible. In the years 1923–4 both political and economic migration to France was high and many well-known activists left during this time. The second wave, from November 1926 until June 1929, began when the government outlawed almost any form of political opposition and created the Special Tribunal of the Fascist Militia. It also instituted the death penalty for political crimes, withdrew passports from suspected anti-Fascists, and created a new crime, 'abusive emigration'. Due to the strict regulation and official discouragement of emigration, it was small and almost entirely political in nature. The economic crisis of 1929, however, did revive the

---

[81] Olga Elaine Rojer, *Exile in Argentina, 1933–1945: A Historical and Literary Introduction* (New York: Peter Lang, 1989), 81.

[82] Simpson, *The Refugee Problem*, 169–71; Marrus, *The Unwanted*, 132.

economic migration somewhat. In the third wave, from June 1929 until July 1936, frontier restrictions were relaxed and emigration assumed a more normal pattern. Political emigration continued sporadically, both legally and illegally. The outbreak of the Spanish Civil War in July 1936 began a fourth wave of emigration. Among these refugees were large numbers of young men going to fight as volunteers with the Republicans.[83]

The Italian government tried several ways of coping with the refugees. In 1926 it made a brief attempt at denationalization, but by 1929 it abandoned this policy and adopted a new, twofold strategy. On the one hand, it would closely watch the political refugees overseas. On the other, it would try to prevent non-political emigrants abroad from joining the anti-Fascist movement. In order to do this, the government formed Fascist groups abroad and then used these societies as propaganda mechanisms. Furthermore, Italian consulates spied on the political refugees. After 1929 it became possible to renew travel documents abroad. Many refugees, however, declined this privilege because they feared persecution.[84]

The refugees, numbering at most 10,000, lived primarily in France as part of a larger community of Italian migrants.[85] Because they drew on the resources of the Italian immigrant community in France, the refugees managed to support themselves and did not constitute a relief burden for the French government. However, they still found themselves in an insecure position legally, because they could not depend on the diplomatic protection of the Italian government. Moreover, their presence proved to be a major source of friction between the Italian and French governments, and worsened Mussolini's ideological hatred of the democratic republic.[86]

Despite the Fascist nature of the Italian government, Italy did not pursue an anti-Jewish policy in the early 1930s. Mussolini even supported the Zionist cause. But, by the middle of the decade, growing German influence and increasing racism in Italy forced a policy change. A decree of 1 September 1938 ordered the expulsion within six months of all foreign Jews who had settled in Italian territory since 1 January 1919. The law applied to Italy, Libya,

---

[83] Simpson, *The Refugee Problem*, 120–1.   [84] Ibid. 121–2.
[85] Ibid. 117–25; Marrus, *The Unwanted*, 124–8.
[86] Adrian Lyttleton, *The Seizure of Power: Fascism in Italy 1919–1929* (Princeton, NJ: Princeton University Press, 1987), 427.

and the Aegean possessions, but not to East Africa, and affected about twenty thousand Jews, some resident since 1919, others more recent refugees from Germany and Austria. Another decree of the same time excluded Italian Jews from universities and government schools.[87] Eventually, native Jews were subjected to racial laws similar to those in the Third Reich.

The Spanish Republicans

In contrast to Portugal and Italy, political change in Spain produced a flood of refugees. At the conclusion of the Spanish Civil War, the Nationalist forces of General Franco, aided by Germany and Italy, stood victorious over the defeated Republican government. As in the Russian Civil War, population movements, both external and internal, accompanied the war. External movements took place early on, the first being a consequence of Franco's conquest of the northern coast of Spain between the autumn of 1936 and the summer of 1937. In this conquest, Irun was the first city to fall. On the night of 30 August 1936 some 2,000 people arrived at Hendaye, France. More followed after the fall of San Sebastian shortly afterwards. By the end of 1936 France was hosting about 10,000 refugees. More were generated by the final phase of the northern campaign, from May to October 1937. On 18 June Bilbao fell to Franco. By this time 30,000 refugees had been safely evacuated by French and British ships. Evacuations continued despite Franco's warning that aerial bombing would continue.[88]

When Santander was threatened in July 1937, it became clear that the refugee problem would be a growing one. In response, the French government instituted a new policy. From then on, refugees would be given the choice of returning to either Republican or Nationalist Spain, provided that the French consul at Santander received a list of prospective refugees, though no men of military age would be accepted. The fall of Santander in August 1937 produced 29,000 refugees. After the fall of Gijon on 21 October, people fled to Catalonia and some 9,500 went to France. By

---

[87] Simpson, *The Refugee Problem*, 124; Susan Zuccotti, *The Italians and the Holocaust: Persecution, Rescue, and Survival* (New York: Basic Books, 1987), 28–51. See also Meir Michaelis, *Mussolini and the Jews: German–Italian Relations and the Jewish Question in Italy, 1922–1945* (Oxford: Clarendon Press, 1978).

[88] Stein, *Beyond Death and Exile*, 7.

October 1937 France hosted almost 70,000 Spanish refugees, despite attempts at repatriation.[89]

Another flood of refugees followed the Nationalist campaign in Aragon. More refugees fled internally to Catalonia, and others went to France. Some 15,000–17,000 refugees entered in April, and 8,000 more entered in June 1938. Among the refugees were 12,000–14,000 soldiers of the Republican army. Once inside France, the men were disarmed and repatriated. Ninety per cent of the soldiers opted for repatriation on the Republican side. The women, children, and the sick and wounded were distributed throughout France. By mid-June 1938 there were 40,000–50,000 refugees in France.[90] Suffering under this burden, France officially closed the border in July 1938.

The Nationalist push into Catalonia began on 23 December 1938. Franco's troops moved quickly, and by the new year much territory had been taken. Thousands fled to Barcelona seeking refuge. By 22 January, less than a month after the invasion had begun, Franco's troops were only 34 kilometres from Barcelona; it became clear that the Republican government would fall. Meanwhile, the French politician Léon Blum successfully pleaded for the frontier to be reopened, and arms shipped in.[91]

Now the pace of events accelerated. On 23 January the Republican government ordered the evacuation of civilians.[92] On 25 January French troops stood ready to prevent a massive influx of refugees. Meanwhile, negotiations were taking place over a proposed plan for a neutral zone pending resolution of the problem. By 26 January, when Franco's forces took Barcelona, civilians were already on the road to France or just near the border waiting to get in. On 27 January plans for the creation of a neutral zone were still floundering. French officials, however, began to allow in 2,000 refugees per day. The following day, 28 January, the French government reversed its policy. Now refugees of military age would be allowed in, though they were to be disarmed immediately.[93]

People flocked across the border. By the evening of 29 January 15,000 had crossed into France, and 80,000 Republican troops were on their way. At the beginning of February 300,000 starving Spanish refugees waited on the French border. About 80,000 had

[89] Stein, *Beyond Death and Exile*, 7.   [90] Ibid. 8–9.   [91] Ibid. 21.
[92] Ibid. 22.   [93] Simpson, *Refugees: A Review*, 54–5.

already been admitted. Of these, 18,000 had been sent further into French territory. Living conditions for the refugees were very poor. Many were dying of exposure, undernourishment, and typhoid. Starving bands crossed the border illegally to avoid placement in a concentration camp. In response, French officials began turning back suspected deserters and arresting suspected criminals.[94] The dire conditions facing many of the refugees did not affect all: some Republican leaders crossed the border in style while their followers walked.[95]

A conference of 5 February between the French and Republican generals generated an immediate solution to the refugee crisis. An agreement was reached whereby Republican soldiers could enter France or join the Nationalists. As a result, some 300,000 soldiers were allowed into France in an orderly manner. Another 17,000 Republicans who had been Franco's prisoners were admitted on 8 February as part of prisoner exchange. On 11 February the first of Franco's troops arrived at the border.[96] A movement of civilians and soldiers that compared with the withdrawal of the Greek army from Anatolia in 1922 was over.

This movement of some 400,000 Spanish Republicans to France was primarily the product of a revolution and civil war. In some respects, however, it can be seen as one episode in the continuing process of nation-state formation: the strongest resistance to Franco's troops came from the non-Castillian regions of Spain, and the refugees included a high proportion of Catalonians. Although the number of Spanish refugees approximated the number from the Third Reich, this exodus differed in that it took place within a much shorter period of time, and the responsibility for assisting the refugees fell to one country, France. Of the refugees, about half were women, children, and old men, and the rest soldiers.[97] They did not have major difficulties in finding temporary asylum in France but, once there, they still needed some form of international legal protection and a means of earning a living while they waited and hoped for revolution in their home country.

[94] Ibid.   [95] Stein, *Beyond Death and Exile*, 23.
[96] Simpson, *Refugees: A Review*, 56.
[97] On 17 Feb. 1939 the French Foreign Affairs Commission estimated there were 340,000 Spanish refugees in France. On 8 Mar. it estimated 440,000. Simpson, *Refugees: A Review*, 57.

THE ERA OF REFUGEES

In inter-war Europe, no two refugee groups had exactly the same experience of flight and exile. Some refugees, such as the Greeks, fled from their homes suddenly; others, most notably the German Jews, made carefully planned travel arrangements. The Greek, Turkish, and Bulgar refugees had ethnic homelands to welcome them, while the Jewish and Armenian refugees had no similar benefit. The Spanish and Italian refugees were just two of the groups who found asylum primarily in a nearby country. In contrast, boats took Portuguese, Jewish, and some Russian refugees to places half-way around the world, making these refugees similar to the 'jet refugees' of the late twentieth century. The Russian exodus was composed primarily of young men, while in the Greek case women and children made up the majority. The typical refugee in some groups, such as the Turks and Bulgars, was an agricultural worker; in others, including the Armenians and Jews, he or she came from an urban occupation.

Although the origins and dimensions of each refugee movement in inter-war Europe were unique, a common refugee experience also existed. For one thing, the mass refugee movements of the era were generated by common causes. In these 'peaceful' years between the two World Wars, revolutionary upheavals and the process of nation-state formation combined to create millions of refugees. These causes, in turn, made it very unlikely that the refugees would easily return to their home countries. The White Russians and Spanish Republicans spent decades in exile hoping for a revolution at home. For the Jews, Armenians, and other refugees from minority groups, the desire of European countries to form ethnically homogeneous nation-states meant that they would never again be welcome as citizens in the lands of their birth. In the process of flight, all inter-war refugees, especially those who fled during the depression years of the 1930s, had to contend with the reality of immigration restrictions world-wide. Once outside their home countries, they shared the common experience of trying to re-establish themselves in a foreign and sometimes hostile land.

Taken as a group, the refugees of inter-war Europe formed an important part of the political, economic, and social history of the period. The refugees came from or went to virtually every country in Europe, and many others world-wide. Their presence significantly affected both refugee-producing and host countries. In some instances, an entire region was affected: the refugee movements following the Greco-Turkish war dramatically changed the ethnic make-up of both countries. Although many contemporary observers conceptualized the refugee problem as a temporary one similar to disaster relief, in retrospect we can see otherwise. Because of the frequent emergence of new groups, and the length of time that they stayed in exile, refugees became a permanent feaure of the domestic and international politics of the Inter-war Period.

PART II
The International Refugee Regime in Inter-War Europe

3

The Emergence of a Regime

T HE emergence of refugees as an international issue in the first quarter of the twentieth century was related to a wider process affecting the globe: the growth of interdependence. In an interdependent world, countries are no longer isolated; what happens in one country affects others, and vice versa.[1] In the case of refugees from and within inter-war Europe, the existence of an interdependent world meant that a mass exodus from one country potentially threatened the economic and social life of a receiving country, even its national security. The creation of immigration restrictions, something normally considered a purely domestic issue, also had profound repercussions in other countries. While increased interdependence has undermined the ability of sovereign states to deal with issues unilaterally, it also has served as a catalyst for the formation of international regimes to manage interdependence.

In everyday language, the term 'regime' refers to a form of government or a regular pattern of action. In international-relations theory, the term 'international regime' has a related but distinct meaning. It refers to the governing arrangements created by a group of countries to deal with a particular issue in world politics. These arrangements are special because they are not simply based on short-term calculations of interest. Instead, they reflect shared principles and norms, and have established rules and decision-making procedures.[2] International regimes are not as

---

[1] Robert O. Keohane and Joseph S. Nye, *Power and Interdependence* (Boston: Little, Brown, 1977). Keohane and Nye build upon earlier works, particularly those which deal with economic issues. See Robert Cooper, *The Economics of Interdependence* (New York: McGraw-Hill, 1968).

[2] The most widely accepted definition of an international regime is given by Stephen D. Krasner, 'Structural Causes and Regime Consequences: Regimes as Intervening Variables', in Stephen D. Krasner (ed.), *International Regimes* (Ithaca, NY: Cornell University Press, 1983), 2. Also published in special issue on international regimes, *International Organization*, 36 (Spring 1982), 185–205.

strong or as comprehensive as a world government would be, but they do indicate a pattern of international co-operation in an otherwise anarchical state system.

In scholarly works, analysis of international regimes has primarily been concerned with economic and, to a lesser extent, security issues.[3] Nevertheless, Jack Donnelly suggests that a regime perspective provides a useful framework for the study of human rights issues because it 'allows us to see what we "know" in a new light'.[4] Refugees constitute a human-rights issue where organized co-operation between governments has taken place since the early 1920s, when the League of Nations first appointed a High Commissioner for Russian Refugees. From this beginning, the scope and functions of international efforts to assist refugees gradually expanded until they included concern for the legal protection and material well-being of the major refugee groups of the inter-war years. Although the economic and political crises of the 1930s made international co-operation extremely difficult, these efforts did not cease until the outbreak of war in 1939. Because this co-operation reflected common principles and norms, and resulted in the creation of rules being written into international law, it is appropriate to speak of it as constituting an international refugee regime. In this chapter, two important questions about this regime will be considered: what was the structure of the regime, and why did the regime begin? A third question—what impact did the regime have?—will be explored in depth in the chapters that follow.

THE STRUCTURE OF THE INTERNATIONAL REFUGEE REGIME

The structure of an international regime consists of four major elements: principles, norms, rules, and decision-making procedures.[5] Principles are core beliefs held by the members of a regime. Norms are standards which define the rights and obligations of the actors

---

[3] For an exception to this rule, see Kim Salomon, *Refugees in the Cold War: Toward a New International Refugee Regime in the Early Postwar Era* (Lund, Sweden: Lund University Press, 1991).

[4] Jack Donnelly, 'International Human Rights: A Regime Analysis', *International Organization*, 40 (Summer 1986), 640.   [5] Krasner, 'Structural Causes', 2.

in the regime. Together, principles and norms form the foundation of a regime. If they are significantly changed, then the regime itself takes on a different character. A regime may have more than one principle or norm, and there may be contradictions between them. Over time the one given primacy may change, depending on the outcome of bargaining between regime members and on overall systemic conditions. There are many rules that can be derived from the principles and norms of a regime. Rules are often more easily identified than norms because they are usually codified into international law, and efforts to implement and enforce them can be readily observed. Decision-making procedures within a regime primarily involve states, the members of a regime. They can also include the activities of non-state actors such as international organizations or multinational corporations.[6] Some regimes are structured around formal institutions, such as a specialized agency of the United Nations, while others have only informal mechanisms.[7] Because there are many rules and decision-making mechanisms that are compatible with the principles and norms of a given regime, they may be frequently revised. Changes of this sort, unlike revisions in principles and norms, do not affect the fundamental character of the regime. The rules of the regime, however, must be taken seriously by states if the regime is to be effective. If rules are consistently ignored or broken, the regime weakens and may eventually collapse.

Principles and Norms

Two basic principles underpinned the international refugee regime that existed in the inter-war years. The first was sovereignty, which, according to Hedley Bull, is still the defining principle of the international system. Bull defines sovereignty as the supreme authority that states assert 'in relation to a particular portion of the earth's surface and a particular segment of the human population'. Moreover, sovereignty entails 'independence of outside authorities' in exercising this supreme authority.[8] Sovereignty has

---

[6] Oran Young, 'Regime Dynamics: The Rise and Fall of International Regimes', in Krasner (ed.), *International Regimes*, 93.

[7] Arthur A. Stein, 'Coordination and Collaboration: Regimes in an Anarchic World', in Krasner (ed.), *International Regimes*, 133.

[8] Hedley Bull, *The Anarchical Society* (London: Macmillan, 1977), 8.

important implications for immigration generally. Aristide Zolberg, for instance, points out that 'it has been universally acknowledged ever since the state system arose in its modern form that, under the law of nations, the right to regulate entry is a fundamental concomitant of sovereignty'.[9] Applied to refugees, sovereignty translates into the authority of a state to control their entry and exit and their treatment while within the boundaries of the state. The second defining principle of the international refugee regime was humanitarianism, the belief in the fundamental worth and dignity of all human life. The fulfilment of the humanitarianism principle required that the needs of refugees be met in an apolitical, non-discriminatory way.[10]

These two principles were compatible in circumstances where sovereignty represents the best hope for the attainment of humanitarian objectives. But, in circumstances where state actions violate humanitarian standards, the principles conflicted. The large refugee movements of inter-war Europe stand as testimony to the inability of some sovereign states to behave according to humanitarian principles. The provision of refugee relief by states and international organizations can be seen as an attempt to satisfy humanitarian imperatives without trampling on state sovereignty.

In the Inter-war Period, three norms characterized the international refugee regime: asylum, assistance, and burden-sharing. These norms were derived from multiple sources rather than from one comprehensive document. In this regard, the international refugee regime of the inter-war years contrasts with the post-1945 international human rights regime: in the latter case, the Universal Declaration of Human Rights explicitly enumerates the norms of the regime.[11] The asylum norm has a long history in both state

[9] Aristide R. Zolberg, 'Dilemmas at the Gate: The Politics of Immigration in Advanced Industrial Societies', unpub. paper (1982), 2–3.
[10] For a general definition of humanitarianism, see Bruce Nichols, 'Rubberband Humanitarianism', *Ethics and International Affairs*, 1 (1987), 194. See also Bruce Nichols and Gil Loescher (eds.), *The Moral Nation: Humanitarianism and U.S. Foreign Policy Today* (Notre Dame, Ind.: University of Notre Dame Press, 1989); Robert C. Johansen, *The National Interest and the Human Interest: An Analysis of U.S. Foreign Policy* (Princeton, NJ: Princeton University Press, 1980), 153. For a formulation of the humanitarian principle by one UNHCR official, see Jean-Pierre Hocke, *Beyond Humanitarianism: The Need for Political Will to Resolve Today's Refugee Problem*, Inaugural Joyce Pearce Memorial Lecture, Oxford University, 29 Oct. 1986 (Oxford: Refugee Studies Programme with the Ockenden Venture, 1986), 8. [11] Donnelly, 'International Human Rights', 606.

practice and international law. It referred to the right of states
to grant sanctuary to any individuals who come to their territory
seeking protection. Contrary to popular usage, the asylum norm
did not guarantee the right of an individual to be granted asylum.
The granting of asylum to the French Huguenots following the
repeal of the Edict of Nantes in 1695 established the practice of
asylum in modern times.[12] The asylum norm also has a long tradition in international law, having been originally developed by
the classical legal scholars Hugo Grotius and Emmerich de Vattel.[13]

In their overall approach to the 'law of nations', the seventeenth-
century Dutchman Grotius and the eighteenth-century Swiss Vattel
represent contrary views: Grotius argues that individuals are essentially subjects of international law, while Vattel maintains that
states are the subjects of international law and individuals only its
objects.[14] Despite these philosophical differences, however, these
two scholars expound remarkably similar views on exile and asylum. In contrast to the feudal concept of perpetual allegiance to
the overlord, both Grotius and Vattel assert the right of individuals
to withdraw from or expatriate themselves from their own state.[15]

[12] Atle Grahl-Madsen, *Territorial Asylum* (London: Oceana Publications, 1980),
3.
[13] Hugo Grotius, *De jure belli ac pacis libri tres*, tr. Francis W. Kelsey (Oxford:
Clarendon Press, 1925), ii; Emer de Vattel, *Le Droit des gens, ou principes de la
loi naturelle appliqués à la conduite et aux affaires des nations et des souverains*
(Geneva: Slatkine Reprints, 1983), i: photographic repr. of bks I and II of the 1758
edn.
[14] Peter Pavel Remec, *The Position of the Individual in International Law
according to Grotius and Vattel* (The Hague: Martinus Nijhoff, 1960).
[15] Grotius qualifies this by arguing that nationals of a state cannot depart in
large bodies as this would endanger civil society itself. Individuals, however, are a
different case; under normal circumstances, they are free to withdraw from the
state. Grotius makes two exceptions to this general rule: if a nation has a heavy
debt or if a siege threatens. The second exception can be overcome if the national
furnishes someone equally qualified to defend the state. After this, the state has no
legal claim on the person (*De jure belli*, ii. 253–4).
Although known as a defender of state sovereignty, Vattel argues that individuals have certain inviolable rights that they can assert against a sovereign state.
Paramount among these is the right to emigrate. Vattel, however, limits this right
by saying that it can only be exercised in certain circumstances, namely when the
person is unable to find support, if the society or sovereign fails to keep its obligations to its citizens, or if the majority establishes laws unacceptable to the minority (*Le Droit des gens*, i. 206). Vattel further stresses that exile does not remove a
person's natural rights: 'Un homme, pour être exilé, ou banni, ne perd point sa
qualité d'homme, ni par conséquent le droit d'habiter quelque part sur la terre'
(ibid. 210).

Nevertheless, for them the essence of the asylum norm concerns the rights of sovereign states. Grotius emphasizes the right of a state to grant asylum to exiles.[16] Vattel maintains that every state has the right to refuse admission to an alien if admission would endanger the state's security. He also points out that an exile does not have the absolute right to settle wherever he chooses.[17]

In the nineteenth century the positivist school of jurists further developed the classical view of asylum as defined by Grotius and Vattel. For instance, Oppenheim, a leading positivist writer, affirms the right of a state to grant or refuse asylum to aliens, and denies the right of the individual to choose a place of exile.[18] Although the asylum norm was not specifically codified in treaty law between the two World Wars, the right of states to grant—or to deny—temporary or permanent asylum to refugees was universally accepted. Moreover, states had the right to decide which refugees would be granted citizenship.

The second norm of the international refugee regime, that of assistance, was an outgrowth of the Judaeo-Christian religious tradition. The assistance norm gave states an obligation to help refugees because of their particularly precarious position. Refugees are often in great material need, but in this regard they do not differ from poor people. What sets refugees apart is the fact that they have undergone a traumatic flight, live in an alien environment, and often have an insecure legal status. In a world organized into territorially defined political units, refugees are especially vulnerable because they have no government to protect them. During the Inter-war Period the assistance norm recognized the special problems of refugees and gave states obligations to refugees beyond those that they have to ordinary migrants and aliens. At the same time, a third norm, that of burden-sharing, governed financial obligations towards refugees. According to its tenets , all

[16] Grotius makes this exception: 'It is clearly not permissible to admit towns or large aggregations, which constitute an integral part of a state', or fugitives from justice, slaves, and those under obligations of service (*De jure belli*, ii. 819–20).

[17] While Vattel urges prudence in the admission of exiles, stating that they may be excluded for reasons of national security and for protection against health risks, he urges that exiles should not be rejected on foolish and unreasonable grounds, but that instead charity and sympathy due to the unfortunate should be kept in mind. (*Le Droit des gens*, i. 210–11).

[18] L. Oppenheim, *International Law: A Treatise*, i (London: Longmans, Green, 1905), 371–2.

countries—not just those offering refugees physical asylum—had an obligation to assist refugees.

The clearest expression of the assistance and burden-sharing norms can be found in a report to the League of Nations by a special committee charged with planning the future of refugee assistance. Presented to the Council in January 1936, the report was the result of an extensive study of refugees world-wide and was based on information from governments, private organizations, and the refugee agencies of the League of Nations. The report stresses the importance of burden-sharing, maintaining that the solution to the refugee problem requires 'close co-operation between all States, whether Members of the League or not'. The report divides states into countries of first asylum, countries of resettlement, countries in a position to donate funds, and refugee-producing countries. It further concludes that all members of the international community have the duty to assist those states most heavily burdened by refugees. The report also expresses the assistance norm: it identifies the humanitarian and legal aspects of refugee problems and speaks of the need to assist refugees in these areas. Finally, the report affirms the duty of all states to help ensure the gradual reintegration of refugees.[19]

Rules

The rules created to enforce the principles and norms of the international refugee regime can be found in various legal documents dealing with refugees that were formulated between 1922 and 1939. The most important of these rules concerned the definition of a refugee. Although refugee definitions may appear to be simple exercises in semantics, in fact they are very important because when written into international law they have a special function: they establish obligations of states towards refugees and entitle those granted refugee status to certain benefits. According to one legal scholar, 'the purpose of any definition or description of the class of refugees is to facilitate, and to justify, aid and protection;

[19] League of Nations, Committee on International Assistance to Refugees, 'Report by the Committee Submitted to the Council of the League of Nations' (3 Jan. 1936) [C.2.M.2.1936.XII], 3–5, 8.

moreover, in practice, satisfying the relevant criteria will indicate entitlement to the pertinent rights or benefits.'[20]

The 1933 and 1938 Refugee Conventions, the two major legal instruments of the Inter-war Period, define the term 'refugee' according to ethnic group or country of origin. The 1933 Refugee Convention, for instance, applies to Russian, Armenian, Turkish, Assyrian, Assyro-Chaldean, and Turkish refugees, while the 1938 Refugee Convention applies to 'refugees coming from Germany'.[21] These definitions add the proviso that refugees are people who are outside their home country, lack the diplomatic protection of their home governments, and have not yet acquired another nationality. They make no mention of the reasons for flight beyond the rather vague exclusion of persons who leave 'for reasons of purely personal convenience' contained in the 1938 Convention. Though not explicitly stated, these definitions implicitly suggest that refugees differ from ordinary immigrants because dire circumstances have forced them to leave their homeland.

Another key rule of the regime can be found in the 1933 Convention, which provides the most authoritative statement of the rule of non-*refoulement*, the 'prohibition of the forcible return of a refugee to a country of persecution'.[22] Article 3 of the Convention prohibits states from expelling or refusing entry to refugees authorized to live in their territory. But this article also contains an escape clause: states could violate the rule of non-*refoulement* if 'national security or public order' required it. This provision justifies a broad range of actions: in recession, employment of native-born citizens may be considered a requirement for national security and a reason to expel refugee workers; or, in wartime, the very presence of foreigners in a society may be considered a threat and make refugees a target for expulsion.

In addition to the rule of non-*refoulement*, the various arrangements and conventions of the Inter-war Period contain rules about the treatment of refugees within countries. Perhaps the best-known rules concern the operations of the Nansen passport

[20] Guy S. Goodwin-Gill, *The Refugee in International Law* (Oxford: Clarendon Press, 1983), 2.

[21] 'Convention Relating to the International Status of Refugees, 28 October 1933', *LNTS*, no. 3663, vol. 159. 'Convention Concerning the Status of Refugees Coming from Germany, 10 February 1938', *LNTS*, no. 4461, vol. 192.

[22] Grahl-Madsen, *Territorial Asylum*, 4. See also Atle Grahl-Madsen, *The Status of Refugees in International Law*, ii (Leiden: A. W. Sijthoff, 1972), 93–8.

system, a series of agreements that extended internationally recognized travel documents to refugees. Another rule asserts that laws governing the national labour market be suspended in the case of refugees (1933 Convention, art. 7). Additional rules prescribe that a state should give refugees 'the most favourable treatment that it accords to the nationals of a foreign country'. The 1933 Convention, for instance, applies this rule to the handling of industrial accidents (art. 8), welfare and relief (art. 9), and education (art. 12).

Decision-Making Procedures

Decision-making within the international refugee regime in the Inter-war Period involved virtually all the independent states to some degree. Because the League of Nations provided a forum for this interaction, the membership of the regime approximated that of the League. Of the sixty-three countries which formed the League, a sizeable majority were found in Europe (28) and the Americas (21). Only a few African (4) and Asian states (10) belonged because of continued colonial domination in these regions.[23] Not all countries, however, participated in the international refugee regime continuously from 1919 until 1939. The German government played an active role in the regime even before joining the League in 1926, but this support ended after Hitler came to power in 1933. The Italian government terminated its participation following its invasion of Ethiopia and subsequent withdrawal from the League in 1936.

Within the international refugee regime, the European countries attached the greatest importance to the League's activities, primarily because most refugees were located in Europe. In this sense, the inter-war regime could be described as Eurocentric in comparison with the more global refugee regime which developed after the Second World War. Outside Europe, countries either supported the international refugee regime or at least did not oppose it. The Latin American republics, Australia, and New Zealand participated, but considered refugees to be primarily a

---

[23] The membership of the League included 28 European countries, 20 Latin American republics, Canada, 4 African and 10 Asian states. For a complete list of the members of the League of Nations, see F. P. Walters, *History of the League of Nations* (London: Oxford University Press, 1960), 64–5.

European concern. Even though the United States did not join
the League of Nations, the American government sometimes participated in the international refugee regime by encouraging the
involvement of American private organizations in refugee assistance and by periodically intervening on behalf of a refugee group.

The Institutional Framework

Although the League of Nations as a whole served as a forum for
decision-making, the international refugee regime was centred on
its refugee agencies. Because these agencies changed shape over
time, it is worthwhile to trace their institutional evolution. For the
first decade (1921–30) the first High Commissioner for Russian
Refugees, Fridtjof Nansen of Norway, dominated the League's
refugee work. Appointed High Commissioner at the age of 60,
Nansen brought a unique set of credentials to the job. From his
daring expedition across Greenland in 1888 and his journey across
the polar ice-cap beginning in 1893, Nansen had learned a proven
recipe for success: careful planning, attention to detail, and deter-
mination. As Norway's first Ambassador to the Court of St James
in 1906 and 1907, Nansen gained negotiating skills. He further
honed them when, in 1917, he headed a mission to the United
States, where he successfully concluded an agreement for the ship-
ment of essential goods to Norway. At the end of the First World
War, Nansen distinguished himself as a humanitarian by arranging
for prisoner-of-war repatriation and organizing aid for victims of
the Russian famine.[24]

---

[24] Nansen initially achieved fame as an explorer when, in 1888, he led five com-
panions across Greenland in the first expedition to do so successfully. In 1893 he
set out across the polar sea in a specially built ship, the *Fram* (meaning 'Forward'),
and lodged it in the ice-cap. Three years later the ship returned, having proved
Nansen's theory of Arctic drift. Meanwhile, Nansen and one companion left the
ship in an attempt to reach the North Pole. Although they failed, they travelled
further north than anyone else had previously done. On his return, Nansen was
welcomed as a hero in Norway. For general biographies of Nansen, see Liv Nansen
Høyer, *Nansen: A Family Portrait*, tr. Maurice Michael (London: Longmans, Green,
1957); Aubrey de Selincourt, *Nansen* (London: Oxford University Press, 1957); J.
Sorensen, *The Saga of Fridtjof Nansen* (London: Allen & Unwin, 1932). On Nansen's
travels, see Fridtjof Nansen, *Episodes from Farthest North* (London, 1927) and *The
First Crossing of Greenland*, tr. H. M. Gepp (London: Longmans, 1923); Edward
Shackleton, *Nansen: The Explorer* (London: H. F. & G. Witherby, 1959). On
Nansen's tenure as High Commissioner, see Claudena Skran, 'Profiles of the First
Two High Commissioners', *Journal of Refugee Studies*, 1 (1988), 277–96.

Nansen began work by gathering a small staff of trusted colleagues to assist him. The High Commissioner appointed delegates in host countries with the job of keeping Geneva in touch with both host government officials and the refugees. In addition, Nansen created an Advisory Committee made up of voluntary agencies. Lastly, he kept in touch with governments through special conferences and direct appearances at Council and Assembly sessions. Although the High Commissioner worked in tandem with a special Refugee Section in the International Labour Organization (ILO) from 1925 until 1929, the basic structure established by Nansen continued to function.[25]

In the decade following Nansen's death in 1930 a series of agencies continued his work. From 1931 until 1938 the Nansen International Office served as the principal organization charged with refugee assistance and protection.[26] In response to the crisis of refugees from Germany, the League first established an independent High Commissioner for Refugees coming from Germany. James G. McDonald, an American, served in this post from 1933 until his resignation in 1935.[27] In 1936 the League placed this position under its own auspices and appointed Sir Neill Malcolm

[25] On this episode in the ILO's history, see G. A. Johnston, *The International Labour Organisation: Its Work for Social and Economic Progress* (London: Europa Publications, 1970), 113–14. For a classic study of the ILO, see Ernst Haas, *Beyond the Nation-State* (Stanford, Calif.: Stanford University Press, 1964).

[26] The Nansen Office was governed by a Governing Body and a Managing Committee, rather than by a High Commissioner. The Governing Body was composed of 12 members, including a President appointed by the League Assembly, 4 delegates appointed by the Intergovernmental Advisory Commission for Refugees, 1 member appointed by the Secretariat, 1 member appointed by the ILO, 3 members appointed by the Advisory Committee for Private Organizations, and 2 members belonging to the principal international relief agencies. The Managing Committee, composed of the President of the Governing Body and two other members of the Governing Body, attended to the day-to-day affairs of the agency. During the lifetime of the Nansen Office, three men served as its President. Dr Max Huber, former President of the ICRC, served from the opening of the office on 1 Apr. 1931 until his resignation for health reasons in Jan. 1933. Dr Georges Werner, Vice-Chairman of the ICRC and a member of the Governing Body, succeeded him in Feb. 1933 and continued until his death in 1935. A Norwegian judge, Michael Hansson, became President of the Nansen Office in Jan. 1936 and continued in the position until the liquidation of the agency in 1938. See 'Constitution of the Nansen International Office for Refugees', *Official Journal* (Feb. 1931), annex 1263, pp. 308–11; Sir John Hope Simpson, *The Refugee Problem: Report of a Survey* (London: Oxford University Press, 1939), 210–13.

[27] For a profile of McDonald as High Commissioner, see Skran, 'Profiles of the First Two High Commissioners', esp. 289–94.

of Great Britain as High Commissioner. On the eve of the Second World War the League finally merged all its refugee work under the authority of a single organization, with Sir Herbert Emerson, a British citizen, assuming the position of High Commissioner for Refugees in 1939.[28]

The refugee agencies had to turn to the Council and Assembly of the League of Nations for funding and approval, and to the Secretariat for expertise. The Council, which gave Britain, France, Italy, Germany, and Japan the special status of permanent members,[29] greatly facilitated the involvement of the leaders of the Great Powers in refugee issues.[30] The Assembly, in contrast, embodied the democratic spirit of the League's founding: a universal body where all countries sent representatives, it made decisions by consensus. Each member had one vote and, on substantive matters, voting required unanimity. Thus, if a particular refugee assistance measure were to be passed, all members of the League had to agree to it. Within the Assembly, committees generally performed the substantive work during an annual session, which usually occurred for three weeks in September.[31]

---

[28] Hans Aufrict, *Guide to League of Nations Publications, 1920–1947* (New York: Columbia University Press, 1951), 190–2; Simpson, *The Refugee Problem*, 214–21.

[29] During the history of the League, the composition of the permanent Council members varied a great deal. Only Great Britain and France served continuously from 1920 until 1946. Japan and Italy belonged during the 1920s but withdrew in 1933 and 1937, respectively. Germany joined in 1926 and departed in 1933. The Soviet Union belonged for only six years, from 1934 until its expulsion in 1939. Aufrict, *Guide to League of Nations Publications*, 72–4.

[30] Originally designed as an instrument of the Great Powers, the Council—as designated under article 4 of the Covenant—was to consist of permanent representatives from the Principal Allied and Associated Powers, and four non-permanent members selected by the Assembly. The failure of the United States to join the League, however, severely hampered the ability of the Council to fulfil its original function. Subsequent enlargements in the number of non-permanent members (from four in 1920 to eleven in 1936) further diluted its strength. Nevertheless, the Great Powers continued to have a greater preponderance in the Council than in the Assembly. See 'Covenant of the League of Nations', art. 4 (1), reprinted in Inis Claude, *Swords into Plowshares* (New York: Random House, 1984), 454. The Principal Allied and Associated Powers consisted of the USA, British Empire, France, Italy, and Japan. For an annotated version of the Covenant, see Walters, *History of the League of Nations*, 40–65; Aufrict, *Guide to League of Nations Publications*, 74–7.

[31] In the 1920s the Fifth Committee (Social and Humanitarian Questions) primarily dealt with refugees. After a reorganization in the early 1930s the Sixth Committee (Political Questions) took over. In addition, the Fourth Committee (Budget) always pronounced on the financial aspects of the refugee question.

Throughout the history of the League of Nations, no clear division of labour concerning refugees developed between the Council and the Assembly.[32] Both bodies, for instance, engaged in the supervision of refugee assistance, received reports from the High Commissioner for Refugees, and provided a forum for their members of discuss refugee issues. However, two significant differences between the Council and Assembly existed. The Assembly exercised exclusive control over the budget of the League of Nations and the creation of new organizations.[33] Yet, despite the ability of the Assembly to control these two important functions, it would be a mistake to assume that the Council was impotent on refugee issues. In fact, the Council had one great advantage over the Assembly: it met four times annually, while the Assembly met only once. Consequently, the Council was much better placed to follow refugee issues throughout the year. By the same token, the League Secretariat had a great advantage over the Council because it worked continuously throughout the year.

The creation of an international Secretariat to provide technical and administrative expertise to the political bodies of the League of Nations constituted an innovation in the history of international organization.[34] At the head of the League Secretariat stood the Secretary-General, a position initially held by Sir Eric Drummond of Great Britain and later by Joseph Avenol of France.[35] As head of the League bureaucracy and as the primary liaison between the permanent staff of the League and temporary government delegates, the Secretary-General was well placed to influence the League's policy towards refugees. The functional sections of the Secretariat also dealt with refugee issues. The Economic and Financial Section, for instance, took charge of all loans raised under League auspices for refugee settlement. In addition, the Legal

---

[32] On the ongoing debate within the League of Nations on the competence of the Assembly and Council to handle particular issues, see Felix Morley, *The Society of Nations: Its Organization and Constitutional Development* (London: Faber & Faber, 1932), esp. 502–5.   [33] Ibid. 516, 521.

[34] Walters, *History of the League of Nations*, 75.

[35] On the office of the Secretary-General in both the League and the UN, see Arthur Rovine, *The First Fifty Years: The Secretary-General in World Politics, 1920–1970* (Leyden: A. W. Sijthoff, 1970). On Drummond see James Barros, *Office Without Power: The Secretary-General Sir Eric Drummond, 1919–1933* (Oxford: Clarendon Press, 1979). On Avenol, see James Barros, *Betrayal From Within: Joseph Avenol: Secretary-General of the League of Nations* (New Haven, Conn.: Yale University Press, 1969).

section gave advice on refugees under international law; the Political Section studied the political ramifications of refugee movements; the International Bureaux Section co-ordinated relations between the Secretariat and the refugee agencies; the Health Section helped fight epidemics in refugee areas; and the Social Section collaborated on areas of joint concern, such as the plight of women and children in the Near East.

In the final months of the Inter-war Period, governments created a new institution in the hope of replacing those seriously affected by the declining prestige of the League of Nations. Responding in 1938 to the Austrian refugee crisis, governments created the Intergovernmental Committee for Refugees (IGCR) as an alternative to the discredited League.[36] Unlike the League, the IGCR dealt specifically with refugees from the Third Reich, not with a variety of international issues. Its membership was also much smaller, being confined to governments that had the potential to receive refugees. Although the IGCR had a director, it lacked an international secretariat and delegates such as those provided by the League of Nations.[37]

The Crucial Role of Private, Voluntary Organizations

In addition to states and intergovernmental organizations, a vast array of private, voluntary organizations (PVOs) participated in the international refugee regime. Over time, the number of PVOs with a direct interest in refugees grew substantially. In 1922 Nansen created the Advisory Committee of Voluntary Organizations with only sixteen members. In 1936 more than forty PVOs reported about their aid programmes to the League of Nations committee charged with reorganizing refugee assistance (see Tables 6 and 7).[38] PVOs distinguished themselves as providers of emergency relief and social services to refugees. In the Refugee Survey, Simpson reports that 'it is fair to say that the greater part of material assistance has been provided by private organizations, some of them set

---

[36] On the IGCR see Tommie Sjöberg, *The Powers and the Persecuted: The Refugee Problem and the Intergovernmental Committee on Refugees (IGCR), 1938–1947* (Lund, Sweden: Lund University Press, 1991).

[37] Simpson, *The Refugee Problem*, 223–6.

[38] 'Report of March 24 1922 by the High Commissioner for Refugees', *Official Journal* (May 1922), annex 321, p. 387; [C.2.M.2.1936.XII], 13–14.

TABLE 6. *Advisory Committee of Private Organizations to the High Commissioner for Refugees, March 1922*

Near East Relief
Comité international de la Croix-Rouge
League of Red Cross Societies
European Student Relief
Comité des Zemstovs et Villes russes
Russian Red Cross (Old)
Jewish Colonization Association
Conférence universelle juive de Secours
Save the Children Fund
Union internationale de Secours aux Enfants
Armenian Refugees Fund
Russian Famine Relief Fund
Imperial War Relief Fund
Russian Relief and Reconstruction Fund
International Committee of American YMCA
World's Committee of YMCA

Source: *Official Journal* (May 1922), annex 321, p. 387.

up *ad hoc*, but some with more general functions of which refugee work is only one'.[39] Although private organizations primarily concerned themselves with relief for refugees, in some instances they took on the role of refugee advocacy in the decision-making process of the international refugee regime.

Private voluntary organizations participating in the international refugee regime can be divided into two major groups. The first includes general-purpose organizations, which provided refugee assistance as only one of their many functions. For instance, the International Committee of the Red Cross (ICRC), a voluntary organization based in Switzerland and primarily concerned with helping victims of armed conflict, maintained an active interest in Russian and other refugees in the inter-war years.[40] A second example is the American Red Cross (ARC), one of the many

[39] Simpson, *The Refugee Problem*, 172.
[40] On the Red Cross Movement see David P. Forsythe, *Humanitarian Politics: The International Committee of the Red Cross* (Baltimore: Johns Hopkins University Press, 1977); James Avery Joyce, *Red Cross International and the Strategy for Peace* (New York: Oceana Publications, 1959).

TABLE 7. *Private Organizations Reporting to the Special Committee on Assistance to Refugees, January 1936*

Group A: Private Organizations Dealing with Refugees

World Alliance of Young Men's Christian Associations, Geneva
World Alliance of Young Women's Christian Associations, Geneva
Society of Friends (Germany Emergency Committee), London
Quakers' Refugee Aid International Service, Paris
League of Red Cross Societies, Paris
European Central Office for Inter-Church Aid, Geneva
Save the Children International Union, Geneva
Save the Children Fund, London
Armenian (Lord Mayor's) Fund, London
Academic Assistance Council, London
International Migration Service, Geneva
International Committee of the Red Cross, Geneva
International Committee to secure Employment for Refugee Professional
    Workers, Geneva
International Students' Service, Geneva

Group B: Organizations for Refugees under the Nansen Office

Commission centrale pour l'étude de la condition des réfugiés russes,
    Paris
Union des Associations des émigrés ukrainiens en France, Paris
Comité de protection des émigrés russes en Pologne, Warsaw
Comité central de patronage de la jeunesse universitaire russe à l'étranger,
    Paris
'Zemgor' Association in Yugoslavia, Belgrade
Comité d'Emigration et Colonisation juive, Paris
Russian Zemstvos and Towns Relief Committee for Russian Citizens
    abroad, Paris
Fédération des invalides mutilés de guerre russes à l'étranger
Comitetul Ukrainian pentru Assistenţa emigratilor Ucrainiene in Romania,
    Bucharest
Union générale arménienne de bienfaisance, Paris
Union des Médecins russes à l'étranger, Paris
Ancienne Organisation de la Croix-Rouge russe
Office central des réfugiés russes en France
Haut Conseil des émigrés ukrainiens
Action orthodoxe, Paris
Comité central des réfugiés arméniens, Paris

Table 7. *(Cont.)*

Group C: Organizations Dealing with Refugees from Germany

Hias–JCA–Emigration Association (HICEM), Paris
Jewish Colonization Association, Paris
Notgemeinschaft Deutscher Wissenschaftler im Ausland, Zurich
Central British Fund for German Jewry, London
Jewish Agency for Palestine, London
Jewish Refugees Committee, London
Comite voor Bijzondere Joodsche Belangen, Amsterdam
Comité d'aide et d'assistance aux victimes de l'antisémitisme en Allemagne,
   Brussels
Comité des délégations juives, Paris
Comité allemand, Paris
Comité national de secours aux réfugiés allemands victimes de l'antisémit-
   isme, Paris
International Federation of Trade Unions, Paris
Agudas Israel, London
Czechoslovak National Committee for Refugees from Germany, Prague
Assistance médicale aux enfants des émigrés, Paris
Jewish Committee for the Relief of Refugees from Germany, Warsaw
American Jewish Joint Distribution Committee, New York
Fédération des émigrés d'Allemagne en France, Paris

Source: League of Nations, Committee on International Assistance to Refugees,
'Report by the Committee Submitted to the Council of the League of Nations'
(3 Jan. 1936) [C.2.M.2.1936.XII], 13–14.

national Red Cross Societies affiliated with the ICRC through the
League of Red Cross Societies. Although the ARC concentrated
on health issues and disaster assistance within the United States,
its overseas wing provided more emergency supplies to Russian
refugees at Constantinople and to Greek refugees after the Smyrna
catastrophe than any other relief agency.[41] Other general-purpose
organizations engaged in refugee assistance between the two World
Wars include the Save the Children Fund, the YMCA, the Society
of Friends (Quakers), and the Roman Catholic Church.[42]

[41] Simpson, *The Refugee Problem*, 172–5; Charles Hurd, *The Compact History of
the American Red Cross* (New York: Hawthorn, 1959).
[42] Simpson, *The Refugee Problem*, 173–80.

The second major category consists of organizations designed to assist members of a particular nationality, including refugees. Some of these organizations were led by concerned outsiders, others by the more fortunate kin within a particular ethnic group, and still others by refugees. The largest number of such organizations dealt with Jewish refugees from the Third Reich. These agencies provided comprehensive services to Jewish refugees and other Jewish emigrants: support in their home countries; funds for travel expenses; financial, legal, and moral support in countries of settlement; and political advocacy. Some Jewish organizations operated solely within the boundaries of host countries, such as local committees in France, Holland, Switzerland, Britain, and the United States. Others operated internationally. Of these, the Central British Fund (later the Council for German Jewry) and the American Jewish Joint Distribution Committee are especially noteworthy because of the large sums of money they spent on Jewish refugees. In addition, the Jewish Agency for Palestine should be mentioned because it spearheaded Zionist efforts to create a Jewish homeland in Palestine.[43]

Private voluntary organizations also provided services for Russian refugees. The Committee of Russian Zemstvos and Town Councils (Zemgor) and the Russian Red Cross maintained diverse services for refugees, including child care, language instruction, and employment training.[44] In addition, phil-Armenian groups in the United States, Britain, and other countries assisted Armenian refugees. Many of these sprang up in response to the Armenian genocide during the First World War and continued to contribute to refugee assistance projects afterwards. The Near East Relief, a US-based organization, specialized in the care of Armenian children and was a major supplier of emergency relief to both Armenian and Greek refugees. In Britain, both the Armenian (Lord Mayor's)

[43] Simpson, *The Refugee Problem*, 186–8; Arieh Tartakower and Kurt R. Grossman, *The Jewish Refugee* (New York: Institute of Jewish Affairs of the American Jewish Congress and the World Jewish Congress, 1944), 429–500. On the history of the Joint Distribution Committee see Yehuda Bauer, *My Brother's Keeper: A History of the American Jewish Joint Distribution Committee, 1929–1939* (Philadelphia: Jewish Publication Society of America, 1974); Moses A. Leavitt, *The JDC Story: Highlights of JDC Activities, 1914–1952* (New York: American Jewish Joint Distribution Committee, 1953). On the Central British Fund, see Norman Bentwich, *They Found Refuge* (London, 1956).
[44] Simpson, *The Refugee Problem*, 181–3.

Fund and the Society of Friends of Armenia contributed to refugee settlement schemes for Armenians. Within the Armenian community itself, the Armenian Benevolent Union, a cultural organization funded in 1905, provided material support for poor Armenians, including refugees.[45]

The Role of Refugees

The international refugee regime was state-centric in the sense that states constituted its membership and were the major decision-makers within it. Though the major purpose of the regime was to solve what governments saw as refugee problems, actual refugees were largely excluded from the decision-making process. Nevertheless, refugees tried to make their voices heard through organizations that claimed to represent their interests. Some private voluntary organizations that engaged in refugee relief were primarily composed of refugees and often spoke out on refugee issues. Other organizations had an overtly political purpose and also claimed to represent refugees. In the case of Armenians, the Central Committee for Armenian Refugees and the government in exile of the defunct Armenian republic—the Armenian National Delegation—fulfilled this position. In the case of Russian refugees, the political fragmentation of the migration prevented one group's emerging with an undisputed claim to leadership. Consequently, groups representing the political left, centre, and right competed for recognition and influence with the League of Nations and host governments. In Germany alone, more than forty such organizations sprouted after the defeat of the White armies.[46]

Refugees also had a formal place in the decision-making process through the refugee agencies of the League of Nations. A number of delegates sent to host countries by the High Commissioner for Refugees and the Nansen Office were refugees or naturalized refugees. In 1934, for instance, four of the thirteen delegates of the Nansen Office were refugees, as were four of the five

[45] Ibid. 184–5. On the history of NER, see James L. Barton, *Story of Near East Relief (1915–1939): An Interpretation* (New York: Macmillan, 1930); John S. Badeau and Georgiana G. Stevens (eds.), *Bread from Stones: Fifty Years of Technical Assistance* (Englewood Cliffs, NJ: Prentice-Hall, 1966).
[46] Robert Chadwell Williams, *Culture in Exile: Russian Emigres in Germany, 1881–1941* (Ithaca, NY: Cornell University Press, 1972), 124–5.

correspondents.[47] In addition, representatives from leading Russian and Armenian refugee organizations filled two of the twelve places on the Governing Body of the Nansen Office.[48] Although refugees were in a minority on the Governing Body, they had added influence because one of them always served on the Managing Committee, a group of three that actually supervised the operations of the Nansen Office. In addition, five of the nine technical advisers to the Nansen Office represented refugee organizations. The presence of these refugee delegates within the League of Nations itself helped to shape the form of refugee assistance, as will be seen below.

THE ORIGINS OF THE INTERNATIONAL REFUGEE REGIME

The international refugee regime did not develop according to a comprehensive plan or a grand design. Instead, it resulted from a series of *ad hoc* responses by governments to successive refugee crises, beginning with the mass exodus of more than one million Russian refugees after the Bolshevik revolution. A group of private, voluntary organizations, led by Gustave Ador, then President of the ICRC, first brought this emergency to the attention of the League of Nations. In a letter of 29 February 1921 to the Council, Ador wrote of 800,000 refugees scattered throughout Europe without legal protection and living in desperate poverty. He called on the League, 'the only supranational political authority capable of solving a problem which is beyond the power of exclusively humanitarian organisations', to appoint a 'General Commissioner for the Russian Refugees'. The Commissioner would have the task of defining the legal status of the refugees and of

[47] League of Nations, Nansen International Office for Refugees, 'Report of the Governing Body for the Year ending June 30th 1934' (20 Aug. 1934) [A.12.1934], 18. Russian refugees, or naturalized Russian refugees, were the representatives to Bulgaria, Greece, Romania, and Yugoslavia, and were correspondents to China, Danzig, Estonia, and Lithuania.

[48] From 1931 until 1938 L. Pachalian of the Comité central des réfugiés arméniens served as the representative for Armenian refugees. From 1931 until 1935 C. Goulkevitch of the Conseil des anciens Ambassadeurs russes represented Russian refugees. He was succeeded by J. Rubinstein of the Commission centrale pour l'étude de la condition des réfugiés russes, who served until the closure of the Nansen Office.

organizing either their employment or repatriation back to Russia.[49] Following an intergovernmental conference on Russian refugees held in August 1921, the Council officially agreed to Ador's suggestion and invited Fridtjof Nansen to become the first High Commissioner for Russian Refugees.[50]

From this starting-point, the international refugee regime gradually increased its scope until it encompassed international efforts to aid Russian, Armenian, Greek, Bulgarian, Turkish, Assyrian, German, and Saar refugees. During the 1930s the regime continued to exist despite the challenges brought by the economic depression and the rise of Fascism. Not until the outbreak of fighting in 1939 and the division of Europe into warring camps did the regime cease to function. While the expansion and operations of the regime will be traced in subsequent chapters, the primary purpose of this section is to explain the initial decision made by governments to assist Russian refugees. Three alternative explanations for the creation of the regime will here be considered.[51]

The Strength of Humanitarianism

The most obvious explanation for the formation of the international refugee regime is that a consensus on humanitarian principles inspired the international community to deal with a pressing relief problem.[52] Certainly, the Council of the League of Nations couched its responses to the appeal of the ICRC in this way. Without humanitarian motivations, governments could have quickly solved their problems by refusing to accept any responsibility for refugees and leaving unwanted ones to starve. Yet the British Minister in Belgrade dismissed the idea of cutting services to refugees because doing so would expose them 'to privations and hunger' and would damage 'the standard of humanity with which the world credits us'.[53] For countries not hosting refugees, humanitarian sympathies generated support for refugee assistance.

[49] League of Nations, *Official Journal* (Mar.–Apr. 1921), 227–8.
[50] Ibid. (Nov. 1921), 1027.
[51] For a concise review of different theories of regime change, see Krasner, 'Structural Causes', 10–20, and Stephan Haggard and Beth A. Simmons, 'Theories of International Regimes', *International Organization*, 41 (Summer 1987), 498–513.
[52] On the impact of principles and norms on regime development see Krasner, 'Structural Causes', 16–18.
[53] Letter of 21 May 1921 from Sir C. Alban Young, British Minister to Belgrade, to Earl Curzon. BFO 371/6867/N6310.

The governments of Belgium and Spain, for instance, declared their support for League intervention despite the fact that they hosted few refugees and had no key political interests in them.[54]

However, the strength of humanitarian values alone does not fully explain these early international co-operative efforts on behalf of Russian refugees. After the First World War, the Russian refugees constituted only one group of millions of needy people, including victims of war, epidemics, poverty, disasters, and persecution. Moreover, international co-operation on humanitarian issues rarely took place. During the 1920s the list of failed attempts at international humanitarian projects included proposals for disaster aid, unemployment support, and the elimination of statelessness. The most poignant example of this was the decision by the League of Nations not to assist some thirty million people threatened by starvation after the failure of the harvest in Russia and the Ukraine. At the Assembly debate of the issue in September 1921, delegates rejected humanitarian pleas from Nansen, acting as the delegate from Norway, and sided with the delegate from Serbia, who argued that Bolshevism posed a greater threat to Russia than the famine; therefore, the League should not do anything to help the Bolshevik government.[55] Because of the strength of anti-Communist sentiments, most delegates agreed with the Serbian argument.

Another reason for the reluctance of governments to assist the needy was the strength of the commonly held assumption that 'charity' should be the exclusive domain of private agencies and national governments. The Covenant of the League of Nations itself reflects this attitude: its preamble states that the goal of the organization is 'to achieve international peace and security', but only 'to promote international co-operation'. In contrast to the Charter of the United Nations, very few articles of the Covenant deal with social and economic issues.[56] Consequently, any

[54] *Official Journal* (July–Aug. 1921), 487.

[55] League of Nations, *Records of the Second Assembly: Plenary Meetings* (Geneva, 1921), 552. European private organizations led by Fridtjof Nansen and American relief agencies under the direction of Herbert Hoover did save many famine victims.

[56] Art. 23 of the Covenant concerned international co-operation in efforts dealing with labour, native populations in colonies, traffic in women, children, drugs, and weapons, communications and transit, and disease. Art. 25 encouraged all League members to co-operate with the Red Cross. For the full text of these articles, see Walters, *History of the League of Nations*, 58–60.

international initiatives in the humanitarian field had to be clearly justified in order for an exception to general practice to be made.

The Influence of a Hegemonic Power

A second theoretical explanation for the creation of the international refugee regime is that it depended on the influence of a hegemon, a country which is significantly more powerful than all others. According to what political scientists call the 'theory of hegemonic stability', a hegemon is necessary for the creation and maintenance of regimes.[57] Such a country will use its resources to make the regime's important rules and to see that they are enforced. If the hegemon's power declines, the regime will lose its influence and probably collapse. It has been argued, for example, that the creation of the inter-American human-rights regime can be best explained with reference to the influence of the United States, the dominant power in the region.[58] Can this explanation be applied to the international refugee regime as well?

One problem with applying hegemonic stability theory to the Inter-war Period is that, in contrast to the Cold War period, a hegemonic power with a willingness to lead is not easily identifiable. Although the United States emerged from the First World War as the dominant economic and military power, its refusal to join the League of Nations signalled its withdrawal into political isolationism. Thus, the only country with the capability to absorb millions of refugees removed itself from a leadership role in the regime. In addition, the Great War severely weakened Germany and the Soviet Union, leaving them temporarily on the sidelines of world politics. Although officially victors, both Britain and France suffered substantial losses in the war and were therefore too weak to be completely dominant. Nevertheless, both countries still considered themselves to be Great Powers and attempted to play a leadership role in world politics.

If, for the sake of argument, we accept that either Britain or

[57] For an explication and evaluation of the theory of hegemonic stability, see Robert Keohane, *After Hegemony* (Princeton, NJ: Princeton University Press, 1984), 31–46; Duncan Snidal, 'The Limits of Hegemonic Stability Theory', *International Organization*, 39 (Autumn 1985), 579–614.
[58] Donnelly, 'International Human Rights', 625. An alternative explanation can be found in David Forsythe, *The Internationalization of Human Rights* (Lexington, Mass.: Lexington Books, 1991), 92–3.

France could have played the role of a hegemonic power in regime creation, we should expect that either one or both of them initiated and dominated the formation of the international refugee regime. The selection of a French rapporteur for the Council report which recommended the appointment of a High Commissioner indicates French support for its proposals. Moreover, a representative from the French Minister of Foreign Affairs attended an initial meeting of private organizations on the refugee question in an advisory capacity. Although this attendance indicates France's interest in the meeting's results, it does not constitute an independent French move. The British, meanwhile, maintained an extremely ambivalent attitude towards the proposal. At the Council's February meeting, Balfour, the British delegate, urged that the letter from the ICRC be forwarded to all League members.[59] But the British delegate to the initial intergovernmental conference on refugees did not even attend the meeting. Thus, the historical record does not provide adequate support for the proposition that a dominant power brought about the formation of the international refugee regime.

The Pursuit of Self-Interest

A third theoretical explanation of the formation of the international refugee regime is that governments built it because they expected to benefit from it. In other words, governments acted primarily out of self-interest, not altruism.[60] Some theorists, called functionalists, argue that the primary function of a regime is to facilitate the making of agreements between states. Without the existence of a regime, agreements that would benefit both parties will often not be made. Economists call this situation 'market failure'.[61] In the political sense, the equivalent happens when negotiations between two actors fail to produce the solution which best serves both parties. This failure may occur because the parties do not have enough information, they mistrust each other,

[59] *Official Journal* (July–Aug. 1921), 486.
[60] The most prominent exponent of this approach is Keohane, *After Hegemony*, esp. 85–109. See also his 'The Demand for International Regimes', in Krasner (ed.), *International Regimes*, 141–71.
[61] Keohane defines market failure as 'situations in which the outcomes of market-mediated interactions are suboptimal, given the utility functions of actors and the resources at their disposal' (*After Hegemony*, 82).

or the costs of negotiating are too high. A regime compensates for the impediments which prevent states with shared interests from co-operating. For instance, one country might have a surplus population while another might need a larger work-force; but a lack of trust between the two countries might prevent an agreement about a transfer of people between them. A regime, if created, could produce a better outcome by helping to establish accepted standards of behaviour, reducing the difficulties in making agreements, and minimizing uncertainty.

A functionalist explanation of the formation of the international refugee regime would begin by examining the national interests of the various governments involved and the obstacles that stood in the way of unilateral solutions to refugee problems. To begin with, both France and Britain had a special interest in the Russian refugees because both countries had unsuccessfully supported the White armies in the Civil War. The two democratic powers shared with the Whites a strong antipathy to Communism. After that war both countries found themselves morally and financially responsible for thousands of Russian refugees, the remnants of the armies they once supported. By August 1921 the French government had spent 150 million francs (approximately £3.8 million), primarily on General Peter Wrangel and his defunct army at Constantinople. The British had spent £1 million pounds on Denikin's group, and in August 1921 still maintained 5,000 refugees in Egypt, Cyprus, and Serbia at a cost of £22,000 per month. In addition, both Britain and France had tried, and failed, to extricate themselves from their predicament. Both had attempted to arrange repatriation agreements with the Soviet Union and had been soundly rebuffed, primarily because of a lack of trust between the parties.[62] Moreover, the British government had been decidedly unsuccessful in trying to convince eastern European countries to accept refugees under British control into their territory. These combined failures led Foreign Office officials to conclude that they would 'have to settle the main questions sooner or later by international methods'.[63] Thus, both Britain and France turned to international co-operative efforts in regard to Russian refugees because national policies failed to provide solutions.

[62] *Official Journal* (Nov. 1921), 1010–17.
[63] Foreign Office note by J. S. Gregory of 28 May 1921. BFO 371/6867/N6097.

In addition to the support of two Great Powers, a core group of League members, mostly European states with Russian refugees within their borders, certainly had an interest in internationalizing their financial burdens. Delegates from Bulgaria, China, Czechoslovakia, Finland, Greece, Poland, Romania, Switzerland, and Yugoslavia showed their interest by attending the intergovernmental conference on Russian refugees held in August 1921, and one held at the Assembly the following month (see Table 8).[64] The German government, though excluded from membership of the League of Nations, also looked favourably on international assistance to Russian refugees.[65] An additional reason for these states, which alone hosted more than half of the Russian refugees, to support intergovernmental co-operation was their inability to count on much more support from international relief agencies. As the ICRC's letter pointed out, the funds of the major private relief organizations of the era were almost exhausted. This was also true of the Russian relief organizations, including the Zemgor and the Russian Red Cross, both of which urged League involvement with refugees. Thus, by 1921 it had become clear that purely national responses to the Russian refugees had severe limitations and that a number of states had a shared interest in international co-operative efforts on their behalf.

Governments also expected to benefit from co-operation because of the past success of the League of Nations in arranging prisoner-of-war repatriation. In 1920 the Council had appointed Nansen to supervise the return of the thousands of prisoners who were dispersed across the former Russian empire and in central Europe. Nansen persuaded governments to contribute money, arranged for shipping, co-ordinated the efforts of private agencies, and negotiated with the Soviet Union. By the time he finished his work, he had managed the repatriation of about 425,000 prisoners at a cost of less than £1 per person.[66] Although unfinished in late summer 1921, repatriation had been largely completed. This success bolstered hopes that co-operation could be repeated in other areas.

[64] League of Nations, 'Russian Refugees' (1 Aug. 1921) [C.126(a).M.72(a).1921. VII], 3; *Journal of the Second Assembly of the League of Nations* (20 Sept. 1921).
[65] *Official Journal* (July–Aug. 1921), 489.
[66] League of Nations, *Records of the Third Assembly: Plenary Meetings* (Geneva, 1922), ii. 145. See also Walters, *History of the League of Nations*, 100.

TABLE 8. *Participation in Intergovernmental Conferences, 1921–1927*

Country	Aug. 1921[1]	Sept. 1921[2]	July 1922[3]	May 1926[4]	June 1927[5]
Argentina					
Australia					
Austria			x	x	
Belgium				x	
Bolivia					
Brazil					
Bulgaria	x	x	x	x	x
Canada				x	
Chile					
China	x	x		x	
Colombia					
Costa Rica					
Cuba				x	
Czechoslovakia	x	x	x	x	x
Denmark				x	
Dominican Republic					
Ecuador					
Egypt					
Estonia				x	
Finland	x	x	x	x	x
France	x	x	x	x	x
Germany		x	x	x	x
Great Britain		x	x	x	x
Greece	x	x	x	x	x
Guatemala					
Haiti					
Honduras					
Hungary			x	x	
India				x	
Ireland				x	
Japan			x		
Latvia				x	x
Luxembourg					
Mexico					
Netherlands					
New Zealand					
Nicaragua					
Norway				x	
Panama					

TABLE 8. *(cont.)*

Country	Aug. 1921[1]	Sept. 1921[2]	July 1922[3]	May 1926[4]	June 1927[5]
Paraguay					
Peru					
Poland	x	x	x	x	x
Portugal					
Romania	x	x	x	x	x
South Africa				x	
Spain			x		
Sweden			x	x	
Switzerland	x	x	x	x	
United States					
Uruguay					
Venezuela					
Yugoslavia	x	x	x	x	x
Totals	10	12	16	25	11

[1] Conference on the Russian Refugee Question, 26 Aug. 1921 [C.277.M.203.1921.VII], 3.
[2] Conference on Russian Refugees, Sept. 1921, *Journal of the Second Assembly of the League of Nations* (20 Sept. 1921).
[3] Conference on Identity Documents for Russian Refugees, 3–5 July 1922, *Official Journal* (Aug. 1922), 926–8.
[4] Conference on Russian and Armenian Refugees, 10–12 May 1926 [A.44.1926], 2.
[5] Conference on the Creation of a Revolving Fund, 15–16 June 1927 [A.48.1927.XII], 3.

While many countries had a shared interest in refugee assistance, only a few opposed the ICRC's proposal. Sweden was the sole League member publicly to oppose the scheme, arguing that the needs of Russian refugees could best be met by a coalition of voluntary agencies.[67] But Sweden's opinion did not carry much weight, as the country lacked Great Power status. Outside Europe, the governments of the Latin American republics and the United States did not take a keen interest in the Russian refugees, but they did not oppose international assistance either. Only

[67] [C.126(a).M.72(a).1921.VII], 5.

the Soviet Union, the source country of the refugees, strongly objected to any aid for the 'counter revolutionaries'; but it could do little to prevent such action at the time because of its own internal weakness and diminished international position.[68] It is also important to note that international co-operative efforts on behalf of refugees did not commence until they had the full support of the refugees themselves. Although Zemgor, the Russian Red Cross,[69] and the National Ukrainian Committee[70] eagerly called for League involvement, General Peter Wrangel, one of the White leaders, opposed 'refugee aid' because he wanted to maintain his troops as a military unit, not see them dispersed or repatriated.[71] Wrangel had brought with him considerable sums of money from Russia that made it possible for him to maintain his army. But eventually these funds dwindled, leaving him in a weakened bargaining position *vis-à-vis* the French and British governments, both of which wanted to disband his army.[72] Finally, by June 1921, Wrangel could see the merits of outside assistance, and he too appealed to the League of Nations on behalf of 10,000 Russian patriots in camps in Gallipoli and Lemnos.[73]

The importance of a weak opposition to the success of efforts on behalf of refugees is especially evident if we consider the ill-fated attempts by governments to address the problems of the stateless, who have been called 'the most symptomatic group in contemporary politics'.[74] The problem of statelessness first became evident after the First World War when, as a result of the territorial

[68] Telegram of 17 June 1921 from Chicherin to Curzon. BFO 371/6867/7072. See also Simpson, *The Refugee Problem*, 191.

[69] Letter to the Secretary-General of the League of Nations, Geneva, from Countess Sophie Panine, Nicolas Astroff of the Russian Zemstovs and Town Councils, and Georges Lodygensky, Russian Red Cross, Geneva, 14 June 1921 [C.126(a).M.72(a).1921.VII], 6–7. These two organizations supported League involvement in improving the legal status and economic position of refugees, but they strongly opposed any plans for repatriation to the Soviet Union.

[70] Letter to the President of the League of Nations, Geneva, from Marcotoune and Tzitovitch, National Ukrainian Committee, Paris, 17 June 1921 [C.126(a).M.72 (a).1921.VII], 10–11. The Russian Financial, Industrial, and Commercial Association and the Conference of Jewish Ukrainian Refugees also advocated League involvement with refugees.

[71] Michael R. Marrus, *The Unwanted: European Refugees in the Twentieth Century* (New York: Oxford University Press, 1985), 59.

[72] T. F. Johnson, *International Tramps: From Chaos to Permanent World Peace* (London: Hutchinson, 1938), 235.   [73] [C.126(a).M.72(a).1921.VII], 12.

[74] Hannah Arendt, *The Origins of Totalitarianism* (New York: Harcourt, Brace, 1951), 276.

revisions that took place in eastern and central Europe, many people lost their former nationality and did not successfully acquire a new one. Among the stateless were included a high proportion of Jews who would not or could not accept the nationality of the successor states. In Romania, for instance, nationality laws passed by the government in 1924 rendered about 100,000 former Jewish citizens stateless.[75] The actions of the totalitarian states in the Inter-war Period compounded the problem of statelessness. For instance, two Soviet decrees enacted in 1921 deprived most Russian refugees of their nationality. In an attempt to solve this problem, governments held a Conference on Communications and Transit in 1927, but they failed to create a uniform travel document for all stateless people, including refugees. One of the primary reasons for the failure of this proposal was that Italy, an important member of the League of Nations and a country that practised denationalization, strongly opposed any aid to the stateless.

Based on the above discussion, it can be concluded that, without a regime, the plight of the refugees resembled a situation of market failure. National solutions alone could not solve the refugee problem and a lack of trust between countries precluded the formation of bilateral agreements that might have done so. Moreover, governments acting according to their own self-interest had a variety of reasons to support international efforts on behalf of Russian refugees. Thus, a functional analysis seems to identify the reasons why governments might demand a regime to deal with refugees. What has not yet been explained, however, is why this regime was created at this particular place and time,[76] and who or what provided the leadership for its formation. In order to answer these questions, the origins of the international refugee regime must be placed in a historical context.

[75] Board of Deputies of British Jews and Council of the Anglo-Jewish Association, 'The Jewish Minority in Roumania', unpub. paper (Apr. 1928), 5–6.

[76] Haggard and Simmons, 'Theories of International Regimes', 506, point out that functional theories 'are better at specifying when regimes will be demanded rather than suggesting how or when they will be supplied'. Similar criticisms are made in Roger K. Smith, 'Explaining the Non-Proliferation Regime: Anomalies for Contemporary International Relations Theory', *International Organization*, 41 (Spring 1987), 275–6. Part of the reason for this problem is the implicit assumption made by functionalists that a hegemonic power is often necessary for regime formation.

The Importance of Leadership

Clearly, the crisis created by the arrival of more than one million dispossessed Russian refugees provided a catalyst for international action.[77] But this human disaster should not be viewed in isolation from the great upheaval created by the First World War and its aftermath. For a generation of political leaders known as the 'idealists', refugees were part of the problem of war. According to Fridtjof Nansen, one of the most eloquent spokesmen for the idealist cause and a Nobel Peace Prize winner, 'all these endless horrors, this misery, these incredible sufferings, these hundreds of thousands of abandoned prisoners of war, these famines, these millions of helpless refugees are the result, direct or indirect, of the war'.[78] Because of the tremendous loss of life and physical destruction caused by the First World War, the idealists challenged prevailing views about international politics and the way the world should be run. They saw in the aftermath of the war the possibility of creating a new world order based on three major building-blocks: disarmament, international law, and international organization.[79]

The idealists criticized the nineteenth century balance-of-power system as a fundamentally corrupt and unworkable method of managing world affairs. They identified the arms race that raged before the First World War as a principal cause of the war, and concluded that a disarmed world would be a peaceful one.[80] In addition to disarmament, the idealists advocated a new way of

[77] Oran Young points out that crises can increase the chances of success in efforts to negotiate international regimes. The 1986 Chernobyl nuclear accident, for instance, motivated governments to reach an agreement on a regime covering nuclear accidents. See Oran R. Young, 'The Politics of International Regime Formation: Managing Natural Resources and the Environment', *International Organization*, 43 (Summer 1989), 371–2.

[78] Fridtjof Nansen, 'No More War', in his *Adventure and Other Papers* (London: Hogarth Press, 1927), 58.

[79] The idealist approach, the dominant theory of international relations in the 1920s and 1930s, is expressed in the writings of Sir Alfred Zimmern, Philip Noel-Baker, Felix Morley, James Shotwell, and David Davies. See Alfred Zimmern, *The League of Nations and the Rule of Law: 1918–1935* (London: Macmillan, 1936); Philip Noel-Baker, *Disarmament* (London: Hogarth Press, 1926); Morley, *The Society of Nations*; James Shotwell, *War and its Renunciation as an Instrument of Policy in the Pact of Paris, 1929* (New York: Harcourt and Brace, 1929).

[80] Noel-Baker, *Disarmament*, 328. See also Philip Noel-Baker, *The League of Nations at Work* (London: Nisbet, 1926), 9–10.

achieving security. Instead of struggling in a system of international anarchy, all states would join together in a League of Nations to form a collective security system.[81] The League also would engage in the peaceful settlement of disputes and establish the rule of law world-wide. Idealists believed that mobilized public opinion would be an effective sanction behind the rule of law. This notion was essentially an outgrowth of the idea, popularized by Woodrow Wilson, that democratic peoples were inherently peace-loving. Hence, in this disarmed world it would be peoples, not despotic governments, that ultimately ruled. In keeping with this thinking, Sir Alfred Zimmern, perhaps the best-known idealist writer, describes international relations as involving not just a knowledge of relations between states, 'but also of the relations between peoples'.[82] He argues that it was the peoples of the world, through world public opinion, who evoked the 'mobilisation of shame' that provided the ultimate sanction for international law.[83] Because of these beliefs, the idealists stressed the desirability of educating the hearts and minds of all people so that peace could become a reality instead of a far-off dream. In addition, some idealists saw the great potential of international organizations for promoting international co-operation on economic and social issues, including refugees.[84]

Since the 1920s the idealists have been criticized by a group of scholars and policy-makers known as 'realists' for neglecting the importance of power and the existence of conflicting interests in international relations.[85] While it is beyond the scope of this

[81] For a concise treatment of the major ideas behind the League of Nations, see David Armstrong, *The Rise of the International Organization: A Short History* (London: Macmillan, 1982), 11–13; Claude, *Swords into Plowshares*, 41–56.

[82] Zimmern, *League of Nations*, 5, 8.

[83] Ibid. 460. For a review of Zimmern's life and work, see D. J. Markwell, 'Sir Alfred Zimmern Revisited: Fifty Years On', *Review of International Studies*, 12 (1986), 279–92.

[84] Zimmern, for instance, describes the League as 'an instrument of co-operation' and 'a standing agency facilitating common actions by states animated by the co-operative spirit', rather than as a body dominated by powerful states. He praises the work of the League in Greek reconstruction following the mass migration of Asia Minor Greeks, and commends the Health Organization for helping to save lives and stop epidemics among refugees in central Europe (1920) and in Greece (1922). *League of Nations*, 313, 320–1.

[85] See e.g. E. H. Carr, *The Twenty Years' Crisis, 1919–1939* (London: Macmillan, 1939); Hans J. Morgenthau, *Politics Among Nations: The Struggle for Power and Peace* (New York: Knopf, 1949).

discussion to decide which side of this ongoing debate has better characterized world politics, it is important to recognize that the beliefs of the idealists formed a crucial part of the intellectual climate of the League of Nations era. Moreover, idealists worked in the Secretariat and the refugee agencies of the League of Nations. In these positions, they played an instrumental role in beginning international assistance to refugees.

Within the Secretariat of the League of Nations, key officials strongly supported the ICRC proposal and took steps to bring it about. The best example of this is Philip Noel-Baker, the member of the Secretariat most directly concerned with the refugee issue.[86] A former Olympic runner and champion of disarmament who later won the Nobel Peace Prize, Noel-Baker argued that the 'problems connected with the refugees are insoluble except by international action'. Similarly, he emphasized that famine relief and refugee assistance could help to 'remove the fear of war and create the "good understanding among peoples" upon which peace depends'. In this venture, Noel-Baker believed that all governments, even refugee-producing ones, had a common interest in helping refugees.[87] He further added that the problem could be quickly solved with only 'a trifling expenditure' on travelling expenses.[88] He and other Secretariat officials not only drew up initial ideas for the office of High Commissioner, but also conducted a search for the first one and asked the Council for approval only after they had agreed on a candidate.[89]

Whether Noel-Baker and others like him correctly linked refugee assistance with the cause of world peace is not important here. What matters is that these men believed the two were linked,

---

[86] Philip Noel-Baker had a long and interesting career. Born on 1 Nov. 1889, as Philip Baker, to a family of Canadian Quakers, he later added his wife's family name to his own. Noel-Baker served as a British delegate to the Paris Peace Conference in 1919 and in the League of Nations Secretariat. He also served as a Labour member of Parliament from 1929 to 1931, and from 1936 until 1970. A leading advocate of disarmament, Noel-Baker championed it at the 1933 Geneva Conference on Disarmament. In his later life he turned his energies to opposing the nuclear arms race, for which he won the Nobel Peace Prize in 1959. Noel-Baker was also an outstanding athlete and supporter of the Olympic movement. He won a silver medal in the 1500 metres at the 1920 Olympics.

[87] Noel-Baker, *The League of Nations at Work*, 113, 121; and P. J. [Noel-]Baker, 'Memorandum on the Possible Action of the League in Connection with Russian Refugees', Secretariat Memo, 6 May 1921 [NBKR 4.450], 3.

[88] NBKR 4. 450.   [89] LNA C1405/R.403.1.0. Also, see below Ch. 8.

and thus became personally motivated to make international co-operation on behalf of refugees a reality. As a result, the Secretariat provided leadership that was necessary in the absence of a hegemonic power.[90] In this regard, private relief agencies led by the ICRC joined them. Despite the many limitations of these non-state actors, they were able to lead, in part because they were seen as neutral brokers. Consequently, the proposal for refugee aid was not closely associated with any one government.

This fate of the ICRC's proposal contrasts sharply with that of one for an International Relief Union (IRU) put forth in 1926 by Senator Giovanni Ciraolo, Italian delegate to the League Assembly and honorary President of the Italian Red Cross. The IRU would have been a multi-purpose emergency relief agency to assist countries in dealing with famine, floods, epidemics, forced migrations, and other disasters on the basis of humanitarian principles, 'lest generosity should become a means of influence and be twisted to benefit the benefactors'.[91] Though this proposal was similar in many ways to that for refugee assistance, the results differed a great deal. Although an international conference met and formally ratified statutes creating an International Relief Union in 1927, the organization died stillborn.[92] One of the major reasons for its failure was that the British and French governments declined whole-heartedly to support a project so closely associated with the Italian government.[93]

The Secretariat of the League of Nations also provided leadership

[90] Oran Young argues that regime formation is more likely to succeed if effective leadership emerges, and is more likely to fail without it. However, he distinguishes (1) 'entrepreneurial leaders'—'actors who are skilled in inventing new institutional arrangements and brokering the overlapping interests of parties concerned with a particular issue-area'—from (2) hegemons, and (3) 'ethically motivated actors who seek to fashion workable institutional arrangements as a contribution to the common good'. What is not clear is why the first and third of these need be mutually exclusive. Noel-Baker would seem to be an example of someone motivated by concern for the common good who also was quite capable of creative thinking and institution-building. Young, 'Politics of International Regime Formation', 373.
[91] League of Nations, International Relief Union, 'Draft Statutes and Statement drawn up by the Preparatory Committee for the Ciraolo Scheme' (Nov. 1926) [C.618.M.240.1926.II], 1–4.
[92] League of Nations, International Relief Union, 'Convention and Statutes' (July 1927) [C.364.M.137.1927].
[93] See memorandum from T. F. Johnson to Albert Thomas, 'Cooperation of the Office in the execution of Ciraolo scheme', 8 July 1927. LNA C1408.

by developing creative proposals that would be acceptable to governments because they required limited means. Though the League made a dramatic departure in appointing a High Commissioner, it also established strict guidelines within which the refugee work of the League had to take place: aid was to be limited to Russian refugees; League funds were to be spent on administration and not on direct relief; and refugee assistance was to be considered a temporary project.[94] In this sense, the proposal for refugee assistance differed substantially from that for the IRU, which saddled governments with 'an absolute rather than incremental declaration of international obligations'.[95] The proposal for refugee aid, in contrast, asked governments for a limited commitment.

The Secretariat's proposal also had limited goals in that it separated refugee assistance from other related issues. In this regard, it differed from failed attempts to link refugee problems with that of general unemployment. Both Nansen and Albert Thomas, President of the International Labour Organization (ILO), hoped to expand international efforts to find jobs for refugees.[96] Governments, however, consistently refused to create a world-wide migration service or co-operate on the problem of general unemployment.[97] The success of the proposal for refugee aid also contrasts with the failure of similar efforts to deal with the problem of statelessness. According to these proposals, Russian and other refugees fitted within a broader category of persons without nationality. Although League of Nations assistance programmes helped only Russian and Armenian refugees and neglected other stateless persons, the fact remains that governments rejected responsibility for this broader segment of humanity.

Without the leadership provided by the Secretariat of the League of Nations and non-governmental organizations, it is unlikely that

[94] Simpson, *The Refugee Problem*, 192.
[95] Nichols, 'Rubberband Humanitarianism', 195.
[96] Johnson, *International Tramps*, 249. Nansen, for instance, writes that 'if we are enabled to develop our settlement work overseas I believe that sooner or later similar measures will be adopted on behalf of the surplus unemployed populations in Europe'. Letter from Nansen to Robert Cecil of 27 May 1927. NP, MS. 2.1988, S5B.
[97] League of Nations, *Official Journal*, Special Supplement no. 38, Sixth Assembly, Fifth Committee (Geneva, 1925), 24–8; ibid., Special Supplement no. 49, Seventh Assembly, Fifth Committee (Geneva, 1926), 34–41.

governments would have joined together to assist refugees, despite the existence of shared interests in doing so. For the initial decision to assist Russian refugees to take place—a decision that proved to be the foundation of the international refugee regime—individuals had to grasp opportunities presented to them by the crisis brought on by the First World War. In doing so, a group of idealists developed an extremely practical proposal to help uprooted people. Their efforts were at least in part accepted by governments because they were modest proposals that excluded other needy people. While justified on humanitarian grounds, this initial response to Russian refugees succeeded where others failed precisely because it placed strict limits on generosity.

It remains to answer the question, 'did the international refugee regime matter?' This question, in turn, raises others about how and in what ways the regime influenced state behaviour towards refugees, and whether its existence improved the lives of refugees or of their hosts. The remaining chapters in Part II examine the impact of the regime on four interrelated aspects of the refugee issue: securing legal protection; providing durable solutions; confronting immigration barriers; and preventing refugee movements. By following a topical rather than a chronological approach, it will be easier to make comparisons about different refugee groups and responses to them. Admittedly, the selection of these four aspects of the refugee problem inevitably involves neglecting other important dimensions of refugee issues, such as providing emergency relief or meeting the special needs of disabled refugees and refugee women. However, the topics chosen here are especially worthy of study because they not only required international action, but also addressed enduring problems. The creation of an internationally accepted travel document for refugees, for instance, required international co-operation because it could not be successfully created by one country acting unilaterally. Furthermore, this system of travel documents helped to supply refugees with a semblance of legal status, a continuing need which lasted long after their basic needs had been met.

4

The Quest for Legal Protection

FROM the beginning of the international refugee regime, one of its primary objectives concerned the legal protection of refugees. Throughout the Inter-war Period, the major actors in the regime grappled with the problems involved in securing this goal. Providing legal protection for refugees was not an easy task, partly because few rules on the subject existed at the time of the regime's founding. Although the asylum norm was well established in international law and state practice, virtually no rules specified how millions of refugees should be treated within host countries. In the nineteenth century, governments concluded treaties dealing with the treatment of aliens and political offenders, but by and large the law of asylum remained unwritten before the First World War.[1] In addition, customary law did not compensate for this paucity of treaty law; it too remained silent on the subject of refugees.[2] Because of the absence of either treaty or customary law dealing with refugees, 'refugee status', defined as the 'sum total of the rights, benefits, and obligations due to refugees by virtue of rules of international law',[3] was ambiguous.

Prior to the Inter-war Period, the ambiguous legal status of refugees did not present major problems. Since the number of exiles was relatively small, states could easily incorporate them into their own legal systems. The traditional legal framework, however, proved to be grossly inadequate when the number of refugees reached the millions in the early twentieth century. Consequently, the need to develop an improved system arose. Legal scholars of the Inter-war Period clearly recognized this. In the

---

[1] Atle Grahl-Madsen, *The Status of Refugees in International Law*, i (Leyden: A. W. Sijthoff, 1966), 9; Jeff Crisp, 'The Challenge of Protection', *Refugees*, 46 (Oct. 1987), 20.

[2] R. Yewdall Jennings, 'Some International Law Aspects of the Refugee Question', *British Yearbook of International Law* (1939), 110.

[3] Grahl-Madsen, *Status of Refugees*, 4–5.

words of R. Yewdall Jennings, 'He [the refugee] is an anomaly for whom there is no appropriate niche in the framework of the general law. It is for this reason that it has been necessary to establish a special conventional regime governing his legal status.'[4]

In order to correct the anomaly about which Jennings writes, the principal actors of the regime embarked on a twofold strategy. On the one hand, they sought to create a legal framework which would define the status of refugees in international law. In this regard, they shared the enthusiasm of the era for the achievement of peace through the development of international law.[5] On the other hand, the refugee agencies of the League of Nations attempted to protect special groups of refugees through the provision of consular services and interventions with host governments on their behalf. In this chapter, this twofold approach is discussed. The development of rules designed to define refugees, enhance freedom of movement, increase economic and social well-being, and prevent expulsions is traced, and the direct impact of these rules on the lives of refugees is assessed. In conclusion, the influence of the international refugee regime on the legal protection of refugees in inter-war Europe is evaluated.

TURNING NORMS INTO RULES: TRAVEL AND IDENTITY DOCUMENTS

Given the lack of specific rules to govern the treatment of refugees by governments prior to 1920, it is not surprising that post-First-World-War refugees found themselves in an insecure legal position. Russian refugees, in particular, faced great difficulties. With no new national state to accept them, they lacked a natural place of permanent asylum. Consequently, they lived scattered throughout Europe and the Far East. A Soviet decree of 15 December 1922 denationalized the vast majority of the refugees, rendering them stateless and invalidating their travel documents.[6] Without a government to defend them, Russian refugees lacked

---

[4] Jennings, 'Some International Law Aspects', 110. See also Louise Holborn, *Refugees: A Problem of our Time: The Work of the United Nations High Commissioner for Refugees, 1951–1972* (Metuchen, NJ: Scarecrow Press, 1975), 154.

[5] The Kellogg–Briand Pact is the clearest example of this. The many international codes developed by the ILO during this time also reflect this general trend.

[6] Sir John Fischer Williams, 'Denationalization', *British Yearbook of International Law*, 8 (1927), 45.

diplomatic protection and physical security. Without passports, they were denied freedom of movement. Writing in May 1921, a Secretariat official noted that 'As things are, they [the Russian refugees] cannot travel, marry, be born, or die without creating legal problems, to which there is no solution.'[7] Russian refugees expressed these sentiments even more strongly:

The Russians enjoy no legal protection such as is accorded to the citizens of every country by their diplomatic representatives. This imposes a heavy burden upon their lives and more especially affects their rights to travel. In some countries the Russians are deprived of all guarantees of personal freedom and of inviolability of their person. They can be cast into prison, ill-treated and forcibly placed in the hands of their political enemies— Soviet Russia. . . . [Thus,] the humiliation of this absence of legal rights is added to the bitterness of exile.[8]

Given the stateless condition of most Russian refugees, the simplest solution to their predicament would have been for their host countries to naturalize them *en masse*. Both the Greek and Turkish governments adopted such a policy towards refugees following the Greco-Turkish war. But, in this case, the refugees concerned shared a similar ethnic identity with their hosts. No such ethnic affinity existed between the Russian refugees and the societies that hosted them. Although host governments might consider individual petitions for naturalization, they rejected granting citizenship to large groups of refugees. Some governments feared that these new citizens might become public charges; others wanted the refugees to leave, not stay. Mass naturalizations also would have undermined ongoing efforts by the newly created nation-states of eastern Europe to achieve ethnic homogeneity. In addition, many of the Russian refugees rejected the option of naturalization because they considered their exile to be a temporary one. For them, acceptance of another citizenship would have been an act of disloyalty to their homeland.[9]

---

[7] Memorandum of 6 May 1921 on the Possible Action of the League in Connection with Russian Refugees. NBKR 4.450.

[8] Letter from Russian Refugee Organizations in London to Lord Robert Cecil of 13 Aug. 1923. NBKR 4/625.

[9] Sir John Hope Simpson, *The Refugee Problem: Report of a Survey* (London: Oxford University Press, 1939), 235–6; Louise Holborn, 'The Legal Status of Political Refugees, 1920–1938', *American Journal of International Law*, 32 (1938), 682. See also Marc Raeff, *Russia Abroad: A Cultural History of the Russian Emigration, 1919–1939* (New York: Oxford University Press, 1990), 42.

The impossibility of mass naturalizations for Russian refugees meant that another method of dealing with their legal status needed to be developed. Gustave Ador realized this when he appealed to the League for the appointment of a High Commissioner to deal with the Russian refugee problem. His letter identifies the need to define 'the legal position of the Russian refugees ... because it is impossible that, in the 20th century, there could be 800,000 men in Europe unprotected by any *legal organisation recognised by international law*'.[10] Governments attending the August 1921 conference on Russian refugees also recognized the need to provide them with some form of legal protection. The conference resolutions stress the necessity of supplying refugees with passports and preventing any from being returned involuntarily to the Soviet Union.[11] Despite acknowledging the desirability of action, governments did not take concrete steps to improve the position of refugees. Instead, the task of developing such documents fell largely on the shoulders of Fridtjof Nansen, the newly appointed High Commissioner for Refugees.

The Nansen Passport System

In March 1922 High Commissioner Nansen used his Council report to draw attention to the problems refugees faced in travel. Calling the matter one of 'importance and urgency', he proposed that recognized refugees be provided with travel and identity documents.[12] Shortly afterwards, in July 1922, Nansen convened an intergovernmental conference which was attended by representatives from sixteen governments (see Table 8). At the conference, these delegates unanimously agreed to the Arrangement of 5 July 1922, which created a special certificate of identity for Russian refugees, commonly called a 'Nansen passport'.[13] Unlike a treaty, this Arrangement was not legally binding, but rather it recommended a certain standard of conduct for signatory states.

Under the terms of the 1922 Arrangement, governments could

[10] League of Nations, *Official Journal* (Mar.–Apr. 1921), 228.
[11] League of Nations, 'Conference on the Russian Refugee Question: Resolutions adopted by the Conference' (26 Aug. 1921) [C.277.M.203.1921.VII], 3.
[12] 'Russian Refugees: Report to the Council on March 24th, 1922 by Dr. Nansen', *Official Journal* (May 1922), annex 321*a*, p. 396.
[13] 'Arrangement of 5 July 1922 Relating to Russian Refugees', *LNTS*, 13/355, 238.

issue the identity certificates but doing so did not confer upon the
bearer citizenship rights. Nevertheless, the documents did allow
refugees to travel legally across international boundaries. They
were valid for one year, stated the bearer was a Russian national
by origin, and became invalid if the bearer adopted another nationality. Interestingly enough, the 1922 Arrangement did not
contain a precise definition of a refugee or specify the causes of
the refugee's flight from his or her home country. It merely stated
that certificates should be granted to refugees of Russian origin
who had not acquired another nationality.[14]

Governments quickly moved to adopt the Nansen passport system. By September 1923 thirty-one governments had signed the
Arrangement; by 1925 forty governments had done so; and by
1929 over fifty governments had (see Table 9).[15] The documents
allowed refugee travel and gave stateless refugees a modicum of
legal status. The system helped governments to collect more accurate statistics on refugees and to reconcile their aid to refugees
and their bilateral relations with the Soviet Union.[16] From the point
of view of the High Commissioner, the identity system facilitated
burden-sharing among host countries. The 1922 Report of the High
Commissioner calls the document 'a great step towards a more
equitable distribution of Russian refugees'.[17] So successful was the
system that the League Council authorized the extension of its
provisions to Armenian refugees in 1924; and by 1929 almost forty
governments had accepted this arrangement (see Table 9).[18]

The beginning of international refugee law can properly be dated
to the creation of the Nansen passport system. In its original form,
however, this method of facilitating refugee travel was not without
defects. In fact, governments readily agreed to issue the identity
certificates because this did not involve a drastic intrusion on their

[14] 'Russian Refugees: Report to the Council of July 20th, 1922 by Dr. Nansen',
Official Journal (Aug. 1922) [C.472.M.297.1922], annex 384, p. 926–8.
[15] League of Nations, 'Report on the Work of the High Commission for Refu-
gees Presented by Dr. Fridtjof Nansen to the Fourth Assembly' (4 Sept. 1923)
[A.30.1923.XII], 1; 'Report by the Director of the ILO, 1925', *Official Journal,
Special Supplement No. 38. Sixth Assembly, Fifth Committee* (Geneva, 1925), 120;
League of Nations, 'Russian, Armenian, Assyrian, Assyro-Chaldean and Turkish
Refugees: Report to the Tenth Assembly' (15 Aug. 1929) [A.23.1929.XII], 13.
[16] [A.30.1923.XII], 4.   [17] [C.472.M.297.1922], 926.
[18] 'Arrangement of 31 May 1924 Relating to Armenian Refugees' [C.L.72(a)1924];
[A.23.1929.XII], 13.

TABLE 9. *Recognition of Arrangements and Conventions Relating to Refugees, 1922–1930*

Country	5 July 1922[1]	31 May 1924[2]	12 May 1926[3]	30 June 1928[4]	30 June 1928[5]
Europe					
Albania	x	x			
Austria	x	x	x	x	x
Belgium	x	x	x	x	x
Bulgaria	x	x	x	x	x
Czechoslovakia	x	x	x	x	x
Denmark	x	x	x		
Danzig	x				
Estonia	x	x	x	x	x
Finland	x		x		
France	x	x	x	x	x
Germany	x	x	x	x	x
Great Britain	x	x			
Greece	x	x	x		x
Hungary	x	x	x		
Ireland	x	x	x		
Italy	x	x			
Latvia	x	x		x	x
Lithuania	x	x			
Luxembourg	x		x		
Netherlands	x				
Norway	x	x	x		
Poland	x	x	x	x	x
Portugal	x	x			
Romania	x	x	x	x	x
Saar	x	x			
Spain	x				
Sweden	x	x	x		
Switzerland	x	x	x	x	x
Yugoslavia	x	x	x	x	x
Americas					
Argentina	x				
Bolivia	x				
Brazil	x	x			
Canada	x	x	x		
Chile	x				
Cuba	x	x	x		

TABLE 9. *(Cont.)*

Country	5 July 1922[1]	31 May 1924[2]	12 May 1926[3]	30 June 1928[4]	30 June 1928[5]
Guatemala	x				
Mexico	x				
Paraguay	x				
United States	x	x			
Uruguay	x	x		x	
Africa					
South Africa	x	x			
Egypt	x	x			
Liberia	x	x			
Asia (including Middle East)					
Australia	x	x			
China	x				
India	x	x	x		
Iraq	x	x			
Japan	x	x			
New Zealand	x	x			
Palestine	x	x			
Siam	x	x			
Turkey	x				
Totals	52	39	22	13	13

Note: x = ratification

[1] Arrangement of 5 July 1922 Relating to Russian Refugees [A.23.1929.XII], 13.
[2] Arrangement of 31 May 1924 Relating to Armenian Refugees [A.23.1929.XII], 13.
[3] Arrangement of 12 May 1926 Relating to Russian and Armenian Refugees [A.44.1926], 3; [A.23.1929.XII], 13.
[4] Arrangement of 30 June 1928 Extending Protection to Assyrian, Assyro-Chaldean, Turkish, and Assimilated Refugees, *Official Journal* (Dec. 1929), 1807, and (Apr. 1930), 323; [A.28.1930.XII], 16, 26.
[5] Arrangement of 30 June 1928 Relating to the Legal Status of Russian and Armenian Refugees, *Official Journal* (Dec. 1929), 1806; [A.28.1930.XII], 26.

sovereignty.[19] Once in operation, the shortcomings of the certificate system rapidly became apparent. In 1925 the Director of the ILO openly admitted that 'the measure of their practical application, in many countries, falls far short of the standard necessary to confer on the refugees the benefits contemplated when these systems were recommended'. His report stresses that the system lacked uniformity, especially in regard to fees, and that the certificate did not guarantee a right to return to the country which originally issued it.[20]

In order to correct these inadequacies, the Sixth Assembly of the League of Nations urged the convening of another intergovernmental conference. At this conference representatives gathered from twenty-five countries, more than double the number in attendance at the first (see Table 8). The conference resulted in the signing of the Arrangement of 12 May 1926, an improvement over the existing travel and identity system because it recognized the right to have a return visa placed on the refugee identity certificate.[21] In all, twenty-two countries adopted the May 1926 provisions (see Table 9).[22]

Almost exactly two years after the signing of the 1926 Arrangement another flurry of rule-making took place. This time governments attempted to create a more stable and secure legal status for refugees. The Arrangement of 28 June 1928, signed by representatives of thirteen states at an intergovernmental conference, recommended that consular services for refugees be carried out by the High Commissioner (see Table 9).[23] These functions included the certification of refugee identity and civil status, attesting to refugee character and conduct, and recommendation of refugees to government and educational authorities. At the same time, France and Belgium signed an agreement designating these quasi-consular functions to the representatives of the High Commissioner.[24] These arrangements, along with the earlier ones, were

---

[19] Simpson, *The Refugee Problem*, 242.   [20] 1925 ILO Report, 120.

[21] 'Arrangement of 12 May 1926 relating to the Issue of Identity Certificates to Russian and Armenian Refugees', *LNTS*, 89/2004, 47.

[22] [A.23.1929.XII], 13.

[23] 'Arrangement of 30 June 1928 Relating to the Legal Status of Russian and Armenian Refugees', *LNTS*, 89/2005, 53; *Official Journal* (Dec. 1929), 1806.

[24] 'Agreement [of 30 June 1928] Concerning the Functions of the Representatives of the League of Nations [in France and Belgium]', *LNTS*, 93, p. 377. Between 1954 and 1988 Belgium continued this tradition. During this period it was the only country to have the UNHCR determine refugee status. Crystal Johnson,

eventually codified into international law in the 1933 Refugee Convention.[25] For signatory states, the provisions of the Convention became legally binding instead of being recommendations for action.

Defining 'Who is a Refugee?'

The first formal definition of a refugee in international law is given in the 1926 Arrangement. It defines the term 'refugee' as follows:

Russian: Any person of Russian origin who does not enjoy or who no longer enjoys the protection of the Government of the Union of Soviet Socialist Republics and who has not acquired another nationality.
Armenian: Any person of Armenian origin formerly a subject of the Ottoman Empire who does not enjoy or who no longer enjoys the protection of the Government of the Turkish Republic and who has not acquired another nationality.[26]

The 1926 Arrangement defines refugee status on the basis of country of origin or ethnic group. In the case of Russian refugees, the term 'Russian origin' means 'from the former Russian Empire': refugees of Russian, Ukrainian, Jewish, Cossack, Georgian, and other ethnic origins were all considered to be 'Russian refugees'. The definitions of both Russian and Armenian refugees reflect the dominant view, held by the Institute for International Law and among legal scholars in the inter-war years, that refugees were persons who had lost the diplomatic protection of their home governments without acquiring another nationality.[27] In contrast to the definition given in the 1951 Refugee Convention, individuals

---

'Refugee Law Reform In Europe: The Belgian Example', *Columbia Journal of Transnational Law*, 27/3 (1989), 592.

[25] 'Convention Relating to the International Status of Refugees, 28 October 1933', *LNTS*, 159/3663, 199.   [26] 'Arrangement of 1926', 49.

[27] In 1936 the Institut de Droit International adopted this definition of a refugee at its Brussels conference: 'Dans les présentes résolutions, le terme réfugié désigne tout individu qui, en raison d'événements politiques survenus sur le territoire de l'Etat dont il était ressortissant, a quitté volontairement ou non ce territoire ou en demeure éloigné, qui n'a acquis aucune nationalité nouvelle et ne jouit de la protection diplomatique d'aucun autre Etat.' *Annuaire de l'Institut de Droit International*, ii (1936), 294. (Eng. tr. in Tartakower and Grossman, *The Jewish Refugee*, 5.) Legal scholars Sir John Hope Simpson, Louise Holborn, and R. Yewdall Jennings hold similar positions. Simpson, for instance, writes that in international law 'the main characteristic of a refugee . . . is the fact that he does not enjoy the protection of the government of his country of origin'. See Simpson, *The Refugee Problem*, 229; Holborn, 'The Legal Status of Political Refugees', 680; Jennings, 'Some International Law Aspects', 99.

did not have to explain their personal motivations for flight or
prove that they had suffered persecution in order to receive refugee status.[28] Though not explicitly stated, the fact that this definition appears in an agreement about international travel documents
implies that the refugee is outside his or her home country. All
other international legal documents adopted during the inter-war
years also identify refugees by their group affiliation, loss of diplomatic protection, and location outside their home country.

After the Second World War, the refugee definitions put forth
by the League of Nations came under fire from legal scholars for
misrepresenting the essence of refugeehood. In part, this criticism
was due to the dramatic impact of the Nazi era on thinking about
human rights. In many minds, refugees became synonymous with
victims of Nazi persecution. As a result, refugees tended to be
thought of as individuals facing persecution for their religious or
political beliefs, or because of their association with a particular
class or racial group. Jacques Vernant, the author of an early post-
war study of refugees, argues that definitions that use lack of diplomatic protection as the litmus test for refugeehood are too broad
in that they include anyone who has left his country for political
reasons, even if he has not been persecuted.[29] Guy Goodwin-Gill
sees interwar definitions as an abstraction, divorced from the events
which actually produced refugees.[30] The distinguished jurist Atle

[28] The 1951 Convention defines a refugee as any person who 'As a result of
events occurring before 1 January 1951 and owing to well-founded fear of being
persecuted for reasons of race, religion, nationality, membership of a particular
social group or political opinion, is outside the country of his nationality and is
unable or, owing to such fear, is unwilling to avail himself of the protection of
that country; or who, not having a nationality and being outside the country of his
former habitual residence as a result of such events, is unable or, owing to such
fear, is unwilling to return to it'. Although this definition is based on individual
characteristics of the refugee rather than on his or her group affiliation, it does
include an optional clause which restricted its application to Europe. 'United Nations Convention Relating to the Status of Refugees, 28 July 1951', *UNTS*,
189/2545, 152.

[29] According to Vernant, 'Before a man can be described as a refugee, the
political events which caused him to leave, or to break with, the State to which
he owed allegiance must be defined. The political events which in the country of
origin led to his departure must be accompanied by persecution or by the threat
of persecution against himself or at least against a section of the population with
which he identifies himself.' Jacques Vernant, *The Refugee in the Post-War World*
(London: Allen & Unwin, 1953), 6.

[30] Guy S. Goodwin-Gill, *The Refugee in International Law* (Oxford: Clarendon
Press, 1983), 4.

Grahl-Madsen writes that definitions which stress lack of diplomatic protection as the distinguishing feature of a refugee are in error because 'the lack of protection is not relevant unless it is caused by a deep-rooted political controversy between the authorities and the individual'.[31]

What these scholars fail to appreciate is the true purpose of the legal definitions put forward by the League of Nations. Their first purpose was to formalize the political consensus which had already been reached within the Council or Assembly of the League of Nations about the groups that should be given refugee status. Their second purpose was to aid governments and international organizations in determining which individuals qualified as members of a given refugee group. In addition, the very existence of these definitions implied that refugees, unlike international migrants who travel primarily for economic reasons, had left their home countries because of extraordinary political circumstances. Inter-war scholars were very much aware of the distinction. In fact, they insisted on it. Simpson, for instance, writes that the 'refugee is distinguished from the ordinary alien or migrant in that he has left his former territory because of political events there, not because of economic conditions or because of the economic attraction of another territory'.[32] Consequently, there was no need to place an elaborate explanation of the reasons for a refugee's flight within a legal definition. The fact that legal definitions did not contain such an explanation actually benefited both refugees and their host countries. Because legal documents did not mention persecution, they did not give the appearance of blaming a particular country for the creation of refugees. This made it easier for host countries both to help refugees and to maintain cordial relations with the Soviet Union, Turkey, and other refugee-producing countries.

Moreover, the inter-war practice of defining refugees on a group basis had several advantages. From a purely practical point of

[31] Grahl-Madsen, *Status of Refugees*, i. 98. Madsen directly attacks Simpson on this point. In all fairness to Simpson, it should be noted that he provides two definitions of refugee status. The first emphasizes that refugees are unique because they flee from political events. The second gives lack of diplomatic protection as the essential quality of a refugee in a general discussion of legal thinking on refugees. See Simpson, *The Refugee Problem*, 3–4, 227.

[32] Simpson, *The Refugee Problem*, 4. See also Tartakower and Grossman, *The Jewish Refugee*, 2–3; Oscar Jaszi, 'Political Refugees', *Annals*, 203 (May 1939), 83.

view, it provided a relatively efficient way of dealing with a mass exodus. Interviewing several million people individually to see if they qualified as refugees under one specific definition was unnecessary; instead, refugee assistance could simply be extended to all members of a particular movement. In addition, the granting of refugee status did not depend on the refugees' proving that they left their home countries because of persecution or some other specific reason.[33] Instead, the group designation gave refugee status to people who fled a variety of life-threatening situations. The Russian refugees, for instance, included all of the following types of people: victims of the Russian and Ukrainian famines of 1920–2; peasants fleeing both the Red and White armies in the Russian Civil War; soldiers of the White armies and their families; and former tsarist officials and aristocrats. Ironically, many legal scholars and refugee advocates now urge abandoning the practice of defining refugees only as those who face persecution as individuals. They argue that this is inadequate to deal with the mass refugee flows produced by the anti-colonial and civil wars which have taken place in the developing world since 1945.[34] The definition of a refugee developed by the Organization of African Unity in its 1969 Refugee Convention makes an attempt to deal with this problem by including both individuals with a well-founded fear of persecution and those fleeing 'events seriously disturbing public order'.[35]

[33] James C. Hathaway argues that the requirement in the 1951 Refugee Convention that a refugee have a well-founded fear of persecution was a deviation from the humanitarian principles of the early phase of refugee law. According to him, 'no longer was it enough to be a member of a group of displaced or stateless persons; rather a particularized analysis of each claimant's motives for flight was requisite to recognition as a refugee.' James C. Hathaway, 'A Reconsideration of the Underlying Premise of Refugee Law', *Harvard International Law Journal*, 31/2 (Winter 1990), 139.
[34] For instance, Elizabeth Ferris contends that refugees should be 'considered as those victims of political violence who seek refuge outside their nation's borders. This definition includes individuals persecuted for their political or religious beliefs, their ethnic or racial background, as well as those fleeing their homelands because of war, whether or not they are singled out for persecution.' Elizabeth Ferris, 'Overview: Refugees and World Politics', in her (ed.), *Refugees and World Politics* (New York: Praeger, 1985), 6. See also Andrew E. Shacknove, 'Who is a Refugee?', *Ethics*, 95 (Jan. 1985), 274–84.
[35] The 1969 Organization of African Unity (OAU) Convention on Refugees defines a refugee as every person fitting the definition given in the 1951 Convention (time-limit exempted) and 'every person who, owing to external aggression, occupation, foreign domination or events seriously disturbing public order in either

Extension of the Nansen Passport System

Although originally designed for Russian and Armenian refugees, the League of Nations expanded its system of legal protection on an *ad hoc* basis to other refugee groups. In 1928 an Arrangement incorporated approximately 19,000 Assyrians and other Christian minorities from the former Ottoman Empire into the Nansen passport system.[36] In the 1930s further extensions of the system brought in more people under the heading 'refugee'. Following the return of the Saarland to Germany in 1935, the Council responded favourably to a proposal from the French government which asked that identity certificates be issued to refugees from the Saar.[37] After an extended debate the Assembly decided not to extend the Nansen passport system to refugees from the Third Reich.[38] However, at the suggestion of Sir Neill Malcolm, High Commissioner for Refugees coming from Germany, an attempt was made to introduce a similar system. The resulting documents, a provisional Arrangement of 1936 and a Convention of 1938, relate to 'refugees coming from Germany', primarily Jews who had been denationalized by the Nazi government, and specify that governments issue them with

part or the whole of his country of origin or nationality, is compelled to leave his place of habitual residence to seek refuge in another place outside his country of origin or nationality'. 'OAU Convention Governing the Specific Aspects of Refugee Problems in Africa of September 10, 1968', *UNTS*, no. 14,691, art. 1 (2).

[36] 'Arrangement of 30 June 1928 Concerning the Extension to Other Categories of Refugees of Certain Measures taken in Favour of Russian and Armenian Refugees', *LNTS*, 89, p. 63. It defines Assyrian, Assyro-Chaldean, and assimilated refugees as 'Any person of Assyrian or Assyro-Chaldean origin, and also by assimilation, any person of Syrian or Kurdish origin, who does not enjoy, or who no longer enjoys, the protection of the State to which he previously belonged and who has not acquired, or does not possess, another nationality'. It also defines a Turkish refugee as 'Any person of Turkish origin, previously a subject of the Ottoman Empire, who, under the terms of the Protocol of Lausanne of July 24th, 1923, does not enjoy, or no longer enjoys, the protection of the Turkish Republic and who has not acquired another nationality'.

[37] 'Extension of the Nansen Passport System to Refugees from the Saar', *Official Journal* (Dec. 1935), 1681; '*Aide-Mémoire* of 18 January 1935 by French government to Secretary-General', *Official Journal* (Feb. 1935), annex 1532, pp. 276–7. Refugees from the Saar were defined as 'all persons who, having previously had the status of inhabitants of the Saar, had left the Territory on the occasion of the plebiscite and were not in possession of national passports'. See League of Nations, Nansen International Office, 'Report of the Governing Body' (29 Aug. 1935) [A.22.1935.XII], 2.

[38] The treatment of Jewish and non-Jewish refugees from Nazi Germany is discussed in more depth in Chs. 5–7.

travel documents.[39] At the suggestion of the British and French delegates, the Council extended protection to refugees from Austria in May 1938.[40] A similar decision by the Council in January 1939 brought refugees from Czechoslovakia under the League's umbrella.[41]

Despite this growth in the number of refugees covered under international law, individual political exiles not associated with a larger migration remained outside the system. In addition, designation of refugee status required a strong consensus about assisting a particular group. The debates about extending refugee status in the late 1920s indicate that such consensus was very difficult to form. These efforts began when, in 1926, the Belgian delegate called the attention of the Seventh Assembly to the plight of people who were in a position similar to Russian and Armenian refugees but lacked legal protection. As a result, the Assembly passed a resolution asking the High Commissioner to investigate the extension of protection to 'other analogous categories of refugees'. Private organizations, rather than governments, then sent petitions to the Refugee Section of the ILO about particular refugee groups. After compiling these appeals, High Commissioner Nansen informed the Council of numerous refugees in need of legal protection: 150 Assyrians and a small number of Montenegrin refugees in France,[42] 19,000 Assyro-Chaldeans in the Caucasus and

[39] 'Provisional Arrangement on the Status of Refugees coming from Germany, 4 July 1936', *LNTS*, 171/3952, 75; 'Convention on the Status of Refugees coming from Germany, 10 February 1938', *LNTS*, 192/4461, 59. The Convention defined refugees coming from Germany as '(a) Persons possessing or having possessed German nationality and not possessing any other nationality who are proved not to enjoy, in law or in fact, the protection of the German Government; (b) Stateless persons not covered by previous Conventions or Agreements who have left German territory after being established therein and who are proved not to enjoy, in law or in fact, the protection of the German Government'.
[40] *Official Journal* (May–June 1938), 368. This decision merely authorized the High Commissioner for Refugees coming from Germany to consult with governments about extending the provisions of the 1936 Arrangement and 1938 Convention to refugees from Austria. A separate Protocol of 14 Sept. 1939 specifically dealt with refugees from Austria. *LNTS*, 198/4634, 141.
[41] 'Minutes of the 104th Session of the Council', *Official Journal* (Feb. 1939), 73.
[42] Forced to leave their homes near Mt. Ararat, the Assyrians, a Christian minority group within the Ottoman Empire, eventually travelled to Marseilles, where they lived in a destitute condition without the right to stay. The Montenegrins fled the kingdom of Serbs, Croats, and Slovenes (Yugoslavia) for political reasons. League of Nations, 'Russian and Armenian Refugees: Report to the Eighth Assembly' (1927) [A.48.1927.XIII], 14. The Montenegrin National Defence Committee

Greece,[43] 9,000 Ruthenes in Austria and Czechoslovakia,[44] 100,000 refugees in central Europe, including 10,000 former Hungarians in Austria, France, and Romania,[45] 16,000 Jews in Romania,[46] and 150 Turks in Greece who had been 'Friends of the Allies'.[47]

In considering Nansen's report, the Council began by restricting its consideration to those people only who became refugees 'as a consequence of the war and of events directly connected with the war'.[48] At a second discussion it made further qualifications. In an official Council report, the Romanian delegate indirectly referred to the appeal by the Jewish Colonization Association that stateless Jews in Romania and Poland be considered refugees. He clearly pointed out that 'the mere fact that certain classes of persons are without the protection of any national Government is not sufficient to make them refugees', a distinction which effectively eliminated any consideration of the stateless, including the many Jews in Romania whom his government refused to accept as citizens. Although the Italian delegate claimed that 'every member of the Council was filled with the most humanitarian feelings', the financial costs concerned him because it would be states which would

in Paris appealed to the League on behalf of the Montenegrins in France. Letter from T. F. Johnson, Refugee Section, ILO, to the Representatives of the High Commissioner, 28 Oct. 1926. LNA C1412/R.409.04.j.1.

[43] The Assyro-Chaldeans fled from areas south of Lake Van to Caucasus and Greece, where they were unable to settle permanently. [A.48.1927.XII], 14.

[44] The Ruthenes originally came from Galicia. [A.48.1927.XII], 14. The International Committee of the Red Cross called the attention of the League to the Ruthenes in Czechoslovakia. Letter from Dr J. M. Linhart, Croix-Rouge, Prague, to M. Johnson, Service des Réfugiés, Bureau international du Travail, Genève of 16 Nov. 1926. LNA C1412/R.409.04.j.1.

[45] The Fédération internationale des Ligues des Droits de l'Homme et du Citoyen brought these refugees to the attention of the Refugee Section of the League. [A.48.1927.XII], 14.

[46] Lucien Wolf of the Jewish Colonization Association wrote to the Refugee Section of the League in regard to the 'Staatenlose' Jews of Romania and Poland. What Wolf really wanted, however, was for the Council to enforce the Minorities Treaties of 1919. See memorandum on 'Staatenlose' from Lucien Wolf, London, to the Refugee Section, ILO, Geneva of 1 Oct. 1926. LNA C1412/R.409.04.j.1.

[47] These Turks had been proscribed by the Turkish government for being 'Friends of the Allies'. [A.48.1927.XII], 14. They were brought to the attention of the Refugee Section by Erik Colban of the Minorities Questions Section, who had been approached by a Turkish refugee while visiting Greece. See letter from Erik Colban to Major Johnson, Refugee Section, ILO, Geneva of 25 Mar. 1926. LNA C1412/R.409.04.j.1.

[48] 'Minutes of the 43rd Session of the Council', Official Journal (Feb. 1927), 155.

be 'called upon to pay the bill'.[49] Certain host countries also objected to increasing aid. The Austrian government, for instance, vetoed the expansion of any efforts on behalf of Ruthenes and Hungarians in its country.[50] Although the French government agreed to the extension of legal protection to the Assyrians, Assyro-Chaldeans, and Turks, it made no initiatives on behalf of Hungarians and Montenegrins in its territory.[51] In the end the League selected only these groups—the Assyrians, Assyro-Chaldeans, and the Turks—from its long list of needy candidates.

Application of the Nansen Passport System

Although not available to all refugees, the Nansen passport system represents an important step in the quest for refugee protection. The identity certificates had a profound effect on the lives of refugees carrying them: they made it possible for them to cross international borders legally. But the identity certificates had more than a utilitarian importance. Over time, the Nansen passport system served as the foundation of a clearly defined legal status for refugees. Russian and Armenian refugees were clearly aware of this, and they jealously guarded their rights to Nansen passports, which they considered to be 'a sign of the legal recognition of their peculiar status'.[52] According to Louise Holborn:

The importance of the Nansen Passport can hardly be overestimated. Through this first international identity paper, refugees of specified categories became the possessors of a legal and juridical status. Thus refugees, who were *de facto* or *de jure* stateless and without protection or representation from their native governments, were provided with both by the High Commissioner for Refugees, who acted for them in a quasi-consular capacity.[53]

[49] 'Minutes of the 46th Session of the Council', *Official Journal* (Oct. 1927), 1137–8.   [50] *Official Journal* (Mar. 1928), 357–9.
[51] Letter from T. F. Johnson, Refugee Section, ILO Geneva, to Dr J. Rubinstein, Paris of 28 Apr. 1928. LNA C1412/R.409.0.4.
[52] Both the Russian and Armenian refugee organizations strongly objected to the extension of the Nansen passport system to all stateless people. Hannah Arendt, *The Origins of Totalitarianism* (New York: Harcourt, Brace, 1951), 280; [A.48.1927], 10–11.
[53] Holborn, *Refugees: A Problem of our Time*, 10. See also Michael R. Marrus, *The Unwanted: European Refugees in the Twentieth Century* (New York: Oxford University Press, 1985), 95.

In the provision of actual protection, the system of delegates begun by Nansen also proved to be of great importance. From 1922 to 1939 the various refugee agencies of the League of Nations maintained representatives in the major refugee host countries of the world (see Table 10). These delegates provided refugees with a variety of services, from recommendations to government officials that refugees be issued with an identity certificate or visa, to certifying professional qualifications or family status. From 1932 to 1938 the Nansen office made an average of more than 18,000 interventions annually relating to the personal status of Russian, Armenian, Assyrian, and Saar refugees (see Table 11).[54] In addition, the representatives of the High Commissioner provided consular services directly in France and Belgium under the terms of their 1928 Accord. Although no other states ratified this accord, it is still significant because of the wide-ranging powers that the two states transferred to the representatives of an international organization.

While most legal scholars agree that the development of the Nansen passport system was an important innovation, the operation of the system in practice has been criticized. In particular, Holborn points out that, as the Arrangements grew more comprehensive, the number of adherents declined.[55] A glance at the total number of acceptances of the various Arrangements supports this observation. In regard to Russian refugees, 52 countries accepted the initial Arrangement instituting the certificate system, 22 countries accepted the Arrangement recommending a right to return, and only 13 accepted the Arrangement on their legal status. However, a closer look reveals a different picture. Although the total number of acceptances declined, it remained steady among the major host countries of Europe. This was important because these countries actually had to apply the terms of the Arrangements. Of the ten major host countries to Russian refugees in Europe, eight adhered to all the Arrangements (see Table 9).[56] The fact that Siam,

---

[54] No comprehensive statistics on consular activities were kept during the 1920s. Reports by the High Commissioner and the ILO indicate that the delegates performed rudimentary consular services, even before the Arrangement of 30 June 1928 on the legal status of Russian and Armenian refugees.

[55] Holborn, *Refugees: A Problem of our Time*, 16.

[56] Bulgaria, Czechoslovakia, Estonia, France, Germany, Poland, Romania, and Yugoslavia all accepted the Arrangements of 1922, 1926, and 1928 relating to Russian refugees. Of the major host countries, only Latvia refused to accept the 1926 Arrangement, and only Finland refused to accept the 1928 Arrangement.

TABLE 10. *Delegates of the Refugee Agencies of the League of Nations, 1922–1938*

Country	HC (1922)[1]	ILO (1927)[2]	NIO (1931)[3]	NIO (1938)[4]
Europe				
Austria	x	x	x	
Belgium			x	x
Bulgaria	x	x	x	x
Czechoslovakia	x	x	x	x
Estonia	x	(with Poland)	(with Poland)	x
Finland	x	x	x	
France	x	x	x	x
Germany	x	x	x	
Great Britain	x			
Greece		x	x	x
Hungary	x			
Latvia	x	(with Poland)	(with Poland)	x
Lithuania		(with Poland)	(with Poland)	x
Poland	x	x	x	
Romania	x			x
Yugoslavia	x	x	x	x
Asia and Middle East				
China		x	x	x
Turkey	x	x	x	x
Syria		x	x	x
South America				
Argentina		x	x	
Total	14	13	14	13

[1] Delegates of the High Commissioner for Refugees, 1922, *Official Journal* (May 1922), 395.
[2] Delegates of the Refugee Section of the ILO, 1927 [A.48.1927.XII], 17.
[3] Delegates of the Nansen International Office, 1931, *Official Journal* (Apr. 1931), 750.
[4] Delegates of the Nansen International Office, 1938 [A.21.1938.XII], 19–20.

TABLE 11. *Interventions by the Nansen International Office, 1932–1938, relating to the personal status of Russian, Armenian, Assyrian, and Saar refugees*

Types of Intervention	1932[1]	1933[2]	1934[3]	1935[4]	1936[5]	1937[6]	1938[7]
Issues & Renewals of Nansen passports (applications to governments)	13,598	12,518	10,412	8,823	7,812	8,506	4,782
Issues of visas (steps taken for obtainment)	1,887	1,278	2,523	1,070	1,159	685	1,295
Establishment of documents as per art. 1, Arr. 30/6/28							
(a) certifying the identity and position of refugees	624	781	1,980	1,852	517	1,981	822
(b) certifying family position and civil status	1,068	1,092	1,084	1,664	1,944	1,930	2,061
(c) testifying to the regularity of documents issued in country of origin	186	263	502	346	775	564	783
(d) certifying signatures	785	551	1,081	1,411	1,488	1,087	1,165
(e) testifying to good character and conduct	495	429	844	479	251	335	314
(f) recommending the refugee to the competent authorities re visas, residence permits, etc.	1,256	1,246	3,238	5211	4,814	3,414	2,560
Totals	19,899	18,158	21,664	20,856	18,760	18,502	13,782

Grand Total: 131,621, or 18,803 per year on average.

[1] [A.24.1932], 7–8.
[2] [A.19.1933], 7–8.
[3] [A.12.1934], 6–8.
[4] [A.22.1935.XII], 22–3.
[5] [A.23.1936.XII], 24–5.
[6] [A.21.1937.XII], 14–15.
[7] [A.21.1938.XII], 11–12.

for instance, did not accept the 1926 Arrangement was of little consequence because of the small number of Russian refugees there.

Of course, the Nansen passport system gave governments—not the delegates of the League of Nations—the authority to issue the identity certificates. This meant that acceptance of any Arrangement did not ensure compliance. Germany, for instance, ratified all the major Arrangements but never issued Nansen passports to the majority of refugees there as the government preferred to deal with the former Russian delegation.[57] The Polish and Finnish governments issued certificates to only a small fraction of the refugees in their territory. A number of countries, however, took full advantage of the system. Latvia, Estonia, Czechoslovakia, and Yugoslavia all issued certificates to more than 90 per cent of the refugees in their territory, while Hungary, Switzerland, Austria, and Bulgaria issued certificates to a considerable number (see Table 12).[58] Russian refugees in France could easily obtain the documents.[59]

It must be admitted that the success of the travel and identity system for refugees from Germany pales in comparison with the Nansen passport system. Less than ten countries adopted the 1936 Arrangement, which severely limited its effectiveness. Moreover, the High Commissioner for Refugees from Germany did not maintain a system of delegates in major refugee-hosting countries. Without these representatives, the High Commissioner could do very little in the way of providing consular services to refugees. Within these limits, the documents did help to improve the legal position of some refugees. Following French ratification of the 1936 Arrangement, the government created a special committee to examine the applications of refugees from Germany who entered France between 30 January 1933 and 5 August 1936 to see if they should be granted travel documents. Based on their recommendations, the government legalized the status of refugees who had entered France illegally.[60]

[57] Robert Williams, *Culture in Exile: Russian Emigres in Germany, 1881–1941* (Ithaca, NY: Cornell University Press, 1972), 145.

[58] League of Nations, 'Armenian and Russian Refugees: Report to the Seventh Assembly' (3 Sept. 1926) [A.44.1926], 9–10.

[59] Robert H. Johnston, *New Mecca, New Babylon: Paris and the Russian Exiles, 1920–1945* (Kingston, Ontario: McGill-Queen's University Press, 1988), 73.

[60] Sir John Hope Simpson, *Refugees: Preliminary Report of a Survey* (London: Royal Institute of International Affairs, 1938), 115; Holborn, 'Legal Status', 695–6.

TABLE 12. *Application of the Nansen Passport System for Russian Refugees, 1926*

Major Host Countries (over 1,000 refugees)	Number of Russian Refugees	Number of Certificates Issued (%)
Austria	2,465	1,030 (42%)
Bulgaria	28,340	6,500 (23%)
China	76,000	no data
Czechoslovakia	30,000	30,000 (100%)
Estonia	19,000	17,209 (90%)
Finland	14,312	800 (6%)
France	400,000	no data
Germany	400,000	no data
Hungary	5,294	3,011 (57%)
Latvia	33,544	33,544 (100%)
Lithuania	7,644	no data
Poland	60,800	4,600 (8%)
Switzerland	2,268	900 (40%)
Turkey	5,000	no data
Yugoslavia	38,000	37,500 (99%)
Total	1,122,667	

Source: [A.44.1926], 9–10.

To a large extent, the strength of the sovereignty principle and asylum norm within the international refugee regime explains why the Nansen passport system was more effective than the travel document system devised for German refugees. None of the rules of the international refugee regime significantly challenged the notion that the state was sovereign over its own territory and retained the right to grant admission to refugees. In the case of refugees protected by the Nansen system, such as the Russian, Armenian, and Saar refugees, governments had already granted the refugees temporary asylum. For these refugees, the problem was one of improving and regularizing their legal status within countries which were already favourably disposed to them. In contrast, the major problem faced by both Jewish and non-Jewish refugees fleeing Nazi Germany was actually finding countries willing to permit them to enter at all. Without this willingness, international agreements on refugee travel certificates did little to improve their desperate situation.

Even though the rules of the international refugee regime did not guarantee a refugee entrance to a particular country, they did make the lives of refugees better. For many refugees, having an internationally recognized identity document helped them to cross international borders legally and gave them a more secure legal status. True, holding a Nansen passport did not guarantee a refugee anything, but it sometimes helped a great deal. Writing in 1938, journalist Dorothy Thompson notes that:

It is a fantastic commentary on the inhumanity of our times that for thousands and thousands of people a piece of paper with a stamp on it is the difference between life and death, and that scores of people have blown their brains out because they could not get it. But there is no doubt that by and large, the Nansen certificate is the greatest thing that has happened for the individual refugee. It returned to him his lost identity. The refugee could never be sure whether he would get a labor permit by means of the Nansen certificate, but he could be sure that *without* the Nansen certificate he would *never* get it.[61]

TURNING NORMS INTO RULES: SOCIAL WELFARE AND EMPLOYMENT

In addition to enhancing freedom of movement and providing consular functions, rule-making efforts in the Inter-war Period focused on improving the general welfare of refugees. In this regard, the year 1928 can be considered a turning-point. As economic depression encompassed countries around the world, many governments adopted legislation prohibiting the employment of foreigners.[62] Usually this resulted in a deterioration of the living conditions for refugees. Anti-alien feelings became particularly acute in France, the major country of immigration in Europe and host to refugees of many nationalities.

[61] Dorothy Thompson, *Refugees: Anarchy or Organization?* (New York: Random House, 1938), 28.
[62] In 1930–1 Albania, Belgium, Brazil, Germany, Malaya, Poland, Portugal, Switzerland, and Tunisia enacted restrictions on the employment of foreign workers. International Labour Office, *Annual Review 1930* (Geneva: Albert Kundig, 1931), 371–3; id., *I.L.O. Year-Book 1931* (Geneva: Albert Kundig, 1932), 357–9.

After the First World War, France alone of the European countries welcomed immigration. By 1930 France had an alien population of nearly three million, made up of Poles, Italians, Belgians, Russians, Armenians, and other nationalities.[63] Eager to replace the manpower lost in the war, the French government encouraged the entrance of foreign workers to fill jobs often rejected by French workers. Consequently, immigrants came to hold an important position in the French economy, especially in mining, construction, and metallurgy. Though Russian, Armenian, and other refugees never constituted more than about ten per cent of the foreign work-force, they played an important role in French industry in the 1920s. Russian refugees worked primarily in the car and metal industries. Armenians held jobs in these sectors and in textiles as well.[64]

Attitudes towards foreign workers in France changed dramatically when the world-wide economic depression began in the early 1930s. As the level of unemployment rose, the French government and people began to seriously question the wisdom of its immigration and asylum policies. Acting in the belief that foreigners took jobs from nationals, the French government enacted the Law for the Protection of National Labour in 1932. The law gave the government the authority to restrict the percentage of foreign workers in industry, commerce, and agriculture.[65] Normally the Ministry of Labour fixed a quota of ten per cent, though the figure could be smaller or larger. In 1935 the French government carried out a revision of all alien work permits, often resulting in the delay and eventual denial of renewals.[66]

The promulgation of these restrictive laws had a dramatic impact on the refugees in France, many of whom had been residents there for over ten years. Russian and Armenian refugees lost their work permits and their jobs, leaving them dependent on the meagre resources of charitable institutions. In 1939 the Refugee Survey reported that the law hurt refugee enterprises, citing

---

[63] Georges Mauco, *Les Etrangers en France* (Paris: A. Colim, 1932), 133; Marrus, *The Unwanted*, 146.

[64] Gary S. Cross, *Immigrant Workers in Industrial France* (Philadelphia: Temple University Press, 1983), 123–6, 187.

[65] International Labour Office, *I.L.O. Year-Book 1932* (Geneva: Albert Kundig, 1933), 255–6.

[66] Id., *I.L.O. Year-Book 1934–35* (Geneva: Albert Kundig, 1935), i. 336; Simpson, *The Refugee Problem*, 275.

the examples of a Russian orchestra that was permitted to employ only 15 per cent Russian musicians and a Russian choir that could have only 10 per cent Russian singers.[67] In 1935 the Save the Children Fund called attention to the dire conditions facing Russian refugees in France:

It has been said—and there is a great deal of truth in this statement—that the beginning of their life as refugees held out much brighter prospects than those which, fifteen years later, confront them in France to-day. Their present situation is so serious, and indeed so tragic, that unless something is rapidly done to remedy the existing state of affairs, thousands of these unfortunate people will be doomed to a premature end by the gradual but terrible process of starvation.[68]

The 1933 Convention

The deteriorating conditions for refugees in France and elsewhere spurred a flurry of rule-making and rule-promoting activities. As early as 1928 the Arrangement on the legal status of Russian and Armenian refugees recommended that restrictives on foreign labour should not be strictly applied to Russian and Armenian refugees.[69] Unfortunately, this provision had little concrete effect, in part because the Arrangement was not legally binding. Gradually a consensus formed around concluding an international convention to remedy the defects of existing Arrangements. In early 1933 a Secretariat memorandum noted that 'with the exception of the Nansen passport, the existing so-called arrangements are producing practically no effect upon the position of the refugees' and suggested consideration of an international convention.[70] The Nansen International Office and the Intergovernmental Advisory Commission also supported the idea of a convention.[71] These two

[67] Simpson, *The Refugee Problem*, 275.
[68] Save the Children Fund, *Report on Russian, Armenian, German, and Saar Refugees in France* (London: Save the Children Fund, 1935), 8. See also League of Nations Union, *Refugees and the League* (London: League of Nations Union, 1935), 29–30.   [69] Arrangement of 30 June 1928, par. 6.
[70] Secretariat memorandum of 3 Feb. 1933. LNA R5614/686.
[71] The Intergovernmental Advisory Commission for Refugees was a special body created by the Council in Dec. 1928 with the express purpose of conducting a general survey on the reorganization of the League's refugee work after Nansen's death. Its membership consisted of delegates from Germany, Bulgaria, China, Estonia, France, Great Britain, Greece, Italy, Latvia, Poland, Romania, Czechoslovakia,

bodies drew up a draft document and submitted it to an inter-governmental conference in October 1933.[72] As a result of these efforts, the first refugee convention came into being.

The 1933 Convention represents the first attempt to create a comprehensive legal framework for refugees.[73] Though limited in its scope to refugees already under the protection of the League of Nations, the Convention deals with a wide variety of concerns, from identity certificates to expulsions.[74] It contains a number of important provisions relating to labour conditions (ch. IV), industrial accidents (ch. V), welfare and relief (ch. VI), and education (ch. VII). In 1935 the Convention came into force after Bulgaria and Norway ratified it. Michael Hansson, President of the Nansen Office from 1936 until 1938, made increasing the number of ratifications a top priority.[75] Eventually Belgium, Czechoslovakia, France, Great Britain, Italy, and Denmark also ratified it. Eight additional countries applied the provisions of the document without formal ratification, bringing the total number of adherents to sixteen (see Table 13).[76] Although the Convention never became applicable world-wide, it must be remembered that it came into force only four years before the outbreak of the Second World War. As the formal ratification of a treaty can be a long and arduous process, the number of acceptances is a considerable accomplishment.

The 1933 Convention formed an important component of the international refugee regime for two reasons. First of all, the document set standards on the treatment of refugees in several areas. These standards had an impact on regime members, whether or not they formally adhered to the Convention. One of the most

and Yugoslavia. After completing its report in May 1929 the Commission continued to advise the refugee agencies of the League of Nations. League of Nations, 'Report by the Secretary-General on the Future Organization of Refugee Work' (30 Aug. 1930) [A.28.1930.XII], 2.

[72] League of Nations, Nansen International Office for Refugees, 'Report of the Governing Body' (30 Aug. 1933) [A.19.1933], 2; id., 'Report of the Governing Body' (20 Aug. 1934) [A.12.1934], 3.   [73] 1933 Convention, 199–217.

[74] The Convention covered Russian, Armenian, Assyrian, Assyro-Chaldean, and Turkish refugees.

[75] Nansen International Office, 'Special Report Submitted to the 17th Assembly by M. Michael Hansson, Acting President of the Governing Body' (7 Sept. 1936) [A.27.1936.XII], 9.

[76] The USA, Estonia, Finland, Greece, Iraq, Latvia, Sweden, and Switzerland did not ratify the 1933 Convention, but applied it in practice. Nansen International Office, 'Report of the Governing Body' (20 Aug. 1937) [A.21.1937.XII], 5.

TABLE 13. *Recognition of Arrangements and Conventions Relating to Refugees, 1931-1938*

Country	28 October 1933[1]	4 May 1935[2]	4 July 1936[3]	10 February 1938[4]
Europe				
Albania				
Austria				
Belgium	X		S	S
Bulgaria	X	X		
Czechoslovakia	X			
Denmark	X	X	S	S
Danzig				
Estonia	A	X		
Finland	A	X		
France	X	X	S	S
Germany				
Great Britain	X	X	S	S
Greece	A			
Hungary				
Ireland		X		
Italy	X	X		
Latvia	A	X		
Lithuania				
Luxembourg				
Netherlands				S
Norway	X	X	S	S
Poland		X		
Portugal				
Romania				
Saar				
Spain			S	S
Sweden	A			
Switzerland	A	X	S	
Yugoslavia				
Americas				
Argentina				
Bolivia				
Brazil				
Canada				
Chile				
Cuba				

TABLE 13. *(Cont.)*

Country	28 October 1933[1]	4 May 1935[2]	4 July 1936[3]	10 February 1938[4]
Guatemala				
Mexico				
Paraguay				
United States	A			
Uruguay				
Africa				
South Africa		X		
Egypt	S			
Liberia				
Asia				
Australia		X		
China				
India		X		
Iraq	A			
Japan				
New Zealand		X		
Palestine				
Siam				
Turkey				
Totals	8(X) 8(A) 1(S) 17	16	7(S)	7(S)

Note: X = ratification; A = applied without ratification; S = signatory

[1] Convention Relating to the International Status of Refugees, 28 Oct. 1933, *LNTS*, 159/199; [A.21.1937.XII], 4–5; [A.21.1938.XII], 4.
[2] Arrangement of 24 May 1935 Relating to Refugees from the Saar [A.23.1936.XII], 11.
[3] Provisional Arrangement Concerning the Status of Refugees Coming from Germany, 4 July 1936 [A.17.1937.XII], 2.
[4] Convention Concerning the Status of Refugees Coming from Germany, 10 Feb. 1938 [A.25.1938.XII], 2.

important standards is spelled out in article 7, which states that 'laws and regulations for the protection of the national labour market shall not be applied in all their severity to refugees' and that they should be suspended altogether in certain circumstances.[77] This standard represents a negotiated compromise. On the one hand, refugee advocates and refugee leaders felt that refugees should be given the same treatment as nationals in matters of employment, asserting that the 'right to asylum' is inseparable from the 'right to work'.[78] On the other hand, government delegates proved reluctant to sanction a major intrusion into this key area of domestic politics.

In relation to social welfare concerns, the Convention establishes the principle that governments should treat refugees as they would other aliens. The Convention states that governments should provide refugees with the 'most favourable treatment that it accords to the nationals of a foreign country' in matters of industrial accidents (art. 8), medical care and hospital treatment (art. 9), social insurance (art. 10), admission to relief associations (art. 11), and education (art. 12). The Convention also contains an important provision on reciprocity: according to article 14, 'The enjoyment of certain rights and the benefit of certain favours accorded to foreigners subject to reciprocity shall not be refused to refugees in the absence of reciprocity'.[79] This article attempts to compensate for the fact that refugees do not have a home government which could provide reciprocity. Without such a provision, refugees could be easily deprived of basic rights such as the rights to inherit, to be a trustee, to obtain a patent, to appear as a plaintiff in court, and others.[80]

Overall, the 1933 Convention establishes the standard that refugees should be accorded the same treatment as that given to aliens in the host country. It does not, however, go so far as to institute

[77] 1933 Convention, art. 7, p. 207. The article states that restrictions designed to protect the national labour market should be suspended for refugees if '(a) The refugee has been resident for not less than three years in the country; (b) The refugee is married to a person possessing the nationality of the country of residence; (c) The refugee has one or more children possessing the nationality of the country of residence; (d) The refugee is an ex-combatant of the great war'.

[78] J. L. Rubinstein, 'The Refugee Problem', *International Affairs* (Summer 1936), 728–9. See also Holborn, 'Legal Status', 690.

[79] Under the reciprocity principle, the government of country A accords certain rights to the nationals of country B within its territory if country B does the same for nationals of country A.   [80] Rubinstein, 'Refugee Problem', 726.

equality of treatment for both refugees and nationals. Nevertheless, the Convention is noteworthy because it set the first universal standard on the treatment of refugees, a standard which accorded refugees better treatment than that which they generally received in host countries.[81]

Application of the 1933 Convention

The 1933 Convention is also important because of its impact on refugee life in the countries adhering to it. After ratifying the Convention, individual governments had responsibility for translating its provisions into their own legal systems. Despite the fact that many governments made reservations on key articles of the Convention,[82] ratifying countries gradually moved to bring their municipal laws into line with its provisions.[83] This is most evident in regard to social services. Following French ratification of the Convention, the government embarked on a major effort to implement articles 8–12. The government upgraded benefits to refugees in the area of medical assistance, unemployment insurance, and old-age pensions so that they would be equal to those aliens receiving the most favourable treatment under French law. For instance, in regard to unemployment insurance, refugees began to receive the same rights as Spanish aliens in France; under the terms of the Franco-Spanish Convention of 1932, Spanish aliens were accorded the same status as nationals. In addition, the government extended special benefits to refugees who were old or very young, pregnant or nursing, or who had large families. It also established a special committee to inform refugees of their new rights. In Belgium, Great Britain, Bulgaria, Italy, Norway, and Denmark, the Convention placed the provision of social services

---

[81] In rare circumstances, the application of this standard meant a reduction in the rights accorded to refugees. In Bulgaria, for instance, Russian refugees had the same rights to social insurance as did nationals until 1935. In that year Bulgaria passed a law excluding aliens from most social insurance benefits. Since by the terms of the 1933 Convention refugees were to be treated as aliens, the Russian refugees lost their rights to social insurance. Simpson, *The Refugee Problem*, 288.

[82] Bulgaria, Czechoslovakia, Denmark, France, and Great Britain placed reservations on art. 7; Czechoslovakia, Denmark, Norway, Great Britain, and Belgium placed reservations on art. 14. [A.22.1935.XII], 4; Nansen International Office, 'Report of the Governing Body' (3 Sept. 1936) [A.23.1936.XII], 4–5.

[83] Simpson, *The Refugee Problem*, 262.

that were already being provided to refugees on a sounder legal
footing.[84]

The impact of the Convention on employment restrictions is
more difficult to ascertain. In many countries, ratification of the
Convention did not bring about dramatic changes in regard to
refugee employment. Some countries, however, did adopt more
lenient policies towards refugees after ratification. In Bulgaria, the
government complied with article 7 and did not strictly enforce its
laws governing foreign labour in the case of refugees.[85] In France,
adherence to the Convention preceded the loosening of labour
restrictions. After taking office in 1936 Léon Blum's Popular Front
government ratified the Convention and proclaimed the principle
that the 'right to asylum' cannot be separated from the 'right to
work'. Although the government did not suspend the provision
of the 1932 quota law for refugees, it did loosen restrictions on
work permits.[86] The new Minister of Labour ordered local labour
boards to grant work permits to refugees and to reissue permits to
refugees with cancelled ones.[87] In this instance, the Convention
reinforced the efforts of the French government to bring about
improved conditions for refugees.

THE FIGHT AGAINST EXPULSION

Of all the legal disabilities facing refugees in the Inter-war Period,
the threat of expulsion, or *refoulement*, presented the greatest
danger to their well-being. Developing rules to govern these two
government practices required venturing near to the heart of
a state's territorial sovereignty.[88] While the legal definitions of

[84] Simpson, *The Refugee Problem*, 285–8. In Belgium, refugees were admitted
to voluntary medical and old-age insurance schemes. In Norway and Great Britain, the government gave refugees with the right of permanent residency the
same social services as nationals. In Italy, hospitals extended welfare and medical
care to refugees on the same terms as nationals. In Bulgaria, refugees received free
treatment in hospitals.   [85] [A.22.1935.XII], 16.
[86] France made the following reservation concerning art. 7 of the 1933 Convention: 'Article 7 shall not preclude the application of the laws and regulations fixing
the proportion of wage-earning foreigners that employers are authorized to employ in France.' [A.21.1937.XII], 4.
[87] Simpson, *The Refugee Problem*, 274–85.
[88] This section will only examine the expulsion of refugees from host countries.
In Ch. 7, the regime's response to the expulsion of nationals by their own governments will be discussed.

expulsion and *refoulement* are slightly different, they both have the same result: the physical removal of a refugee from a country of asylum. Expulsion is an administrative measure whereby a government orders a refugee to leave the country, where he or she has been resident for a considerable length of time. *Refoulement* is an act in which the police physically return and conduct someone over the frontier shortly after his or her arrival. In the case of a refugee, non-admission at the frontier is also considered a case of *refoulement*. Throughout the Inter-war Period, governments periodically expelled unwanted aliens, including refugees, and sometimes turned back asylum-seekers at the border. In the 1920s these practices formed the exception rather than the rule. Unfortunately, the reverse was true in the 1930s.

As economic crisis encompassed the world, governments increasingly turned to expulsion as a way to rid their countries of unwanted foreigners. In doing so, they were fully within their rights as sovereign states. International law had little to say on the subject of expulsions, except that they were to be governed by municipal law.[89] In the early 1930s many governments strengthened legislation and enforcement mechanisms designed to facilitate expulsion measures. France, for instance, issued regulations that increased the powers of the Ministry of the Interior to enforce existing laws on expulsions.[90] In 1931 the United States government allocated more funds for the enforcement of its expulsion laws. According to this legislation, any immigrant who became a public charge within five years of admission to the country could be expelled.[91] The Romanian government went so far as to give notice to all foreign workers who had entered the country after 1 January 1923 that they must leave the country within three months. Even Norway, a country known for its humanitarian treatment of aliens, passed a law in 1932 that provided for the expulsion of any alien who became a public charge or lacked an authorized occupation.[92]

As few countries made special provisions for refugees, expulsion laws aimed at foreigners affected refugees as well. This impact varied a great deal between countries. In 1935 the Nansen Office reported that the governments of Australia, the United

---

[89] L. Oppenheim, *International Law: A Treatise*, i (London: Longmans, Green, 1905), 378–9.   [90] *I.L.O. Year-Book 1932*, 256.
[91] *I.L.O. Year-Book 1931*, 359.   [92] *I.L.O. Year-Book 1932*, 257.

Kingdom, Bulgaria, Cyprus, Czechoslovakia, Denmark, Iraq, Ireland, Lithuania, the Netherlands, Norway, Romania, and the United States did not expel Nansen refugees unable to obtain entry visas to other countries.[93] In 1938 the Refugee Survey made a more tentative claim: it noted that the governments of the United Kingdom, Sweden, Norway, Estonia, Lithuania, Yugoslavia, Bulgaria, Romania, and Greece rarely expelled refugees. But the report went one step further and identified Turkey and Poland as countries making frequent use of expulsion measures. Moreover, it singled out France as the country resorting to expulsion the most often.[94]

In France, the practice of expulsion rested on an established legal tradition. A law of 3 December 1849 gave the Ministry of the Interior, through the police, the authority to expel undesirable aliens and to imprison those who failed to comply with an expulsion order. In theory, the expulsion order came from the Minister of the Interior; in practice, orders could be issued by local policemen. Vagrancy, unemployment, irregularity in identity papers, and many trivial offences, such as the unauthorized wearing of decorations and insignia, served as grounds for expulsion.[95] The expulsion law, originally designed to protect the French people from undesirable foreigners, had the reverse effect and actually created criminals. The following case of a Russian can be regarded as typical fo the plight of many refugees in France:

The man worked in a garage. In March 1932 he lost his job. He received the dole for five months. After that he tried to earn a living selling papers. Early in 1934 he had nowhere to live and no work. He was arrested for

---

[93] The Office also reported that the governments of Finland, Latvia, Monaco, and Sweden admitted to expelling refugees in exceptional cases. [A.23.1936.XII], 7.   [94] Simpson, *The Refugee Problem*, 251–61.
[95] The Refugee Survey lists 17 different causes for expulsion: (1) non-compliance with identity paper regulations; (2) conviction for an offence however trivial; (3) delay in renewing an identity certificate; (4) unauthorized employment; (5) not having found work; (6) non-payment of taxes; (7) because permission to work had been applied for and was refused; (8) not having applied for a permit to work or a change of occupation; (9) non-renewal of identity certificate owing to lack of means; (10) denunciation or complaint by third persons; (11) inability to obtain a visa admitting to another country; (12) vagrancy; (13) no adequate means of support; (14) disorderly and noisy conduct in public places; (15) drunkenness; (16) wearing of decorations and insignia without authorization; (17) offences against property. Simpson, *The Refugee Problem*, 252–3.

vagabondage, convicted and given one month. His history henceforth was as follows:—1st conviction: March 1934. 2nd conviction: July 1934. 3rd conviction: August 1934. 4th conviction: October 1934. 5th conviction: December 1934. 6th: conviction January 1935. 7th conviction: February 1935. The man has committed no offence except that of being without work and having no fixed place of abode. He has no papers because as soon as a foreigner is convicted—no matter how trifling the offence—his papers are taken away and an expulsion order is issued. On being liberated from prison, he is unable to get work, having no papers. So he wanders about or hides until the day comes when the police ask for his papers and he is marched off to prison again.[96]

In the 1930s governments not only expelled unwanted foreigners but also used *refoulement* to prevent the entry of refugees, especially in response to refugees from Nazi Germany. Initially the countries bordering Germany welcomed these refugees. But, as their numbers increased, more and more governments closed their doors to entry. As governments could not completely seal their borders, they used *refoulement* as a way to return those who had crossed them secretly. The incidence of this practice became more frequent after the annexation of Austria and Czechoslovakia in 1938. The Nazi practice of rounding up Jews and dumping them across the border aggravated the situation. According to the asylum norm, states maintained the right to grant or deny asylum to refugees. This meant that there was no prohibition against *refoulement* in international law. Nevertheless, *refoulement*, especially to a refugee's country of origin, seriously called into question the humanitarian foundation of the regime because it placed the lives of refugees in great jeopardy.

Developing Rules against Expulsion

The increased frequency of expulsions and *refoulement* spurred rule-making activities on a topic previously ignored by the actors of the international refugee regime. The first mention of the physical protection of refugees came in paragraph 7 of the Arrangement of 30 June 1928 relating to the legal status of Russian and Armenian refugees, which recommends that governments suspend measures to expel a Russian or Armenian refugee if it

[96] Save the Children, *Report*, 10.

was not possible for the person to enter another country legally.[97] In the early 1930s the Assembly of the League of Nations, the Intergovernmental Advisory Commission, and the Nansen Office sought to develop more binding rules on expulsion and *refoulement*.

The Assembly took up the issue of expulsions in earnest in 1932, when delegates to the Sixth Committee noted the alarming increase in this practice.[98] The Thirteenth Assembly then passed a resolution urging governments not to expel refugees unless they had obtained permission to enter an adjoining country.[99] At the Fourteenth Assembly the following year, the Norwegian delegate woefully pointed out that expulsions were still on the increase. This time, the Assembly passed a stronger resolution calling attention to the dangers which expelled refugees faced and the problems they caused for the countries they entered; it then repeated the plea that governments not expel refugees without permission to enter an adjacent country.[100] From 1934 until 1937 the issue of expulsions remained on the Assembly's agenda and it continued to pass resolutions condemning the practice. Although these resolutions did little to curb the practice, they did contribute to the growing body of rules prohibiting it.

A second body, the Intergovernmental Advisory Commission for Refugees, also addressed the expulsion issue. This organization differed from the League Assembly in that delegates both from governments and from private organizations attended its sessions. In addition, Russian and Armenian refugee organizations played a prominent role in its activities.[101] Because of the presence of refugee advocacy groups at its meetings, the Commission took

---

[97] Par. 7 reads: 'It is recommended that measures for expelling foreigners or for taking other such action against them be avoided or suspended in regard to Russian and Armenian refugees in cases where the person concerned is not in a position to enter a neighbouring country in a regular manner. This recommendation does not apply in the case of a refugee who enters a country in intentional violation of the national law. It is also recommended that in no case should the identity papers of such refugees be withdrawn.' 'Arrangement of 30 June 1928', 53.

[98] *Official Journal*, Special Supplement no. 109, Thirteenth Assembly, Sixth Committee (Geneva, 1932), 17.

[99] *Official Journal*, Special Supplement no. 104, Thirteenth Assembly, Plenary Meetings: Text (Geneva, 1932), 58–9.

[100] *Official Journal*, Special Supplement no. 120, Fourteenth Assembly, Sixth Committee (Geneva, 1933), 19, 64–5.

[101] For instance, the session of the Commission held on 16 May 1929 included representatives from the governments of Germany, Bulgaria, China, Estonia, France, Greece, Italy, Latvia, Poland, Romania, Serbia, and Czechoslovakia, and technical

the task of formulating rules against expulsion and *refoulement* more seriously than did the Assembly. The Commission first discussed expulsions in September 1930, when delegates from private organizations raised the subject. After the Commission made clear that it meant 'no interference with the sovereign rights of States in this domain', it stated that refugees should only be expelled under serious circumstances, not simply for the violation of police regulations.[102]

The topic of expulsion remained at the top of the Commission's agenda throughout the 1930s. At the Commission's seventh session, held in March 1935, it formulated a comprehensive statement on the subject. This statement included recommendations about the conditions under which refugees could be expelled, the methods by which they could be removed, and ways to regularize the status of refugees threatened by expulsions.[103] One of the most important of these recommendations was contained in paragraph 2, which urged that governments 'create an internal authority to assist the refugee and enable him to submit his case'. This recommendation attempted to correct one of the most insidious aspects of expulsion proceedings: the fact that they were generally carried out in secret. Under the expulsion laws of many states, an unsubstantiated denunciation often resulted in an expulsion order being issued. In including this suggestion, the Commission hoped to make expulsion proceedings more public and give refugees a chance to defend themselves.[104]

Following the recommendation of the Commission, some governments changed their expulsion procedures. By a royal decree of 20 February 1936, the Belgian government established a commission composed of delegates from the Foreign Office, the Economic Department, the Department of Labour and Social Assistance, and a representative of a refugee relief organization chosen by the refugee concerned. This commission gave refugees threatened by expulsion the right to defend themselves,

---

experts from the Council of Former Russian Ambassadors, the Committee of Russian Zemstvos and Town Councils, the Central Committee for Armenian Refugees, the Armenian Republic in Exile, the League of Red Cross Societies, and the Jewish Colonization Association. LNA C1406/R.403.6.0.

[102] *Official Journal* (Nov. 1930) [A.34.1930.XIII], annex 1232, p. 1404.
[103] *Official Journal* (June 1935), annex 1541, pp. 656–9; [A.22.1935.XII], 6; Simpson, *The Refugee Problem*, 249.
[104] Simpson, *The Refugee Problem*, 250–1.

something denied to them previously in Belgium and in other countries. In France, the government revised regulations so that refugees could not be expelled without the personal decision of the Ministry of the Interior. This helped to protect refugees from the whims of lower-level officials and police officers.[105]

In conjunction with the Nansen International Office, the Intergovernmental Commission of Refugees also developed the provisions on expulsion contained in the 1933 Convention. Though far less extensive than the 1935 recommendations, article 3 of the Convention contains the first prohibition against expulsion and *refoulement* in treaty law:

Each of the Contracting Parties undertakes not to remove or keep from its territory by application of police measures, such as expulsions or non-admittance at the frontier (*refoulement*), refugees who have been authorised to reside there regularly, unless the said measures are dictated by reasons of national security or public order. It undertakes in any case not to refuse entry to refugees at the frontiers of their countries of origin.[106]

From a purely humanitarian point of view, article 3 only provides limited protection for refugees. Under its provisions, governments can still legally expel refugees if they threaten national security and public order. Moreover, host governments retain the right to define what constitutes a national security threat. In addition, the second paragraph of the article was generally interpreted to apply only to refugees who had already been admitted by the host country, not to all refugees seeking asylum.[107]

Nevertheless, government policy did change after the creation of the Convention in some countries. Of the eight countries ratifying the treaty, only Italy and Czechoslovakia made reservations on this article.[108] After ratification, several countries amended their municipal laws to bring them in line with the 1933 Convention. Belgium, for instance, incorporated the provisions of the Convention into municipal law through a decree of 29 June 1937.[109] In addition, the French government adopted a new law on expulsions

---

[105] [A.27.1936.XII], 10; [A.23.1936.XII], 5.   [106] 1933 Convention, 205.

[107] Grahl-Madsen, *Status of Refugees*, ii. 98–9; Goodwin-Gill, *Refugee in International Law*, 74.

[108] The Czechoslovakian government reserved the right to expel people who threatened public safety and order and to carry out expulsions ordered by their courts. The Italian government reserved the right to expel refugees for reasons of national security and public order. 1933 Convention, 201, 203.

[109] Simpson, *The Refugee Problem*, 257.

on 2 May 1938, practically reversing its earlier legislation. According to this new law, aliens who were unable to leave French territory legally would be assigned a place of residence and be required to report periodically to the police authorities there. Moreover, a circular of 28 May 1938 stated that refugees recognized by the League of Nations would be presumed unable to leave the country, and therefore not be subject to expulsion proceedings.[110] In addition, ratification of the Convention placed existing practice in Denmark, Norway, and the United Kingdom on a firmer legal footing; at the time of ratification, these countries had already renounced expulsion as a method of dealing with refugees.[111]

The 1938 Convention on Refugees coming from Germany also includes provisions on expulsion and *refoulement*. According to article 5:

2. Without prejudice to the measures which may be taken within any territory, refugees who have been authorised to reside therein may not be subjected by the authorities to measures of expulsion or reconduction unless such measures are dictated by reasons of national security or public order.

3. (a) The High Contracting Parties undertake not to reconduct refugees to German territory unless they have been warned and have refused, without just cause, to make the necessary arrangements to proceed to another territory or to take advantage of the arrangements made for them with that object.

(b) In such case, the travel document may be cancelled or withdrawn.[112]

The concrete impact of article 5 of the 1938 Convention was limited. The Dutch government, for instance, increasingly avoided deporting refugees back to Germany even though they knew this might have the indirect effect of encouraging the Nazis to dump more Jews across the border.[113] But only six countries signed the Convention and it was available for ratification less than one year before the Second World War erupted. Nevertheless, its provisions, combined with those of article 3 of the 1933 Convention,

---

[110] Nansen International Office, 'Report of the Governing Body' (10 Aug. 1938) [A.21.1938.XII], 5.
[111] [A.27.1936.XII], 10; Simpson, *The Refugee Problem*, 257.
[112] 1938 Convention, 59.
[113] Bob Moore, *Refugees from Nazi Germany in the Netherlands, 1933–1940* (Dordrecht: Martinus Nijhoff, 1986), 89–90.

contributed to the development of the rule of non-*refoulement*, 'the prohibition of the forcible return of a refugee to a country of persecution'.[114] Non-*refoulement* is an essential rule if the physical protection of refugees is to be assured. While this rule does not establish a refugee's right to be granted asylum—this remained the prerogative of governments—it does provide a limited form of asylum, because it prohibits the return of refugees to their country of origin.[115] After the Second World War this rule was firmly incorporated into the new international refugee regime: it became article 33 of the 1951 Refugee Convention.[116]

Fighting Expulsion in Practice: The 1920s

Since the end of the international refugee regime, the legacy of the rules developed between the wars can still be seen in both municipal and international law. But the regime did more than simply influence the creation of rules: actors in the regime also helped to enforce these rules by providing a rudimentary form of physical protection to refugees. While this protection did not equal that provided to citizens by their own government, it is still noteworthy because it gave individuals and groups the opportunity to appeal to an authority beyond sovereign states. The principal actor in the regime's protection mechanism was the League of Nations, especially its special refugee agencies. Not only did the delegates of the High Commissioner for Refugees and the Nansen Office help to provide refugees with travel documents and identification papers, they also helped to save their lives.

Interventions on behalf of refugees threatened with expulsion began long before the prohibitions against the practice sprung up in legal arrangements and conventions. At the end of 1922 the Polish government threatened the expulsion of approximately 6,000 Jews from the Russian Empire, allegedly in the country for commercial reasons rather than political ones. As the Soviet Union had already denationalized the refugees, they faced punishment

---

[114] Atle Grahl-Madsen, *Territorial Asylum* (London: Oceana Publications, 1980), 4.   [115] Grahl-Madsen, *Status of Refugees*, ii. 11.

[116] Article 33 (1) reads: 'No Contracting State shall expel or return ("refouler") a refugee in any manner whatsoever to the frontiers of territories where his life or freedom would be threatened on account of his race, religion, nationality, membership of a particular social group or political opinion.' Convention Relating to the Status of Refugees, 28 July 1951, *UNTS*, 189/2545, 150.

if they returned to their former homes. Lucien Wolf, representative of the Jewish Colonization Association, urged the League of Nations to rescue the refugees. Based on these conversations, a Secretariat official reported to Nansen in February 1923 that 'a very large number of these wretched people are congregated between the Polish and Russian frontiers and are altogether in a very desperate situation'.[117] After negotiations with the Polish government, Nansen gained a reprieve. The Polish government agreed to delay expulsions until visas to the United States and other countries could be obtained.[118] During the same year, the High Commissioner also intervened on behalf of 10,000 refugees threatened with return to Russia by the Romanian government. In this case, the Romanian government agreed to delay action until private organizations arranged for the evacuation of the refugees.[119]

The League of Nations also intervened on behalf of Russian refugees in Turkey. In 1927 over 3,000 White Russians still remained there, primarily in Constantinople. Although the Russians contributed to the Turkish economy, their presence became a source of friction in Soviet–Turkish relations. Initially the Turkish government demonstrated its displeasure by expelling several White Russians for engaging in anti-Soviet propaganda.[120] Then, in August 1927, the Turkish government issued a decree stating that all Russian refugees must either obtain Turkish or Soviet citizenship or leave Turkey. In exchange for assistance in helping the refugees to move elsewhere, Major Johnson, Chief of the Refugee Section of the ILO, gained a temporary suspension of the decree in negotiations held in Ankara.[121] By 1929 over 1,700 Russians had been evacuated to other countries; and the majority of those remaining opted for Turkish citizenship.[122] Afterwards the Nansen Office continued to monitor their fate and periodically intervened on their behalf with Turkish authorities.[123]

Despite these successful interventions by the League of Nations in Poland, Romania, and Turkey, it would be misleading to imply

[117] Letter from Philip Baker (?) to Dr Nansen of 22 Feb. 1923. NBKR 4/620.
[118] [A.30.1923.XII], 14; Marrus, The Unwanted, 65–6; Tartakower and Grossman, The Jewish Refugee, 404.
[119] Official Journal (May 1922), 390–1; [A.30.1923.XII], 14.
[120] 'White Russians in Turkey under Notice to Quit', The Times (10 Jan. 1928).
[121] For Johnson's account of his trip, see T. F. Johnson, International Tramps (London: Hutchinson, 1938), 246.   [122] [A.23.1929.VII], 15.
[123] See e.g. [A.22.1935.XII], 11.

that all refugees could rely on this protection. These interventions involved confronting relatively minor countries, not questioning the practices of a Great Power. Moreover, the High Commissioner's organization was simply too small and inadequately funded to protect all refugees, even if it had chosen to do so. What is remarkable about these interventions is the humanitarian spirit in which they were carried out. Under Nansen's leadership, the office of the High Commissioner willingly assisted diverse refugee groups, even without special authorization or a mandate from international law. The record of the 1930s is more mixed. During this decade, the refugee agencies of the League had to cope with both a dramatic increase in the number of expulsions and the expulsion practices of some of the most powerful states in Europe.

Fighting Expulsion in Practice: The 1930s

In contrast to the 1920s, a High Commissioner for Refugees was not responsible for refugee protection during most of the 1930s. Following Nansen's death in 1930, the League of Nations charged the Secretariat with the legal protection of refugees and created the Nansen International Office to handle matters of relief and settlement. In practice, this strict division of labour never existed. The Nansen Office continued to supervise the application of legal arrangements for refugees using the system of delegates originally established by Nansen. These representatives often provided refugees with their first and only line of defence against an expulsion order. The number of cases dealt with by the office soared during the height of the economic recession. In 1932 the Office made only 722 interventions; the following year it dealt with 1,664 cases; and in 1935 it handled 3,203 cases (see Table 14).[124] The 1934 report of the Governing Body stresses that dealing with expulsions had 'become one of the major daily preoccupations of the Office'. It went on to say that 'the desperate situation of some of these refugees, and the sacrifices they are prepared to make to remedy it, may be gauged from the fact that many of them have travelled hundreds of kilometres on foot to Geneva in the hope that

---

[124] League of Nations, Nansen International Office for Refugees, 'Report of the Governing Body' (16 Aug. 1932) [A.24.1932], 8; [A.19.1933], 8; [A.22.1935.XII], 23.

TABLE 14. *Interventions by the Nansen International Office, 1932–1938 to prevent the expulsion of Russian, Armenian, Assyrian, and Saar Refugees*

Country	1932[1]	1933[2]	1934[3]	1935[4]	1936[5]	1937[6]	1938[7]
Austria	1	0	1	0	0	1	0
Baltic states	*	80	*	1	0	0	6
Belgium	11	95	97	111	147	112	108
Bulgaria	7	0	2	0	0	1	2
Czechoslovakia	30	0	67	248	141	261	64
France	233	761	1,141	2,219	1,126	403	920
Germany	308	658	663	493	359	308	211
Greece	2	2	112	0	0	0	0
Poland	119	27	52	nd	nd	nd	nd
Romania	0	9	0	1	1	0	0
Turkey	0	0	0	117	0	0	0
Yugoslavia	11	32	7	13	4	0	0
Total	722	1,664	2,142	3,203	1,778	1,086	1,311

* Data for Baltic countries included in figure for Poland.
nd = no data available
[1] [A.24.1932], 8.
[2] [A.19.1933], 8.
[3] [A.12.1934], 7.
[4] [A.22.1935.XII], 23.
[5] [A.23.1936.XII], 25.
[6] [A.21.1937.XII], 15.
[7] [A.21.1938.XII], 13.

the Office might be able to extricate them from their distressing dilemmas'.[125]

In addition to assisting individual refugees in fighting expulsion orders, the Office drew attention to the problem of expulsions in general. The annual reports of the Office featured a special section on expulsions throughout the 1930s. While head of the Nansen Office, Michael Hansson continually highlighted the inhumane nature of expulsions, calling them a 'game with the refugee as a human tennis ball' and 'one of the greatest scandals of our times'.[126]

[125] [A.12.1934], 4.
[126] Michael Hansson, *The Refugee Problem* (Granchamp: Annemass, 1936), 19.

The Office, however, did not go so far as to identify flagrant violators, especially France, by name. Instead, it attempted to constrain such countries through the development of legally binding conventions on the treatment of refugees.

The actors in the international refugee regime responded to the German refugee crisis in a similar manner: they concentrated on rule-making rather than confronting the governments that frequently expelled the refugees. In this regard, the Secretariat of the League of Nations played a decisive role in determining the regime's direction. In January 1934 Major Johnson, Secretary-General of the Nansen Office, wrote to Joseph Avenol, Secretary-General of the League of Nations, asking that the Secretariat make representations to the French and German governments urging them to stop expelling people without visas to enter another country. This request generated a Secretariat investigation and resulted in the announcement of a general policy on the subject. Legal advisers in the Secretariat informed Avenol that he had full authority to make such a representation. Other advisers quickly dismissed the idea that a representation to Germany would do any good, but urged approaching France. In fact, M. de Navilles, a French Foreign Office official and president of the Intergovernmental Advisory Commission on Refugees, made it clear that the intervention of the Secretariat would strengthen his position domestically in the fight against expulsion. Despite this advice, the Secretary-General declined to intervene.[127]

As Secretary-General, Avenol still maintained strong sympathies for right-wing forces in his native France. Moreover, as a member of the 'appeasement' school, he went out of his way not to offend Germany.[128] Therefore, it is not surprising that he refused to challenge French and German expulsion policies directly. Avenol's decision successfully quashed any further initiatives to prevent expulsions, and it stands in sharp contrast to earlier initiatives taken by the Secretariat in order to assist refugees. As a result, the Nansen Office never brought up the subject of government intervention again, and Sir Neill Malcolm devoted his tenure as High Commissioner for Refugees coming from Germany to the creation of the 1936 Arrangement and 1938 Convention.

[127] LNA R5626/9111.
[128] James Barros, *Betrayal from Within: Joseph Avenol, Secretary-General of the League of Nations, 1933–1940* (New Haven, Conn.: Yale University Press, 1969), 18; F. P. Walters, *A History of the League of Nations* (London: Oxford University Press, 1960), 809.

CONCLUSION

To refugee advocates of the late Inter-war Period, there seemed to be one overwhelming problem with the existing system of legal protection for refugees: it only applied to specified categories of refugees. Under this system, some refugees received international assistance, while others with equal needs did not, a deviation from the humanitarian principle of the regime. By the mid-1930s some associations and legal scholars argued for a change. The Institute of International Law, for instance, prepared a universal definition of a refugee and a draft treaty that would apply to all refugees.[129] The Refugee Survey identified Italian, Spanish, and Portuguese refugees as major groups without a defined legal status.[130] Legal scholars, including Louise Holborn, argued against the belief that a general definition of a refugee would both encourage the creation of new refugees and perpetuate refugeehood. According to Holborn, 'refusal to grant a legal status to those who have been forced out of their countries has had no deterring effect upon governments'. She also pointed out the benefits of a 'clearly defined status for refugees' by saying that it 'would aid efforts to make refugee status transitory in character and would facilitate settlement'.[131]

In 1935, the year when the Italian–Ethiopian conflict preoccupied the membership of the League of Nations, a group of government delegates and private organizations spearheaded an attempt to create a more universal system of dealing with refugees. At the Sixteenth Assembly, Halvdan Koht, Minister of Foreign Affairs and the first Norwegian delegate, proposed the creation of a single refugee organization under the authority of the League of Nations, an organization that would protect all refugees.[132] In addition, six major refugee relief organizations petitioned the League to provide legal protection for all refugees and stateless people.[133] The

---

[129] Institute of International Law, *Annuaire*, ii (1936), 294.

[130] Simpson, *The Refugee Problem*, 239.

[131] Holborn, 'Legal Status', 702–3.

[132] *Official Journal*, Special Supplement no. 138, Sixteenth Assembly, Plenary Meetings: Text (Geneva, 1935), 57–8.

[133] League of Nations, 'International Assistance to Refugees' (13 Sept. 1935) [A.36.1935.XII]. Officials from the International Committee of the Red Cross, the European Central Office for Inter-Church Aid, the International Migration Service, the Friends' International Service, the International Federation of League of Nations Societies, and the Save the Children International Union signed the petition, which was submitted to the Assembly by Halvdan Koht, first delegate from Norway. LNA R5615/686(18558).

delegates of Sweden, Switzerland, the Netherlands, Poland, Belgium, Czechoslovakia, and Yugoslavia strongly supported the Norwegian proposal, but the Great Powers offered only opposition. Viscount Cranborne, delegate for the United Kingdom, and M. Berenger of France both warned of creating a permanent class of refugees dependent on the League and of signing blank cheques which the League could not pay off. The delegates from Italy and the Soviet Union opposed the further expansion of refugee assistance. The Bulgarian delegate, M. Stoyanoff, also expressed a popular sentiment when he said that creating a new organization to deal with all types of refugees would 'call forth fresh hordes of refugees'.[134] Consequently, the Assembly referred the matter to a committee, effectively postponing the debate until the post-war era.

Despite the failure of the Norwegian proposal at the 1935 Assembly, gradual increases in the scope of the international refugee regime brought virtually all the major refugee groups of inter-war Europe within its parameters. Originally formed to assist only Russian refugees, by 1939 Armenian, Assyrian, Assyro-Chaldean, Turkish, Saar, German, Austrian, and Czech refugees also stood under its umbrella of legal protection. Although certain refugees remained outside the regime's boundaries, this does not detract from the growth that did take place. In fact, quite the reverse is true. Calls for further expansion demonstrate the importance of the international refugee regime. They indicate that it had had an impact on how governments treated refugees and that some actors wanted its scope broadened.

Even though the actors in the international refugee regime did not develop a system of universal protection for refugees in the Inter-war Period, they left a lasting legacy in the legal arena. The League of Nations and other actors in the regime developed a comprehensive body of rules governing refugee identity and travel, economic and social well-being, and physical protection. In addition, the authority of international organizations to defend refugees and intervene on their behalf was established, a unique tradition in the field of human rights. Perhaps most importantly, as a result of the regime, refugees became defined as a special

---

[134] *Official Journal*, Special Supplement no. 143, Sixteenth Assembly, Sixth Committee (Geneva, 1935), 10–26, 52–4.

category of international migrant. In particular, refugees came to be seen as being different from traditional economic migrants because they were forced to flee their home countries and could not easily return. Before 1920 few countries made provisions for refugees in their municipal laws. Twenty years later a dramatic change had taken place. In 1939 the Refugee Survey reported: 'The discrimination between aliens who are refugees and other aliens is becoming increasingly common in the practice of national administrations, and is indeed inevitable as a sequence to those international agreements and conventions which provide for special treatment of aliens who are recognized as refugees.'[135]

In effect, the existence of the international refugee regime led to the creation of the refugee as a special category of person deserving preferential treatment. Indeed, the increasingly common usage of the word 'refugee' was a sign of this process. Given the relatively short history of the regime, this development must be considered a major accomplishment.

---

[135] Simpson, *The Refugee Problem*, 230.

5

In Search of Durable Solutions

W HEN Gustave Ador first appealed to the Council of the League of Nations on behalf of approximately one million Russian refugees, his letter stressed the great need to define the legal position of these refugees. But Ador and the private organizations that he represented did not stop here. They added that 'the next step will be to organise their employment . . . and, above all, their repatriation to Russia'. In this sentence, Ador mentions what became a major preoccupation of the actors of the international refugee regime: achieving durable solutions for refugees.[1]

A durable solution contrasts with emergency relief, which only aims to meet the physical needs of refugees for a short time. In the medium term, a durable solution helps to make refugees self-supporting and free from charity. The final goal of a durable solution is to re-establish refugees within the state system. This can be achieved by repatriating refugees to their home country or by integrating them into other countries. One of the most important concomitants of a durable solution is the creation of a secure legal status for refugees: without a right to travel, to hold employment, or to be protected from expulsion, it is very difficult for refugees to become self-sufficient. In the previous chapter, efforts of actors in the international refugee regime to develop a clear legal status for refugees were discussed. With this as a background, the focus of this chapter shifts to the influence of the regime on promoting durable solutions directly.

The most desirable solution to a mass exodus is for the refugees simply to return to their home countries. But, if circumstances prevent the safe return of refugees, other durable solutions need to be found. Under the regime's division of labour, the primary responsibility for facilitating this process fell on host governments.

---

[1] The term 'durable solution' is used today by those involved in refugee work. In the inter-war years, the term 'final solution' was generally used to connote the same idea.

Only they could fulfil the obligations of the assistance norm by granting refugees permanent residence, giving them work permits, and eventually naturalizing them as citizens. Nevertheless, this responsibility did not rest on host governments alone. The regime's burden-sharing norm stressed the obligation of all members of the regime to assist refugees, not simply host governments. In the preceding chapter, we saw how the norms of the regime became translated into explicit rules through the development of international law; here, we will see the same norms implicitly expressed in international assistance projects.

The League of Nations played an influential role in international assistance projects for refugees. Although the refugee agencies of the League were prohibited from spending money directly on the relief and settlement of refugees, they acted as important policy-making and planning bodies. In addition, the refugee agencies co-ordinated projects aimed at the achievement of durable solutions involving the resources of host governments, donor governments, private organizations, and individual refugees. Moreover, they channelled money from funding sources directly to host governments and refugees. More than any other actor, the League's activities expressed a spirit of international co-operation—the essence of the regime's burden-sharing norm.

Private, voluntary organizations, including ones primarily composed of refugees, also acted to carry out the assistance and burden-sharing norms of the international refugee regime. These organizations primarily devoted themselves to helping refugees integrate into host countries through the provision of social services at the national and local levels. Nevertheless, they sometimes operated at the international level. Private agencies also acted as refugee advocates in the intergovernmental forum provided by the League of Nations and the IGCR. Moreover, they helped to fund international settlement projects sponsored by the League of Nations, and occasionally carried out smaller projects entirely on their own. In the 1930s private organizations distinguished themselves by assisting individual refugees to emigrate to new countries.

During the twenty-year lifetime of the international refugee regime, the League of Nations, in co-operation with other actors, pursued numerous and diverse strategies aimed at the achievement of durable solutions. In general, they devised them on an *ad hoc* basis to meet the needs of a particular refugee group, such as Russian or Greek refugees. Their record is appropriately characterized as an experimental one in which new ideas were constantly applied to refugee issues. Although it is beyond the scope of this work to examine in detail all the refugee assistance projects conducted in the inter-war years, what will be presented here is a survey of the two most important strategies pursued for dealing with refugees: repatriation and promoting local integration through refugee settlement. In each case, the effect of the durable solution on the refugees, the host countries, and the wider political environment will be considered. At the end of each section, the efficacy of each strategy as a method of solving refugee problems will be evaluated.

ARRANGING REPATRIATION FOR RUSSIAN REFUGEES

Without exception, all the actors in the international refugee regime regarded voluntary repatriation—the uncoerced return of refugees to their country of origin—as the most desirable durable solution. Governments in particular viewed repatriation as the best solution to their refugee problems. Despite this, repatriation did not play a significant part in the achievement of durable solutions for refugees in the Inter-war Period.[2] More often than not, refugee-producing countries would not accept refugees back into their territories, and the refugees did not want to return to their home countries because of the danger of persecution there. After the First World War, few of the ethnic migrants returned to the lands of their birth; they would have been considered an unwelcome minority in foreign lands. For example, following the mass exodus from Asia Minor, the Turkish government made it clear that it would not welcome the Greek or Armenian refugees home. Similarly, the Greek and Bulgarian governments did not wish to see the return of ethnic minorities to their countries.[3] In

---

[2] See the special report by the Intergovernmental Advisory Commission for Refugees on the subject of repatriation. League of Nations, 'Russian, Armenian, Assyrian, Assyro-Chaldean and Turkish Refugees: Report to the Tenth Assembly' (15 Aug. 1929) [A.23.1929.VII], 1–2.

[3] Sir John Hope Simpson, *The Refugee Problem: Report of a Survey* (London: Oxford University Press, 1939), 527–9.

the early years of Hitler's rule, some refugees fleeing Germany did return to the Third Reich, but as time progressed this option became increasingly dangerous because the Nazis placed returnees in concentration camps.[4] The only organized repatriation effort, an attempt by the League of Nations to return Russian refugees to the Soviet Union, yielded little fruit. Under its terms, only a fraction of the total number of refugees returned to their homeland. Nevertheless, this scheme evoked great controversy and brought important actors in the regime in conflict with one another, demonstrating both the pressures for repatriation and the obstacles against it.

The Nansen–Soviet Repatriation Plan

When the Council of the League of Nations initially appointed Nansen as High Commissioner for Refugees, it was with the hope that he would quickly solve the Russian refugee problem. To all concerned, the return of the vast majority of Russian refugees to their homeland appeared to be the best solution. Both of the Great Powers, France and Great Britain, favoured this solution because they thought it would free them of their financial obligations to the defeated soldiers of the White armies whom they had armed in the Russian Civil War. In April 1921 the French government reported to the League that it had already spent 150 million francs (about £3.8 million) and further urged the appointment of a High Commissioner to arrange the repatriation of refugees to the Soviet Union.[5] The following month Under-Secretary of State for Foreign Affairs Cecil Harmsworth declared to the British Parliament that His Majesty's Government hoped to see the return of refugees to Russia and an end to their drain on British revenues. Privately, he was even more outspoken: for him, the 'Cossacks, Kalmucks, Priests, generals, judges and ladies' constituted 'nothing but an intolerable nuisance'.[6] In the Foreign Office, diplomats held

---

[4] From 1933 to 1938 an estimated 6,000 Jews returned to Germany from Poland. In addition, several thousand more returned from other countries. Michael R. Marrus, *The Unwanted: European Refugees in the Twentieth Century* (New York: Oxford University Press, 1985), 135.

[5] *Official Journal* (July–Aug. 1921), 488, 1011.

[6] Parliamentary question of 2 May 1921 by Cecil Harmsworth, Under-Secretary of State for Foreign Affairs; note by Cecil Harmsworth of 20 June 1921 on Russian refugees. BFO 371/6867/N6310.

a similar view: 'We are only too anxious that any scheme for repatriating the refugees should be successful, especially as our own expenses for the upkeep of four thousand and eight hundred of them amount to something over twenty thousand pounds a month.'[7]

Nansen, for his part, passionately believed in repatriation as a solution to the Russian refugee problem, not only for the sake of the refugees, but also for the sake of European reconstruction. In the High Commissioner's view, the Soviet Union should be an integral part of Europe and it needed the refugees to help with internal reconstruction. In 1922 he wrote:

No foreign labour imported into Russia can take the place of Russian labour; and no foreign country can provide the economic general staff necessary for the real restoration of the country. There is no better means of speedily providing such a staff than by utilising the hundreds of thousands of Russian children and young people at present in the territory of the States which are interested in the reconstruction of Russia.[8]

Russian refugees generally agreed that repatriation was the most desirable way to end their exile. Refugee opinion, however, was divided as to when and under what conditions repatriation should take place. Throughout 1921 and 1922 the office of the High Commissioner received petitions from refugees in Romania, Serbia, and Egypt asking to be repatriated immediately. In these cases, the refugees either came from the lower classes or were ethnic Cossacks.[9] Other strata of Russian refugee opinion strongly objected to any return to a country under Bolshevik rule. The Cossack leader, General Peter Krasnov, for instance, wrote an open letter to Nansen imploring him not to negotiate with the Bolsheviks.[10] In a letter to the League of Nations, two major Russian refugee organizations called repatriation 'the measure

[7] Note by J. Gregory, Superintending Assistant Secretary, of 16 June 1921 on proposal by League of Nations to assist Russian refugees. BFO 371/6867/N6972.
[8] Official Journal (Apr. 1922), 339.
[9] Letter to Dr Nansen from Dr Bacilieri, Delegate of the ICRC in Romania of 3 Dec. 1921; petition of 27 Dec. 1921 to the High Commission from Russian refugees in Alexandrie, Sidi-Bishr, and Camp B, Egypt; petition of 10 Feb. 1922 to the High Commission from the old men of the colony of Russian refugees in Shabatz, Serbia. LNA C1105/187(N1).
[10] 'Open Letter to Dr. Nansen' from Peter Krasnoff, former Ataman of the Don, Novoe Vremia, Belgrade, 3 Aug. 1922. Tr. in NBKR 4/620. General Krasnov fought against the Soviets in the Second World War. After surrendering to the British at the age of 76, he was forcibly repatriated to the USSR, where he was executed. Marrus, The Unwanted, 314–16.

which inspires the greatest hope of finally solving all difficulties' but rejected any guarantees about it by the Soviet Union. The letter concluded that repatriation was not possible under existing conditions.[11]

Despite general agreement on the desirability of repatriation, the League of Nations did not attempt to arrange the return of Russians to their homeland during 1921 because of the famine conditions prevailing in both the Ukraine and Russia. In March 1922 Nansen reported to the Council that 'in the long run there can be no final and satisfactory solution of the problem created by the presence in Europe of one and a half million refugees except by their repatriation to their native land'. But he concluded that the Russian famine and other reasons precluded such a plan.[12] In May of the same year Nansen repeated his evaluation of the situation.[13] Not until the summer of 1922 did his assessment of the prospects for repatriation begin to change. During this time he received appeals from associations representing a large number of Cossacks in Bulgaria asking to be repatriated, and famine conditions within the Soviet Union began to improve. Finally, in August 1922, Nansen began negotiations with Krestinsky, the Soviet representative in Berlin, about a repatriation agreement.[14]

The very mention of repatriation created an uproar at the Third Assembly in September 1922. In a plenary session, Gustave Ador, still President of the ICRC, announced that a large number of protests had been received from associations claiming to represent 1.5 million Russians. Ador implored the Assembly that 'We cannot allow a single refugee to be compelled to return to his country against his will'. Nansen responded to Ador's speech by outlining the proposed repatriation plan to the Assembly. Under the plan's provision, the Soviet government agreed to state explicitly that the provisions of the general amnesty of November 1921 applied

---

[11] League of Nations, 'Russian Refugees', annex 4: Letter from the United Committee of the Russian Zemstovs and Town Councils and the Russian Red Cross Society of 14 June 1921 (1 Aug. 1921) [C.126(a).M.72(a).1921.VII], 6–8.

[12] 'Report to the Council of March 24th, 1922 by Dr. Nansen', *Official Journal* (May 1922), 392.

[13] 'Russian Refugees: Report to the Council of 13 May 1922 by Dr. Nansen', *Official Journal* (June 1922), 612.

[14] 'Interim Report on the Repatriation of Russian Refugees by Mr. J. H. Gorvin, Dr. Nansen's representative in Russia', LNA C1105/187(N6); 'Russian Refugees: Report to the Council of 1 September 1922 by Dr. Nansen', *Official Journal* (Nov. 1922), 1226.

to all returnees. In addition, Nansen would be allowed to appoint representatives in Russia who would have free access to the refugees after their return. Provisions would also be made for small groups of refugees who had already returned to Russia to visit other countries and tell their compatriots about life there. Finally, all refugees would be required to sign a declaration saying that they had returned of their own free will. Nansen further added that at most 20,000 refugees would be sent home, and only to non-famine areas of Russia.[15] The comprehensiveness of the Nansen–Soviet agreement did a great deal to calm Ador's fears. In practice, however, the repatriation plan failed to fulfil initial expectations.

Implementation of the Nansen–Soviet Plan

In October 1922 repatriation began with small groups of refugees from Bulgaria, the only host country willing to allow in a Soviet Red Cross delegation to supervise the process. At the time, the peasant leader Alexander Stamboliiski led a coalition government in Bulgaria. Though not a Communist, Stamboliiski looked with favour on the newly formed Soviet Union.[16] Moreover, the presence of armed White Russian soldiers with contacts with the pre-1914 political and military leaders threatened Stamboliiski's government.[17] From the High Commissioner's point of view, the close proximity of Bulgaria reduced transportation costs, an important consideration for an organization dependent on voluntary contributions.[18] In the beginning, repatriation proceeded according to the terms of the agreement. A Nansen delegate supervised the arrival of the refugees in Southern Russia. A month later a Nansen representative visited the Don and Kuban regions and had personal interviews with men who had previously returned on their own. The representative reported that conditions were difficult for returnees, but that they had no desire to leave Russia.

---

[15] League of Nations, *Records of the Third Assembly: Plenary Meetings, Text of the Debates* (Geneva, 1922), i. 297, 302.

[16] Joseph Rothschild, *East Central Europe between the Two World Wars* (Seattle: University of Washington Press, 1974), 334.

[17] R. J. Crampton, *A Short History of Modern Bulgaria* (Cambridge: Cambridge University Press, 1987), 95.

[18] LNA C1105/187(N3). See also T. F. Johnson, *International Tramps: From Chaos to Permanent World Peace* (London: Hutchinson, 1938), 283.

Moreover, delegations of repatriated refugees travelled to Bulgaria to tell others of their experiences in the Soviet Union.[19] Within a few months, however, the mutual agreement began to unravel. Although the Soviets initially allowed refugee delegations to return to Bulgaria, they soon took the position that reports from the High Commissioner should be sufficient to inform potential returnees about conditions in the Soviet Union. In addition, the Russian *émigré* press began reporting that the Soviets shot many of the returning refugees. One paper, for instance, reported that 'among returned Denikin and Wrangel refugees, officers who had taken a greater or lesser part in the war were shot. A large percentage of Cossacks were shot. The indulgence of the bolsheviks is only extended to soldiers.'[20] In response to these charges, the office of the High Commissioner investigated a number of missing-persons reports but found no evidence of mass killings. However, it did confirm that a number of former officers had mysteriously disappeared.[21] Despite these factors, pressures for repatriation increased; the governments of Poland, Romania, Albania, and France approached the High Commissioner about extending the agreement to refugees in their territories.[22] This momentum, however, came to an abrupt end because of unexpected political events in Bulgaria.

On 9 June 1923 opponents of the peasant government, aided by some White Russians from Wrangel's army, overthrew the Stamboliiski regime and began a reign of 'White Terror'.[23] Stamboliiski himself was brutally tortured and murdered. In early July 1923 the Soviets withdrew their Red Cross representatives because of charges of espionage against their mission and the deaths of two Red Cross officials while under arrest by the Bulgarian government. In a personal communication with Nansen, Maxim Litvinov, Soviet Minister of Foreign Affairs, lambasted the High Commissioner for not protesting against the incident. J. W. Collins, Nansen's delegate in Sofia and a British subject, refuted these charges and reported to Geneva that extensive propaganda materials had been found in the Soviet mission. Nansen, for his part, insisted that he must 'remain neutral and impartial' and that a proper

---

[19] Gorvin, 'Interim Report', 7.   [20] *Roul* (7 Nov. 1922).
[21] Gorvin, 'Interim Report', 10; LNA C1105/187(N5) and (N6).
[22] LNA C1105/187(N5).   [23] Rothschild, *East Central Europe*, 339–42.

investigation be carried out.[24] In an attempt to appease the Soviets, the High Commissioner offered to replace his delegate in Sofia. But the damage had been done. Both the Bulgarian and Soviet governments refused to restart the repatriation plan.[25] After this incident, Soviet relations with Bulgaria and other European countries never became cordial enough to allow mass repatriation to take place. In all, only about 6,000 refugees from Greece and Bulgaria returned under the terms of the Nansen–Soviet agreement.[26]

The abrupt end to the repatriation agreement prompted a controversy about Nansen's role as High Commissioner. Shortly after the expulsion of the Red Cross delegation from Bulgaria, *The Times* of London reported that a group of Russian refugee organizations wanted Nansen to resign. In particular, they accused him of conflict of interest because his work for the Russian famine victims required that he have good relations with the Bolshevik leaders. Moreover, he had written articles and made speeches urging *rapprochement* with the new government, and had been made an honorary member of the Moscow Soviet.[27] The Russians garnered some support from Sir Samuel Hoare, who had directed refugee assistance efforts for the British government in the Balkans. He considered the complaints to have been made from 'the most reasonable and representative Russian emigrants in London' and thought it was a mistake to combine the duties of famine and refugee relief in one person.[28] However, Lord Robert Cecil, British delegate to the League of Nations, staunchly defended Nansen against all charges. He called the contention that 'Nansen is the tool of the Soviet Government' ridiculous and pointed out that, in any case, his work with famine relief had already finished. Moreover, he accused the critics of forgetting all the efforts Nansen had made on behalf of the refugees, including preventing forced expulsions from Romania and Poland. Other defenders pointed

---

[24] LNA C1105/187(N6).   [25] LNA C1105/187(N7).

[26] League of Nations, 'Report on the Work of the High Commission for Refugees presented by Dr. Fridtjof Nansen to the Fourth Assembly' (4 Sept. 1923) [A.30.1923.XII], 18.

[27] 'Russian Refugees and the Soviet: Dr. Nansen's Position', *The Times* (27 Aug. 1923). See also memorandum of 13 Aug. 1923 to Lord Robert Cecil from the Russian Red Cross (Old Organization), Russian Refugees Relief Association, Russian Self Help Association, Russian Children's Welfare Association, Russian Relief Fund, the Russian Army and Navy ex-Service Mens Association, the Russian Academical Group, and the Northern Association. NBKR 4/625.

[28] Letter from Samuel Hoare to Lord Robert Cecil, 24 Aug. 1923. NBKR 4/625.

out that Nansen had rejected the award from the Moscow Soviet because he wanted to remain neutral.[29] With these supporters, the debate eventually subsided and Nansen continued as High Commissioner.

Evaluation of the Repatriation Plan

The failure of the League of Nations repatriation plan reveals the major obstacles that often prevent repatriation from becoming a viable durable solution. For such a scheme to work, the government of the host country, that of the country of origin, and the refugees must agree on its desirability. In this case, the Soviet government initially expressed interest in the return of Russian refugees as part of its wider strategy aimed at preventing former Russian citizens from participating in anti-Soviet organizations abroad.[30] Then, after the Bulgarian incident, the Soviets lost their enthusiasm for politically suspect returnees. Moreover, once Bulgaria and other host countries refused to co-operate, the repatriation plan became operationally impossible.

Most importantly, the Russian refugees needed to be willing to return home. Their readiness to do so depended primarily on conditions in the Soviet Union, especially guarantees for their personal safety. In this regard, the Nansen–Soviet agreement had many admirable features. It required that refugees sign a statement declaring that they left of their own free will. Moreover, the agreement went beyond many repatriation plans sponsored by the United Nations in that it allowed both for periodic checks on the refugees after their return home and for delegations of repatriated refugees to report to refugees still in host countries. But the actual history of the Nansen–Soviet agreement shows the limitations of paper promises. Ultimately, the Soviet Union, a country which refused to participate in the international refugee regime at this time, controlled access to the refugees once they returned to its territory. The High Commissioner could do little to change

---

[29] Letter from Robert Cecil to Dawson, 27 Aug. 1923; letter from Robert Cecil to Sir Samuel Hoare, 28 Aug. 1923; response to the appeal addressed to Lord Robert Cecil by the Russian Refugee Relief Association of England, n.d. NBKR 4/625.

[30] Yuri Felshtinsky, 'The Legal Foundations of the Immigration and Emigration Policy of the USSR, 1917–27', *Soviet Studies*, 34 (July 1982), 335.

this. Though perhaps exaggerated, allegations of the mass killings of returnees reflected the very real fears of refugees for their personal safety.

The repatriation controversy also shows that such an agreement needs to be negotiated by an impartial source. Though Nansen's work for both famine relief and refugee assistance used scarce resources efficiently, it was bound to raise suspicions about his loyalty. These concerns grew even greater when Nansen's relief organization became a business venture that promoted agricultural development in the USSR. Although there is no convincing evidence that either Nansen or his staff tried to profit from this, or that they forced anyone to return to the Soviet Union, they failed to gain the trust of prominent refugee organizations. The High Commissioner, a political liberal who personally disliked dealing with the conservative White Russian leaders, generally left the task of dealing with them to his assistants. A large part of the repatriation controversy could have been avoided if Nansen had adopted the attitude of Sir Samuel Hoare: 'the active co-operation of the Russian 'emigrés' is essential to the success of any relief or protection schemes.'[31]

More than anything else, the failure of the Nansen–Soviet agreement demonstrates that a successful voluntary repatriation plan cannot be carried out in isolation from its wider political environment. The first prerequisite for a repatriation agreement is the elimination of the conditions that produced the refugee movement in the first place. In other words, a successful repatriation plan may require intervention in the domestic affairs of a sovereign state by international organizations or other actors. Given the strength of the sovereignty principle, this is an extremely difficult task. The attempts by certain actors in the international refugee regime to confront the root causes of refugee flows will be discussed in Chapter 7.

PROMOTING LOCAL INTEGRATION THROUGH REFUGEE SETTLEMENT

Because repatriation was not a viable option for the vast majority of refugees, other durable solutions needed to be found for them.

[31] Hoare to Cecil, 24 Aug. 1923.

An obvious answer was to integrate the refugees into the countries into which they initially found asylum. To this end, many host governments unilaterally developed extensive programmes to assist refugees.[32] In a few instances, co-ordinated efforts between the major actors in the regime—host governments, donor governments, and private relief agencies—took place under the auspices of the League of Nations. In Greece and Bulgaria, the League actively promoted local integration by sponsoring refugee settlement. It also carried out smaller settlement projects in Syria and Paraguay. All these projects attempted to combine what is now known as 'development aid' with refugee assistance.[33] Heralded at the time as examples of 'international co-operation', over time they helped establish both the assistance and burden-sharing norms of the international refugee regime.

Refugee Settlement in Greece

In the early 1920s the Greco-Turkish war resulted in an unprecedented disruption of the population and the creation of over one million refugees. Following the conclusion of the conflict and the population exchange that followed, Greece faced the enormous job of caring for more than one million refugees from Asia Minor. In addition, Turkey received 400,000 Muslim refugees who were former residents of Greek Macedonia. Both governments quickly naturalized their respective refugees so that these people did not face the legal disabilities of Russian and Armenian refugees.[34] Nevertheless, both countries confronted the prospect of resettling homeless people. Of the two countries, Greece faced the larger task: it added about 20 per cent to its population of 5.5 million almost overnight.

The involvement of the actors in the international refugee regime in providing durable solutions for refugees in Greece began as a response by the League of Nations to the mass exodus. On 18

---

[32] For a comprehensive survey of the status of refugees in major host countries, see Simpson, *The Refugee Problem*, esp. chs. 13–20. For similar information on the position of Jewish refugees, see Arieh Tartakower and Kurt R. Grossman, *The Jewish Refugee* (New York: Institute of Jewish Affairs of the American Jewish Congress and World Jewish Congress, 1944), esp. chs. 4–10.

[33] For a recent study on linking refugee and development assistance, see Robert F. Gorman, *Coping with Africa's Refugee Burden: A Time for Solutions* (Dordrecht: Martinus Nijhoff for UNITAR, 1987).

[34] Simpson, *The Refugee Problem*, 235–6.

September 1922 Colonel Proctor, head of the Nansen Office in Constantinople, telegraphed Nansen in Geneva, reporting that the Turkish army appeared to have forced the Greek army to retreat from Asia Minor. As a consequence of this, thousands of Greeks and Armenians who had been under the protection of Greek forces were fleeing their homes in Anatolia for Constantinople and Greece. Disregarding normal procedures, Nansen read the telegram to the Assembly and asked the League to intervene.[35] Up until then the League had not taken any action regarding the war. This time, however, it acted swiftly under the leadership of the British delegation. Lord Balfour, the chief British delegate, successfully urged the Council to put 100,000 Swiss francs, about £4,000, at Nansen's disposal.[36] Within twenty-four hours the Assembly extended the High Commissioner's mandate to include refugees from the Near East.[37] A few days later Balfour offered £50,000 for emergency relief, provided other governments contributed the same amount. Although the French and Italian governments, both of which had reached agreements with Kemalist Turkey,[38] never contributed, twelve other League members joined the relief effort.[39]

Not an armchair High Commissioner, Nansen left immediately for the scene of the conflict.[40] Once there, the great physical energy which had once been devoted to conquering polar ice was now turned to other purposes. Apparently not used to such a pace, Philip [Noel-]Baker, his secretrary for the mission, complained that 'I have been having a devil of a time with Nansen—twelve hours a day since we left Geneva, and no Sundays'.[41] With

[35] *Records of the Third Assembly: Plenary Meetings*, i. 124.
[36] 'Minutes of the 21st Session of the Council', *Official Journal* (Nov. 1922), 1195–6. The delegates from France, Spain, and Italy agreed, but they made it clear that the Council accepted no further responsibilities.
[37] *Records of the Third Assembly: Plenary Meetings*, i. 137–42.
[38] See above, Ch. 2.
[39] *Records of the Third Assembly: Plenary Meetings*, i. 226. The British government eventually donated £19,208 for refugee relief in Asia Minor. An equivalent amount was raised by Canada (£5,500), Greece (£5,000), Japan (£1,036), New Zealand (£1,000), Denmark (£1,000), Sweden (£1,000), Norway (£1,000), Brazil (£1,000), Switzerland (£625), Spain (£2,000), Poland (30 large military tents), and Belgium (1,000 tents and 1,000 blankets). *Official Journal* (Jan. 1923), 126.
[40] For an account of Nansen's trip, see Philip Noel-Baker, *The League of Nations at Work* (London: Nisbet, 1926), 107–11. Noel-Baker, then a member of the Secretariat, accompanied Nansen as his secretary.
[41] Philip J. [Noel-]Baker, Constantinople, to Bevil Rudd, London, 30 Oct. 1922. NBKR 4/471.

the grant from the British government, Nansen assisted the major American and British relief agencies in providing food, shelter, and medical supplies for both Greek and Turkish refugees.[42] Although the Turkish government accepted some emergency relief, it opted to tackle the task of long-term settlement on its own.[43] At the time, the Turkish government was pursuing a strategy of independence and did not want to be dependent on outside sources of assistance. Moreover, if the government had desired assistance, its non-membership in the League of Nations eliminated this organization as a potential donor.[44] In Greece, however, the government quickly realized that its resources alone could not solve its refugee problem.

Once again an initiative by the High Commissioner resulted in an expansion of the international refugee regime's functions. Nansen began by urging the Greek leader, Venizelos, of the necessity of helping the refugees to re-establish themselves: 'I am further convinced that the rapid settlement of as many as possible of these refugees on the vacant lands of Greece is urgently desirable in the interests of the peace of the world.'[45] In his report to the League Council of 18 November 1922, Nansen recommended that an international loan be raised under League auspices for

[42] Nansen's organization provided food to refugees on the Greek islands and helped co-ordinate the fight against epidemics. This initiative might have been the start of a new regime aimed at the provision of emergency relief for natural and man-made disasters. This, in fact, did not happen, partly because the League could not establish itself *vis-à-vis* the better-endowed private agencies. For instance, the League spent a total of £38,000, a figure that pales in comparison with the 2.6 million dollars (£520,000) spent on food and clothing by the American Red Cross. Moreover, the British relief agencies bitterly resented that the British government should distribute aid through the Nansen organization and not through them. See BFO 371/7954/E10693 and E 10735. In addition, membership of the League was divided on how emergency relief should be conducted. The Italian delegation proposed the creation of a new organization, an International Relief Union, to deal with all types of emergencies. This proposal, however, never came to fruition. See above, Ch. 3.

[43] Nansen sent 200 tons of flour to Smyrna to be distributed by the Turkish Red Crescent, and provided transport for some Turkish refugees. The Epidemics Commission of the League of Nations provided the Turkish Red Crescent with medical supplies. The ICRC sent blankets to Smyrna, and the American Red Cross and Near East Relief also offered assistance. 'Relief Measures for Refugees in Greece and Asia Minor: Report by Dr. Nansen of 18 November 1922', *Official Journal* (Jan. 1923), 133.

[44] Arnold J. Toynbee and Kenneth P. Kirkwood, *Turkey* (London: Ernest Benn, 1926), 206, 209. Turkey eventually joined the League in July 1932.

[45] Letter from Nansen to Venizelos of 10 Oct. 1922, in Jacob Worm-Müller (ed.), *Fridtjof Nansen Brev* (Oslo: Universitetsforlaget, 1966), iv. 153.

refugee settlement.[46] Although this proposal resembled that of the reconstruction project already undertaken by the League for Austria, great scepticism greeted Nansen's idea:

At that moment every practical policitian denounced the scheme as wild and foolish; six months later they were saying that it was wrong, that there could be no solution unless the refugees returned to Asia Minor; Nansen saw, calmly, steadily and all the time, that only his plan could possibly succeed; only he foresaw that within a generation it would make a new and greater Greece.[47]

In early 1923 the Greek government took up the loan proposal with vigour. After consulting with Sir Eric Drummond, Secretary-General of the League,[48] Venizelos put forth a proposal for a loan to the Council at its February meeting. The Council referred the matter to the Financial Committee, the technical organ of the League responsible for developing economic reconstruction plans for Austria and Hungary.[49] Meanwhile Nansen continued to follow the loan with interest. He reported to the Council in April 1923 on the success of a pilot settlement scheme for 10,000 refugees in western Thrace. He also informed the Council that the American government had announced that American relief agencies, principally the Red Cross, would withdraw from Greece by June 1923 and leave their work supporting refugees. Nansen urged the Council to fill this gap and adopt a humanitarian response by authorizing the loan quickly.[50]

Although Nansen played an important role in advocating international support for refugee settlement in Greece, other actors in

[46] 'Report of 18 November 1922', 135.
[47] P. J. Noel-Baker, 'Nansen: The International Statesman', in J. H. Whitehouse (ed.), *Nansen: A Book of Homage* (London: Hodder & Stoughton, 1930), 105.
[48] Record of conversation of 25 Jan. 1923 between Venizelos, Michalopoulis, and Drummond. LNA R1763/25486.
[49] 'Minutes of the 23rd Session of the Council', *Official Journal* (Mar. 1923), 234–5.
[50] 'Near East Refugees: Report by Dr. Nansen of 23 April 1923', *Official Journal* (June 1923), 696, 701. The departure of the American Red Cross from Greece signalled a general withdrawal from its relief activities in Europe. In the early 1920s the failure of an overseas fund drive forced a realignment along domestic lines. The drive failed because the local chapters refused to support the National Red Cross, which was criticized for many sins: charging soldiers for supplies, the immoral behaviour of its nurses, distributing cigarettes, helping reactionary Russians, feeding Communists, and mismanagement of funds. See Charles Hurd, *The Compact History of the American Red Cross* (New York: Hawthorn, 1959), 182–3.

the regime actually determined the fate of the loan. Initially the French and Italian delegates to the Council opposed any loans to Greece because they feared that the money would be spent for military purposes. In the United States, however, Secretary of State Charles E. Hughes expressed support for the idea of refugee settlement and authorized a government official to attend the meetings of the League on the subject in a consultative capacity. In addition, Lord Robert Cecil, British delegate to the Council, strongly advocated the loan scheme.[51] Ultimately, the weight of Britain and the United States, the two major financial powers of the era, proved to be decisive.

On 29 September 1923 the Council formally approved a Protocol establishing a Greek Refugee Settlement Commission (GRSC), a unique institution that combined international and national resources for the express purpose of achieving a durable solution.[52] According to its statutes, the major function of the GRSC was 'to promote the establishment of refugees in productive work either upon the land or otherwise in Greece'. Moreover, in keeping with overall League policy, the statutes prohibited it from spending any funds on relief. The Commission was to be headed by a Chairman, a representative of American relief agencies, who cast the deciding votes in all decisions, and also included two members nominated by the Greek government and one member nominated by the League of Nations.[53] Under the terms of the Protocol, the Greek government agreed to donate 500,000 hectares of land to be used for refugee settlement.[54]

The creation of the GRSC signalled an important step in the achievement of a durable solution for refugees in Greece, but it

---

[51] Dimitri Pentzopoulus, *The Balkan Exchange of Minorities and its Impact upon Greece* (Paris: Mouton, 1962), 79–81. See also Johnson, *International Tramps*, 306.

[52] Previously, in July 1923, a special Sub-Committee, composed of the British, French, and Italian delegates to the Council and a representative from Greece, approved the plan. 'The Settlement of Greek Refugees', *Monthly Summary of the League of Nations: Supplement* (Nov. 1924), 2.

[53] The following people served on the GRSC during its lifetime. As Chairman: Henry Morgenthau, Sept. 1923–Dec. 1924; Charles P. Howland, Feb. 1925–Sept. 1926; Charles B. Eddy, Oct. 1926–Dec. 1930. Appointed by the League of Nations: Sir John Campbell, Sept. 1923–Jan. 1927; Sir John Hope Simpson, Jan. 1927–Dec. 1930. Appointed by the Greek government: Pericles Argyropoulos, Sept. 1923–Aug. 1924; Etienne Delta, Sept. 1923–Aug. 1925; Theodore Eustathopoulos, Aug. 1924–Aug. 1925; Alexander Pallis, Sept. 1925–Dec. 1930; Achilles Lambros, Sept. 1925–Dec. 1930.   [54] 'The Settlement of Greek Refugees', 26–30.

did not guarantee success. Although the Protocol authorized the Greek government to raise a loan to finance refugee settlement, it did not provide funding for this loan. The Bank of England did offer an advance of £1 million, but the rest of the money still needed to be raised.[55] Responsibility for securing the loan fell primarily on Henry Morgenthau, the newly appointed Chairman of the GRSC.[56] Nominated on the suggestion of Near East Relief, the former American Ambassador to Turkey was both a successful financier and well-known philanthropist who had previously helped the Armenians.[57] Described as a 'small man, with a small pointed beard, rather reminiscent of the traditional portraits of Uncle Sam', Morgenthau vigorously tackled the job of advocating the Greek cause.[58] This was not an easy task because Greece was undergoing a period of acute political instability brought about by clashes between monarchists, republicans, and militarists.[59]

After his appointment as Chairman, Morgenthau travelled first to London to meet with Montague Norman, Governor of the Bank of England, and Sir Otto Niemeyer, Comptroller of Finance, prior to appearing before the Council in Geneva. In public, Morgenthau left aside appeals to humanitarian concerns and announced, 'This is a business proposition, and not charity.'[60] In private meetings with Norman and Niemeyer, Morgenthau found them to be 'friendly, but skeptical about a big loan'.[61] In the course of negotiations over the next year Morgenthau consistently argued that any future Greek government would support the GRSC. In raising the loan, Morgenthau worked in conjunction with Sir Arthur

---

[55] 'The Settlement of Greek Refugees', 3.

[56] For Morgenthau's account of his role, see Henry Morgenthau, *I was Sent to Athens* (New York: Doubleday, Doran, 1929). Also printed as *An International Drama* (London: Jarrolds, 1930). For an alternative view, see Johnson, *International Tramps*, 308.

[57] Letter from Gordon L. Berry, European Representative of Near East Relief, to Major T. F. Johnson, High Commission for Refugees of 19 Sept. 1923. LNA R1764/29451. During his tenure as Ambassador to Turkey, Morgenthau urged the involvement of the United States in assisting Armenians suffering from genocide in Turkey. His appeal eventually led to the creation of Near East Relief in 1919. See James L. Barton, *Story of Near East Relief (1915–1930): An Interpretation* (New York: Macmillan, 1930), 4–5, 17.

[58] 'Mr. Morgenthau Takes Over', *Manchester Guardian* (3 Nov. 1923).

[59] A brief period of stability did follow the declaration of a Hellenic Republic in Apr. 1924. See William Miller, *The Ottoman Empire and its Successors, 1801–1927* (Cambridge: Cambridge University Press, 1936), esp. 541–64.

[60] 'Help for Greek Refugees', *Daily News* (2 Nov. 1923).

[61] Morgenthau, *I was Sent to Athens*, 79–80, 176–8.

Salter, the British economist who headed the Financial Committee.[62] Salter advocated the loan primarily because it would help the Greek government to balance its budget and achieve currency stability, not for humanitarian reasons.[63] On 12 September 1924 the Financial Committee issued a favourable report, paving the way for the loan.[64]

A little more than a year after the creation of the GRSC, the body successfully concluded negotiations for a loan of £12.3 million, raised in London (£7.5 million), Athens (£2.5 million), and New York (£2.3 million).[65] Although the loan carried a nominal rate of 7 per cent, the addition of commissions and duties produced a real rate of 8.71 per cent, a figure significantly higher than the prevailing interest rate 4–5 per cent for government loans.[66] But this loan did not solve Greece's financial problems. When the first loan proved to be insufficient, it had to be supplemented with a second one. In 1927 the Greek government floated a loan for £6.5 million at a real interest rate of 7.05 per cent. The bulk of this loan went towards stabilization of the Greek economy and only £0.5 million was given to the GRSC. At the same time, the United States government lent the Greek government a further £2.5 million at an interest rate of 4 per cent to be entirely turned over to the GRSC.[67]

The relatively high rate of interest on the Greek loans calls into question their 'humanitarian' nature. Stephan Ladas writes that 'this is a tragic-comic commentary on the high-sounding discussion of the Refugee Loan as a humanitarian and philanthropic work. Greece could probably have raised such a loan without the intervention of the League.'[68] Other contemporary observers held the opposite view. For instance, Charles Eddy, Chairman of the GRSC from 1926 until 1930, contends that, 'after the Smyrna catastrophe of 1922, it would have been impossible for Greece to obtain the

[62] Ibid., 83; LNA R1767/38170.
[63] Letter from O. E. Niemeyer, Treasury, to Orme Sargent, Foreign Office of 21 Mar. 1926. BFO 371/12162/C3215.
[64] 'The Settlement of Greek Refugees', 20–5. The Committee endorsed the raising of a loan of up to £10 million. This was important because many regarded the £6 million loan authorized by the original Protocol to be insufficient to finance refugee settlement.
[65] 'Participation in League Loans', *The Economist* (22 Dec. 1928), 1156.
[66] Pentzopoulos, *Balkan Exchange of Minorities*, 89.
[67] Stephen P. Ladas, *The Exchange of Minorities: Bulgaria, Greece, and Turkey* (New York: Macmillan, 1932), 638; Charles B. Eddy, *Greece and the Greek Refugees* (London: Allen & Unwin, 1931), 63–8.
[68] Ladas, *Exchange of Minorities*, 635.

funds necessary for that settlement, except with the help of the League of Nations'.[69] The latter presents the more plausible view; if the Greek government could have raised a loan without League assistance, it would presumably would have done so. The relatively high interest rates on the loans, however, did add to Greece's already large external debt burden. Though not the sole cause, this contributed to the bankruptcy of the Greek state in 1932.[70]

The GRSC had a positive impact on the lives of thousands of Greek refugees during its seven years of operation, 1924 until 1931. Following the plans originally drawn up by Nansen and the Greek government, it concentrated on agricultural settlement, even though the majority of Asia Minor refugees came from urban backgrounds.[71] With the 500,000 hectares of land provided by the Greek government, primarily land in Macedonia vacated by Turks and Bulgarians, the GRSC built villages and helped establish farms.[72] The Commission provided each smallholding family with maintenance for one year, seed, animals, and tools. It also provided infrastructure by building schools, hospitals, wells, and model farms.[73] By December 1930 almost 600,000 refugees had been established in agricultural settlements.[74] The GRSC also made a significant contribution in settling urban refugees, spending twenty per cent of its resources for this purpose. Rather than supplying refugees with jobs, the GRSC concentrated on the easier task of building houses for them in the major cities of Greece. By the end of 1929 it had build over 27,000 homes, primarily in Athens, Piraeus, and Salonica.[75]

One of the reasons for the accomplishments of the GRSC was the close relations it maintained with the Greek government and Greek refugees.[76] Virtually all of its staff was Greek. Indeed, during

[69] Eddy, *Greece and Greek Refugees*, 230. See also, 'Land Settlement for Greek Refugees', *Manchester Guardian* (2 Oct. 1923).
[70] Simpson, *The Refugee Problem*, 21.
[71] League of Nations, *Greek Refugee Settlement* (Geneva, 1926), 16.
[72] The land came from three major sources: land belonging to the Greek state (50,000 ha); land vacated by Turks under the population exchange (350,000 ha); land expropriated by the Greek government under agrarian reform laws (100,000 ha). Ladas, *Exchange of Minorities*, 648.
[73] Simpson, *The Refugee Problem*, 18.
[74] Pentzopoulus, *Balkan Exchange of Minorities*, 105.
[75] Ibid. 112; Ladas, *Exchange of Minorities*, 672–9; Simpson, *The Refugee Problem*, 20.
[76] During its lifetime, one major dispute did occur between the GRSC and the Greek government. Eventually this matter was taken to the Council of the League

the early years of its work the Commission employed only three foreign officials. As a result of this policy, the organization helped create a well-trained staff of approximately two thousand people to spearhead the future economic development of Greece.[77] The policy can be credited, in part, to the first Chairman of the GRSC, who viewed the refugees not as 'hapless dependents' but as equals. Morgenthau insisted that every post created by the Commission should be given, if possible, to one of the Greek refugees. Almost every position was filled in this way. For instance, refugees made up ninety per cent of the labour force involved in constructing urban housing.[78]

The arrival of the refugees from Asia Minor had a profound impact on Greece, influencing the demographic, economic, political, cultural, and social aspects of Greek life. This would have been true with or without the existence of an international refugee regime. Nevertheless, the GRSC, the concrete expression of the regime, channelled the impact of the refugee influx on Greece in several important ways. To begin with, the work of the Commission had a dramatic effect on the demography of Macedonia. In 1912 Macedonia had a Greek population of only 43 per cent but, by 1926, its population had increased to nearly 90 per cent Greek.[79] In this regard, the Commission helped the Greek government to achieve the political goal of a more ethnically homogeneous state.

In social terms, the existence of the GRSC may have helped to perpetuate a separate 'refugee' identity for Asia Minor Greeks. In 1931 Charles B. Eddy optimistically hoped that the word 'refugee' would quickly disappear from the everyday vocabulary of Greeks.[80] In fact, the reverse happened: the continuation of a 'refugee consciousness' has been documented long after the exodus from Anatolia.[81] According to Dimitri Pentzopoulus, this

of Nations for arbitration. See 'Minutes of the 35th Session of the Council', *Official Journal* (Oct. 1925), 1359–61. See also Eddy, *Greece and Greek Refugees*, 79–81.

[77] League of Nations, *Greek Refugee Settlement*, 9–10; Ladas, *Exchange of Minorities*, 630–1, 703; Pentzopoulus, *Balkan Exchange of Minorities*, 86.

[78] Morgenthau, *I was Sent to Athens*, 103, 108, 238.

[79] Richard Clogg, *A Short History of Modern Greece* (Cambridge: Cambridge University Press), 121; Ladas, *Exchange of Minorities*, 699.

[80] Eddy, *Greece and Greek Refugees*, 234.

[81] See, for instance, Renée Hirschon, *Heirs of the Greek Catastrophe: The Social Life of Asia Minor Refugees in Piraeus* (Oxford: Clarendon Press, 1988).

is in part because the term serves as a basis for claims against the Greek government derived from the population exchange agreement. Moreover, the term binds people together who share a common heritage.[82] Although this may have occurred without the influence of the international refugee regime, the treatment of refugees as a special category of persons contributed to this result. The GRSC had its greatest impact on the Greek economy. This was most evident in the agricultural sector, where the Commission accelerated economic development by bringing land under cultivation and introducing modern farming techniques and new products.[83] After conducting a comprehensive survey of the Greek economy in the late 1920s Eliot Mears concluded that:

> The refugees have caused vast changes in rural Greece. Wastelands have been transformed into orchards, vineyards, grain fields, and tobacco plantations, while in Macedonia alone two thousand new villages have been built for the refugee farmers with about one hundred and fifty families in each village . . . better breeds of livestock are being introduced, and nomadic shepherds are being replaced by stock breeders who raise forage crops on their own land. Fallowing has given place to artificial fertilization, and new tools supplied by the Refugee Settlement Commission are gradually causing the peasants to discard antiquated methods of agriculture. As a consequence, production of almost all kinds of agricultural products has increased enormously since the refugees began to flood the country in 1922–23.[84]

Mears concludes that 'contrary to all expectations, the refugees have actually proved a benefit to Greece'.[85] In large part, this transformation can be attributed to the work of the GRSC. In the words of Stephan Ladas: 'while, undoubtedly, the success of the refugee settlement is due primarily to "the courage, effort, and energy of the refugees," it is impossible not to notice the intelligence

---

[82] Pentzopoulus, *Balkan Exchange of Minorities*, 201–5. In 1930 Greece and Turkey cancelled the population exchange agreement and signed the Treaty of Ankara. Under its terms, each government took over the obligations to the refugees within its territory. In addition, the Greek government paid the Turkish government the difference between the value of the Greek and Turkish properties, indicating that the losses of 400,000 Turks exceeded those of 1.5 million Greeks. This settlement continues to be a source of friction between Greek refugees and the Greek government to the present day.

[83] Simpson, *The Refugee Problem*, 21; Pentzopoulos, *Balkan Exchange of Minorities*, 253.

[84] Eliot G. Mears, *Greece Today: The Aftermath of the Refugee Impact* (Stanford, Calif.: Stanford University Press, 1929), 279.   [85] Ibid. 275.

and devotion, the admirable and enlightened activity displayed by the Refugee Settlement Commission in the work.'[86]

Refugee Settlement in Bulgaria

The success of refugee settlement in Greece inspired other countries to apply for similar loans. In February 1926 the representative of Albania formally requested the Council to authorize a loan for the settlement of 7,500 refugees, but the proposal was rejected after failing to gain adequate support from the Financial Committee.[87] Shortly afterwards, in May 1926, the Bulgarian government appealed to the League for a £3 million loan to assist 24,000 Bulgarian refugee families.[88] On this occasion the League responded favourably for both humanitarian and political reasons.[89] As in the case of the Greek refugee settlement, involvement of key actors in the international refugee regime began as an *ad hoc* response to a crisis and coincided with the desire of League members for political stability in a turbulent region.

From 1903 until 1926 approximately 500,000 ethnic Bulgars, 50 per cent of whom arrived after 1918, flooded into Bulgaria from surrounding areas. Although Russian and Armenian refugees within Bulgaria had access to external assistance, the plight of Bulgar refugees received little international support.[90] Then, in October 1925, a border incident with Greece brought the two countries to the brink of war and threatened the peace of Europe.[91] Though the Council successfully intervened, it became obvious that the presence of unsettled refugees on both sides of the frontier had aggravated the conflict.[92] Partly in response to this,

[86] Ladas, *Exchange of Minorities*, 703.

[87] 'Minutes of the 37th Session of the Council', *Official Journal* (Feb. 1926), 182–3.　　　　[88] *Official Journal* (July 1926), annex 892, pp. 1002–3.

[89] On 10 June the Council agreed to be associated with a scheme for refugee settlement in Bulgaria and the raising of an international loan. 'Minutes of the 40th Session of the Council', *Official Journal* (July 1926), 886. In Sept. 1926 the Seventh Assembly also endorsed the plan. *Official Journal*, Special Supplement no. 44, Plenary Meetings: Text (Geneva, 1926), 112–13.

[90] A model refugee village sponsored by the Save the Children Fund was an exception to this. Simpson, *The Refugee Problem*, 176.

[91] James Barros, *The League of Nations and the Great Powers: The Greek–Bulgarian Incident, 1925* (Oxford: Clarendon Press, 1970).

[92] F. P. Walters, *A History of the League of Nations* (London: Oxford University Press, 1960), 314.

the Bulgarian government asked the ILO to undertake a study of refugees in its economy.[93] Officials from the government of Aleksandŭr Tsankov, the economics professor placed in power by the army after the fall of Stamboliiski, argued that the refugees would easily fall prey to Macedonian and Communist extremists. Moreover, the only way to avoid the threat of instability in the Balkans was to give the refugees a social and political stake by settling them on their own land.[94]

Albert Thomas, the French Director of the ILO, took up the proposal with vigour and sent Colonel Proctor, the man who designed the first refugee villages in Greece, to investigate the conditions facing Russian and Armenian refugees there.[95] On his own initiative, Proctor enlarged the scope of his work to consider the possibility of settling Bulgarian refugees, and then communicated the information to the interested parties.[96] After the ILO issued its report, the Bulgarian government took up the issue with the Council. Support for the Bulgarian proposal came quickly from those primarily concerned with humanitarian issues. The Twelfth Conference of the International Committee of the Red Cross adopted a resolution in favour of the Bulgarian proposal, and Gustave Ador personally campaigned for it.[97] In addition, Nansen also informed the Secretariat of his support for the loan.[98]

But agreement from other quarters proved to be more difficult to achieve. The Financial Committee of the League of Nations had little interest in Bulgarian refugee settlement until the British Foreign Office convinced it that the financial stability of the country was at stake.[99] Bulgaria's neighbours initially opposed the loan. The governments of Romania, Yugoslavia, and Greece all suspected the Bulgarian government of supporting the IMRO, a

[93] Telegram of 4 Dec. 1925 from Kiril Propoff, President of the Labour and Social Insurance Council of Bulgaria, to Albert Thomas, Director of the ILO. LNA C1411. At the time, only Russian and Armenian refugees fell under the ILO's mandate.   [94] Crampton, *Short History of Modern Bulgaria*, 102–3.
[95] Letter from Albert Thomas to Proctor, 10 Dec. 1925. LNA C1411. At about the same time, other organizations investigated the refugee situation there. See, for instance, Friends' Council for International Service, *Report of the Delegation to Bulgaria* (17 Nov. 1925).
[96] Note by the Secretariat to the Financial Committee, May 1926. LNA C1411.
[97] Letter from G. Ador to Nansen, 3 June 1926. LNA C1411.
[98] Letter from T. F. Johnson, Refugee Service, to Sir Eric Drummond, Secretary-General of the League of Nations, 5 June 1926. LNA C1411.
[99] Letter from O. E. Niemeyer, Treasury, to Orme Sargent, Foreign Office, 21 Mar. 1927. BFO 371/12162/C3215.

terrorist nationalist organization trying to establish an independent Macedonia.[100] The governments of these three countries eventually agreed to support a loan for humanitarian purposes, provided that refugees would not be settled near Bulgaria's frontiers.[101] In the end, the British government and pro-refugee actors proved to be decisive. A loan of £3.325 million at an interest rate of 7 per cent was floated in Britain (£1.75 million), the United States (£925,000), and three other countries (£650,000).[102]

In approving the loan, the Council and the Assembly acknowledged both its humanitarian and political purposes. M. Vandervelde, Rapporteur for the Council, pointed out that the establishment of refugees would improve external relations between Bulgaria and its neighbours and decrease social agitation in which refugees played a part.[103] The Assembly resolution passed in favour of the scheme expressed 'the belief that the execution of this plan will not only alleviate widespread suffering but will also benefit economic and social order within Bulgaria, and consolidate and improve the political relations of Bulgaria with neighbouring countries'.[104]

In Bulgaria, the work of refugee settlement was carried out under the supervision of a Commissioner appointed by the Council, rather than by a settlement commission.[105] The plan of refugee settlement greatly resembled the operation going on in Greece at the time. A number of factors, however, made refugee settlement more difficult than in Greece. For one, the refugees did not arrive in one wave, but in a series of small ones between 1903 and 1926. In addition, most of the cultivable land in Bulgaria was already occupied. Since the settlement of refugees less than 50 kilometres from Bulgarian frontiers was prohibited, there was even less land available for settlement. Despite these constraints, the Bulgarian government turned over 132,000 hectares of land for settlement. With the proceeds of the loan, the Commissioner supervised road

---

[100] Simpson, *The Refugee Problem*, 24.

[101] *Official Journal* (Oct. 1926), annex 906, p. 1391; annex 906a, pp. 1392–3; annex 906b, p. 1394.

[102] 'Participation in League Loans', 1156. The three other countries were Holland (£250,000), Italy (£200,000), and Switzerland (£200,000).

[103] 'Minutes of the 40th Session of the Council', 884.

[104] League of Nations, 'Settlement of Bulgarian Refugees: Report Submitted by the Second Committee to the Assembly' (21 Sept. 1926) [A.84.1926.II], 2.

[105] The Council appointed Rene Charron, formerly of the General Commissariat for Hungary, to the post as from 31 Oct. 1926.

construction, swamp drainage, land clearance, and the establishment of farms. By the time work was turned over to the Bulgarian government on 1 January 1933, about 125,000 refugees had been established.[106]

Despite the difficulties encountered, refugee settlement in Bulgaria had a positive impact on both the refugees and their host country. The loan enabled over half the refugees to end their landless status, an important accomplishment in an essentially agricultural society. In addition, the settlement scheme helped to improve economic conditions within Bulgaria by increasing the area of land under cultivation, improving health services, and providing infrastructure for transportation and communications.[107] Contemporary observers also stressed that refugee settlement helped to alleviate political tensions within Bulgarian society. In the Refugee Survey, Simpson writes that 'the settlement, with its promise of land and work, prevented the creation of a lawless class which would have constituted a serious political danger'.[108]

Refugee settlement in Bulgaria, however, had little impact on the country's position in the prevailing international political order. After the conclusion of the First World War, Bulgaria, an ally of the defeated Central Powers, was punished by the victorious Allied Powers through loss of territory: by the punitive Treaty of Neuilly, it lost much of Macedonia to Yugoslavia and parts of Thrace to Greece. This left the country without an outlet to the Aegean Sea and smaller territorially than before 1914. Although the refugee settlement programme did help to reduce border squabbles between Bulgaria and its neighbours, it did not redress all grievances. Bulgaria remained committed to irredentism and linked to the revisionist camp.[109]

Armenian Refugee Settlement in Erivan

The existence of the international refugee regime helped to achieve a durable solution for thousands of Greek and Bulgarian refugees during the Inter-war Period. In regard to Armenian refugees, the

[106] Simpson, The Refugee Problem, 25; Ladas, Exchange of Minorities, 591–617.
[107] Ladas, Exchange of Minorities, 616.
[108] Simpson, The Refugee Problem, 25.
[109] Raymond Pearson, National Minorities in Eastern Europe, 1848–1945 (London: Macmillan, 1983), 170, 174; C. A. Macartney and A. W. Palmer, Independent Eastern Europe (London: Macmillan, 1962), 230.

regime's influence was more ambiguous. From 1923 until 1929 the principal actors in the regime pursued an ambitious scheme for the settlement of Armenian refugees in Erivan, the Armenian republic in the Soviet Union. This plan received strong support from a coalition of pro-Armenian groups but lacked a powerful government sponsor. Although the scheme failed, a smaller but still significant settlement plan was carried out for Armenian refugees in Syria.[110]

The international refugee regime's dealings with Armenian refugees must be seen in relation to Armenia's position in world politics. During the First World War the Armenians, a Christian minority in the Ottoman Empire, supported the Allied cause against the Turks. This act of defiance on the part of the Armenians prompted Turkish retaliation. As a result, thousands of Armenians were murdered and still more fled as refugees. At the conclusion of the war, survivors who gathered in Erivan established an Armenian republic. Sandwiched between Turkey and the Soviet Union, the fledgeling state turned to the League of Nations for protection from its hostile neighbours. Although great sympathy for the Armenian cause permeated the Assembly, the Council refused to place the republic under the mandate system. Unable to stand alone, it collapsed and became incorporated into the Soviet Union. In 1923 the Treaty of Lausanne confirmed this result—the document contained no mention of an independent Armenia.[111] After this failure to create an Armenian national homeland, advocates of the Armenian cause turned to the next best alternative: assistance to Armenian refugees.

Interestingly enough, the Soviet Union opened the door for debate on Armenian refugee settlement by offering to donate territory for this purpose in January 1923.[112] A coalition of private, voluntary organizations, working in conjunction with the Armenian National Delegation, quickly took advantage of this opportunity. Private organizations took a special interest in Armenian refugees because they had been involved in aid to victims of the Turkish genocide against the Armenian people. At a

[110] The Nansen Office also built homes for 600 Armenian refugees in Greece. League of Nations, Nansen International Office for Refugees, 'Report of the Governing Body' (10 Aug. 1938) [A.21.1938.XII], 9.

[111] Walters, *History of the League of Nations*, 109–23.

[112] Letter from Nansen to Tchitcherine, Russian Embassy, Berlin, 10 Feb. 1923. LNA C1428.

deeper level, many of the organizations had a tradition of Christian missionary work in the Middle East, giving them both a heightened awareness of and sympathy towards Armenian refugees. Representatives of Near East Relief, one of the largest American relief agencies, and the Ligue Internationale Philarménienne, a French-based organization, led the efforts of private organizations to gain support from the Council, the Secretariat, and the High Commissioner for Refugees.[113] They sought the involvement of Nansen especially because of his experience in negotiating with the Soviets.[114] Based on these preliminary talks, the Armenian National Delegation made a formal appeal to the governments of France, Great Britain, and Italy proposing the settlement of 50,000 Armenian refugees on the Sardarabad plain at a cost of five million dollars (£1 million).[115]

The Armenians found a willing ally in the French government. On 25 September 1923 M. Hanotaux, the French delegate, brought the proposal to the Council. At this time the High Commissioner expressed strong reservations. Nansen said that it would be easy to provide the Armenian refugees with identity certificates but that financing the settlement scheme would be a problem. Nevertheless, the Council authorized an appeal for funds and agreed to furnish technical assistance if sufficient funding became available.[116] Privately, members of the Secretariat shared Nansen's reservations: F. P. Walters of the Political Section expressed the view that 'it seems almost unimaginable that one single farthing will be given by any European Government for this cause'.[117]

For the following year, the scheme proceeded at a snail's pace, in part because of the preoccupation of the League with the creation of the GRSC. Finally, in September 1924, the Fifth Assembly passed a resolution inviting the ILO, in conjunction with Nansen,

[113] Letter from Ed. Naveill, President of the Ligue Internationale Philarménienne to the Council, 27 Jan. 1923. LNA C1428; 'Minutes of the 23rd Session of the Council', *Official Journal* (Mar. 1923), 235.

[114] Memorandum by Eric Drummond, Secretary-General of the League of Nations, 10 Feb. 1923; memorandum of a conversation between M. de Morsier, International Philarmenian League, Major Johnson, representing Dr Nansen, and Mr Berry, Near East Relief, 6 Feb. 1923. LNA C1428.

[115] Letter to M. Hanotaux from Gabriel Noradounghian, President of the Armenian National Delegation, 24 Aug. 1923. LNA C1428.

[116] 'Minutes from the 26th Session of the Council', *Official Journal* (Nov. 1923), 1325–7, 1349.

[117] Letter from F. P. Walters to Major Johnson, 18 Oct. 1923. LNA C1428.

to make a formal inquiry into the prospects for Armenian refugee settlement in the Caucasus. At this time, strong support for the scheme was expressed by two leading British politicians. Conservative and Liberal party leaders Baldwin and Asquith sent a letter to Labour Prime Minister Ramsay MacDonald urging that the British government make a grant to aid Armenians.[118]

The task of planning the inquiry fell on the newly formed Refugee Section of the ILO.[119] Albert Thomas, Director of the ILO, took a keen interest in the plan. In Paris, he sought out representatives of the Soviet Armenian republic and gained their support.[120] In assembling the survey team, he stressed the necessity of including British, French, and Italian members and urged Nansen to head it.[121] Initially Nansen refused; he believed that the key to a successful project rested in utilizing the best technical experts, not in his own participation.[122] Thomas then presented one final argument, that the Soviets would not deal with a League venture, only an independent commission led by Nansen.[123] Faced with this dilemma, the 65-year-old Nansen postponed his retirement and agreed to lead the mission.

In the late spring of 1925 Nansen and the survey team travelled to Erivan, where the Armenian government, people, and landscape all left a deep impression.[124] To Nansen, Erivan was 'a wonderful land which only needs one thing, and that is *water* to become a garden of Eden'.[125] On their return, the Commission issued a favourable report, recommending the raising of an international loan to finance the settlement of 15,000 Armenian refugees

---

[118] 'Help for Armenians: Party Leaders Appeal to Mr. McDonald', *The Times* (27 Sept. 1924).

[119] League of Nations/ILO, 'Report by Dr. Fridtjof Nansen, President of the Commission Appointed to Study the Question of the Settlement of Armenian Refugees' (Geneva, 28 July 1925), 1.

[120] Letter from Johnson to Nansen, 29 Jan. 1925. LNA C1428.

[121] Letter from Thomas to Nansen, 6 Apr. 1925. LNA C1428.

[122] Letter from Nansen to Thomas, 13 Apr. 1925. LNA C1428.

[123] Letter from Thomas to Nansen, 24 Apr. 1925. LNA C1428.

[124] In addition to Nansen, the Commission consisted of G. Carle, a French agricultural specialist, C. E. Dupois, an English cotton expert, Lo Savio, an Italian irrigation expert, and V. Quisling, a Norwegian who acted as secretary to the Commission. 'Report by Dr. Nansen of 28 July 1925', 1. Quisling later became infamous for his role as a collaborator with the Nazis during the German occupation of Norway. He was executed by the Norwegian government in October 1945.

[125] Letter from Nansen, Tiflis, to Lili Sulzer, 4 July 1925, in Worm-Müller, *Fridtjof Nansen Brev*, no. 955.

currently living in Greece and Constantinople on newly irrigated land in Erivan.[126] Nansen believed that the loan would not be difficult to raise; he counted on rich Armenians in France to finance the project.[127]

In September 1925 the Sixth Assembly debated the merits of the proposal. Nansen, acting in his capacity as first Norwegian delegate, argued that the plan represented the only practical way to fulfil past promises by the League to the Armenian people. Mrs MacKinnon, the Australian delegate, spoke in favour of the plan and urged Christian solidarity, saying that 'it should never be forgotten that when John Ziska and the champions of Christendom held the gates of Vienna against the oncoming Muslims there were with them many thousands of Armenians'. When delegates from both France and Britain also indicated their support, passage of the plan in the Assembly was assured.[128]

Despite this hopeful beginning, raising the loan for Armenian settlement in Erivan proved to be impossible. The American government and relief organizations shunned any part of the scheme.[129] The French and Italian governments stated that they would only take part if the British did, leaving the fate of the loan in British hands. Despite Baldwin's earlier support for Erivan, no financial contribution was forthcoming during his tenure as prime minister. The British Treasury adamantly opposed the loan because of past defaults by both the Soviet and Armenian governments. Although Foreign Office officials found the scheme to be practical, they considered the loan to be risky because of Soviet control over Erivan.[130] Without British support, the Financial Committee rejected any possibility of a loan and suggested the funds be raised privately.[131]

After the announcement of the Financial Committee's decision in September 1926, support for the Erivan scheme began to erode.

[126] 'Report by Dr. Nansen of 28 July 1925', 4.

[127] Letter from Nansen to Johnson, 28 July 1925. LNA C1428.

[128] *Official Journal*, Special Supplement no. 33, Sixth Assembly, Plenary Meetings (Geneva, 1925), 152–3.

[129] Notes on report given to the Executive Committee by General Secretary of Friends of Armenia, 25 Nov. 1925. BFO 371/10865/E7568.

[130] Memorandum by the Treasury on the settlement of Armenian Refugees in Armenia, 24 Nov. 1925. BFO 371/10865/E7348. Also BFO 371/10865 and 371/11550.   [131] *Official Journal* (Oct. 1926), annex 901, pp. 1339–40.

The Refugee Section of the ILO and British relief agencies began to direct their attention to the conditions of Armenian refugees living in Syria. The French government joined in this project, and refused further participation in the Erivan scheme.[132] The government of the United States also refused to help.[133] Only the High Commissioner continued to work undaunted. Over the next three years Nansen conducted a one-man fund-raising drive in an attempt to salvage his plan.

Nansen's greatest efforts went into trying to convince the British, the leading European financial power, of the merits of the scheme. Philip Noel-Baker had urged him to do this, saying 'try to get the Foreign Ministers—Chamberlain and Stresemann especially—to face the fact that they must now put the loan through or kill it—and that they will have to face the responsibility of the thing at the next Assembly'.[134] Nansen hoped to use his friendship with Austen Chamberlain, the Conservative Foreign Minister, to win a British donation. Within the Foreign Office, the plan did have supporters who argued that they had a 'moral obligation' not to 'endanger the whole scheme by a refusal'. To the Foreign Minister himself, the two key factors engaging British responsibilities were the Allied encouragement to the Armenians during the war and the earlier support of Prime Minister Baldwin for refugee settlement. On the strength of these considerations, Chamberlain authorized a request to the Treasury for a donation of £50,000.[135] Treasury officials countered with humanitarian arguments of their own, in particular that it was not in the interest of the refugees to be under a Communist regime. Moreover, they also cited objections from the refugees, which had been garnered from reports of British relief agencies operating in Greece and Syria.[136] But the decisive arguments linked refugee assistance with the broader issue of British foreign policy towards the Soviet Union: in effect, the

---

[132] *Official Journal*, Special Supplement no. 70, Ninth Assembly, Sixth Committee (Geneva, 1928), 31.

[133] Letter from Charles P. Howland to Nansen, 31 Jan. 1927. LNA C1429.

[134] Letter from Philip Noel-Baker, Greece, to Nansen, 10 May 1927. NP. MS fo. 1988.A1.

[135] Foreign Office notes on documents relating to Council discussion of 16 and 17 June on Dr. Nansen's proposals. BFO 371/12324/E3380.

[136] Treasury's reply of 19 Aug. 1927 to Lord Monteagle's letter of 15 Aug. 1927. BFO 371/12324/E3624.

scheme would contribute to the economic development of an enemy. Winston Churchill, then a member of the Treasury, stated this argument in no uncertain terms: 'it would be quite impossible to ask Parliament to vote money to turn Armenians into Communists and develop any part of Soviet Russia.'[137]

At the next Council meeting, held in September 1927, Chamberlain went personally to represent the British government. There he had the difficult task of telling Nansen, a man he personally admired, that the British would not contribute. In his own words, his position 'was not a pleasant one'.[138] Discouraged by the lack of British support, Nansen asked the Council to support the plan or end the League's connection with it. But the Council did not want to take responsibility for jettisoning the Armenian cause, and they begged Nansen to continue his efforts.[139] Eventually, a group of Armenian organizations, led by Nubar Pacha of the Union Générale Arménienne de Bienfaisance, offered to provide £100,000.[140] The government of only one Great Power, Germany, agreed to make a major donation, but their £50,000 alone was not enough. The governments of Romania, Norway, and Switzerland also gave small contributions. Eventually £155,000 was promised, but this amount was too small to make the scheme workable.[141]

The difficulties over the Armenian loan took their toll on Nansen. He confided in his friend and colleague Robert Cecil that: 'I must admit that I often feel very lonely there [Geneva], as hardly any of the other small countries do much to support our struggle, although they say they agree, and if one looks round there are indeed very few from whom I can expect much support. . . . I do not know where the knights for the good causes may be found. . . . So you see I have not much hope that much can be done, but

---

[137] Letter from Winston Churchill, Treasury Chambers, to Austen Chamberlain, 31 Aug. 1927. BFO 371/12324/E3762.

[138] Austen Chamberlain, Geneva, to Sir W. Tyrrell, 16 Sept. 1927. BFO 371/12324/E3972.

[139] 'Minutes of the 47th Council', *Official Journal* (Oct. 1927), 1415–17.

[140] Note from Union Générale Arménienne de Bienfaisance to Nansen, Nov. 1928. LNA C1429.

[141] This sum included £100,000 from Armenian organizations, £50,000 from the German government, £2,680 from governmental and private sources in France, £2,000 from the Norwegian government, £1,000 from the Romanian government, and £40 from the Albanian government. The Greek government offered to provide transportation at a reduced rate. In addition, the Luxembourg government donated £200, and private sources in Britain donated £700. [A.23.1929.VII], 20.

nevertheless one has of course to try.'[142] When Nansen finally had to inform the Assembly that it was time to discontinue the Erivan settlement scheme, he spoke with 'a bleeding heart' as he conducted the 'last act in a great tragedy'.[143] This was Nansen's last appearance at the Assembly of the League of Nations; he died the following May at the age of 68.

Armenian Refugee Settlement in Syria

Although the ambitious Erivan scheme produced meagre results, several smaller settlement projects for Armenians were carried out in Syria and Greece. The plight of these refugees first became widely known because of information gathered by several private organizations. The English Society of Friends (Quakers) first called attention to the precarious conditions facing Armenian refugees in Syria. After a mission conducted in the summer of 1925 they reported that, of the 100,000 Armenians living in Syria, only 10 per cent had permanent employment, 50 per cent lived 'hand to mouth', and 40 per cent lacked both jobs and adequate food.[144] In early 1926 delegates of the ICRC called attention to the poor health experienced by Armenian refugees in Syria.[145] At about the same time, the British consulate in Damascus informed the Foreign Office of the grim conditions facing Armenian refugees there. The refugees' problems included unsanitary refugee camps, epidemics of typhoid fever, overcrowding, and extreme poverty. Despite this and other similar reports, Foreign Office staff considered the conditions of Armenians in Syria to be a 'French concern' and declined to take any action.[146] The French mandatory government agreed; they invited the Refugee Service to co-oper-

[142] Letter from Nansen to Robert Cecil, 15 July 1927, in Worm-Müller, *Fridtjof Nansen Brev*, v, no. 1034.

[143] Alfred Zimmern, *The League of Nations and the Rule of Law: 1918–1935* (London: Macmillan, 1936), 376. *Official Journal*, Special Supplement no. 75, Tenth Assembly: Text (Geneva, 1929), 129–31.

[144] Joseph Burtt, 'Report on Armenian Refugees in the Near East' (Society of Friends, 1925). LNA C1428.

[145] Raymond Schlemmer, 'Mission en Syrie', *Revue Internationale de la Croix-Rouge* (Jan. 1926), 1–15; Georges Burnier, 'Les secours en Syrie', *Revue Internationale de la Croix-Rouge* (Feb. 1926), 94–104.

[146] Letter from Vaughan Russell, Acting Consul, British Consulate, Damascus, Syria, to the Secretary of State for Foreign Affairs, London, 31 May 1926. BFO 371/11550/E3549.

TABLE 15. *Armenian Sub-Committee of the Advisory Committee of Private Organizations, 1927*

Fridtjof Nansen, High Commissioner for Refugees, Chairman
Albert Thomas, Director of the ILO, Vice-Chairman
T. F. Johnson, Head of the Refugee Section of the ILO, General Secretary
Senator Victor Berard, French Phil-Armenian organizations
M. Vandervelde, Minister, Belgian Phil-Armenian organizations
Senator G. Ciraolo, Italian Phil-Armenian organizations
L. Pachalian, Armenian organizations
M. Schlemmer, Comité international de la Croix-Rouge
G. L. Berry, Near East Relief
A. Krafft-Bonnard, International Near East Association
A. Hacobian, British Armenian organizations
M. Thiebaut, Minister, Comité central de la Croix-Rouge française
Edith Pye and Mr. Blackhouse, United British Committee: Save the Children Fund, Armenian (Lord Mayor's) Fund, Society of Friends (Quakers), Friends of Armenia

---

Source: [A.48.1927], 5.

ate in establishing destitute Armenian refugees, a proposal that the ILO took up with enthusiasm.[147]

In November 1926 the ILO convened a special Armenian Sub-Committee of the Refugee Advisory Committee (see Table 15). It asked relevant private organizations interested in Armenian refugees to participate, including representatives of the British, French, Belgian, and Italian phil-Armenian societies, Armenian refugee groups, the ICRC, Near East Relief, and the International Near East Association.[148] At the invitation of this group, Major Johnson, head of the Refugee Section, travelled on a fact-finding mission to Syria. On his trip, Johnson visited Beirut, Aleppo, and Alexandretta, the three places with the largest concentrations of Armenian refugees in the Middle East. He met with Armenian

---

[147] 'Mémorandum relatif aux propositions de coopération du BIT et du Haut-Commissaire de la Société des Nations pour les Réfugiés à l'établissement des réfugiés arméniens dans les Etats de Syrie et du Liban, 15 Octobre 1926'. LNA C1429. See also League of Nations, 'Armenian and Russian Refugees' (3 Sept. 1926) [A.44.1926], 31.

[148] League of Nations, 'Russian and Armenian Refugees: Report to the Eighth Assembly' (1927) [A.48.1927.XIII], 5.

leaders and representatives of Near East Relief and other private agencies, and received a warm welcome from the mandatory authorities. Johnson found that the living conditions of the majority of the approximately 90,000 Armenian refugees living in the French mandated territories constituted a 'grave danger to public health and security'. In describing the camps, he writes:

I have never during the course of a fairly wide experience of refugee conditions in many countries, during and after the war, encountered refugees in such an unsatisfactory permanent situation as that of the refugees in the Beyrouth and Alexandretta camps. The Beyrouth camp, constructed mostly of petrol cases and tins, presents the appearance of a town of cards or at best of match boxes; the streets, or rather alleys, are so narrow as to make it difficult for two persons to pass each other, and are the receptacles for the draining and refuse of the houses. The effect of this state of affairs is reflected in the unsatisfactory health reports of the camp, and especially by the recent outbreak of plague.[149]

Based on Johnson's findings, the ILO recommended immediate settlement of the 20,000 most needy Armenian refugees at a cost of £120,000, a much smaller sum than the £10 million needed for the Erivan scheme. According to the plan, refugees would be settled along the coastal regions of Lebanon and Syria, near existing Armenian communities and the protection of foreign troops. The French mandatory government immediately supported the plan; it quickly donated 3 million French francs (£25,000) towards it.[150] But not every actor in the international refugee regime shared this enthusiasm. Although Johnson urged the High Commissioner for Refugees to authorize a grant of £3,000, Nansen had serious reservations. He felt that the necessity of settling refugees near military installations called into question the desirability of Syria as a location for refugee settlement. Most importantly, Nansen still advocated the Erivan scheme, and he feared that a rival plan would undermine it. Despite his reservations, Nansen agreed to the expenditure because of his concern for Armenian refugees in Syria.[151]

---

[149] T. F. Johnson, 'Report to the Director on Mission Undertaken to Study the Problem of the Armenian Refugees in the Mandated States of Lebanon and Syria of 18 December 1926'. LNA C1429. See also [A.48.1927.VII], 6; Johnson, *International Tramps*, 329–32.   [150] [A.48.1927.VII], 6.

[151] Letter from Nansen to Thomas, 11 Jan. 1927. LNA C1429. Nansen was not the only one who objected to the settlement locations. Gilbert Murray and Arnold Toynbee suspected that the French had ulterior motives in agreeing to these sites since they had been recently annexed to Lebanon by the French government, over the objections of the local population. See letter from Gilbert Murray to John Harris, 4 Mar. 1927. LNA C1430.

The Armenian refugee organizations essentially shared Nansen's view of settlement in Syria. They saw the plan as complementary to the more important goal of achieving an Armenian homeland in Erivan through refugee settlement there.[152] Their financial contributions reflect this position. Although Armenian organizations promised £100,000 for Nansen's plan, they only donated £500 for the Syrian project.[153]

Initially the ILO hoped to win a large contribution from the British government for Armenian refugee settlement in Syria. Although the Foreign Office approved of the plan in principle, the government refused to contribute because they considered the French to be primarily responsible for the Armenians.[154] The blessings of the Foreign Office, however, did pave the way for the support of private organizations. The United British Committee, a coalition made up of four phil-Armenian groups, initially donated £5,000 for the scheme and then launched a major fundraising appeal. This appeal also had the support of prominent leaders of the Church of England, including the Archbishop of Canterbury.[155]

With these initial contributions, the ILO immediately began construction of new homes for refugees in Lebanon and Syria. Less than two years after Johnson's study the ILO reported to the Ninth Assembly of the League of Nations that 1,500 families, or about 8,000 refugees, had been placed either in agricultural colonies or in urban settlements.[156] With this proven success, the Refugee Section of the ILO pressed the French government for a major contribution. Over the winter of 1928–9 Johnson and Thomas conducted negotiations with the Ministry of Foreign affairs, especially its representative to the League of Nations, J. Fouques-

---

[152] Minutes, First Meeting of the Armenian Sub-Committee of the Advisory Committee to the High Commissioner, 6 Nov. 1926: Statement by L. Pachalian, representing Union Générale Arménienne de Bienfaisance. LNA C1430.
[153] A wealthy Armenian also donated £1,000. [A.48.1927.VII], 6.
[154] Letter from Austen Chamberlain, Foreign Office, to Rt. Revd Charles Gore, Chairman of the United Committee of the British Armenian Societies, 4 May 1927 (BFO 371/12323/E1520); House of Commons, *Parliamentary Debates*, 206/65 (18 May 1927).
[155] [A.48.1927.XIII], 6. The United British Committee was composed of the Armenian (Lord Mayor's) Fund, the Save the Children Fund, the Friends of Armenia, and the Society of Friends. BFO 371/12323; LNA C1430.
[156] League of Nations, 'Measures in Favour of Russian, Armenian, Assyrian, Assyro-Chaldean and Turkish Refugees' (Geneva, 1928) [A.33.1928.VIII], 5.

Duparc. With his support, the French government authorized a credit of 3 million French francs (£25,000), an amount sufficient to finance the rest of the scheme.[157] For the next ten years Armenian refugee settlement continued in Syria and Lebanon under the supervision of a Central Committee, composed of officials of the mandatory government and representatives from the ILO, the ICRC, Armenian organizations, and British and American relief agencies.[158] These efforts were noteworthy for at least two reasons. First of all, the Committee made an attempt to place refugees in an environment that would be most familiar to them. For instance, it placed refugees who had been town-dwellers in urban settlements and those who had been farmers in agricultural settlements.[159] As most of the refugees came from urban areas in Turkey, this policy resulted in an emphasis on urban housing. By 1938 over 36,000 refugees had been placed in urban settlements, and only 1,100 in agricultural colonies.[160]

The second policy of interest here relates to financing. In total, about 11 million French francs (£88,000) were donated to the project, about half from the French government and half from private organizations.[161] This money was lent to refugees and then had to be repaid. Once refugees repaid the grant, they received title to their land or home, and the money was then used to finance someone else. This revolving fund reflected the 'no-charity' philosophy of the refugee agencies of the League of Nations. Instead, administrators thought that they should 'act as benevolent bankers to refugees and make them loans to set themselves up in productive employment, on the principle of helping them to help themselves'.[162] For urban refugees, this system worked remarkably well: almost all borrowers returned their money. For refugees in agricultural colonies, however, the repayments proved to be a heavy burden. Successive crop failures during the mid-1930s reduced their

[157] Correspondence between T. F. Johnson of the Refugee Section of the ILO and J. Fouques-Duparc, Ministère des Affaires Etrangères, from Jan. to June 1929. LNA C1429.
[158] Haut Commissariat de la République Française auprès des États de Syrie, du Grand Liban, arrêté no. 694, 3 Sept. 1926.
[159] League of Nations, Nansen International Office for Refugees, 'Report of the Governing Body' (16 Aug. 1932) [A.24.1932], 26.   [160] [A.21.1938.XII], 7.
[161] League of Nations, Committee on International Assistance to Refugees, 'Report by the Committee Submitted to the Council of the League of Nations' (3 Jan. 1936) [C.2.M.2.1936.XII], 7, 15.   [162] Johnson, *International Tramps*, 334.

ability to repay the loans. In addition, political disturbances in rural areas forced some refugees to seek protection in the cities, proving Nansen's predictions to be correct.[163]

Refugee settlement in Syria and Lebanon had a positive impact on the lives of Armenian refugees there. This is most evident in the area of health and sanitation. Before the construction of new urban housing, the refugees lived in malaria-prone makeshift camps. Under the direction of the Central Committee, new quarters were constructed on sites where refugees would be less vulnerable to disease. In each new town, a water sanitation and waste disposal system was included.[164] Although the League-sponsored settlement scheme did not include provisions for refugee employment, its efforts to provide decent housing did facilitate this. Many Armenian refugees found jobs in public works projects and in the local economy.[165]

Armenian refugee settlement in Syria and Lebanon had less of an impact on the economies of these two mandates than did refugee settlement in Greece. This is not surprising, given the fact that the number of refugees involved was much less (100,000 versus 1.5 million). Nevertheless, the project did remove a serious danger to the health of both refugees and native inhabitants. In addition, the refugee settlement facilitated the modernization of the major cities in these areas by bringing electricity and more efficient sanitation and water systems. As in Greece, refugee settlement also affected the ethnic politics of Syria and Lebanon. The Armenian refugees, primarily Christian in religion, added to the Christian population of Lebanon, in keeping with the long-term French strategy in this region.

CONCLUSION

From the above account of the influence of the international refugee regime on facilitating local integration through refugee settlement projects, an important conclusion can be drawn: refugee

[163] [A.21.1938.XII], 8.
[164] 'Extract from a Report by Colonel-Doctor Jude, Chief of the Sanitary Service of the High Commissariat for Syria, M. Burnier, Representative of the Nansen International Office for Refugees, and Major-Doctor Lubt, on the Armenian Refugees Problem in Syria' [A.24.1932], appendix IV, 24–6.
[165] [A.24.1932], 10.

settlement in Greece, Bulgaria, and Syria and Lebanon did have a positive impact on both the lives of refugees and their host countries. Although the governments concerned probably would have managed to assist the refugees without any outside help, the availability of support from the League of Nations, private organizations, and other actors in the regime proved to be a considerable benefit. In the case of Greece, the arrival of more than one million refugees could have been a devastating burden on this relatively poor country. Instead, with the assistance of the GRSC, the refugee influx soon began to contribute in a postive way to the Greek economy. Though the results of refugee settlement in Bulgaria and Syria were less dramatic, these projects also contributed to the well-being of both the refugees and their hosts.

Given that the successful settlement schemes in Greece, Bulgaria, and Syria all depended heavily on the support of one or more Great Power, one might reach the conclusion that the Great Powers were the driving force behind them. It is true that the financial support of Britain, France, and the United States was crucial in bringing major refugee projects to fruition. If a Great Power strongly objected to a scheme, as the British did to settlement in Soviet Armenia, this opposition contributed greatly to failure. It would be a mistake, however, to equate the refugee settlement projects in Greece, Bulgaria, or Syria solely with the Great Powers. In each of the cases reviewed above, private, voluntary organizations and the refugee agencies of the League of Nations literally enticed the governments of France, Britain, and the United States into the projects, often urged on by representatives from smaller countries. Nansen, Thomas, and their staffs provided policy-makers with options that became the basis for bureaucratic debates within governments. In doing so, they harnessed national interests for the achievement of their own humanitarian goals and convinced the Great Powers to do something that otherwise they would not have done.

Undoubtedly, the failure of states in the international refugee regime to provide durable solutions for all refugees represents a divergence from the original humanitarian ideal of the regime. Nevertheless, what was accomplished constitutes a significant, albeit partial, fulfilment of the regime's principles and norms. Individually, each project aimed at a durable solution helped refugees in a particular place and time. Taken as a whole, the various attempts at arranging repatriation and refugee settlement had an even greater impact. Over time they established the legitimacy of international efforts aimed at securing the material needs of refugees, not just their legal status. Although this concept may be taken for granted now, it must be remembered that this was not always true. In the early 1920s many thought that refugee aid and other 'charity' projects were not legitimate concerns for international activity. By the time of the Second World War this idea had been gradually eroded, in large part because of the refugee projects sponsored by the League of Nations. As a result, the IRO directly distributed aid to the millions of people displaced by the conflict. In retrospect, the successful achievement of durable solutions for millions of refugees in the 1920s and 1930s began a tradition now being carried out by the current international refugee regime through the work of UNHCR.

6

Confronting Barriers to Immigration

IN Greece, Bulgaria, and Syria, the major actors in the international refugee regime joined together to sponsor refugee settlement projects. In each of these cases, the refugees had already been welcomed by a host country. Not all refugees, however, were so lucky. Some only managed to find a country of temporary asylum, while others struggled to locate even this. This situation presented a dilemma within the norms of the international refugee regime. On the one hand, the asylum norm gave states the authority to grant or deny asylum to refugees. On the other, the assistance norm required that states help refugees in need. During the history of the international refugee regime, key actors tried to reconcile these two norms by attempting to reduce barriers to immigration for refugees. Finding countries of permanent asylum for Russian refugees was one of the first problems Nansen confronted as High Commissioner for Refugees. Later in the 1920s the Refugee Section of the ILO helped Russian and Armenian refugees to emigrate to and find employment in a country of permanent settlement. In the 1930s the League of Nations, private organizations, and certain governments helped refugees fleeing the Third Reich to find asylum. Although these initiatives did little to change the overall restrictive character of world migration in the Inter-war Period, they contributed to the development of the idea that refugees should be treated as a special kind of migrant in immigration law.

NANSEN AND THE CRISIS AT CONSTANTINOPLE

Shortly after Nansen began his job as High Commissioner, he was confronted by a refugee crisis at Constantinople, the dumping-ground for the White armies evacuated from South Russia. At the time, the Allied powers jointly administered the city and cared for refugees there. In late September 1921 both the French government and the American Red Cross threatened to withdraw; at the time, they were feeding approximately 25,000 refugees. Dealing with this crisis did not properly fall under Nansen's mandate; he had been appointed as High Commissioner to deal with the legal protection, repatriation, and employment of Russian refugees. Nevertheless, Nansen accepted the challenge because 'it seemed to him useless to endeavour to find productive employment for people who were actually starving'. He appealed to the French government and they agreed to continue feeding the remnants of General Wrangel's army temporarily. The American Red Cross, however, refused to continue its work because it could no longer afford to do so. All in all, the situation in the refugee-swamped city was grim. Nansen calculated that there were '25,000 refugees without visible means of support, of whom 15,000 were in actual danger of starvation'.[1]

In order to ward off almost certain death for many refugees at Constantinople, Nansen first moved to secure emergency relief, then arranged for their transportation elsewhere. He asked the British, French, and Italian governments and private organizations to contribute. Because the British government considered the French responsible for Wrangel's army, it had previously rejected appeals on behalf of Russian refugees in Constantinople.[2] In early December 1921, however, the British changed their policy because of the combined influence of the League of Nations appeal and the urging of Sir Horace Rumbold, British High Commissioner in Constantinople. In a desperate appeal to the Foreign Office, Rumbold stressed that deaths from starvation were a daily occurrence and that private charity, including a relief committee led by Lady Rumbold, only touched the fringe of the problem. Apart from the humanitarian element, Foreign Office officials were moved to action by fears that large numbers of desperate refugees would become a catalyst for the spread of Bolshevism, public disorder, and increased crime. Moreover, they saw the refugees as a direct threat to the British garrison at Constantinople because of the 'grave danger' posed to British troops by female Russian prostitutes and the spread of epidemic diseases such as typhus, cholera,

---

[1] 'Russian Refugees: Report to the Council on March 24th, 1922 by Dr. Nansen', *Official Journal* (May 1922), annex 321, 387.
[2] Foreign Office Minutes. BFO 371/N12256 and N12416.

and smallpox.[3] Consequently, the British government authorized a donation of £20,000 in cash and kind. In addition, private organizations, including a coalition of women's groups, the Jewish Colonization Association, and the ICRC, contributed a further £9,000. With this money, Nansen bought enough flour to feed 10,000 people for two months, and established a special office of the League of Nations at Constantinople.[4]

But emergency measures alone did not provide a lasting solution to this refugee problem. Sir Samuel Hoare, the new head of the office at Constantinople, clearly stated what was needed: £30,000 more to finance the evacuation of 15,000 Russian refugees from Constantinople.[5] The British and French governments, having already contributed significant sums for Russian refugees, gave Hoare's idea a lukewarm reception.[6] Unexpectedly, support for the proposal came from outside Europe when, in March 1922, representatives of the American Relief Administration and the American Red Cross appeared before the Council, the first United States citizens to do so. They offered to feed the refugees for four months provided the League paid for their evacuation.[7] This generous offer bought the time the High Commissioner for Refugees needed. Nansen raised £50,000 to pay for the evacuations, including £11,700 from governments, £15,000 from the American Red Cross, and £23,000 from the High Commissioner's private fund.[8]

With the above contributions, the High Commissioner paid the

[3] Foreign Office Minute, Eastern Department, re Appeal of League of Nations for £30,000 from France, Britain, and Italy for starving in Constantinople, 7 Dec. 1921. BFO 371/6872/N13517.

[4] The National Council of Women of Norway, Danish National Council of Women, Swedish National Council of Women, and Women of Iceland donated £1,000 earmarked for Russian refugee women. The Jewish Colonization Association donated £1,000 and made a short-term loan of £3,000. The ICRC promised a gift for credit equal to 200,000 French francs (£3,450) and the Conférence universelle juive made a gift of 25,000 French francs (£430). 'Report to the Council of 24 March 1922 by Dr. Nansen', 388. (French francs converted to pounds at the rate of £1 = 58 French francs, the franc's high for 1921.)

[5] 'Russian Refugees in Constantinople: Report by Sir Samuel Hoare Presented to the Council on March 24th, 1922', Official Journal (May 1922), annex 321(b), p. 401.

[6] 'Minutes of the 17th Session of the Council', Official Journal (May 1922), 375–9.

[7] 'Minutes of the 18th Session of the Council', Official Journal (June 1922), 530; Sir John Hope Simpson, The Refugee Problem, Report of a Survey (London: Oxford University Press, 1939), 175.

[8] 'Russian Refugees: Report by Dr. Nansen, Submitted to the Council of 7 July 1923', Official Journal (Aug. 1923), annex 542, pp. 1041–2.

188 CONFRONTING BARRIERS TO IMMIGRATION

travel expenses of the refugees to countries willing to accept
them. In addition, its delegates often helped refugees get visas or
identity papers. International and national private organizations
also aided in the evacuation, either by contributing money or by
arranging for entrance to a host country. The American Red Cross,
for instance, arranged for 1,800 Russian refugees to emigrate to
the United States. Once inside the country, the Russian Refugee
Relief Society of America helped to ease their transition. Similarly, in France, a private organization called Placement Familial
received over fifty orphan refugee boys who emigrated under the
auspices of the High Commissioner. As a result of these efforts by
multiple actors in the international refugee regime, a successful
example of international co-operation was achieved. Nansen reported to the Council in July 1923 that over 20,000 refugees had
been evacuated to over forty-four different countries worldwide.[9]
This achievement even surprised sceptics at the British Foreign
Office, bureaucrats who had tried unsuccessfully for over a year
to get eastern European countries to accept refugees under their
control.[10]

Although refugees from Constantinople emigrated to countries
all over the world, host countries in eastern Europe were crucial
to the success of the programme because they accepted the majority of the refugees. The peoples of eastern Europe generally shared
with the Russian refugees a common Slav heritage and a distrust of the newly formed Soviet Union. Within this region, Yugoslavia distinguished itself as a host country for Russian refugees.
Because Serbs, the dominant ethnic group within the pan-Slav
republic, had strong ethnic, religious, and political ties to Tsarist
Russia, the Yugoslavian government considered itself specially
obligated to assist Russian refugees. Thousands of Russians went
from Constantinople to Yugoslavia, bringing the total number of
refugees in the country to over 40,000. Many of these refugees
went to work in the army and civil service, fulfilling the newly
created government's need for professionals. In addition, the
Yugoslavian government, aided by religious institutions and other
philanthropic groups, devised an extensive network aimed at

[9] 'Report to the Council of 7 July 1923', 1042.
[10] Memorandum by P. V. E. Evans on Russian Refugees in Serbia, 19 Oct. 1921.
BFO 371/6870/N11574.

assisting the refugees, making it 'one of the most striking examples of government hospitality to refugees' in inter-war Europe.[11]

THE ILO AND RUSSIAN AND ARMENIAN REFUGEES

At the time of Nansen's appointment as High Commissioner, it was widely believed that the experiment in Communism taking place in the Soviet Union would soon collapse and mass repatriation of Russian refugees would be possible. By the mid-1920s, however, it became clear that the Russian refugees would have to continue their exile for an undetermined period and longer-term arrangements were required. In 1924 Nansen recommended to the League of Nations that the ILO be entrusted with the task of promoting the emigration and employment of refugees, while the High Commissioner continued to be responsible for their legal protection.[12] In making this suggestion, Nansen had the support of Albert Thomas, the fiery Socialist Frenchman who headed the ILO and had the confidence of the large Russian refugee community in Paris.[13] Both Nansen and Thomas shared an interest in combating the problem of general unemployment. They hoped to use the ILO's work for jobless refugees as a basis for tackling this greater project.[14]

Although most members of the international refugee regime approved of the ILO's direct involvement in the area of refugee employment, not all of them desired movement in this direction. In discussions at the Fifth Assembly in September 1924, the French Delegate, M. Sarraut, spoke in favour of transferring refugee work to the ILO, saying that it constituted an inherently international service because of the variety of nationalities involved and the number of states receiving them. Delegates from Italy, Britain,

[11] Sir John Hope Simpson, *Refugees: Preliminary Report of a Survey* (London: Royal Institute of International Affairs, 1938), 123–7; Marc Raeff, *Russia Abroad: A Cultural History of the Russian Emigration, 1919–1939* (New York: Oxford University Press, 1990), 39.

[12] 'Minutes of the 29th Session of the Council', *Official Journal* (July 1924), 904–6.

[13] Robert H. Johnston, *New Mecca, New Babylon: Paris and the Russian Exiles, 1920–1945* (Kingston, Ontario: McGill-Queen's University Press, 1988), 73.

[14] T. F. Johnson, *International Tramps: From Chaos to Permanent World Peace* (London: Hutchinson, 1938), 249; letter from Nansen to Robert Cecil, 27 May 1927. NP, MS fo. 1988. S.5.B).

Poland, Czechoslovakia, Austria, Romania, Brazil, Yugoslavia, Bulgaria, Ireland, Belgium, Spain, Switzerland, and Uruguay all supported the French resolution. But a vocal minority disagreed. The delegate from South Africa, supported by delegates from Australia and Venezuela, argued that finding jobs for refugees did not properly fall within the scope of the League of Nations. The British representative, Mrs Swanwick, strongly objected to the South African position. She insisted that refugee assistance fell within the broad mandate 'to promote international co-operation' given in the preamble of the Covenant of the League of Nations.[15] In the end the Fifth Assembly approved the transfer and allocated 203,000 gold francs (about £8,000) for administrative expenses.[16] Shortly afterwards the Governing Body of the ILO concurred, on condition that the ILO concern itself only with the 'investigation, co-ordination and communication of offers of employment' to refugees and not provide any funds for direct relief.[17]

From 1925 until 1929 the ILO provided a service unique in the history of the international refugee regime. The Refugee Service, headed by T. F. Johnson, Nansen's former assistant, matched refugees looking for jobs with employers in other countries looking for workers. The Refugee Service helped by arranging for refugee emigration and transportation. The process whereby refugees were selected for jobs took place under the watchful eye of the local agents of the Refugee Service, agricultural and medical advisers, prospective employers, and representatives of refugee organizations. In this way, the Service hoped both to prevent the exploitation of refugees by their future employers and to preclude the formation of a monopoly by refugees of one political persuasion.[18] Though simple in conception, the existence of a myriad of immigration restrictions made the practical implementation of this durable solution difficult. In Europe, France alone sustained a significant demand for labour.

In an effort to overcome immigration restrictions in European countries, the Refugee Service turned to Latin America as a place

[15] *Official Journal*, Special Supplement no. 23, Fifth Assembly, Fifth Committee (Geneva, 1924), 18–30.

[16] *Official Journal*, Special Supplement no. 23, Fifth Assembly, Plenary Meetings: Text of the Debates (Geneva, 1924), 153.

[17] ILO, Governing Body, Resolution of 10 Oct. 1924.

[18] 'Report of the Work for the Refugees by the Director of the ILO', *Official Journal*, Special Supplement no. 38, Sixth Assembly, Fifth Committee (Geneva, 1925), 120–1.

for refugee colonization. In 1925 the ILO sent a mission, headed by Colonel Proctor, to Latin America.[19] After a five-month visit to Argentina, Brazil, Paraguay, and Uruguay, the team optimistically reported that 'the possibilities of obtaining suitable employment for refugees in these countries are considerable'.[20] Acting on this favourable report, the ILO set up two offices in Latin America and commenced negotiations with governments there. In order to finance the project, the ILO, in conjunction with the High Commissioner for Refugees, offered a unique and creative idea: the establishment of a revolving fund.

The idea of a revolving fund was an attempt to rationalize spending on refugee assistance. In 1926 nine governments reported to the League of Nations that they spent 20 million gold francs (£800,000) on refugees in their countries annually, a sum one hundred times that allotted to the Refugee Section of the ILO. High Commissioner Nansen bemoaned this state of affairs; he firmly believed that the money would be much better spent on securing settlement and employment for refugees rather than on providing short-term relief. To overcome this problem, he urged the creation of a revolving fund of 2.5 million gold francs (£100,000) to be used for major projects, including colonization in Latin America.[21] In order to solicit contributions to the revolving fund, Nansen convened an intergovernmental conference in June 1927, primarily attended by the major host countries of Europe (see Table 8). At the conference, the German delegate took the lead by offering a contribution of 100,000 RM (£5,000) but others were slow to follow.[22] A year later Nansen had only one addition to report: an offer by the Czechoslovakian government to provide £12,500 for the transfer of unemployed refugees from its country.[23]

[19] The mission also included Professor Varlez, Chief of the Migration Service of the ILO, Professor Brunst, selected by the refugee organizations, an agricultural expert, and representatives of the Jewish Colonization Association and the Conférence universelle juive de Secours.

[20] 'Report on the Work for Refugees by the Director of the ILO', 122.

[21] High Commissioner for Refugees and the Director of the ILO, 'Russian and Armenian Refugees: Report to the Seventh Assembly' (3 Sept. 1926) [A.44.1926], 7–8. The nine countries consisted of Bulgaria, Estonia, Finland, Greece, Latvia, Poland, Yugoslavia, Switzerland, and Czechoslovakia.

[22] High Commissioner for Refugees and the Director of the ILO, 'Russian and Armenian Refugees: Report to the Eighth Assembly' (1927) [A.48.1927.XIII], 3.

[23] High Commissioner for Refugees and the Director of the ILO, 'Measures in Favour of Russian, Armenian, Assyrian, Assyro-Chaldean and Turkish Refugees: Report to the Ninth Assembly' (1928) [A.33.1928.VIII], 7.

Without adequate financing, the plans for refugee colonies in Latin America faltered; the Refugee Service placed only 450 refugees there, primarily in Argentina. In his report to the Ninth Assembly in 1928, Thomas acknowledged the high cost of transporting and establishing a refugee family in an agricultural setting as the primary reason for this result.[24] But the report neglected to mention one other important reason for this failure: the strong opposition of most Russian refugees to the scheme. After the publication of Colonel Proctor's report, Russian refugee organizations in Paris, the intellectual centre of the migration, launched a series of meetings on the subject. The plan, which put Russian refugees into the role of agricultural colonists in tropical areas, proved to be unpopular for a variety of reasons. Prominent Russian refugee organizations listed political disturbances, a hostile local population, unfamiliar climate, and working conditions akin to slavery as reasons for rejection of the plan.[25] Perhaps most importantly, relocating to Latin America would have been tantamount to giving up hope of return to their beloved homeland, something few Russian refugees were prepared to do in 1925.

Although the prospects for colonization did not meet initial expectations, the Refugee Service achieved better results elsewhere. From 1925 until the end of 1928 the Refugee Service placed 50,000 refugees directly into employment and a large number indirectly.[26] These refugees came from European countries and China, and found employment primarily in France. In addition, the Service found refugees jobs elsewhere in Europe, in North and South America, the Middle East, and Asia.[27] Overall, the ILO claimed credit for reducing the total number of able-bodied unemployed Armenian and Russian refugees by fifty per cent, from 400,000 to 200,000.[28] Although these efforts were never transferred to the

---

[24] [A.33.1928.VIII], 15–16.

[25] For instance, see minutes of the Russian Red Cross meeting held in Paris in Jan. 1926; report by Zemgor (Russian Zemstvos and Towns Relief Committee) of 1 Aug. 1925. LNA C1383.

[26] [A.33.1928.VIII], 11–12. In 1929 refugee assistance was placed under the direction of the Secretariat of the League of Nations.

[27] [A.48.1927.XIII], 18–19. The Service placed refugees in Argentina, Armenia, Australia, Belgium, Brazil, Canada, Cuba, Egypt, France, Luxembourg, Mexico, Paraguay, Russia, Syria, the USA, and Uruguay.

[28] [A.33.1928.VIII], 11. ILO statistics on the number of unemployed refugees are not consistent. In his 1925 report to the Assembly the Director of the ILO listed 200,000 unemployed Russian and Armenian refugees. In his 1927 report he

problem of general unemployment, the Refugee Service succeeded in providing a durable solution for the refugees that it placed. This was a significant accomplishment given the immigration restrictions and lack-lustre economic conditions of the period.

Although the plan for a revolving fund did not produce the hoped-for results, the League of Nations successfully implemented a more modest financing scheme. Under this system, every non-indigent refugee paid a small sum for the issue of a Nansen passport; then this money could be used to assist other refugees. Because the fund came from refugees, a special sub-committee made up of representatives of refugee organizations helped to determine how the money should be distributed.[29] Although this method of financing generated complaints from refugees who objected to paying an annual fee for their papers, it did benefit refugees as a group.[30] By the 1930s the Nansen stamp fund formed the nucleus of a humanitarian fund large enough to help refugees become self-supporting. In 1934, for instance, the Nansen Office assisted 782 refugees through the provision of small loans. The refugees used the loans to establish businesses, including twelve restaurants, five laundries, five tobacco shops, five rabbit farms, and a doll factory.[31] Unfortunately, this worthwhile programme was eventually discontinued because officials of the League of Nations found it required a 'complicated system of accounts'. In its place, High Commissioner Emerson adopted the policy of only giving grants to organizations, not to individual refugees.[32]

writes that 'at the time of the transfer of the refugee work to the Office, it was estimated that there were approximately 400,000 unemployed Russian and Armenian refugees'. The report goes on to say that this estimate could be revised to a grand total of 304,650 unemployed refugees, in the light of recent returns of the ILO census. But the report later contradicts this by concluding that 'at the time of the transfer of the work to the Office, their number [Russian refugees] had been reduced to 200,000, to which had to be added 200,000 Armenian refugees'. The 1928 report repeats the estimate that there were 400,000 able-bodied unemployed Russian and Armenian refugees in 1925 and that this had been reduced to approximately 200,000.

[29] [A.48.1927.XIII], 2.
[30] Johnston, *New Mecca, New Babylon*, 73.
[31] League of Nations, Nansen International Office for Refugees, 'Report of the Governing Body' (20 Aug. 1934) [A.12.1934], 10.
[32] League of Nations, 'International Assistance to Refugees: Report by Sir Herbert Emerson, High Commissioner for Refugees' (24 July 1939) [A.18.1939.XII], 3.

194 CONFRONTING BARRIERS TO IMMIGRATION

THE RESPONSE TO REFUGEES FROM THE THIRD REICH: 1933-1937

After Hitler's rise to power in 1933, the actors in the international refugee regime confronted yet another mass exodus: the flight of refugees from Germany. Unlike the Greek, Turkish, and Bulgarian refugees, these had no national homeland willing to accept them *en masse*. Consequently, they had to find new homes through the process of individual migration. Unlike the Russian and Armenian refugees, these fled their home country during the worst global economic depression of the century. In response to record levels of unemployment, many governments made their immigration restrictions even tighter.[33] Since virtually all countries treated refugees just like other immigrants, refugees from Germany had to compete with economic migrants in their search for new homes. In this process, the refugees were severely disadvantaged because they often lacked the financial resources and vocational skills desired by countries of immigration.

In addition, the pervasiveness of anti-Semitism world-wide made immigration difficult for refugees from Germany, the majority of whom were Jews.[34] Although the governments of eastern Europe had welcomed thousands of Russian refugees, they opposed the entry of Jewish refugees from Germany; to admit more Jews would only have added to their already large, unwanted Jewish minorities.[35] The Soviet Union, also a country with a significant Jewish population, refused to accept Jewish refugees as well. In Latin America, some countries—including Bolivia, Chile, Peru, and Venezuela—explicitly restricted the entry of Jews.[36] Even in the democratic countries of the world, including the United States, Great Britain, France, the Netherlands, Australia, and Canada,

[33] See above, Ch. 2.

[34] In 1933 about 60,000 refugees fled the Third Reich. Of these, about 9,000, or 15 per cent, were non-Jews. As time progressed, however, the migration became increasingly Jewish. By Dec. 1937, 150,000 had fled Germany, including 15,000 non-Jews, or about 10 per cent of the total. By August 1939 the total number of refugees from the Third Reich had reached 400,000, including 40,000 non-Jews, or about 10 per cent of the total. This meant that 90 per cent of the total number of refugees were Jews. See above, Ch. 2, and Simpson, *The Refugee Problem*, 140-1.

[35] See Ezra Mendelsohn, *The Jews of East Central Europe between the World Wars* (Bloomington, Ind.: Indiana University Press, 1983).

[36] See above, Ch. 1.

anti-Semitism was a factor which mitigated against the entry of Jews.[37]

Moreover, in contrast to most refugees of the 1920s, refugees fleeing the Third Reich in the 1930s had the misfortune to be from a Great Power on the rise in world politics. Although the Russian refugees fled a Great Power, they did so at a time when the Soviet Union was a weak and isolated state, unable to affect significantly the policies of other countries towards its former citizens. In contrast, the German government in the 1930s had increasing influence throughout Europe and Latin America. The ascendancy of Germany particularly affected the ability of the League of Nations to respond effectively to refugees from there. Because the League operated on a consensus basis, the German delegation could exercise a unit-veto over the refugee policies of the organization as long as it was a member. Even after Germany withdrew from the League, a desire on the part of France, Britain, and other members to appease Germany hindered the organization's ability to deal with the problem.[38] As a result, the League of Nations, the actor in the international refugee regime which had done so much for refugees in the 1920s, lacked a strong mandate from its leading members for dealing with the German refugee crisis. Moreover, the death of Nansen in 1930 meant that the greatest humanitarian of the era would not be there to guide the League through this crisis.

[37] While there seems to be general agreement among scholars that anti-Semitism was a factor in the response of the democratic countries to Jewish refugees, its importance relative to other considerations is a matter of debate. In writing of the United States, David Wyman argues that unemployment, nativistic nationalism, and anti-Semitism combined to create public resistance to refugees. In contrast, Richard Breitman and Alan Kraut identify 'bureaucratic indifference to moral or humanitarian concerns' as the key factor shaping refugee policy during the Roosevelt years. See David Wyman, *Paper Walls: America and the Refugee Crisis, 1938–1941* (New York: Pantheon Books, 1985), 3–23; Richard Breitman and Alan M. Kraut, *American Refugee Policy and European Jewry, 1933–1945* (Bloomington, Ind.: Indiana University Press, 1987), 1–10; Bernard Wasserstein, 'The British Government and the German Immigration 1933–1945', in Gerhard Hirschfeld (ed.), *Exile in Great Britain* (Leamington Spa: Berg Publishers, 1984), 64; Timothy P. Maga, 'Closing the Door: The French Government and Refugee Policy, 1933–1939', *French Historical Studies*, 12 (Spring 1982), 430; Bob Moore, *Refugees from Nazi Germany in the Netherlands 1933–1940* (Dordrecht: Martinus Nijhoff, 1986), 106–7; Michael Blakeney, *Australia and the Jewish Refugees, 1933–1948* (Australia: Croom Helm, 1985), 161; Gerald E. Dirks, *Canada's Refugee Policy: Indifference or Opportunism?* (Montreal: McGill-Queen's University Press, 1977), 53–5.

[38] Marrus, *The Unwanted*, 128–9; Maga, 'Closing the Door', 432.

The Action of the League of Nations

Despite the reluctance of the Great Powers to place refugees from Germany under the protection of the League of Nations, other members urged action.[39] At the Fourteenth Assembly, held in October 1933, M. de Graeff, Minister of Foreign Affairs of the Netherlands, advocated that the League take action because its 'competence to deal with them [refugee problems] was an accepted fact'. De Graeff further stressed that the border states and private organizations alone could not meet the needs of the refugees for material assistance, employment, and travel documents. De Graeff's proposal grew out of the Dutch government's desire that some international aid be given to the 'front-line' states, the countries bordering Germany which thus far had hosted most of the refugees. It also reflected its desire not to offend the German government at a time when the primary issue before the Assembly was disarmament. Consequently, de Graeff described the problem as a purely technical one and stressed that the Assembly in no way wanted to intervere in Germany's internal affairs.[40] Initially the Dutch government wanted the League to assist only Jewish refugees, because they believed this would interest the German government in the proposal. Moreover, the Dutch government was reluctant to assist Socialist and Communist refugees, whom they viewed as a political threat. This plan, however, also created the fear that if the League improved the welfare of Jewish refugees, then Germany, Poland, and other countries would take advantage of it and encourage more of their Jewish minorities to leave.[41] Representatives of the Jewish community eventually persuaded the Dutch to broaden their proposal because they did not want the refugees to be seen as purely a 'Jewish problem'.[42]

In discussions in the Second Committee, delegates from Czechoslovakia, France, Poland, Spain, Denmark, Portugal, and Italy all spoke favourably of the Dutch proposal but the German delegate

[39] The first reference to the German refugee problem in an IGO came when the General Labour Conference passed a resolution relating to refugees and the labour markets of the receiving states in June 1933. See Louise W. Holborn, 'The League of Nations and the Refugee Problem', *Annals*, 203 (May 1939), 133.

[40] *Official Journal*, Special Supplement no. 117, Fourteenth Assembly, Second Committee (Geneva, 1933), 22–9. Moore, *Refugees from Nazi Germany*, 99–101.

[41] Moore, *Refugees from Nazi Germany*, 100–1.

[42] Barbara McDonald Stewart, *United States Government Policy on Refugees from Nazism, 1933–1940* (New York: Garland Press, 1982), 98.

strongly objected to it. Using the threat of a veto, the German government managed to win major concessions in a compromise arrangement essentially worked out by the British and French delegates. In particular, it won the concession that the refugees would not be placed within the mandate of the Nansen Office, but rather under the auspices of a separate organization which the League would not directly finance. Although the Dutch government had originally stressed that it was of capital importance to establish a very close link between the organization and the League, they gave this up because of their desire to have some action taken.[43]

In October 1933 the Council of the League of Nations appointed an American, James G. McDonald, to be the High Commissioner for Refugees (Jewish and other) coming from Germany. In selecting a national of a powerful but neutral country, it was hoped that McDonald could increase the involvement of the United States government in the League, win major funds from wealthy American Jews, and transcend European political divisions. Since McDonald had assisted Jewish leaders in lobbying for the establishment of a High Commission, he seemed to be a logical choice. Moreover, McDonald had extensive knowledge of and experience in foreign affairs. A former professor of history and politics, McDonald had served as Chairman of the Foreign Policy Association since 1919. This work brought him into contact with the major political issues of the day, and with key New York and national leaders. McDonald had the confidence of the New York Jewish community. He counted among his personal friends Felix Warburg, a member of the Schiff banking family by marriage, and the head of the Joint Distribution Committee, the largest Jewish relief agency.[44]

From the beginning of his tenure as High Commissioner, McDonald's work was hampered by his separation from the League. Headquarters had to be set in Lausanne, rather than in Geneva, the seat of the League. Joseph Avenol, Secretary-General of the League, made McDonald's independent status clear to him in their

---

[43] *Official Journal*, Special Supplement no. 117, Fourteenth Assembly, Second Committee (Geneva, 1933), 22–9, 47–8; Moore, *Refugees from Nazi Germany*, 101.

[44] For information on McDonald's career, see his obituary in the *New York Times*, 27 Sept. 1964. On his appointment as High Commissioner, see Stewart, *US Government Policy*, 103–9; Yehuda Bauer, *My Brother's Keeper: A History of the American Jewish Joint Distribution Committee, 1929–1939* (Philadelphia: Jewish Publication Society of America, 1974), 142.

first meeting. Avenol stressed the separate status of the High Commissioner, who was to report to the Commission's own Governing Body, not to the League Assembly.[45] To add insult to injury, Avenol insisted that the initial 25,000 Swiss francs given by the League to begin operations was only a loan and had to be repaid within a year.[46] At the time, Avenol, a member of the appeasement school with strong sympathies towards the extreme right, wanted to placate the German government.[47]

As High Commissioner, McDonald had a twofold task: (1) coordination of relief and settlement efforts; (2) negotiations with governments to facilitate refugee travel and settlement. Under this division of labour, voluntary agencies still maintained responsibility for financing the relief, emigration, and settlement of refugees. Because McDonald lacked strong support from the League, the help of private organizations became even more important than it had been for High Commissioner Nansen and the Refugee Section of the ILO. Following the Nansen model, McDonald established an Advisory Council of private organizations made up of twenty-five Jewish and non-Jewish agencies (see Table 16). With only lukewarm support from governments, the private organizations, especially the Anglo-American Jewish ones, became the major source of funds for the High Commissioner.[48] With their support, McDonald paid the loan back within a year.

During his tenure as High Commissioner, McDonald concentrated his meagre resources on facilitating refugee immigration; he did not control sufficient funds to propose major refugee settlement projects. McDonald and his staff conducted negotiations on refugee travel and emigration with all the governments

---

[45] The Governing Body included government representatives from Great Britain, Denmark, the United States, France, Italy, the Netherlands, Poland, Sweden, Switzerland, Czechoslovakia, and Uruguay. See minutes of the Governing Body, Dec. 1933–Oct. 1935. LNA C1616/13.

[46] James G. McDonald, 'Refugees', in Harriet Eager Davis (ed.), *Pioneers in World Order: An American Appraisal of the League of Nations* (New York: Columbia University Press, 1944), 218.

[47] James Barros, *Betrayal from Within: Joseph Avenol, Secretary-General of the League of Nations, 1933–1940* (New Haven, Conn.: Yale University Press, 1969), 24–6.

[48] In its first six months of operations the High Commissioner operated on a budget of about £10,000. This included a loan from the League of £1,560 and contributions of £1,250 from the Central British Fund for German Jewry, £4,000 from the JDC, £2,500 from the Jewish Colonization Association, and £700 from individual donors. See Statement from 1 Nov. 1933 to 31 Mar. 1934 of the High Commissioner for Refugees (Jewish and other) coming from Germany. JGM H6.

TABLE 16. *Advisory Committee to the High Commissioner for Refugees Coming from Germany, 1933–1935*

Jewish Organizations (12)
American Jewish Joint Distribution Committee
Jewish Colonization Association
Jewish Agency for Palestine
Alliance Israélite Universelle
American Jewish Community
French Jewish Community
Anglo-Jewish Community
Belgian Jewish Community
Netherlands Jewish Community
Polish Jewish Community
Comité des Délégations Juives[1]
Agudas Israel

Non-Jewish Organizations (14)
Catholic organizations
Conseil Œcuménique du Christianisme pratique
L'Office central d'Entr'Aide des Eglises
Society of Friends
International Federation of Trade Unions
International Migration Service
International Committee for the Placement of Intellectual Refugees
International Save the Children Fund
Emergency Committee in Aid of Displaced German Scholars
Academic Assistance Council
Netherlands Academic Committee
International Student Service
Comité national (français) de secours aux réfugiés
Comité national tchécoslovaque pour les réfugiés provenant d'Allemagne.

Source: 'Liste des organisations israélites etc. représentées au Comité Consultatif, mai 1934', LNA C1616/no. 13.

[1] Representing the Jewish Communities of central and eastern Europe, Greece, and Italy.

of Europe and North America.[49] In 1934 he and an associate visited several South American republics to discuss the possibility of Jewish colonization there. But this mission repeated the earlier experiences of the ILO; the Jewish colonists proved to be unsuitable for positions as agricultural workers in this tropical

[49] LNA C1609, C1610, C1611.

area.[50] In negotiations with his home country, McDonald also found himself rebuffed. Despite a personal appeal to President Roosevelt, the State Department refused to increase the number of visas for German refugees. At the time, only a small fraction of the quota for Germany was being utilized. In addition, the United States government never followed through on promises of financial support for the High Commissioner.[51]

McDonald did produce results in one key area: convincing governments to accept academic refugees. In this regard, the High Commission acted as a co-ordinating body for several organizations assisting intellectual refugees, including the Academic Assistance Council in Britain and national committees in France, Holland, Switzerland, Denmark, Sweden, and the United States. Together, national committees and private foundations contributed over £250,000 for the placement of academic refugees. By October 1935 almost 700 displaced German scholars had been placed, including 212 in Great Britain, 143 in the United States, and 47 in France.[52]

Although McDonald did not reverse the general trend towards more restrictive immigration policies, his High Commission facilitated the placement of almost two-thirds of the 80,000 refugees who left Germany between 1933 and 1935.[53] Of these, over 25,000 people, approximately one-third of the total, found asylum on the European continent. About the same number of refugees, 27,000, migrated to Palestine. About 9,000, 10 per cent of the total, settled permanently in the Americas. In addition, 18,000 people, slightly over 20 per cent of the total, went to Poland; this group primarily consisted of Polish Jews who had been naturalized by Germany after the First World War but were deprived of their citizenship by the Nazis (see Table 5).[54]

[50] LNA C1608/9 (Brazil, 33–6); Bauer, *My Brother's Keeper*, 145.

[51] LNA C1611/3 (USA, 33–6); Bauer, *My Brother's Keeper*, 148; Stewart, *US Government Policy*, 152–9. In 1933 only 5.3 per cent of the total quota for Germany and Austria was utilized. In 1934 this figure rose to 13.7 per cent. See Wyman, *Paper Walls*, 221.

[52] Norman Bentwich, *The Rescue and Achievement of Refugee Scholars: The Story of Displaced Scholars and Scientists, 1933–1952* (The Hague: Martinus Nijhoff, 1953), 10–20. See also Gerhard Hirschfeld, 'German Refugee Scholars in Great Britain, 1933–1945', in Anna C. Bramwell (ed.), *Refugees in the Age of Total War* (London: Unwin Hyman, 1988), 152–63.

[53] James G. McDonald, *Letter of Resignation... Addressed to the Secretary-General of the League of Nations* (London, 1935), 33–4; Simpson, *The Refugee Problem*, 562.   [54] Simpson, *The Refugee Problem*, 562–3.

In September 1935 the promulgation of the Nuremburg Laws forced still more refugees to flee. To McDonald, this event made it clear that the promotion of any durable solution for refugees from Germany now required that the Nazi policies which forced people to flee needed to be confronted directly. Consequently, he urged the League of Nations to deal with the root causes of the German refugee crisis; to emphasize his point, he resigned from his post in a dramatic protest. The outcome of his attempt to deal with the root causes of the German refugee crisis will be discussed further in the following chapter.

After McDonald's resignation, the League of Nations appointed a new High Commissioner for Refugees from Germany, Sir Neill Malcolm. Unlike McDonald, Malcolm was a League official and received his administrative expenses from the League budget. As High Commissioner, Malcolm concentrated his efforts on developing a legal status for German refugees. In effect, this meant that the League of Nations left questions of emigration and settlement for refugees from Germany entirely to private organizations, with the one exception of refugees who fled the Saar just before the return of this territory to Germany after the plebiscite of 1935. At the request of the French delegate on the Council, the Nansen Office was given charge of approximately 7,000 Saar refugees. In this case, the League deviated from its own rules and accepted responsibility for both the legal protection and settlement of the refugees. It did so because of its prior role in administering the Saar territory and because the French government offered to provide the funds for settlement.[55] Moreover, these refugees, both Jewish and non-Jewish, brought with them more financial resources than the Jews who fled non-Saar Germany itself; they were able to depart with their property intact because of intervention on their behalf from Mussolini.[56] With the approval of the Council, the Nansen Office arranged for the emigration and settlement of Saar refugees in Paraguay. Despite having full advantage of these services, fewer than two hundred people settled in the colony. In explaining why so few Saar refugees moved to Paraguay, the Nansen Office reported that 'the Saar refugees, being mostly

---

[55] 'Minutes of the 84th Session of the Council', *Official Journal* (Feb. 1935), 276–7; 'Minutes of the 86th Session of the Council', *Official Journal* (June 1935), 633–6.

[56] Meir Michaelis, *Mussolini and the Jews: German–Italian Relations and the Jewish Question in Italy 1922–1945* (Oxford: Clarendon Press, 1978), 68.

labourers or miners who have always lived in industrial centres, were not qualified for the heavy work, or able to endure the hardships, which a colonist's life entails'.[57]

The Role of Private, Voluntary Organizations

Among the refugees from the Third Reich, the Saar refugees were a privileged class. The vast majority of German refugees could not tap the resources of the Nansen Office but had to rely solely on the assistance of private organizations in the emigration process. From 1933 until 1937 these organizations effectively managed the orderly emigration of refugees from Germany to Palestine and other locations. Although a variety of sources supported these endeavours, the Anglo-American Jewish communities provided the majority of the financial resources. From 1933 until 1939 British Jewry spent a total of £3 million on refugee assistance, primarily dispersed through the Central British Fund (1933–5) and the Council for German Jewry (1936–9).[58] In the United States, the American Jewish Joint Distribution Committee (JDC), the largest American-Jewish relief agency, spent over 20 million dollars (£4 million) on assistance to Jews in Europe and elsewhere over the same period.[59]

The largest private organization in the field of emigration aid was the Jewish organization HICEM. Originally formed in 1926 out of three immigrant aid organizations,[60] HICEM derived most of its financing from the JDC, the Jewish Colonization Association, and the British Council for German Jewry. In the first three years of the Nazi regime HICEM assisted 14,000 refugees to leave Germany at a cost of 600,000 dollars (£120,000). By 1940 HICEM had assisted almost 40,000 refugees, at a cost of nearly one million dollars (£250,000). In helping refugees to emigrate, HICEM provided a variety of services, including giving advice to prospective emigrants, helping to obtain visas, and financing transportation costs. Within Germany, HICEM collaborated closely with the

[57] League of Nations, Nansen International Office for Refugees, 'Report of the Governing Body' (10 Aug. 1938) [A.21.1938.XII], 9.
[58] Norman Bentwich, *They Found Refuge* (London, 1956), 41.
[59] Bauer, *My Brother's Keeper*, 25.
[60] HICEM combined the initials of its three component groups: HIAS (Hebrew Sheltering and Immigrant Aid Society), ICA (Jewish Colonization Association), and Emigdirect.

Hilfsverein der Juden in Deutschland, an organization which helped Jews emigrate to other countries. From 1934 until 1938 this organization arranged and paid for the departure of almost 30,000 German Jews to countries around the world, excluding Palestine. Like HICEM, the Hilfsverein received its funding from the JDC and the British Council for German Jewry.[61]

The Jewish Agency for Palestine organized the emigration of German Jews to Palestine. Established at the end of the nineteenth century, the Jewish Agency was a Zionist organization attempting to build a Jewish homeland in Palestine. Since the creation of a British mandate in Palestine after the First World War, the Jewish Agency had been actively involved in helping Jews from Europe to emigrate there. Like HICEM, it provided a variety of services for German emigrants, including arranging for entry permits, subsidizing transportation, and providing job training. A special branch of the organization, the Youth Aliyah, specifically concentrated on the emigration of German youth. Overall, the Jewish Agency helped a substantial number of the German Jews emigrate. In 1934, for example, almost half of the 8,500 German emigrants to Palestine received funding from it.[62] Because of the efforts of the Jewish Agency and the unwillingness of other countries to admit Jewish refugees, Palestine became one of the major places of refuge for Jewish refugees from Germany. By the end of 1937 approximately 42,000 people, or nearly 30 per cent of the total number of refugees, had settled in Palestine (see Table 5).[63]

The extensive emigration services available for Jewish refugees contrasted sharply with the paucity of assistance available for the approximately 15,000 non-Jewish refugees. Of these, many had ties to the Social Democratic and Communist parties and found themselves unwelcome in host countries because of their leftist views. For instance, in the Netherlands, a country which hosted thousands of Jewish refugees, the government harrassed, interned, and deported Marxist refugees in a deliberate attempt to make the country seem as unwelcome as possible.[64] Consequently, the

[61] Tartakower and Grossman, *The Jewish Refugee*, 457–63; Marrus, *The Unwanted*, 182–3.

[62] Tartakower and Grossman, *The Jewish Refugee*, 463–4; Simpson, *The Refugee Problem*, 188, 435–8.   [63] Simpson, *The Refugee Problem*, 562–3.

[64] One of the few extensive treatments of government policy towards Socialist and Communist refugees can be found in Moore, *Refugees from Nazi Germany*, 139–79.

primary source of assistance for left-wing refugees came from politically sympathetic groups. The Matteotti Funds, especially in Denmark and Sweden, provided aid to Social Democrats. Communist refugees had to turn to the European Secretariat of Red Help for aid.

The non-Jewish refugees also included people labelled as 'non-Aryans', often Jews who had converted to Catholicism. Assistance for these and other Christian refugees was not well organized. In the early 1930s many of the British religious organizations which had been so helpful to the Armenian refugees were totally absorbed in the plight of the Assyrians, a Christian minority forced to become refugees after Iraq became an independent state.[65] In the United States, both Catholic and Protestant voluntary organizations failed to raise significant amounts of money to assist Christian refugees from Germany.[66] In Europe, some Catholic organizations, particularly the Catholic Committee at Utrecht, did assist Catholic refugees. Internationally, it was not until January 1936 that an International Christian Committee for German Refugees was created. An exception to the generally slow response on the part of Christian organizations was that of the Society of Friends (Quakers). Shortly after refugees began to flee Germany, the Quakers set up an Emergency Committee to help all types of refugees, including Jews, Christians, Social Democrats, and Communists.[67]

Overall, the outstanding work of the private organizations, especially Jewish ones, helped to manage effectively the first four years of the exodus from Germany. Approximately one-half of the people who fled Germany during this time did so with the

---

[65] After the termination of the British mandate and the declaration of an independent Iraqi state, clashes between the Christian Assyrians and Muslim Iraqis emerged. Afterwards several thousand Assryians fled to Syria. Simpson, *Refugees: Preliminary Report*, 30–4; R. S. Stafford, 'Iraq and the Problem of the Assyrians', *International Affairs*, 13/2 (1934). On the work of British private organizations for these refugees, see Captain G. F. Gracey, 'The Truth about the Assyrians: Their Appeal to the Conscience and Sympathy of Christendom', *Evangelical Christendom: Organ of the World's Evangelical Alliance (British Organisations)* (Nov.–Dec. 1934), 205–8; *The Assyrian Settlement National Appeal*, address given by His Grace the Archbishop of Canterbury (London, 31 Mar. 1936). See also LNA C1533.

[66] Haim Genizi, *American Apathy: The Plight of Christian Refugees from Nazism* (Jerusalem: Bar-Ilan Press, 1983).

[67] Simpson, *The Refugee Problem*, 141–2, 180, 188–9.

assistance of a private organization.[68] In the Refugee Survey, Simpson praises the work of Jewish organizations from 1933 until 1937: 'Their work has been extremely efficient, and . . . the organizations were able to cope with the exodus in an orderly manner and to prevent dangerous accumulations of refugees in various centres.'[69] High Commissioner Malcolm also gave high marks to private organizations. In speaking of the first four years of the German exodus, Malcolm reports that 150,000 refugees had left Germany. Of these, about 120,000, or 80 per cent, had found permanent asylum overseas or in Europe. Based on these results, Malcolm concludes that 'this is a record which is highly creditable to the private organizations which have concerned themselves for many years with this problem of emigration and settlement'.[70]

Based on their record, it is fair to say that non-governmental organizations outpaced governments in fulfilling the obligations of the assistance norm of the international refugee regime. But it would be a mistake to see these efforts as totally independent of the activities of governments. For one, private organizations only flourish in particular types of societies, most notably democratic countries which allow for freedom of association. Moreover, a number of Jewish organizations carried out their work on the basis of agreement with national governments. Both the British and Dutch Jewish communities, for instance, guaranteed that any admitted to those countries would not become a public charge.

THE RESPONSE TO REFUGEES FROM THE THIRD REICH: 1938-1939

Until 1938 the actors in the international refugee regime successfully managed the exodus of refugees from Germany. Then, in

---

[68] Estimates of 'free' versus 'organized' emigration vary considerably. The Refugee Survey concludes that 'free emigration has been at least as great as organized emigration, and at times has been twice as great'. Simpson, *The Refugee Problem*, 143. Bauer estimates that 129,000 Jews left Germany between 1933 and 1937 and about two-thirds of these received help in emigration (*My Brother's Keeper*, 139).

[69] Simpson, *The Refugee Problem*, 186. Walter Adams reaches a similar conclusion in 'Extent and Nature of the World Refugee Problem', *Annals*, 203 (May 1939), 32.

[70] 'Speech of Sir Neill Malcolm', *Proceedings of the Intergovernmental Committee, Evian, July 6th to 15th, 1938: Verbatim Record of the Plenary Meetings of the Committee, Resolutions and Reports* (July 1938), 33.

1938, what had been an orderly exodus turned into a refugee crisis. In March of that year, Germany declared *Anschluss* with Austria, a move with devastating consequences for the 180,000 Jews living there. The implementation of an anti-Jewish programme, developed in Germany over a period of five years, took place in Austria in a few months. Thousands desperately tried to flee the country only to find their exit blocked.[71] Already struggling to cope with an influx, France, Switzerland, the Netherlands, and Belgium tightened immigration restrictions. Hungary and Yugoslavia, countries sharing borders with Austria, closed their doors completely. In Great Britain, the government introduced a visa requirement for Austrian immigrants.[72]

Unlike earlier refugees from Nazi Germany, Austrian refugees could not rely on an open door to Palestine. In reaction to the 1936 Arab rebellion in Palestine, the British government reversed its previous policy of allowing the admission of Jewish immigrants up to the 'economic capacity' of the country without numerical limits. In 1937 the government decided to limit Jewish immigration to not more than 12,000 per year for the next five years. This quota had to accommodate refugees from Germany and Austria, as well as Jewish immigrants from eastern Europe and the Soviet Union.[73] The quota sharply curtailed immigration to Palestine at a time when many desperately sought asylum. From 1933 until 1936 an average of over 41,000 Jews immigrated into Palestine each year. By 1937 the number of legal entrants dropped to 10,536. Legal immigration continued at the rate of 10,000–12,000 people for the rest of the decade.[74]

Despite increases in immigration restrictions, many Austrian Jews still tried to escape life under the Nazis by crossing international borders secretly, greatly increasing the number of illegal immigrants in Europe. For those who did manage to leave legally, they faced the difficult prospect of starting a new life virtually penniless. After paying flight taxes, emigrants from Austria left with only about 6 per cent of the value of their property.[75] Even

---

[71] See above, Ch. 2.   [72] Marrus, *The Unwanted*, 148, 169.

[73] Wasserstein, 'British Government', 69; Simpson, *The Refugee Problem*, 434–5.

[74] David H. Hopper, 'A Homeland for Refugees', *Annals*, 203 (May 1939), 170; Simpson, *The Refugee Problem*, 434.

[75] League of Nations, 'Refugees Coming from Germany: Report Submitted to the Nineteenth Assembly by Sir Neill Malcolm, High Commissioner' (22 Aug. 1938) [A.25.1938.XII], 6.

such a famous Viennese as Sigmund Freud did not escape paying the 'refugee tax'.[76]

The aftermath of *Anschluss* demonstrated that the resources of private organizations alone could not effectively deal with the refugee crisis. Private organizations providing refugee assistance had been calling for increased government assistance for German refugees since 1933. Now this need became acknowledged by governments, the official members of the international refugee regime. Faced with a similar situation in the Russian and Greek refugee crises, the governmental actors in the regime had turned to the League of Nations for leadership. In this instance, however, the League did not fulfil this role. This is not surprising given that the League's prestige had been badly damaged by the withdrawal of Germany, Japan, and Italy from the organization, and by its inability to resolve the Manchurian and Ethiopian conflicts. As the League's credibility declined in the political sphere, its competence to deal with technical and humanitarian issues also decreased. While the League stood silent, a response to events in Austria came from an unexpected source: the United States of America.

Prior to March 1938 the United States government had been a supportive but relatively inactive member of the international refugee regime. After the *Greco*-Turkish war, the American government helped to assist refugees through the work of the American Red Cross, an organization which received significant government funding. American banks also provided financial backing for the Greek refugee settlement loan. Throughout the rest of the 1920s, however, the United States remained in the background on refugee issues. Since it did not belong to the League of Nations, it did not even participate in the annual discussions on refugee affairs held each September at the Assembly sessions. Not until 1933, when the Roosevelt administration approved the appointment of an American as the High Commissioner for Refugees, did it appear that the United States would take a more active interest in refugees. Despite hopes that this would encourage greater American participation in League and refugee activities, the State Department avoided active involvement.[77] Instead of designating

---

[76] For Freud's own account of his escape, see *The Diary of Sigmund Freud, 1929–1939* (London: Hogarth Press, 1992).

[77] Stewart, *US Government Policy*, 146.

a government official to serve on the Governing Body of the High Commission, Professor Joseph Chamberlain of Columbia University received the appointment. After McDonald's resignation, the United States government faded into the background once again, preferring to allow American philanthropic agencies to carry out refugee assistance programmes.[78]

Then, on 25 March 1938, President Franklin D. Roosevelt startled much of the world by inviting twenty-nine governments to participate in a special conference to deal with the refugee crisis.[79] Among the invited guests were Great Britain, France, Italy, Belgium, the Netherlands, Denmark, Norway, Sweden, Switzerland, and twenty American republics. According to Roosevelt, the conference's purpose was to deal with the settlement of 'political refugees', refugees from Germany and Austria and those who might leave these areas in the future. Spokesmen from the State Department stressed that the conference was not intended to interfere with the work of any existing agency, a reference to the activities of the League of Nations. In addition, all settlement costs would still be paid by private organizations, not governments. Most importantly, no country would be asked to admit more immigrants than its current legislation allowed.[80]

Other members of the international refugee regime responded favourably to Roosevelt's proposal. The governments of Britain and France quickly voiced support for the conference, as did those of Belgium and the Netherlands. The Swiss government replied

---

[78] In Oct. 1934 over 15 agencies involved in refugee assistance formed the National Coordinating Committee for Aid to Refugees and Emigrants coming from Germany. The Committee helped to provide a variety of social and legal services for the refugees in the United States. See Eric Estorick and Erica Mann, 'Private and Governmental Aid of Refugees', *Annals*, 203 (May 1939), 142.

[79] Roosevelt's motives for calling the conference are not entirely clear. Several historians credit journalist Dorothy Thompson and Congressmen from certain metropolitan areas for convincing Roosevelt to take the initiative. Others believe that Roosevelt convened the conference on the advice of the State Department as a way to forestall moves to liberalize American immigration policy. In other accounts, Roosevelt was moved by humanitarian motives. See Arthur Morse, *While Six Million Died: A Chronicle of American Apathy* (New York: Random House, 1968) 211–12; Wyman, *Paper Walls*, 44; Henry Feingold, *The Politics of Rescue: The Roosevelt Administration and the Holocaust, 1938–1945* (New Brunswick, NJ: Rutgers University Press, 1970), 23.

[80] 'US Asks Powers to Help Refugees Flee from Nazis', *New York Times* (25 Mar. 1938), 1; Eric Estorick, 'The Evian Conference and the Intergovernmental Committee', *Annals*, 203 (May 1939), 136.

CONFRONTING BARRIERS TO IMMIGRATION 209

that it would send a delegate, but declined President Roosevelt's suggestion that the conference be held in Switzerland. Neighbouring France then agreed to host the meeting. Acceptances came from the Latin American republics, usually accompanied by reservations about increasing refugee immigration. Though eastern European countries had not been invited to the conference, Poland and Romania volunteered to attend as 'refugee producer' countries and indicated a desire to assist the departure of their own Jewish minorities. The United States State Department rejected their applications because they were not potential receiving countries. Officials of both Germany and the Soviet Union ridiculed the planned conference, confirming the State Department's decision not to invite either country.[81]

Only the Italian government declined Roosevelt's invitation outright. This refusal coincided with an end to a relatively liberal policy towards refugees from Germany. From 1933 until 1935 Italian delegates worked closely with High Commissioner McDonald, despite Italy's dispute with the League of Nations over Ethiopia.[82] Even after Italy's withdrawal from the League Assembly in October 1936,[83] the government continued to welcome approximately 5,000 refugees from the Third Reich.[84] By mid-1938, however, the Italian government increasingly emulated the anti-Semitic policies of Germany. Finally, in September 1938, the Italian government instituted a series of laws against foreign Jews, many of whom were refugees, and moved to prevent the entrance of new refugees.[85]

The Evian Conference

After several months of preparation, delegates from thirty-two countries convened in Evian-les-Bains, France, on 6 July 1938 (see Table 17). Myron C. Taylor, a personal friend of Roosevelt's and a former head of US Steel Corporation, chaired the meeting; and James G. McDonald served as one of his assistants.[86] Taylor

[81] 'Refugees Board Gets Wide Acclaim', *New York Times* (26 Mar. 1938), 4; Feingold, *Politics of Rescue*, 26–7. [82] LNA C1609/6 (33–6).
[83] The Italian delegates left the Assembly in anger after the Credentials Committee accepted the papers of the Ethiopian delegation, but did not formally withdraw until Dec. 1937. See Walters, *History of the League of Nations*, 65, 623–91.
[84] Marrus, *The Unwanted*, 169. [85] See above, Ch. 2.
[86] Robert T. Pell and George L. Brandt of the State Department and George L. Warren of the President's Advisory Committee on Political Refugees also acted as assistants. Estorick, 'Evian Conference', 136.

TABLE 17. *Participation in Intergovernmental Conferences, 1928–1938*

Country	June 1928[1]	Oct. 1933[2]	July 1936[3]	Feb. 1938[4]	July 1938[5]
Argentina					x
Australia					x
Austria	x	x			
Belgium	x	x	x	x	x
Bolivia					x
Brazil					x
Bulgaria	x	x			
Canada					x
Chile					x
China		x			
Colombia					x
Costa Rica					x
Cuba				x	x
Czechoslovakia	x	x	x	x	
Denmark			x	x	x
Dominican Republic					x
Ecuador			x		x
Egypt	x	x			
Estonia	x	x			
Finland	x	x	observer	observer	
France	x	x	x	x	x
Germany	x				
Great Britain			x	x	x
Greece	x	x			
Guatemala					x
Haiti					x
Honduras					x
Hungary					
India					
Ireland			x		x
Japan					
Latvia	x	x	x		
Luxembourg				x	
Mexico					x
Netherlands			x	x	x
New Zealand					x
Nicaragua					x
Norway			x	x	x

TABLE 17. *(Cont.)*

Country	June 1928[1]	Oct. 1933[2]	July 1936[3]	Feb. 1938[4]	July 1938[5]
Panama					x
Paraguay					x
Peru					x
Poland	x	x	x	x	
Portugal				x	
Romania	x	x	x		
South Africa					
Spain				x	
Sweden			x	x	x
Switzerland	x	x	x	x	x
United States			observer	observer	x
Uruguay			x		x
Venezuela					x
Yugoslavia	x	x		observer	
Totals	15	15	17	17	32

[1] Conference on the Legal Status of Russian and Armenian Refugees, and the Extension of Legal Protection to Other Refugees, 28–30 June 1928, *Official Journal* (Mar. 1929), 483.
[2] Intergovernmental Conference for the Adoption of a Refugee Convention, 26–8 Oct. 1933 [A.12.1934], 3.
[3] Conference on the Legal Status of Refugees coming from Germany, 2–4 July 1936 [A.19.1936.XII], 3.
[4] Conference on the Adoption of a Convention for Refugees coming from Germany, 7–10 Feb. 1938 [A.25.1938.XII], 2.
[5] Evian Conference, July 1938 [A.25.1938], 3.

quickly pointed out that the ultimate objective of the conference should be to establish an organization to deal with all refugees, but their immediate goal must be to deal with the pressing problem of refugees from Germany and Austria.[87] In order to accomplish this, government delegates made speeches and held discussions over the next nine days. In addition, the conference made special provisions for short presentations by private organizations.

In his keynote speech, Taylor exposed a fundamental problem

[87] 'Speech of Myron C. Taylor, USA', *Proceedings of the Evian Conference*, 12.

of the international refugee regime: that of reconciling the principles of sovereignty and humanitarianism. On the one hand, Taylor expressed support for the humanitarian principle, saying that 'discrimination and pressure against minority groups and the disregard of elementary human rights are contrary to the principles of what we have come to regard as the accepted standards of civilisation'. On the other hand, he stressed the sovereignty principle, especially in matters of immigration. He said all actions must take place 'within the framework of existing laws and practices'. He then tried to reconcile the competing principles by explaining that his government combined the German and Austrian quotas so that a total of 27,370 people could now enter the United States in one year.[88] Astute observers quickly realized, however, that the United States had not actually increased the quota.

In the course of the conference, other delegates also attempted to balance humanitarian concern for refugees with sovereignty over immigration. Speaking for the British government, Lord Winterton characterized the refugee problem as 'mainly a humanitarian one'. He then stressed that 'the United Kingdom is not a country of immigration' and for 'economic and social reasons, the traditional policy of granting asylum can only be applied within narrow limits. But within these limits, the people of the United Kingdom are ready to play their part.' Since immigration into Britain itself was difficult, Winterton said that his government was 'carefully surveying the prospects of the admission of refugees to their colonies and overseas territories'. In particular, he seemed hopeful about the prospects for settlement in East Africa, a place far away from England itself.[89] Nevertheless, Winterton, a staunch anti-Zionist, disappointed many because he neglected to mention Palestine as a possible source of settlement. The Foreign Office had declared this subject 'off-limits' because the British mandatory government had recently moved to restrict Jewish immigration there.

Speaking on behalf of the French government, Henry Berenger,

---

[88] 'Speech of Taylor', 12–13. On the American role at Evian, see Feingold, *Politics of Rescue*, 22–44.

[89] 'Speech of Lord Winterton, United Kingdom', *Proceedings of the Evian Conference*, 13–15. On the British position at Evian, see A. J. Sherman, *Island Refuge: Britain and Refugees from the Third Reich: 1933–1939* (London: Paul Elek, 1973), 112–36.

a prominent French Jew who had previously served on McDonald's Governing Body, recalled the humanitarian record of his country in the treatment of refugees. He assured the conference that 'France continues to be true to the long-standing tradition of universal hospitality which has characterized her throughout all her history'. But he went on to say that France had reached 'the extreme point of saturation as regards admission of refugees'. In other words, he essentially reversed previous French policy and indicated that France should not be considered as a country of permanent settlement for future refugees. Berenger then voiced support for the burden-sharing norm, saying that 'France considers the refugee problem to be an international political problem, which can only be finally solved by the joint and collective action of the Governments of the world'.[90]

After presentations by the major powers, officials from the smaller countries gave the positions of their governments. Delegates from Belgium, Denmark, the Netherlands, Sweden, and Switzerland expressed sympathy for the refugees, but added that because of their small geographic size they could not admit a large number of refugees. They were also prepared to provide transitory service pending resettlement elsewhere. Representatives from the South American republics also expressed their desire to welcome immigrants, but regretted that their economic conditions at that time made it difficult for them to do so. Only the delegate from the Dominican Republic made a concrete offer for agricultural settlers.[91] The Canadian delegation adopted the position that it was prepared to participate in a discussion of the refugee question, but under no circumstances would it agree to a special admissions quota for refugees.[92] The Australian spokesman emphasized that his government was only interested in British immigrants and made the infamous declaration that his country did not have a racial problem and did not want to import one.

Near the end of the conference, Sir Neill Malcolm made an obvious but unpopular observation. He noted that the speeches of

[90] 'Speech of Henry Berenger, France', *Proceedings of the Evian Conference*, 15–16. On the French position at Evian, see Maga, 'Closing the Door', 436–8.
[91] Feingold, *Politics of Rescue*, 30–3; Wyman, *Paper Walls*, 49–50; Bauer, *My Brother's Keeper*, 233–4; 'Speech of M. V. T. Molina, Dominican Republic', *Proceedings of the Evian Conference*, 32.
[92] Dirks, *Canada's Refugee Policy*, 56.

the previous two days had essentially confirmed an opinion he had already reached while carrying out his job as High Commissioner for Refugees coming from Germany. Malcolm said that 'in the present condition of labour markets in the countries of the world, any large-scale scheme of migration could only arouse hostility'. Malcolm further stated that the greatest hope for the refugees lay in a process of individual migration such as had been carried out by private organizations for the previous five years. He concluded that the Committee would be doing 'good work' if it helped to finance emigration and settlement schemes conducted by private organizations.[93]

At Evian, over twenty private organizations also presented their view of the refugee crisis.[94] In general, the outcome of the Evian conference disappointed the representatives of both Jewish and non-Jewish groups. Although the government officials in attendance used humanitarian rhetoric, very few offered any assistance to the refugees. The Evian conference produced only one concrete accomplishment: the Intergovernmental Committee on Refugees (IGCR). The American delegation strongly advocated the creation of a new institution to deal with the refugee problem, despite the objections of the British and French delegations. Both the British and French preferred to continue working through the League of Nations, a body they had been active in since its creation. The United States, however, showed little desire to work with an organization it had never joined. In the end both the British and French deferred to the United States and agreed to the creation of the Committee.[95] Although the IGCR took great pains not to pre-empt the existing refugee work of the League, in fact 'the weight of moral and political authority' shifted to it from the League.[96]

The IGCR and the Search for Refugee Havens

Headquartered in London, the IGCR met for the first time in August 1938. George Rublee, an American with a reputation as a

[93] 'Speech of Sir Neill Malcolm', 32–3.
[94] On the position of private organizations at the Evian conference see below, Ch. 7. [95] Bauer, *My Brother's Keeper*, 235; Feingold, *Politics of Rescue*, 29.
[96] Louise W. Holborn, 'The League of Nations and the Refugee Problem', *Annals*, 203 (May 1939), 135.

skilled negotiator, served as Chairman of the new institution. Officially, the Chairman of the IGCR had a twofold task: (1) negotiating 'to improve the present conditions of exodus and to replace them by conditions of orderly emigration' and (2) approaching 'the Governments of the countries of refuge and settlement with a view to developing opportunities for permanent settlement'.[97] In practice, Rublee devoted most of his efforts to negotiating with the German government over the exit conditions for refugees, a topic which will be discussed in detail in the following chapter. The governmental members on the IGCR, however, spent considerable time trying to find places of permanent settlement for the refugees from the Third Reich. In the autumn of 1938 the importance of their work greatly increased because of the creation of still more refugees and a further tightening of immigration laws.

On 1 October 1938 the German occupation of the Sudetenland forced thousands more to flee their homes. One month later the Czech government reported that over 90,000 refugees had come to the rump state seeking refuge. Then, in early November, *Kristallnacht* dealt a crushing blow to the Jews remaining in Germany. On that night the Nazis escalated their persecution of the Jews from gradual economic deprivation to physical violence directed against Jewish persons, property, and communal institutions. As a result of these two events, the departure of refugees from the Third Reich quickly accelerated. In the year ending June 1939 approximately 120,000 refugees fled the Third Reich, almost as many as had fled over the previous four years.[98]

In Europe, governments responded to the flight of refugees from Czechoslovakia and Germany as they had to the Austrian exodus: they moved to further restrict immigration. Perhaps the greatest change in the refugee policy of a government was in that of France. In the Refugee Survey, Simpson describes France as *'par excellence* the country of refuge in western Europe'.[99] As a liberal, democratic country bordering Germany, France was the preferred country of asylum for many refugees. In the first two years of the German migration, neighbouring France accepted over 40 per cent of them. A significant number eventually went overseas but, by

[97] 'Resolution Adopted by the Intergovernmental Committee at Evian on July 14th 1938' [A.25.1938.XII], 10. [98] See above, Ch. 2.
[99] Simpson, *The Refugee Problem*, 297.

the end of 1937, France still hosted about 10,000 refugees, the largest German refugee population in Europe.[100] While not as well received as the Russian refugees, the refugees from Germany benefited from the liberalism of a succession of governments, most notably that of Léon Blum's Popular Front. Then, in April 1938, a new government led by Edouard Daladier came to power. Daladier saw refugees primarily as a security threat; since 1933 he had consistently advocated restrictionist policies for this reason. In addition, many French Jews considered Daladier's views to be anti-Semitic. Under his influence, the French government's policy became increasingly restrictive. A decree of 2 May 1938 prohibited the expulsion of refugees already in France but increased the authority of border guards to refuse entry to new refugees. After *Kristallnacht* the French government established detention centres along its borders to house illegal immigrants. In the spring of 1939 Daladier issued decrees requiring refugees to perform military service and to do forced labour. As a result of these measures, the border became effectively closed to legal immigration. Nevertheless, illegal immigration still continued. An estimated 40,000 German refugees were in France just before the outbreak of the Second World War.[101]

Other European countries followed the French example. Shortly after *Kristallnacht* the Belgium government declared that illegal refugees who arrived in the country after 27 August 1938 would be expelled. In nearby Holland, the government gave strict orders that illegal immigrants found after 23 December 1938 would be deported. In Switzerland, the government reached a special agreement with the German government. Under the terms of the agreement, the passport of all non-Aryan Germans would be marked with a 'J' so that their movements could be easily controlled. After October 1938 all non-Aryan Germans needed special permission to enter Switzerland. In February 1939 the Swiss government further restricted the influx of refugees by strengthening police orders on controlling the borders. As a result of these actions, the number of refugees in Switzerland actually declined: in December 1938 approximately 12,000 refugees were in Switzerland; by

[100] Simpson, *The Refugee Problem*, 322–3, 562.
[101] Maga, 'Closing the Door', 424–42; Marrus, *The Unwanted*, 145–9.

August 1939 this number had been reduced to 8,000, including 5,000 Jews.[102]

In Latin America, governments also moved to further restrict immigration. An overview of the prospects for immigration in mid-1939 reported that Argentina, Brazil, Colombia, Uruguay, Venezuela, Mexico, Barbados, Trinidad, and Jamaica were practically closed to refugees, especially Jewish ones.[103] In Colombia and Venezuela, laws specifically restricted the entrance of Jews. The immigration laws of several other countries, including Brazil, Bolivia, Chile, Uruguay, Mexico, and Panama, favoured agricultural immigrants. In addition, the laws of Brazil constrained the entrance of professionals, and those of Mexico limited the entrance of petty merchants. A number of countries, including Argentina, Bolivia, and Colombia, also charged immigrants an entrance fee. After November 1938 the Mexican government went so far as to prohibit the entrance of all 'labouring immigrants': that is, those hoping to work in the country. These provisions particularly hurt Jewish refugees, because most came from professional and commercial backgrounds and had to flee the Third Reich with meagre resources.[104]

The increase in the number of people looking for asylum combined with the decrease in the number of countries admitting refugees made swift action on the part of the IGCR imperative. The governments composing the IGCR realized this and increased their efforts to find refugee havens. Treading a path taken earlier by the Refugee Section of the ILO, the United States State Department pursued proposals for the establishment of a Jewish homeland in Angola, Ethiopia, Kenya, and the Central African highlands. President Roosevelt advocated a settlement in the Orinoco River valley in Venezuela. In Britain, the Foreign and Colonial Offices explored the possibility of refugee settlement in British Guiana, Northern Rhodesia, Tanganyika, and other colonies.[105]

[102] International Labour Office, The I.L.O. Year-Book 1938–39 (Geneva, 1939), 260; Bauer, My Brother's Keeper, 265–8; Marrus, The Unwanted, 154–8; Simpson, The Refugee Problem, 346–7, 352, 397.

[103] Estorick and Mann, 'Private and Governmental Aid', 151–2.

[104] I.L.O. Year-Book 1938–39, 260–3; Samuel Guy Inman, 'Refugee Settlement in Latin America', Annals, 203 (May 1939), 187–91.

[105] International Labour Office, The I.L.O. Year-Book 1939–40 (Geneva, 1940), 230; [A.18.1939.XII], 7–8; Marrus, The Unwanted, 186–7; Wyman, Paper Walls, 57–60.

Of the various proposals, only a plan for refugee settlement in the Dominican Republic actually came to fruition. According to the scheme, 50,000–100,000 refugees would be established in an agricultural colony. In 1940 an initial group of settlers finally arrived. The settlement, however, never became a success. Despite high expectations, the supply of fertile land proved to be extremely limited. In addition, some refugees used the colony as a way of immigrating into the United States. In total, less than 500 refugees ever settled in the colony.[106]

Overall, the IGCR did little to arrange the settlement of refugees before it discontinued operations at the outbreak of the Second World War. Partly as a result of this failure, Zionists began to call for large-scale refugee settlements in Palestine. Before 1938 only radical Zionists had advocated this policy, while moderates called for gradual development of the Jewish homeland. As the refugee crisis worsened and alternative settlement projects faltered, mainstream leaders such as Chaim Weizmann, head of the World Zionist Organization, called for mass settlement in Palestine. The British mandatory power, however, remained committed to its policy of limiting Jewish immigration there. At the same time, Zionists who advocated illegal immigration to Palestine gained widespread acceptance within the movement. As a result of their efforts, over 18,000 illegal immigrants went to Palestine between 1938 and 1941.[107]

Changes in Immigration Policies

Although the IGCR did not secure areas of mass settlement for refugees, a number of countries unilaterally moved to fulfil the obligations of the assistance norm by liberalizing their own immigration policies. The governments of both Holland and Belgium eventually stepped back from hard-line policies declared in late 1938. In 1939 the Dutch government established emergency camps for legal immigrants without funds and for illegal immigrants whom they agreed not to deport. In Belgium, the government agreed to help finance refugee relief. Although the amount provided was

---

[106] Wyman, *Paper Walls*, 61–2.   [107] Marrus, *The Unwanted*, 185–6.

much smaller than that provided by Jewish organizations, its action established an important precedent.[108]

In the year between Evian and the outbreak of war in Europe, the United States government also improved its treatment of refugees. Moved by the excesses of *Kristallnacht*, President Roosevelt used his executive powers to announce that the visitor visas of approximately 12,000–15,000 refugees from Germany would be extended. In addition, the government reversed its previous policy and began to allocate fully the immigration quota of 27,370 for Germany and Austria. From 1933 until 1937 the United States admitted slightly more than 26,000 refugees from Germany, a number equal to only about twenty per cent of the total quota available. In contrast, the German–Austrian quota was filled 85 per cent in 1938 and completely used in 1939. When the Second World War began, the United States hosted the largest German refugee population, about 100,000 refugees, or 25 per cent of the total migration from the Reich.[109]

Despite this relaxation in immigration restrictions, the United States government remained committed to the quota system because of the strength of anti-immigration feeling. Although a public opinion poll taken after *Kristallnacht* showed that 94 per cent of Americans disapproved of the Nazis' treatment of the Jews, 77 per cent of them thought that the United States should not allow a larger number of German Jews to come to the United States.[110] Congress reflected anti-immigration sentiments and consistently refused pleas for preferential arrangements on behalf of refugees. One of the hardest-fought battles over immigration concerned the Wagner–Rogers bill, a proposal which would have allowed the entrance of 20,000 German refugee children outside the existing quotas for 1939 and 1940. Although representives of several Christian Churches, the YMCA, the Boy Scouts, and the

---

[108] Bauer, *My Brother's Keeper*, 265–7. In 1939 the Belgium government allocated the sum of 6 million Belgian francs ($20,000) for the assistance of 3,000 refugees. In the same year, the JDC spent almost $700,000 in Belgium, providing about two-thirds of the budget of the Brussels Jewish Aid Committee.

[109] Breitman and Kraut, *American Refugee Policy*, 62–7; Simpson, *The Refugee Problem*, 473, 563; Wyman, *Paper Walls*, 73, 221, 274; Sherman, *Island Refuge*, 264–5.

[110] Hadley Cantril (ed.), *Public Opinion 1935–1946* (Princeton, NJ: Princeton University Press, 1951), 382–5.

AFL-CIO strongly supported the bill, the opposition of the Daughters of the American Revolution, the American Legion, and other patriotic groups killed it. One of the principal arguments made by the restrictionists was that special treatment for refugee children would divert needed attention from poor children already in the United States.[111]

The United States State Department also used its influence with various South American republics to encourage them to admit more refugees. In response to these pressures, Argentina and Brazil both modified their policies slightly. In 1938 Argentina admitted only 1,050 Jewish refugees. The following year it allowed the admission of 4,300. Afterwards, however, the Argentinian government once again curtailed the influx, but illegal immigration into the country still continued. Immigration policy in Brazil followed a similar pattern. After admitting only 530 Jewish refugees in 1938, the Brazilian government increased the number admitted to 4,601 in 1939. Once war broke out, however, Brazil began to restrict immigration again. By 1944, Jewish immigration had been reduced to nil.[112]

In contrast to its posture at Evian, the Australian government also adopted a more welcoming attitude towards refugees. In late November 1938 S. M. Bruce, the Australian High Commissioner to Great Britain, recommended to his government that they adopt a special quota of 30,000 refugees over the next three years. In advocating this policy, Bruce noted that he felt increasing pressure from the governments of the United Kingdom, United States, Scandinavian countries, Holland, and France to take action on behalf of Jewish refugees from Germany. Bruce further stressed that a humanitarian move by Australia would help to cement ties with the United States, the government which placed the highest priority on the refugee issue. In Australia, the Cabinet responded favourably to Bruce's suggestion, but reduced the amount of the quota by half so as not to greatly upset Australia's established immigration policy. Consequently, the Australian government amended its immigration laws to include a special quota allowing

---

[111] Norman L. Zucker and Naomi Flink Zucker, *The Guarded Gate: The Reality of American Refugee Policy* (San Diego: Harcourt Brace Jovanovich, 1987), 19–21.
[112] Feingold, *Politics of Rescue*, 49.

the entrance of 15,000 refugees from Germany over a three-year period.[113]

By far the greatest transformation in a country's response to the German refugee crisis took place in Great Britain. Before 1938 the British government remained relatively aloof from the German refugee crisis. In 1933 the British Jewish community had promised the government that no Jewish refugees from Germany would become a public charge, a promise they kept until the outbreak of the war. Nevertheless, only a relatively small number of refugees, most coming from the middle class, were admitted to the British Isles. At the end of 1937 the British hosted only 5,000 refugees, less than 4 per cent of the total migration. By the time of the Evian conference the German refugee population had grown to 8,000 but was still relatively small compared with that of other host countries. In writing of the situation, Simpson reports in the Refugee Survey that 'Great Britain's record in the admission of refugees is not distinguished if it be compared with that of France, Czechoslovakia, or the United States of America'.[114]

Although the British government initially responded to *Anschluss* by requiring visas for Austrians, public pressure soon forced it to adopt a more favourable policy. In April 1938 the Home Office asked the major British voluntary organizations to form a committee on refugees. This committee acted as an advisory body and helped to facilitate the processing of visa applications. In the summer of 1938 the government further streamlined its procedures in regard to refugees. Previously both the Ministry of Labour and the Home Office had to be consulted before an employment permit for an alien could be granted. After the reorganization, the Home Office alone dealt with applications from refugee aliens. These two measures helped to create a distinction in British immigration policy between refugees and ordinary aliens, a change which facilitated the admission of refugees.[115]

The German annexation of the Sudetenland proved to be another impetus in the liberalization of British refugee policy. Because of the British role at Munich, the government and public

[113] Blakeney, *Australia and Jewish Refugees*, 142; C. Hartley Grattan, 'Refugees and an Underdeveloped Economy', *Annals*, 203 (May 1939), 181.
[114] Simpson, *The Refugee Problem*, 340–1, 562–3.   [115] Ibid. 337–8.

felt a special responsibility for refugees from Czechoslovakia. Urged on by a coalition of Churches, the press, and voluntary organizations, the British government admitted *en bloc* the members of the Social Democratic Party from what had been the Sudetenland. In addition, it guaranteed a loan to the Czech government of £8 million and made a cash contribution of £4 million. Although most of the money was spent on relief within Czechoslovakia, about one-quarter was used to finance refugee emigration. In this process, the British Embassy at Prague and the British Quakers helped to arrange the swift departure of refugees.[116]

Initially the British government maintained that the Czech refugees constituted a special case. After *Kristallnacht* and the progressive worsening of the refugee crisis, this position became impossible to maintain. Moreover, the Zionists and their supporters pressed for more immigration to Palestine. The British government, however, rejected this method of solving the refugee problem. A White Paper published in early 1939 stated that Jewish immigration to Palestine was to be limited to 75,000 people. Over the next five years 10,000 people would be admitted annually, and an additional 25,000 would be allowed to enter.[117] In part because of its policy towards Palestine, the government decided to facilitate the entry of refugees into Britain itself. Under this new policy, the Home Office authorized the admission of thousands of refugees, especially children and domestic servants. At a time when many countries had shut their doors completely, the number of refugees within Britain mushroomed. By the outbreak of the Second World War Britain hosted 50,000 refugees from Germany and Austria, and 6,000 from Czechoslovakia.[118]

The British example of adhering to the assistance norm of the international refugee regime influenced other governments, particularly through the movement to save children. The movement began in England under the direction of the Council for German Jewry, the Quakers, and other Christian groups. Under the programme, approximately 10,000 children under the age of 18 were

---

[116] Wasserstein, 'British Government', 74–5; Sherman, *Island Refuge*, 262; Tarkakower and Grossman, *The Jewish Refugee*, 38; Bauer, *My Brother's Keeper*, 263.

[117] Wasserstein, 'British Government', 75; Fred J. Khouri, *The Arab Israeli Dilemma* (Syracuse, NY: Syracuse University Press, 1976), 26–7.

[118] Sherman, *Island Refuge*, 262, 264–5; Marrus, *The Unwanted*, 152–3.

admitted to Britain. Of these, approximately 90 per cent were Jewish. Once in Britain, private organizations guaranteed that the children would not become public charges and arranged for their care in foster homes. The success of the programme in England inspired other countries to do the same. Under similar programmes, the Netherlands admitted 2,000, Belgium 800, and France 700. In all, over 13,000 children found refuge in this way.[119]

A BALANCE SHEET

Most accounts of refugee problems of the Inter-war Period sharply criticize the major actors in the international refugee regime for their failure to provide asylum for more Jewish refugees.[120] This failure is especially tragic because many Jews unable to escape the Third Reich later perished in the Holocaust. It would be a mistake, however, to base an assessment of the international refugee regime solely on the experience of one refugee group in the last year before the outbreak of the Second World War. Taken as a whole, the Inter-war Period is 'remarkable for the very large numbers of refugees *not* in fact *sent back* to their countries of origin, whether they fled Russia after the revolution, Spain, Germany, or the Ottoman Empire'.[121] The relatively poor countries of eastern Europe and the Near East provided refuge to over 1 million Russians, 350,000 Armenians, 2 million Greeks and Bulgars, and 400,000 Turks. France alone served as a haven for about 10,000 Italians and 400,000 Spanish Republicans. Even in the case of refugees from the Third Reich, approximately 400,000 people, or about 50 per cent of the Jewish population of greater Germany in 1933, escaped and found asylum elsewhere. Based on this record, it must be concluded that states belonging to the international refugee regime generally fulfilled their obligations under the assistance norm.

Of course, most members of the international refugee regime

[119] Bentwich, *They Found Refuge*, 38; Bauer, *My Brother's Keeper*, 272–3; Wasserstein, 'British Government', 76.

[120] See e.g. Yehuda Bauer, *American Jewry and the Holocaust: The American Jewish Joint Distribution Committee, 1939–1945* (Detroit: Wayne State University Press, 1981), 31.

[121] Guy S. Goodwin-Gill, *The Refugee in International Law* (Oxford: Clarendon Press, 1983), 71. (Emphasis added.)

did not consistently abide by the humanitarian ideals embodied by the international refugee regime, especially in regard to Jewish and non-Jewish refugees fleeing Nazi Germany. In response to this, other actors in the regime tried to breach immigration barriers facing refugees. While the IGCR's ill-fated search for refugee havens is well known, its failure was not unique. The Refugee Section of the ILO and the Nansen Office also made searches on behalf of Russian, Armenian, and Saar refugees and produced meagre results. In addition, from 1933 until 1935, a special committee of the League of Nations tried unsuccessfully to arrange the emigration and settlement in South America of 20,000 Assyrians forced to flee Iraq.[122] While one historian concludes that the 'desperate lack of any other solution induced the often unrealistic discussion of refugee havens' by the IGCR,[123] what these different ventures actually reflect is the unwillingness of Western policymakers to let go of the idea that 'surplus populations', including refugees, minorities, and the unemployed, could be exported from Europe.

All the attempts made to export refugees to locations in Africa and Latin America, whether for Jewish or non-Jewish refugees, encountered similar obstacles. One of the primary impediments to such schemes was the existence of immigration policies that favoured particular ethnic or cultural groups. As noted in Chapter 2, the United States encouraged the immigration of people from western and northern European ethnic groups, Commonwealth countries wanted migrants from the British Isles, and the countries of South America desired migrants sharing a common Latin culture. Lack of adequate funding also proved to be a major obstacle to any scheme which required refugees to move great distances and begin settlements. This paucity of funding, in turn, reflected the unwillingness of governments to spend tax revenues on refugees rather than on their own citizens. In addition, a mismatch between the skills of Europeans and the job opportunities

---

[122] The League tried to find a country willing to accept this refugee group and the British government offered to finance their settlement. Despite investigations into settlement in Brazil, British Guiana, and elsewhere, no government proved willing to accept the Assyrians. Eventually, alternative arrangements for their settlement in Syria had to be made. Simpson, *Preliminary Report*, 30–4; League of Nations, *The Settlement of the Assyrians: A Work of Humanity and Appeasement*, League of Nations Questions, pamphlet no. 5 (Geneva: Information Section, 1935).

[123] Wyman, *Paper Walls*, 57.

available in underdeveloped countries mitigated against mass migration.

But the most important obstacle to the large-scale emigration and settlement schemes for refugees was opposition from local populations. While the native inhabitants of Asia, Africa, and the Americas had always opposed colonization efforts, in the interwar years these concerns began to be taken more seriously. Although much of the world was still under colonial rule, nationalist movements were gaining strength in the Middle East, the Indian subcontinent, China, Africa, and elsewhere. In Palestine, for instance, Arab resistance to the arrival of European Jews became a major influence on British policy towards the mandate. Moreover, an anti-colonial norm was developing and being promoted by the League of Nations itself. The classic example of this was the decision of the 1936 Assembly to seat Haile Selassie as the legitimate representative of Ethiopia after the Italian conquest. Much to Mussolini's consternation, the right of white Europeans to rule over black Africans was no longer automatically accepted.

Given the many obstacles to overcoming immigration barriers without disregarding the sovereignty principle of the international refugee regime, the accomplishments of intergovernmental and private organizations in this area are considerable. In the short run, without their efforts more refugees would have succumbed to starvation at Constantinople, languished on the dole in eastern Europe, or died in concentration camps during the Holocaust. In the long run, the operations of the international refugee regime also began to have an impact on the immigration laws of some countries. Gradually governments began to distinguish between refugees and economic migrants. In some cases, these changes were administrative and eased the procedures by which visa applications by refugees were processed. In others, they resulted in a relaxation of restrictions or a preferential quota for refugees. In the last days before the Second World War these amendments did not completely solve the refugee crisis, but they did enable thousands of additional refugees to reach a safe haven. Over time these changes contributed to the acceptance of special treatment for refugees within a country's immigration policy.

7

The Attempt to Deal with Root Causes

IN the preceding chapters, the attempts of actors in the international refugee regime to secure legal protection, provide durable solutions, and overcome immigration barriers for refugees have been explored. From this discussion, it is evident that the scope and functions of the regime increased considerably over time. Originally formed to deal with the Russian refugee problem, the international refugee regime grew to encompass other refugee groups. At first the regime's rules only dealt with refugee travel. By the end of the Inter-war Period, a comprehensive system of rules covering personal status and security, employment, and social services had been developed for refugees. The regime's functions also expanded so that they included refugee settlement, increasing employment opportunities, and facilitating immigration. This growth increased the relevance of the international refugee regime to government policies towards refugees. Moreover, it demonstrates that the actors in the international refugee regime were both flexible and creative in finding solutions for refugee problems.

Nevertheless, all of the refugee assistance efforts mentioned above were superficial in that they only dealt with refugees after they had left their home countries. None of them addressed the deeper problem of how to prevent refugee movements from occurring in the first place. Given the many successful expansions of the scope and functions of the international refugee regime, it is not surprising that some actors tried to expand the regime's boundaries even further to include dealing with the root causes of refugee movements. In this chapter, the outcome of efforts to prevent and control refugee movements in the inter-war years will be discussed.

THE LEAGUE OF NATIONS AND THE CAUSES OF
REFUGEE MOVEMENTS

Logically, the first step in preventing a refugee movement is determining the cause of the mass exodus. In their evaluation of causality, the major actors in the international refugee regime overlooked the primary reason for mass refugee movements in the Inter-war Period, the transformation of multi-ethnic empires into homogeneous nation-states. At the time, the creation of nation-states was viewed as a positive development that both promoted democracy and contributed to world peace, not as a process that produced refugees and other undesirable side-effects. In addition, the actors in the international refugee regime responded to refugee crises on an *ad hoc* basis. Consequently, they focused on the immediate causes of refugee movements, such as war and the persecution of minorities.

The major actors in the international refugee regime did not directly try to eliminate war, one of the most obvious causes of refugee movements. Instead, they left this task to the League of Nations as a whole. Indeed, the primary purpose of the organization was to 'achieve international peace and security by the acceptance of obligations not to resort to war'.[1] In the 1920s the League dealt successfully with almost fifty political disputes, and in three instances was actually able to stop fighting before it had begun. All of these cases, however, involved only minor powers.[2] But in the 1930s two major countries directly challenged the League's prohibition against aggression. First, the League's prestige suffered when it responded to the Japanese invasion of Manchuria with only verbal condemnations. Then the Italian invasion of Ethiopia in 1935 brought the League's doctrine of collective security its greatest challenge. Although the League members joined together and imposed partial economic sanctions on Italy, they failed to prevent a victory for Mussolini. With the League's prestige badly damaged and its Covenant torn up in Africa, the

---

[1] 'Covenant of the League of Nations, Preamble', reprinted in F. P. Walters, *A History of the League of Nations* (London: Oxford University Press, 1960), 43.
[2] The League successfully resolved conflicts between Yugoslavia and Albania in 1921, between Greece and Bulgaria in 1925, and between Turkey and Iraq in 1924.

way was paved for Germany's challenge to the status quo in Europe.[3]

The League of Nations addressed a second immediate cause of refugee movements—the persecution of minorities—through a special system of international treaties which guaranteed the civil rights of minorities without regard to language, race, or religion. In order to enforce the provisions of the Minorities Treaties, the League of Nations established a special Minorities Commission, which heard complaints and publicized violations of the treaties. Other than embarrassment, it lacked the sanctions necessary to enforce the minority protection provisions of the treaties on sovereign states. Though the treaty system offered international protection for the minorities of Europe, it only applied to those living in some of the countries defeated in the First World War or created in its aftermath; it did not cover Germany, Italy, and the other Great Powers. Consequently, the Minority Treaties offered no international protection for the Jews of Germany.[4]

Beyond the Minority Treaties, the League system had no provisions for addressing other causes of refugee movements, most notably governmental abuse of 'human rights', those rights which accrue to everyone by virtue of their humanity.[5] The members of the international refugee regime did not challenge this approach because a consensus existed among them that a government's treatment of its own people was essentially a domestic concern and not an issue for the international community. Governments were reluctant to condemn another government because one day their own policies might be sanctioned. In general, the major private organizations, such as the ICRC and the national Red Cross societies, also confined themselves to the task of emergency relief and assistance, and did not take up the issue of human rights.

The refugee agencies of the League of Nations also avoided addressing the government policies that produced refugees. In this

---

[3] See Walters, *History of the League of Nations*; George Scott, *The Rise and Fall of the League of Nations* (London: Hutchinson, 1973); Elmer Bendiner, *A Time for Angels: The Tragicomic History of the League of Nations* (New York: Alfred A. Knopf, 1975).

[4] The Minority Treaties or similar declarations covered Poland, Czechoslovakia, Romania, Greece, Yugoslavia, Albania, Estonia, Latvia, and Lithuania.

[5] For a discussion of the meaning and content of human rights, see R. J. Vincent, *Human Rights and International Relations* (Cambridge: Cambridge University Press and the Royal Institute of International Affairs, 1986), 7–18.

regard, the first High Commissioner for Refugees set a precedent which has been continued by the United Nations. Nansen interpreted the humanitarian principle to mean that his office must remain politically neutral if it was to be effective in providing humanitarian assistance. Though Nansen himself blamed the Turkish government for the creation of Greek and Armenian refugees, he took pains not to let this affect his work. While in the Near East conducting relief operations, he wrote that 'I cannot in any way denounce the proceedings of the Turkish authorities, whatever my personal opinion may be. I am obliged to confine myself to appealing on strictly humanitarian grounds for assistance for the refugees.'[6] Nansen's neutrality was appreciated by both sides and it was one of the factors which enabled him to act as a negotiator at the Lausanne Conference.

Michael Hansson, president of the Nansen Office from 1936 until 1938, also shared Nansen's view of the appropriate role of a refugee agency. In speeches and reports, he continually stressed the humanitarian and non-political character of refugee work. Hansson made these comments in response to criticisms made by the Soviet Union that the Nansen Office was controlled by White Russian refugees and was being used as a mechanism to spread propaganda. Although the Nansen Office did employ refugees, especially at the local level, there is no substantive evidence that it was being used as a political tool. Nevertheless, the Soviet government, after it joined the League of Nations in 1938, objected to the employment of refugees by the Nansen Office for this reason. By underscoring the non-political nature of refugee work, Hansson was attempting to protect his agency from attacks by a refugee-producing country.[7]

In contrast to Nansen and Hansson, some actors in the international refugee regime challenged the idea that the refugee agencies should be politically passive. In effect, they argued that fulfilment of the humanitarian principle sometimes required infringing on state sovereignty. In these circumstances, assisting refugees necessitated addressing the causes of a refugee movement, even if that meant censuring a government for abusing its

---

[6] Letter from Nansen to N. Politis, 9 Nov. 1922 in Jacob S. Worm-Müller (ed.), *Fridtjof Nansen Brev* (Oslo: Universitetsforlaget, 1966), iv. 170.

[7] League of Nations, Nansen International Office for Refugees, 'Report of the Governing Body' (20 Aug. 1937) [A.21.1937.XII], 7.

own people. The person most closely associated with this position is James G. McDonald, the first High Commissioner for Refugees coming from Germany.

JAMES G. MCDONALD AND HUMAN RIGHTS IN NAZI GERMANY

When James G. McDonald took up his appointment as High Commissioner for Refugees coming from Germany in October 1933, he appeared to be an unlikely candidate to challenge the human rights record of the Third Reich. Throughout his career McDonald had developed a record as a person sympathetic to German interests. As a young assistant professor at Indiana University, he defended Germany against indiscriminate charges of atrocities made during the First World War. Later on, as Chairman of the Foreign Policy Association, he tried to counteract popular hatred and prejudice against Germany and the German people.[8] Nevertheless, McDonald has the distinction of being the only refugee administrator in the Inter-war Period to publicly criticize the German government for its inhumane treatment of Jews and other 'non-Aryans', and to call for international intervention to deal with the root causes of the refugee exodus. In making his appeal, McDonald did not receive a great deal of encouragement from the governments composing the League of Nations. In fact, the reverse is true. They took great pains to avoid confronting the German government on the refugee issue.

When the issue of refugees from Germany first came up at the League of Nations in October 1933, the Minister of Foreign Affairs for the Netherlands proposed that the League assist the refugees, but without interfering in German internal affairs. In his keynote speech, he stressed that 'we have no wish to examine the reasons why these people have left their country, but we are faced with the undeniable fact that thousands of German subjects have crossed the frontiers of neighbouring countries and are refusing to return to their homes, for reasons which we are not called upon to judge. For us, therefore, it is a purely technical problem.'[9]

[8] James G. McDonald, *Christian Responsibility toward German Refugees* (1934), 2.

[9] *Official Journal*, Special Supplement no. 115, Records of the Fourteenth Assembly: Text (Geneva, 1933), 48.

The Assembly agreed. It referred the matter to the Second Committee (Technical Organizations) rather than to the Sixth Committee (Political Questions), the body that normally dealt with refugees.[10] Once the High Commissioner began operations, the League continued to distance itself from the organization.[11] Despite a lack of support from the League itself, McDonald began his work with great enthusiasm. In November 1933 he wrote, 'This is an adventure! Exciting and exhilarating, and so far as one can see it promises to continue to be.'[12] In taking up the job as High Commissioner, McDonald brought both energy and experience to his work. Described as a 'young man, full of initiative and foresight, and one who has always made a success of everything he has been keen on',[13] he drew on his knowledge of politics and public relations garnered while serving as Chairman of the Foreign Policy Association. In addition, he approached his position with a deep moral commitment to the Jewish people. A devout Christian, humanist, and friend of the American Jewish community, McDonald believed that Christians had an obligation to address the 'Jewish problem'. He argued that 'Christians have a special responsibility because those who persecute boast that they are Christians while violating the elementary ethical principles taught and practised by the founder of Christianity'.[14]

Initially McDonald accepted the mandate given to him by the League of Nations and was content to stay within strict guidelines. From the time of his appointment in late 1933 and throughout 1934 he devoted his energies to negotiating with governments on refugee immigration and co-ordinating the activities of private organizations. Though this work yielded small successes, McDonald because increasingly frustrated with his own inability to solve the refugee crisis. In particular, he found that he lacked the authority necessary to deal with governments.

When McDonald took up his post as High Commissioner, he had hoped to negotiate directly with top officials in the German

---

[10] The Fifth Committee (Humanitarian Questions) also dealt with refugee issues.   [11] See above, Ch. 6.

[12] Letter from James G. McDonald to Esther G. Ogden, 27 Nov. 1933. JGM H1.

[13] Letter from Marie Ginzberg, Geneva, to Mildred Wertheimer, Foreign Policy Association, 31 Oct. 1933. JGM H1. Ginzberg was active in the women's international movement and refugee relief circles in Switzerland.

[14] McDonald, *Christian Responsibility*, 8.

government about the conditions under which Jewish refugees left the country. Because of this, McDonald muted his public criticism of the Nazis because he believed it would reduce his ability to negotiate with them. But a meeting with Nazi leaders never materialized, despite McDonald's 'quiet diplomacy' and promises of intervention from both the American and British ambassadors in Berlin.[15] By November 1934 McDonald realized that little would result from talks with the Germans. He reached the conclusion that 'so far as our work is concerned we cannot expect any really effective cooperation from the Reich'.[16]

As time progressed, McDonald's relationships with other governments also deteriorated. This was particularly apparent with the government of France, the European country hosting the largest number of refugees. When McDonald first met French officials in November 1933 they greeted him warmly: 'I could not have asked for a better attitude on the part of the French government.'[17] But, before long, McDonald's stock of goodwill ran out. Henry Berenger, French delegate to the Governing Body and the most important Jew in the French government, did not take an active interest in the organization and rarely attended meetings. His position was that France had already fulfilled its obligations by caring for almost half the refugees and that it was up to the United States to do its fair share.[18] By the autumn of 1935 French officials came to regard the High Commission as a useless body and made it clear that they no longer desired McDonald's services. According to one historian, he was 'too independent, too demanding, and too energetic. He was moving to radical positions.'[19]

Although McDonald maintained a close relationship with Lord Robert Cecil, British delegate to the Governing Body and its chairman, he fared no better with the British government. Despite repeated pleas from the High Commissioner, the government

---

[15] Barbara McDonald Stewart, *United States Government Policy on Refugees from Nazism, 1933–1940* (New York: Garland Press, 1982), 112, 121.

[16] Letter from James G. McDonald to Sir Osmond d'Avigdor Goldschmidt, 17 Nov. 1934. JGM H3. Goldschmidt was a leading member of the Jewish Colonization Association and Chairman of the Allocations Committee of the Central British Fund.

[17] Letter from James G. McDonald to Esther Ogden, 27 Nov. 1933. JGM H1.

[18] Stewart, *US Government Policy*, 119–29.

[19] Correspondence with French government, 1933–5. LNA C1609/1 (33–6); Bauer, *My Brother's Keeper*, 149.

steadfastly refused to contribute more than moral support towards the cost of refugee relief and settlement.[20] In addition, Cecil, a close friend of Nansen and a strong advocate of the League of Nations, did what he could to influence the British government. But his efforts came to naught as well. In early 1935 he led a futile debate in the House of Lords on His Majesty's Government policy towards refugees. Afterwards Cecil declared in frustration that the Governing Body was 'quite useless'.[21]

In addition to his problems with governments, McDonald became increasingly disenchanted with the High Commissioner's separation from the League of Nations. He realized that, as an independent official, the High Commissioner had little authority with which to negotiate with governments. In order to correct this problem, McDonald and his staff lobbied for a compete reorganization of all refugee work under one central agency. Partly as a consequence of their efforts, the Norwegian delegation made a proposal to centralize all refugee assistance programmes at the September 1935 Assembly.[22] The Assembly reacted by establishing an expert committee to study the problem and report back to the League in the near future.[23]

McDonald, however, clearly realized that institutional changes alone would not solve the refugee problem. In the spring of 1935 he and an associate travelled to Latin America in the hope of increasing refugee immigration to the region, but the expedition produced few results. Discouraged, McDonald reached the conclusion that 'the more I face the refugee problem at close range, the more I am convinced that it is utterly insoluble unless and until the governments and private individuals concerned are prepared to make more sacrifices than heretofore. And no scheme of reorganization can, I feel, change this stubborn and unpleasant fact.'[24]

[20] Letter from O. Sargent, Foreign Office, to James G. McDonald, 29 Oct. 1934. LNA C1609/4 (34–6).
[21] Letter from Cecil to J. G. McDonald, 7 Feb. 1935. LNA C1609/5 (33–6). See also House of Lords, 'Official Report', *Parliamentary Debates*, 95/18 (6 Feb. 1935), 828–45. Cecil expresses similar sentiments in his autobiography: Lord Robert Cecil, *A Great Experiment: An Autobiography* (London: Jonathan Cape, 1941), 252–4.
[22] See above, Ch. 4.
[23] *Official Journal*, Special Supplement no. 138, Records of the Sixteenth Assembly: Text (Geneva, 1935), 57–8.
[24] Letter from James G. McDonald to Lord Robert Cecil, 18 May 1935. LNA C1609/5 (33–6).

The promulgation of the Nuremberg Laws by the Third Reich in September 1935 deepened McDonald's sense of frustration with existing efforts to assist Jewish refugees. Among other things, these laws deprived German Jews and other non-Aryans of their citizenship. An increase in persecution accompanied the Nuremberg legislation and, as a result, a new wave of refugees began to flee the country. Soon afterwards, in October 1935, McDonald confided to a close friend that his emotions had become involved in what he called 'the fundamental problem of Jewish–Christian relationships'. He added that his two years as High Commissioner had increased his conviction that 'each of us who has a sense of the terrible responsibility which Christians have for the "Jewish problem", must do everything he can to redress the balance of centuries of wrongs perpetrated against the Jewish people'.[25]

At the time of the Nuremberg legislation, McDonald had already decided to tender his resignation as High Commissioner in the near future. But the new laws gave him and his staff an extra incentive to draw attention to Nazi policies towards Jews and other minorities. The High Commissioner decided to make his latter of resignation a political appeal. Work began on the letter several months in advance. Oscar Janowsky, a professor of history from New York, and Melvin Fagen, a specialist on international law, actually drew up the letter.[26] In addition, McDonald consulted leading experts in various fields and key Jewish leaders. In writing the letter, the High Commissioner sought to accomplish two major goals: (1) to mobilize public opinion against Nazi policies towards Jews and other non-Aryans and (2) to induce the League of Nations to intervene on behalf of persecuted minorities within Germany.[27]

On 27 December 1935 James G. McDonald officially resigned and submitted to the Secretary-General of the League of Nations a 3,000-word letter of resignation, including an annex with documentary evidence on Nazi persecution of non-Aryans.[28] The letter

[25] Letter from James G. McDonald to Lewis L. Strauss, 28 Oct. 1935. JGM H6. Strauss was a prominent New York Jew who served on the Board of Directors of the JDC.
[26] These two men later wrote a book on the subject. See Oscar I. Janowsky and Melvin M. Fagen, *International Aspects of German Racial Policies* (New York, 1937).
[27] Statement of Resignation and Drafts. JGM H13.
[28] James G. McDonald, *Letter of Resignation . . . Addressed to the Secretary-General of the League of Nations. With an Annex.* (London, 1935). A copy of the letter, without the annex, is reprinted in Norman Bentwich, *The Refugees from Germany, April 1933 to December 1935* (London: Allen & Unwin, 1936), 119–228.

begins by calling attention to the source of the refugee problem: 'more than half a million persons, against whom no charge can be made except that they are not what the National Socialists choose to regard as "Nordic", are being crushed.' The letter argues that resolution of the refugee crisis requires greater efforts on the part of philanthropic bodies, but that this alone would not solve the problem. The letter also rejects immigration as a solution to the refugee problem, stating that 'in the present economic conditions of the world, the European States, and even those overseas, have only a limited power of absorption of refugees'.[29] What is needed, the letter argues, is for the causes of the refugee exodus to be addressed: 'efforts must be made to remove or mitigate the causes which create German refugees', and this should be done by the League of Nations itself.[30]

The letter then documents Nazi policies towards Jews and other non-Aryans, and labels the German government as a violator of the common principles of humanity and law. It further declares that collective action, through the League of Nations, should be brought to bear against Germany. According to the letter, 'the growing sufferings of the persecuted minority in Germany and the menace of the growing exodus call for friendly but firm intercession with the German Government, by all pacific means, on the part of the League of Nations, of its Member-States and other members of the community of nations'.[31] The letter concludes with a plea that state sovereignty be set aside in favour of humanitarian imperatives:

When domestic policies threaten the demoralization and exile of hundreds of thousands of human beings, considerations of diplomatic correctness must yield to those of common humanity. I should be recreant if I did not call attention to the actual situation, and plead that world opinion, acting through the League and its Member-States and other countries, move to avert the existing and impending tragedies.[32]

---

[29] McDonald, 'Letter', p. ix, point 15.   [30] Ibid., pp. v–vi, point 3.
[31] Ibid., p. ix, point 14.
[32] Ibid., p. x, point 17. Given the apocalyptic tone of McDonald's letter, it is worth considering whether he foresaw the Holocaust. His daughter, Barbara McDonald Stewart, says that 'McDonald sought to convince governments and individuals that the Nazis meant what they said when they promised a "final solution"'. But there is no reason to assume that McDonald's letter specifically referred to a potential genocide. Because of his extensive knowledge of German politics, McDonald realized that Nazi ideologues would not be satisfied by the Nuremberg Laws. Consequently, stronger measures against the Jews were likely in some form. Stewart, *US Government Policy*, 123.

McDonald's letter of resignation drew the attention of newspapers world-wide, especially in the English-speaking world. In London, *The Times* printed the letter in full and advocated that the League carefully consider McDonald's suggestion that representations be made to Berlin, the source of the flow of refugees.[33] The *Manchester Guardian* called McDonald's resignation a 'powerful letter' and asked Germany to relent in its persecution of 'non-Aryans'.[34] The *Daily Telegraph* hoped that Germany would 'not neglect to consider the advice of world opinion'.[35] In the United States, the *New York Times* printed McDonald's letter of resignation in full and praised McDonald for being a 'statesman as well as a humane agent'.[36] In the nation's capital, the *Washington Post* called the letter 'one of the most powerful indictments of the Nazi regime of terrorism yet given to the outside world'. In the American heartland, the Cleveland *Plain Dealer* said: 'This studied and legalized persecution cannot be allowed to continue in the midst of a world which calls itself civilized . . . If his resignation forces the Nazi terror to the front as a world problem demanding united humanitarian action he will have accomplished much good.' In Canada, the Ottawa *Citizen* said: 'It is high time that the world became better informed on these atrocities, and that the nations which still cherish civilized traditions considered the proposal of Mr. McDonald that political action be applied to Nazi Germany.'[37] Overall, the press reacted favourably to McDonald's letter and helped the High Commissioner to increase public awareness about Nazi policies.

Despite initial public reaction to the letter, McDonald was never personally satisfied with the response, because it was quickly forgotten and never generated direct intervention from the League of Nations.[38] But his letter did influence the League's actions.[39]

---

[33] *The Times* (30 Dec. 1935), 6, 11.

[34] *Manchester Guardian* (30 Dec. 1930), 8, 13. The newspaper also printed the letter in full.   [35] *Daily Telegraph* (30 Dec. 1935), 10–11.

[36] *New York Times* (30 Dec. 1935), 1, 12.

[37] Memorandum on Repercussions of the McDonald Letter of Resignation. JGM H13.

[38] Stewart, *US Government Policy*, 166. Stewart concludes that the Council of the League of Nations never seriously considered the letter and simply passed it on to the Assembly. While the Council clearly did not act on McDonald's major recommendations, their decision to bring the High Commissioner directly under League auspices does reflect that they took parts of the letter to heart.

[39] McDonald, 'Letter', p. vi, point 4.

The Council took seriously the comment that the separation of the High Commissioner from the League severely hampered its ability to assist refugees and, at its meeting of 24 January 1936, it agreed that a High Commissioner for Refugees coming from Germany should be officially appointed by the League. The new High Commissioner would have three major duties: (1) to arrange a system of legal protection for refugees from Germany; (2) to consult with governments on refugee settlement and employment; (3) to establish liaison with private associations dealing with refugees. Under the revised arrangements, the Nansen Office would continue to deal with non-German refugees.[40]

The Council's action gave the position of High Commissioner more authority than it previously had, partially fulfilling the demands made in McDonald's letter of resignation. However, other actions taken by the Council severely limited the powers of the new High Commissioner. First, the Council rejected any intrusion into what they considered to be Germany's internal affairs. They made it clear that the High Commissioner's mandate only referred to refugees who had already left Germany. In addition, the Council carefully limited the new High Commissioner's relations with governments to seeking their assistance, thereby excluding potential criticisms of government refugee policies. Although the Council agreed to finance the new office, they only allocated 50,000 Swiss francs (£2,000) for its operations and prohibited the High Commissioner from receiving money from private organizations.[41]

More important than creating institutional impediments, the Council deliberately appointed a High Commissioner who would willingly stay within his official mandate. Early on, the Council agreed that someone of British nationality should be named as High Commissioner, reflecting the growing interest of the British government in refugee issues.[42] With the approval of British officials, the Council named Major-General Sir Neill Malcolm as the new High Commissioner.[43] An elderly gentleman with a distinguished military career, Malcolm made it immediately clear that

[40] '90th Session of the Council', *Official Journal* (Feb. 1936), 126–9.
[41] Ibid. See also League of Nations, 'Refugees Coming from Germany: Report to the Seventeenth Assembly by High Commissioner, Sir Neill Malcolm' (1 Sept. 1936) [A.19.1936.XII], 2; Marrus, *The Unwanted*, 164.
[42] Letter from F. P. Walters, Secretariat, to Mr Bruce, President of the Council, 3 Feb. 1936. LNA R5719/7100 (22107).
[43] *Official Journal* (Mar. 1936), 296.

he would not challenge the German government.[44] In a press interview he declared that 'I have no policy, but the policy of the League is to deal with the political and legal status of the refugees. It has nothing to do with the domestic policy of Germany. That's not the affair of the League. We deal with persons when they become refugees and not before.'[45]

As High Commissioner, Malcolm fulfilled the expectations of his supporters and disappointed those of refugee-advocates. He devoted most of his efforts to working with governments to improve the legal situation of refugees from Germany. Although he created a Liaison Committee of private organizations, he did not chair its meetings or become actively involved in the humanitarian side of refugee work. In fact, Malcolm stressed that 'we no longer deal with individual cases of hardship, or, indeed, with what we may call the philanthropic and charitable side of refugee work'.[46] On only a few occasions did he take any independent initiatives. After the incorporation of Austria into the Third Reich, he asked the Secretary-General of the League of Nations for the authority to establish temporary camps for refugees in bordering countries. Avenol, in keeping with his general approach to refugees, rejected the proposal as being beyond the scope of the League. Malcolm, unlike Nansen, was a man who took 'no' for an anwer. Whatever his personal feelings, he accepted Avenol's verdict and did not bring up the subject again.[47]

The appointment of the last High Commissioner in the League era followed the Malcolm model. In late 1938 the League finally combined services for all refugees into one High Commissioner for Refugees. This time the League appointed Sir Herbert Emerson, an ailing British civil servant who had retired from the Indian civil service for health reasons.[48] In selecting Emerson, the League

[44] *Who Was Who, 1951–1960* (London: Adam & Charles Black, 1961), 726. Malcolm had served in India, Uganda, South Africa, Somaliland, Europe, and Malaya and had been severely wounded in combat twice. See also Stewart, *US Government Policy*, 231–2.

[45] Quoted in Arthur D. Morse, *While Six Million Died: A Chronicle of American Apathy* (New York: Random House, 1968), 198.

[46] Simpson, *The Refugee Problem*, 217; letter from Malcolm to Avenol, 20 Feb. 1936. LNA R5719/7100 (22107).

[47] Memorandum to the Secretary-General, 1 July 1938. LNA R5721/7100 (34423).

[48] *Official Journal*, Special Supplement no. 189, Nineteenth Assembly, Sixth Committee (Geneva, 1938), 57; *Official Journal*, Special Supplement no. 183, Nineteenth Assembly: Text (Geneva, 1938), 136–8. Emerson resigned from his post

passed over Sir John Hope Simpson, author of the refugee survey published by the Royal Institute of International Affairs in 1938. Though Simpson had worked with refugees in Greece and with disaster victims in China, the Foreign Office thought him to be too critical of British immigration policy.[49] In particular, Simpson advocated greater Jewish immigration to Great Britain because 'in whatever direction you look—politics, economics, professions, literature, art—the Jew is an outstanding feature. And they make excellent citizens.' Moreover, Simpson thought it was both *immoral and unwise* to express sympathy for Jewish refugees without taking action on their behalf.[50] By choosing Emerson instead of a potentially more outspoken person like Simpson, the League could avoid a repeat of McDonald's performance. As High Commissioner, Emerson did not disappoint his sponsors. Privately he voiced the complaint to a Secretariat official that 'It seems to me entirely unworthy of the League of Nations to appoint an officer with a high-sounding title, and beyond his administrative budget to give him no money at all with which to deal with this enormous problem'.[51] In public, however, his comments supported the official policy of the League of Nations and its member states.

Thus, McDonald's attempt to expand the boundaries of the international refugee regime to include dealing with the immediate causes of refugee movements produced a mixed result. On the one hand, his letter of resignation resulted in increased publicity about Nazi atrocities and in assistance to refugees from Germany being brought directly under the authority of the League of Nations. On the other hand, members of the international refugee regime rejected any intrusion into the domestic policies of Germany and

---

as Governor of the Punjab in 1938 because of a prolonged illness. For a short biography see *Who Was Who, 1961–1970* (London: Adam & Charles Black, 1972), 351, and *Obituaries From the Times, 1961–70*, 250–1.

[49] A. J. Sherman, *Island Refuge: Britain and Refugees from the Third Reich: 1933–1939* (London: Paul Elek, 1973), 128; Marrus, *The Unwanted*, 166. Simpson served as a member of the Greek Refugee Settlement Commission from 1926 until 1930. In 1930 he undertook a special mission to Palestine. From 1931 until 1933 he served as Director-General of the National Flood Relief Commission in China. For a short biography see *Who Was Who, 1961–1970*, 1035–6, and *Obituaries from the Times, 1961–70*, 729–30.

[50] Letter from Sir John Hope Simpson to Alfred Zimmern, 1 Aug. 1944. MS Zimmern 48, fos. 135–9.

[51] Confidential letter from Emerson to F. P. Walters, 21 July 1939. LNA R5635/ 35482 (38870).

took action to prevent future refugee administrators from delving too deeply into the causes of refugee movements. This set-back had little impact on McDonald's views: he remained unrepentant. Writing during the Second World War, he still advocated stopping refugee movements at their source: 'The only real solution for the problems of refugees and displaced persons is to eliminate the causes which force these innocent victims from their homes. That these causes must be eliminated is the deepest conviction gained during the writer's experiences with German refugees.'[52]

ORGANIZING THE FLIGHT OF REFUGEES

McDonald's efforts to expand the functions of the international refugee regime to deal directly with the causes of refugee movements was the only serious attempt to do so during the Inter-war Period. Other actors in the regime, however, proved willing to negotiate with refugee-producing countries under special circumstances. These discussions did not try to prevent human-rights abuses but rather to organize the departure of refugees. While this strategy would not stop refugee movements, it sought to improve the conditions under which refugees left their home country. Potentially, organizing flight could improve the material lot of refugees by enabling them to depart with their property. Even though it offered great benefits, this method of dealing with refugees was tried only twice in the Inter-war Period: (1) the exchange of populations after the 1922 Graeco-Turkish war and (2) the flight of refugees from the Third Reich in the 1930s. Though the outcome of these two schemes differed, they heralded the same lessons for the international refugee regime.

Nansen and the Graeco-Turkish Population Exchange

The Greco-Turkish population exchange was only one component of a radical solution to minority problems in the area now encompassing Greece, Turkey, and Bulgaria. In the early twentieth

---

[52] James G. McDonald, 'Refugees', in Harriet Eager Davis (ed.), *Pioneers in World Order: An American Appraisal of the League of Nations* (New York: Columbia University Press, 1944), 226–7.

century this region experienced repeated ethnic conflicts and large population displacements. The largest refugee movement followed the Greco-Turkish war of 1922, in which Greece failed in an attempt to capture Smyrna and its ethnic Greek population. After the Turkish army recaptured the area in September 1922, over one million Anatolian Greek and Armenian refugees fled to Greece. This disastrous turn of events not only affected the Greek minority in Turkey, but also threatened the future of the Turkish Muslim minority in Greece.[53]

In response to the refugee crisis in the Near East, the League of Nations sent High Commissioner for Refugees Nansen to oversee emergency relief efforts. While in Constantinople, the Allied High Commissioners asked Nansen to help negotiate a population exchange between the two belligerents. Such an arrangement was not without precedent, as several similar ones had already been carried out in the Balkans.[54] Nansen began negotiations immediately, but was unable to complete them before the peace conference met at Lausanne in November 1922.[55] At the conference, both the Greek and Turkish governments agreed to a compulsory exchange of Turkish nationals of the Greek Orthodox religion and Greek nationals of the Muslim religion. According to the agreement, the emigrants could take their movable property with them and a Mixed Commission would arrange compensation for their immovable property. In effect, this agreement meant that the Greek refugees who had already fled Asia Minor would not be allowed to return to their homes. In addition, the exchange sanctioned the removal of about 200,000 ethnic Greeks still in Turkey and 400,000 Turkish Muslims living in Greece.

The compulsory nature of the population exchange necessarily created controversy. Asia Minor Greeks opposed it because they

[53] See above, Ch. 2. A small number of Muslims of Albanian ethnicity also lived in Greece, but they were exempted from the population exchange.

[54] The Turco-Bulgarian Convention of 1913 provided for a voluntary exchange of populations within 15 km. on either side of the border between the two countries. The Greeks and Turks signed a similar agreement in 1914, but it was never carried out because of Turkey's entry into the First World War. In 1919 Greece and Bulgaria signed a convention for a voluntary, reciprocal population exchange in conjunction with the Treaty of Neuilly. See Stephen Ladas, *The Exchange of Minorities: Bulgaria, Greece, and Turkey* (New York: Macmillan, 1933), 18–20.

[55] For Nansen's own account of these negotiations, see 'Reciprocal Exchange of Racial Minorities between Greece and Turkey: Report by Dr. Nansen of 15 November 1922', *Official Journal* (Jan. 1923), 126–9.

hoped one day to return to their birthplace. The Turkish Muslims in Greece also objected to it because they did not want to leave their ancestral homes. In addition, outside observers criticized the exchange as 'unsatisfactory' and 'unnecessarily harsh'.[56] The compulsory aspect of the exchange was so controversial that no one would take responsibility for it. At the Peace Conference in Lausanne, delegates from the Greek and Turkish governments both blamed Nansen for suggesting the idea.[57] Nansen claimed that he only presented options to the two governments and did not make a recommendation himself.[58] Lord Curzon, chief negotiator at the conference, and Sir Horace Rumbold, British High Commissioner in Constantinople, both blamed the Turkish government for making the exchange mandatory.[59] While the mystery surrounding the compulsory provision of the exchange may never be completely unravelled,[60] one fact remains: all parties at the conference eventually agreed to a compulsory exchange.

In accepting the compulsory exchange, the government delegates primarily acted in accordance with their national interests. Venizelos, the Greek delegate, supported a solution he labelled 'repugnant' because it enabled his government to settle Asia Minor refugees on land then owned by ethnic Turks.[61] Speaking on behalf of the Turkish government, Ismet Pasha openly stated that his government did not want to see the return of a minority which

---

[56] Arnold J. Toynbee and Kenneth P. Kirkwood, *Turkey* (London: Ernest Benn, 1926), 207; Ladas, *Exchange of Minorities*, 340; Philip Noel-Baker, *Nansen's Place in History*, Nansen Memorial Lecture, 11 Oct. 1961 (Oslo: Universitetsforlaget, 1962), 12.   [57] *Parliamentary Papers* (1923), i. 210, 217.
[58] Nansen defends his role at the Peace Conference in 'Refugees in the Near East: Report by Dr. Nansen to the Council of 2 February 1923', *Official Journal* (Mar. 1923), 383–4.   [59] *Parliamentary Papers* (1923), i. 210, 227.
[60] Historical research since the Lausanne Conference has not ended the controversy. Both Ladas and Pentzopoulus present detailed accounts of the negotiations for the population exchange. Ladas reaches the conclusion that Venizelos first suggested a compulsory exchange. Pentzopoulus disagrees with this and identifies Nansen as the originator of the compulsory exchange. Other scholars place the blame on Turkey for not allowing the return of its Greek minority. Pearson, for instance, writes that 'there was never any doubt that the convention was a cynical attempt by Turkey to legitimise the forcible expulsion of its Greek minority'. See Ladas, *Exchange of Minorities*, esp. 336; Dimitri Pentzopoulus, *The Balkan Exchange of Minorities and its Impact upon Greece* (Paris: Mouton & Co., 1962), esp. 63, 66; Raymond Pearson, *National Minorities in Eastern Europe: 1848–1945* (London: Macmillan, 1983), 140.
[61] *Parliamentary Papers* (1923), i. 210, 223; Pentzopoulus, *Balkan Exchange of Minorities*, 63.

might provoke foreign intervention in the future.[62] Though not explicitly stated, the government welcomed the arrival of ethnic Turks. For over ten years it had been encouraging ethnic Turks residing in Bulgaria, Greece, and elsewhere to move to the new nation-state of Turkey. Although Lord Curzon considered the exchange to be a 'thoroughly bad and vicious solution', he advocated it on pragmatic grounds. He reasoned that a compulsory exchange could be carried out with greater speed and that it would facilitate payments for property.[63]

At the conference, only High Commissioner Nansen presented a case for the population exchange on humanitarian grounds. In his speech, Nansen acknowledged that the population exchange, even under the best circumstances, would impose hardship and poverty on many individuals. Nevertheless, he argued, 'these hardships, great though they may be, will be less than the hardships which will result for these same populations if nothing is done'. Nansen went on to predict economic disaster for both Greece and Turkey if the exchange did not take place.[64] Because the agreement required international supervision and required that compensation be paid to the people involved, Nansen viewed the exchange as a success for the refugees.[65] It should also be noted that Nansen shared the popular wisdom of the era that the 'unmixing' of populations reduced political turmoil and helped to create lasting peace.[66] Based on this belief, Nansen felt that the Greco-Turkish population exchange would dramatically improve the departure conditions of Greek and Turkish refugees and contribute to peace in the region.

In practice, implementation of the population exchange failed to fulfil the convention's original intent. Despite signing the agreement, the Turkish government did not abide by all its provisions. Government officials 'encouraged' the remaining Greek minority to leave quickly and often confiscated their property. As a consequence, the Greeks left in a disorderly fashion and many arrived in Greece just as penniless as those who had fled earlier.[67] In

---

[62] *Parliamentary Papers* (1923), i. 204.   [63] Ibid. 121, 212.
[64] Ibid. 115.   [65] Noel-Baker, *Nansen's Place in History*, 13.
[66] Fridtjof Nansen, 'Refugees and the Exchange of Populations', *Encyclopaedia Britannica*, 14th edn. (1939), xix. 59. See also letter from P. J. [Noel-]Baker, Nansen's assistant, to Harold Nicolson, Foreign Office, 20 Oct. 1922, explaining Nansen's viewpoint on the exchange. NBKR 4/471.
[67] Ladas, *Exchange of Minorities*, 430; Pearson, *National Minorities*, 140.

244 THE ATTEMPT TO DEAL WITH ROOT CAUSES

regard to the departure of the Turkish minority from Greece, the convention worked as anticipated: most refugees left in an orderly manner with their movable property. Once inside Turkey, however, they encountered grim conditions. Instead of moving into vacant houses and farms, they found that many of their promised homes had already been occupied by Turkish citizens. In addition, many refugees died for lack of food, clothing, and shelter.[68]

Most importantly, the Mixed Commission failed to arrange effectively the liquidation of immovable property and the payment of compensation to the refugees. This provision was especially important for the over one million Greeks who fled Turkey before the signing of the convention. To them, the sections in the agreement on movable property mattered little since they had already fled without their possessions. Only the clauses on immovable property offered them hope of receiving compensation for their great financial and personal losses. Although the Greek and Turkish governments negotiated for over five years, the Mixed Commission never liquidated the properties or paid any compensation. The basic stumbling-block in negotiations was the unequal terms of the exchange. No amount of haggling could change the fact that fewer than 400,000 Turks had been exchanged for over one million Greeks. Finally, in 1930, the Greek and Turkish governments reached a bilateral settlement outside the framework of the Mixed Commission. For most of the refugees this settlement was too little and too late.[69]

In theory, the Greco-Turkish population exchange offered a viable method of bringing order to refugee movements and solving a troublesome minority problem. In practice, however, the agreement failed to accomplish these goals. Although the agreement did improve the departure conditions of Turkish refugees from Greece, most of the other provisions were either ignored or not implemented. Moreover, League of Nations sponsorship of the agreement gave an aura of legitimacy to the forcible uprooting of almost two million people. Consequently, it is not surprising that the Greco-Turkish population exchange was destined to be the last one sponsored by the League of Nations. Thereafter, the League preferred to deal with minority problems through the system established in the Minorities Treaties.[70]

[68] Toynbee and Kirkwood, *Turkey*, 208.
[69] Ladas, *Exchange of Minorities*, 720; Pentzopoulus, *Balkan Exchange of Minorities*, 117–19.   [70] Pearson, *National Minorities*, 141–2.

In retrospect, the unhappy experience of the Greco-Turkish population exchange stands in stark contrast to the success of refugee settlement in Greece and Bulgaria. This lesson was not lost on the major actors in the international refugee regime. They preferred to fulfil the principles and norms of the regime by assisting refugees after they fled their home countries; only in desperate circumstances would organizing flight be considered seriously.

The Rublee Plan and Refugees from the Third Reich

Until 1938 the plight of refugees from Germany was not generally considered to be a desperate situation. Despite the warnings of High Commissioner McDonald, many concerned observers anticipated that the German refugee problem could be solved through normal migration channels. Writing about the extent of the problem at the end of 1937, Simpson reports that there were approximately 150,000 refugees from Germany and that the great majority had already settled in overseas countries. Only about 30,000–35,000 needed to be moved from countries of first asylum to permanent homes. Although Simpson calls the problem 'urgent' and 'difficult', he concludes that 'these problems, though intractable, could be solved by concerted efforts and the best use of existing institutions'.[71]

Jewish leaders essentially shared Simpson's evaluation. Officials of the Jewish Agency for Palestine and other Jewish organizations planned on the gradual evacuation of central European Jewry over a twenty-year period.[72] In November 1933 the Jewish Agency concluded an agreement with the German government aimed at carrying out this purpose. Under the terms of the agreement, a special institution, the Haavarah, was established for the express purpose of transferring Jewish capital from Germany to Palestine. From November 1933 until July 1939 the Haavarah transferred 105 million RM to Palestine to be used by German Jewish immigrants there.[73] In Great Britain, leading British Jewish groups continued to lobby the British government to support direct negotiations by the League of Nations with the German government on departure conditions. Meanwhile, they devised an ambitious

[71] Simpson, *The Refugee Problem*, 139–40, 515–16.
[72] Marrus, *The Unwanted*, 167; Bauer, *My Brother's Keeper*, 25.
[73] Tartakower and Grossman, *The Jewish Refugee*, 443.

scheme of assisted emigration for about 100,000 young people at a cost of £3 million and took steps to implement it.[74]

All plans for the orderly departure of refugees from Germany had to be completely revised in 1938. In March of that year Germany annexed Austria, bringing approximately 180,000 more Jews under its rule. Afterwards the swift application of anti-Semitic policies created a mass exodus, primarily composed of Austrian Jews. This transformed what had been a manageable problem into an official 'refugee crisis'. When governments gathered at Evian, France, in July 1938 to discuss ways of dealing with the crisis,[75] the topic of controlling the flight of refugees from the Third Reich was raised both implicitly and explicitly. Indeed, this had been one of the top American objectives in calling the conference.

At Evian, Myron C. Taylor, the chief American delegate and conference chairman, began his keynote speech by defining the scope of the problem before the assembled delegates. Adopting a liberal approach, he established the competence of the conference to include all 'political refugees' and defined this term to include two types of persons: (a) those still inside Germany (including Austria) who wanted to leave because of ill-treatment based on their racial origins, political opinions, or religious beliefs; and (b) those who had already left Germany or were in the process of migration for the same reasons.[76] This definition of the term 'refugee' significantly expanded the scope of international efforts to assist refugees. By including potential refugees, Taylor indicated the need to negotiate with the Third Reich on the departure conditions of refugees.

The American definition, however, did not go so far as to expand the potential refugee problem beyond Germany. In fact, the Roosevelt administration took great pains to define the problem as that of 'political refugees' rather than a 'Jewish problem'. This eliminated the large Jewish population of eastern Europe from the course of discussions. To some, it was obvious that these Jews were just as much at risk as those in Germany. In the Refugee Survey, for instance, Simpson stresses that 'the whole of Eastern

---

[74] Norman Bentwich, *They Found Refuge* (London, 1956), 30; Sherman, *Island Refuge*, 65–8. [75] See above, Ch. 6.
[76] 'Speech of Myron C. Taylor, USA', *Proceedings of the Intergovernmental Committee, Evian, July 6th to 15th, 1938: Verbatim Record of the Plenary Meetings of the Committee, Resolutions and Reports* (July 1938), 12.

Jewry is in an insecure position'.[77] The desire of Romania and Poland to attend the Evian Conference as potential refugee-producers was just one indication that Simpson was correct. At Evian, Dr Nahum Goldmann, representative of the World Jewish Congress, was the only one who advocated that the Jews of eastern Europe and Germany be considered as a whole. His position, however, was considered to be a radical one by delegates from both governments and private organizations.[78]

Surprisingly enough, all the government representatives at Evian followed the American lead and utilized the expanded definition. Even British officials accepted the notion of negotiating with Germany, despite the fact that they led a conservative faction which strenuously objected to dealing with potential refugees. Their view reflected the fear that any agreement to help Jews who had not left their home country would encourage Germany and other countries to pressure their Jewish minorities to leave.[79] In agreeing to the American definition, the British pursued a broader strategy. Sir Neville Henderson, British Ambassador to Berlin, advised the delegates to avoid making any overt references to Germany's policies and to try instead to 'bring pressure to bear on the German government by making the reception of German and Austrian Jews in England dependent on the amounts of property they be permitted to export'.[80] At the conference itself, the British delegation followed this suggestion. In his keynote speech Lord Winterton said that 'no thickly populated country can be expected to accept persons who are deprived of their means of subsistence before they are able to enter it'. Winterton ruled out the possibility that private sources alone could finance the emigrants. Instead he argued that 'if countries of immigration are to do their best to facilitate the admission of emigrants, then they are entitled to expect that the country of origin, on its side, will equally assist in creating conditions in which the emigrants are able to start life in other countries with some prospect of success'.[81]

---

[77] Simpson, *The Refugee Problem*, 517; Bauer, *My Brother's Keeper*, 235–6.
[78] Henry Feingold, *The Politics of Rescue: The Roosevelt Administration and the Holocaust, 1938–1945* (New Brunswick, NJ: Rutgers University Press, 1979), 34–6.   [79] Stewart, *US Government Policy*, 306–7.
[80] Sherman, *Island Refuge*, 112–13; Michael Blakeney, *Australia and the Jewish Refugees, 1933–1948* (Australia: Croom Helm, 1985), 128.
[81] 'Speech by Lord Winterton, United Kingdom', *Proceedings of the Evian Conference*, 15.

At Evian, almost forty private organizations made speeches before the conference; of these about half had ties to the Jewish community (see Table 18). Despite sharing a common concern for the plight of refugees, the private organizations failed to present a united front on the topic of organizing the departure of refugees from Germany and Austria. Indeed, the perfromance of the Jewish organizations has been described by one historian as 'a spectacle of disunity and confusion'.[82] In general, the private organizations were divided between those who advocated the need for planned and orderly emigration and those who wanted more protection for minorities in their own countries.[83]

After the Evian conference, the newly formed IGCR took on the dual task of negotiating with Germany over departure conditions for refugees and arranging with host governments for places of settlement. In fact, George Rublee, the director of the new organization, devoted most of his time to the former assignment. In his career with the United States government, Rublee had developed a reputation as an astute political negotiator. He needed these diplomatic skills because the problem before him was indeed formidable: the German government confiscated from 60 to 100 per cent of an emigrant's capital before he or she fled the country during the period 1937-9.[84]

Rublee began his work with enthusiasm, but negotiations quickly stalled. Initially differences between the American, British, French, and other governments on how to organize the IGCR had to be resolved. Then, in October 1938, the German take-over of the Sudetenland disrupted the international scene. Rublee's diplomatic efforts could not be resumed until the Munich agreement had been reached, and then *Kristallnacht* took place. The 'Night of Broken Glass' and its aftermath greatly increased the need for Rublee's mission to succeed. After the great loss of life and property which took place during the pogrom, it became clear to the Jews remaining in Germany that they would have to leave the country quickly or face dire consequences. Moreover, refugees leaving Germany after November 1938 did so with even less property than before because of the collective fine of one billion RM

---

[82] Bauer, *My Brother's Keeper*, 235.
[83] Feingold, *Politics of Rescue*, 34; Eric Estorick and Erika Mann, 'Private and Governmental Aid of Refugees', *Annals*, 203 (May 1939), 151.
[84] Sherman, *Island Refuge*, 25.

TABLE 18. *Private Organizations in Attendance at the Evian Conference, July 1938*

International Christian Committee for Non-Aryans, London
Central Bureau for the Settlement of German Jews, London
German-Jewish Aid Committee, London
Society for the Protection of Science and Learning, London
The Joint Foreign Committee of the Board of Deputies of British Jews
  and the Anglo-Jewish Association, London
Agudas Israel World Organization, London
Council for German Jewry, London
Notgemeinschaft Deutscher Wissenschaftler im Ausland, London
Society of Friends (German Emergency Committee), London
New Zionist Organization, London
Emigration Advisory Committee, London
Freeland Association, London
League of Nations Union, London
Jewish Agency for Palestine, London
Royal Institute of International Affairs, London
Jewish Colonization Association, Paris
Comité d'assistance aux réfugiés, Paris
Fédération internationale des emigrés d'Allemagne, Paris
American Joint Distribution Committee, Paris
HICEM, Paris
Bureau international pour le respect du droit d'asile et l'aide aux réfugiés
  politiques, Paris
World Jewish Congress, Paris
Alliance israélite universelle, Paris
International ouvrière et socialiste, Paris–Brussels
'Ort', Paris
Centre de recherches de solutions au problème juif, Paris
Comité pour la défense des droits des Israélites en Europe centrale et
  orientale, Paris
Union des Sociétés 'Ose', Paris
Fédération des émigrés d'Autriche, Paris
Société d'émigration et de colonisation juive 'Emcol', Paris
Comité d'aide et d'assistance aux victimes de l'anti-sémitisme en
  Allemagne, Brussels
Comite voor Bijzondere Joodsche Belangem, Amsterdam
Centre suisse pour l'aide aux réfugiés, Basel
Comité central tchécoslovaque pour les réfugiés provenant d'Allemagne,
  Prague
International Migration Service, Geneva

TABLE 18. *(Cont.)*

International Student Service, Geneva
Comité international pour le placement des intellectuels réfugiés, Geneva
Comité pour le développement de la grande colonisation juive, Zurich

---

Source: *Proceedings of the Intergovernmental Committee, Evian, July 1938:
Verbatim Record of the Plenary Meetings of the Committee; Resolutions and
Reports*, annex 1. Representatives from the English, Belgian, Dutch, and Swiss
Catholic Committees for Aid to Immigrants also attended.

levied on the German Jewish community in atonement for vom
Rath's murder. In addition, the Nazis enacted other measures aimed
at the complete pauperization of German Jewry. A decree of 3
December nationalized all Jewish-owned business enterprises at a
price set by the German government. It further mandated the sale
of all Jewish-owned agricultural land and other real estate. Jews
also had to surrender all their securities, jewels, and art objects to
Reich banks.[85]

Ironically, the excesses of *Kristallnacht* renewed the interest of
the German government in negotiating the departure of the Jewish minority. Reaction against the huge property losses that occurred during the pogrom temporarily discredited German radicals
who advocated violent means of dealing with the Jews and
strengthened the position of moderates who wanted to negotiate
with the IGCR. In December 1938 Hjalmar Schacht, a conservative nationalist who engineered the German economic miracle and
rearmament, visited London with a proposal for the evacuation of
German Jewry.[86] In negotiating, Schacht hoped to increase German exports and gain much needed foreign exchange for the
Reichsbank.[87] According to the Schacht Plan, 150,000 German

---

[85] Sir John Hope Simpson, *Refugees: A Review of the Situation since September
1938* (London: Oxford University Press, 1939), app. 1, 111–13.

[86] Schacht held various economic posts, including President of the Reichsbank
and Minister of Economics, from 1933 until 1943. In 1944 he was placed in a
concentration camp for his alleged involvement in an anti-Hitler plot. At the Nuremberg Tribunal, Schacht was acquitted because it was determined that his role
in the rearmament programme was not criminal in and of itself. He later became
a successful German businessman. Robert Wistrich, *Who's Who in Nazi Germany*
(New York: Macmillan, 1982), 267–70.

[87] Robert E. Conot, *Justice at Nuremberg* (New York: Harper & Row, 1983),
175–6.

Jewish men and single women of working age would emigrate over a three-year period, another 250,000 dependants would follow once the original emigrants were established, and the remaining 200,000 elderly Jews would stay in Germany but be allowed to live in peace. Under the terms of the Schacht Plan, Jewish emigration would be financed by a trust fund within Germany of 1.5 billion marks, an estimated 25 per cent of the total assets of German Jewry, and by a fund of equal value created outside Germany by 'international Jewry'. This fund would then be used to lend German emigrants money in foreign currencies necessary to settle elsewhere. In order to garner the needed foreign exchange, Schacht proposed that the non-German currencies come from an increase in German exports.[88]

Reaction to the Schacht Plan was both swift and hostile. The United States State Department objected to the promotion of German exports and called the plan a ransom scheme. Jewish leaders in the United States, Great Britain, France, and Holland refused to meet to consider the plan because they did not want to lend credence to the idea that 'international Jewry' existed.[89] Nevertheless, George Rublee and the IGCR saw some hope in the proposal and wanted to continue negotiations. By this time, however, Schacht had resigned because of disagreements with Hitler over management of the German economy. Consequently, when Rublee travelled to Berlin to secure modifications on Schacht's initial proposal, he had to negotiate with Hermann Goering, who made it clear that he considered that Jews were 'exports' with which to raise foreign exchange.[90] Rublee's efforts produced a revised agreement, which he presented to the IGCR at its meeting of 13 February 1939 in London.

Under the terms of the Rublee Plan, 150,000 Jewish men and women of working age would emigrate from Germany over a five-year period. After they had established themselves, 250,000 of their dependants would be allowed to follow. Their emigration would be partially financed from a trust fund set up in Germany equal to about one-quarter of the value of all Jewish property in the Reich. This fund would be used to purchase travel tickets and German-made equipment to help the emigrants settle elsewhere.

[88] David S. Wyman, *Paper Walls: America and the Refugee Crisis, 1938–1941* (New York: Pantheon Books, 1985), 53; Feingold, *Politics of Rescue*, 50–1.

[89] Feingold, *Politics of Rescue*, 51–2.

[90] Conot, *Justice at Nuremberg*, 176.

In addition, emigrants would not be subject to special flight taxes and they would be allowed to take all their personal belongings except jewellery with them. Outside Germany, a private international corporation would be established to finance settlement and manage relations with Germany. The 200,000 elderly Jews not covered by the agreement would be allowed to live out their old age in Germany without persecution.[91]

The Rublee Plan improved on the original German proposal because it allowed emigrants to leave Germany with significantly more of their capital. Moreover, it removed the concerns of the United States State Department that the plan would help to promote German exports: the new plan specified that German-made equipment could only be used in colonization, not for sale abroad. Nevertheless, the Rublee Plan still had serious defects. The trust fund to be established in Germany was be composed of property confiscated from German Jewry. Although emigrants could salvage more of their property, they still had to pay their share of the atonement fine for vom Rath's murder. In addition, the German government refused to extend the plan to non-Jewish refugees, frustrating the American desire to assist all 'political refugees'. Most importantly, the balance of power within the Nazi regime once again shifted in favour of radical elements. After Schacht, the leading moderate, resigned his position in late January 1939, hard-liners urged the removal of German Jewry almost immediately, not in three to five years. At the same time, a bureaucratic reorganization merged all the emigration agencies and effectively placed them under the control of the Gestapo. Given this, the willingness of the German government to abide by the terms of the Rublee Plan became highly questionable.[92]

The Rublee Plan received a favourable response from the United States government, the leading member of the IGCR, which was moved by a combination of humanitarian and political motives.[93] Yehuda Bauer explains that humanitarian concerns influenced

---

[91] 'Company to Steer German Refugees', New York Times (15 Feb. 1939), 4; Estorick, 'The Evian Conference and the Intergovernmental Committee', Annals, 203 (May 1939), 139–40. [92] Feingold, Politics of Rescue, 55.

[93] Henry Feingold offers an even more cynical explanation for US motives: he suggests that State Department officials advocated the Rublee Plan not because they wanted to help the Jews, but because they desired the 'extrication of the Roosevelt Administration from the embarrassing position created by the Evian initiative'. Politics of Rescue, 68.

Roosevelt but that they were combined with a political purpose, 'possibly that of gaining international prestige by attempting a settlement of the refugee problem—outside of the U.S., of course.' Richard Breitman and Alan Kraut add that negotiators were serious about the agreement but did not want to benefit Germany at the expense of the United States, or encourage Poland and Romania to follow suit.[94] With the strong support of the United States, the IGCR quickly approved the Rublee Plan. Afterwards Rublee felt that he had accomplished his task and resigned his office. Sir Herbert Emerson, the High Commissioner for Refugees of the League of Nations, then became director of the IGCR as well.

In contrast to the governmental response, non-governmental actors in the international refugee regime were deeply divided about the worth of the Rublee Plan. In Britain, Jewish leaders supported it and began to press for the creation of the independent settlement corporation. Across the Atlantic, support from the American Jewish community was much less forthcoming. The Jewish Labour Committee and the American Jewish Congress both came out against the plan because it frustrated their ongoing boycott of German-made goods. The JDC hesitated to reject or approve the plan. Its leaders realized that they would be called on to help finance large-scale settlement efforts through the independent corporation, a task they thought impossible without government assistance.[95]

Shortly after the announcement of the Rublee Plan, the refugee crisis intensified. In March 1939 the German army invaded Czechoslovakia, sending thousands more on the refugee road. In addition, the Nazis began to use more draconian tactics to rid the Reich of its Jewish population. The Gestapo loaded refugees without visas onto ships destined to wander from port to port seeking refuge. The voyage of the *St Louis* to Cuba was but one of the refugee boats to attract international attention. The Gestapo also dumped groups of Jews across the border into neighbouring France and Switzerland. At the same time, the German government still maintained its interest in the Rublee Plan because it offered a way to remove a large proportion of the Jewish population.[96]

[94] Bauer, *My Brother's Keeper*, 284; Richard Breitman and Alan Kraut, *American Refugee Policy and European Jewry, 1933–1945* (Bloomington, Ind.: Indiana University Press, 1987), 68.   [95] Bauer, *My Brother's Keeper*, 276–7.
[96] Marrus, *The Unwanted*, 217.

Despite the urgency of the situation facing German Jews, nego-tiations on the Rublee plan progressed at snail's pace. In order to muster support for the plan, Myron C. Taylor met with American Jewish leaders on behalf of the Roosevelt administration. In par-ticular, Taylor worked to overcome the reasonable fears of Jewish leaders that the formation of an independent corporation would conform to the Nazis' idea of 'international Jewry'. Moreover, they worried that the Rublee Plan would encourage other coun-tries, especially those in eastern Europe, to increase persecution of their Jewish populations. After repeated pleas from Taylor and Roosevelt himself, representatives of the JDC agreed to go to London and negotiate with the British government and leading British Jews. Finally, five months after the announcement of the Rublee Plan, an agreement to establish an independent settlement corporation was reached: the Coordinating Foundation came into being on 20 July 1939.[97]

For the refugees, however, the formation of the Coordinating Foundation came too late. Less then two months after its forma-tion, the Second World War began. In effect, the Rublee Plan became null and void as soon as German troops entered Poland. Given the fate of German Jewry during the Second World War, the slow pace of the major actors in the international refugee regime in attempting to organize the flight of refugees has been sharply criticized. David Wyman, for instance, writes that 'it is tragic that so little was accomplished in the year before the war began'.[98] Undoubtedly, the Rublee Plan must be termed a failure because it did not achieve its main objective—facilitating the de-parture of Jews from Germany. But, even if the Coordinating Foundation had been established sooner, the successful imple-mentation of the Rublee Plan would not have been assured.

To begin with, it was unknown whether or not the Third Reich would have actually abided by the terms of the agreement. With constant changes and increasing radicalization taking place within the Nazi regime, it is difficult to imagine that it could have effec-tively guaranteed its commitments on Jewish emigration. It is also unknown whether Hitler ever took the negotiations seriously. In interviews after the Second World War, Schacht claimed that Hitler

---

[97] Bauer, *My Brother's Keeper*, 277–8; Wyman, *Paper Walls*, 56; Breitman and Kraut, *American Refugee Policy*, 69.   [98] Wyman, *Paper Walls*, 56.

agreed that he should negotiate but never revealed his true thoughts about Jewish emigration.[99] In any case, Hitler did not share Schacht's view that foreign exchange was needed to combat inflation and control the money supply. He thought the fine of atonement would provide ample backing for a stable currency.[100] In addition, places of asylum still needed to be found for the refugees. Without definite settlement offers, the Rublee Plan could not be properly carried out.[101] If these places had been secured, then refugee settlement might have been limited by the financial resources of private organizations. The success of the Haavarah agreement indicates that emigration and settlement agreements could be orchestrated on a small scale, but conducting a much larger project without government funding would have been much more difficult. Thus, the practical application of the Rublee Plan, if implemented, would probably have resembled that of the Graeco-Turkish population exchange.

REFUGEES AND HUMAN RIGHTS

This chapter has examined the efforts of certain actors in the international refugee regime to expand the functions of the regime to include dealing with the causes of refugee movements. In this regard, James G. McDonald's dramatic resignation represents an important departure in the history of the regime. For the first time, a High Commissioner called attention to the immediate cause of a refugee movement: human-rights abuses by a government. Although McDonald's resignation succeeded in increasing public awareness of Nazi policies, it did not spur international action against the German government. This was primarily because the governments belonging to the international refugee regime opposed such an infringement on state sovereignty. In this instance, a direct approach to preventing refugee movements failed.

Other actors in the international refugee regime attempted to deal with the causes of refugee movements by controlling flight. These initiatives consciously avoided criticism of government policies. Instead, they tried to deal with the departure of refugees in

---

[99] Breitman and Kraut, *American Refugee Policy*, 69.
[100] Conot, *Justice at Nuremberg*, 176–7.
[101] On the IGCR's ill-fated search for refugee havens, see above, Ch. 6.

a purely pragmatic way. From the above accounts of the Graeco-Turkish population exchange and the Rublee Plan, it becomes readily apparent that organizing the departure of refugees in a humane way was an extremely difficult task to accomplish for a number of reasons. First, an orderly departure agreement had as its prerequisite the presence of a reliable government willing to conclude and keep international agreements. Often a refugee-producing government is both unstable and untrustworthy. Controlling the exodus of Russian refugees would have been virtually impossible because of the civil war raging within the former Russian Empire. Prior to November 1938 the unwillingness of the German government to negotiate frustrated attempts to control flight. Once the Germany government did decide to negotiate, its continual escalation of persecution towards Jews seriously called into question its desire to meet its commitments. In addition, the failure of both the Greek and the Turkish governments to fulfil completely the terms of the population exchange agreement further indicates the difficulty in assuring compliance with an orderly departure plan.

Second, flight cannot be successfully organized unless a place of settlement is available for the refugees. The governments of Greece and Turkey carried out their population exchange agreement because each was willing to provide asylum to refugees it considered to be its own. In the Refugee Survey, Simpson declares a population exchange for the Jews of Germany to be 'impractical', probably because no Jewish state existed to enter into an exchange with Germany.[102] If it had been implemented, the Rublee Plan probably would have floundered because of the unwillingness of many countries to accept more refugees. The success of the Haavarah agreement in Palestine indicates that an emigration and settlement plan can be successful if a place of refuge is available. The successful results of the orderly departure agreement concluded between the government of Vietnam and the United Nations in the 1980s lead to the same conclusion.[103]

Even if agreements on organizing flight can be concluded, they risk sanctioning human-rights violations by refugee-producing countries. In the controversial debates about the Greco-Turkish

[102] Simpson, *The Refugee Problem*, 525.
[103] See Astri Suhrke, 'Indochinese Refugees: The Law and Politics of First Asylum', *Annals*, 467 (May 1983), 102–15.

population exchange, some actors in the international refugee regime argued that organizing flight could be considered humanitarian because it helped to save lives and property. Others rightly pointed out that any co-operation with a refugee-producing country legitimated the expulsion of innocent people. In the case of the Rublee Plan, even its supporters feared that it would encourage more governments to persecute Jews. They knew that what was at stake was not simply the several hundred thousand Jews of Germany but rather the ten million in eastern Europe. Over sixty years later the risk inherent in organizing flight remains. In the Yugoslavian Civil War of the 1990s, efforts to help Bosnian Muslims escape to safe havens were challenged by those who said this practice simply encouraged more expulsions by the Serbs.

While agreements on orderly departure may be necessary under dire circumstances, they always involve collaboration between refugee-producing countries and those trying to assist refugees. In an effort of this type, it is all too easy to overlook completely the desires of the refugees themselves. The Graeco-Turkish population exchange, for instance, was carried out against the wishes of both the Greek and Turkish refugees. In negotiations for the Rublee Plan, German Jewry was virtually excluded from the negotiations conducted between the IGCR and the German government.

Given the many obstacles to the successful organization of flight, it is not surprising that only two departure agreements were concluded during the inter-war years. The experiences of the Graeco-Turkish population exchange and of the Rublee Plan indicate that the implementation of departure agreements in a humanitarian way is possible, but highly improbable. The attempt of McDonald and other actors in the international refugee regime to expand its functions to include preventing or controlling refugee movements failed. This meant that dealing with the root causes of refugee movements would remain outside the scope of the international refugee regime in the inter-war years.

Nevertheless, McDonald's call for an end to human-rights abuses within Germany was not completely in vain. With the benefit of hindsight, it becomes evident that he was one of the first people to advocate international measures to protect human rights. He believed that the abuse of human rights concerned the entire international community, not just the government involved. Although his viewpoint gained widespread acceptance only after the Second World War, he should be credited for demanding adherence to the norms now expressed in the United Nations Declaration on Human Rights.[104] McDonald's ideas about the linkage between refugee assistance and the root causes of refugee flows also proved to be ahead of his time. In 1986 Jean-Pierre Hocke, the then UN High Commissioner for Refugees, stressed that 'today's refugee problem can no longer be tackled through humanitarian assistance alone'. He argued that concern for the causes of refugee movements was essential if repatriation efforts were to succeed.[105] Shortly after her appointment as High Commissioner in 1991, Sadako Ogata stated that 'an effective and humanitarian aproach to the refugee issue must focus on causes as much as effects'.[106] Both High Commissioners share a common philosophy that refugee problems cannot always be resolved without also addressing the human-rights abuses that cause them. The United Nations' decision to create a 'protective zone' for Kurdish refugees in Iraq after the 1991 Persian Gulf war represents an unprecedented attempt to translate this philosophy into action.

[104] On the international human-rights regime of the post-1945 era, see John Gerard Ruggie, 'Human Rights and the Future International Community', *Daedalus*, 112/4 (1983), 93–110; Jack Donnelly, 'International Human Rights: A Regime Analysis', *International Organization*, 40 (Summer 1986), 599–642.

[105] Jean-Pierre Hocké, *Beyond Humanitarianism: The Need for Political Will to Resolve Today's Refugee Problem*, Inaugural Joyce Pearce Memorial Lecture, Oxford University, 29 Oct. 1986 (Oxford: Refugee Studies Programme with the Ockenden Venture, 1986), 10. On the topic of root causes and repatriation, see also 'Voluntary Repatriation of Refugees', *Refugees* (Aug. 1987), 5.

[106] Sadako Ogata, 'A Safer World', *Refugees* (Mar. 1991), 3.

PART III
The International Refugee Regime:
An Evaluation

8

The Influence of the
International Refugee Regime

THROUGHOUT this book, our primary concern has been with whether the international refugee regime influenced the way governments treated refugees in the Inter-war Period. In other words, did the regime matter? After reviewing its role over nearly two decades, it becomes clear that the regime did affect how governments behaved towards refugees in the inter-war years. For some refugee groups, the existence of the regime resulted in concrete assistance, including consular services, protection from expulsion, settlement aid, employment opportunities, and help in finding a country of permanent asylum. Overall, the most important outcome of the regime's operation was the establishment of the idea that refugees should be treated as a special category of migrant deserving preferential treatment.

In the area of legal protection, the Nansen passport system and the 1933 and 1938 Refugee Conventions provided a comprehensive body of rules governing refugee identity and travel, economic and social well-being, and protection from expulsion. Although these rules did not apply to all refugees, they helped to make the legal status of designated groups more secure. The High Commissioner's system of delegates in host countries also helped to establish the idea that international organizations have a special role in protecting the rights of refugees. In the long run, the cumulative effect of these rules helped to create a distinction between refugees and other aliens in both international and municipal law. This in turn meant that the existence of the regime reinforced the idea that refugees should not be subject to the same rules as other aliens.

The international refugee regime also facilitated the provision of durable solutions for refugees. In Greece, Bulgaria, Syria, and elsewhere the major actors in the regime joined together to sponsor settlement projects for about 800,000 refugees. These projects had a direct effect on the refugees whom they helped by providing them with housing and, in some cases, a livelihood. But their impact went beyond individual refugees because they improved the economic, social, and political climate in their host countries. In Greece, for instance, refugee settlement proved to be a great benefit to the country's troubled economy. In Bulgaria, similar efforts helped to stabilize the country by giving dispossessed refugees a stake in the political system. Not every attempt at the achievement of durable solutions made by the actors in the international refugee regime was a success: the Nansen–Soviet repatriation plan and the Erivan refugee settlement scheme are cases in point. Nevertheless, all these attempts undermined the idea that refugee aid was simply charity and not the proper concern of governments. And they simultaneously legitimized international efforts aimed at improving the material well-being of refugees.

The most difficult task that the members of the international refugee regime faced involved helping refugees struggling to find a place of permanent, or even temporary, asylum. In some instances, key actors in the regime facilitated the admission of a refugee to a country of asylum. Nansen's efforts to evacuate over 20,000 Russian refugees from Constantinople and the ILO's refugee employment service are two examples of successful ventures in this regard. For the most part, however, the actors in the regime did not significantly affect the overall trend towards increasing control of migration by governments. The unwillingness of many governments to provide asylum for all refugees fleeing the Third Reich stands as testimony to the limitation of the regime in matters of immigration. Although the regime's impact on immigration laws in the inter-war years was limited, its existence did result over time in the modification of those laws to favour refugees in some instances. This change coincided with and reinforced a similar trend in international and municipal law towards treating refugees as a special group not subject to the same restrictions as other migrants and aliens.

Thus, the international refugee regime mattered both because it facilitated refugee assistance in the short run and because it led to the acceptance of refugees as a special category of migrant in the long run. The rest of this chapter will be devoted to an exploration of three questions that are related to this conclusion. First, in what ways did the regime influence how governments treated refugees? This is not immediately obvious because the regime could not directly assist refugees, finance settlement, or control immigration. It could only influence the activities of governments and other actors, but how was this influence exerted? Second, why was the impact of the regime uneven? The regime's influence varied over time, among refugee groups, and by issue. Since this result was contrary to the humanitarian ideals of the regime, it needs to be explained. Third, who or what provided leadership for the regime? In Chapter 3 it was established that a variety of individuals and organizations rather than one hegemonic power provided the impetus for the creation of the regime. But the sources of leadership for its development and operation still need to be considered. In conclusion, we will take a fresh look at the refugee issue and the legacy of the international refugee regime.

IN WHAT WAYS DID THE INTERNATIONAL REFUGEE REGIME INFLUENCE GOVERNMENTS?

International regimes influence state behaviour towards a particular issue in two primary ways. First, regimes make co-operation between states more likely by changing the environment in which negotiations take place. If a regime includes a formal institution, such as an intergovernmental organization, the cost of making agreements can be reduced because governments can be brought together on a regular basis to discuss common concerns. An intergovernmental organization also can provide unbiased information to all members of the regime. This facilitates co-operation by reducing uncertainty and enhancing trust between the members of the regime. Because a regime includes norms, or mutually accepted standards of behaviour, it becomes more likely that governments will keep the agreements they make; failure to do so would violate a clear standard and damage a state's reputation.[1]

[1] Stephan Haggard and Beth A. Simmons, 'Theories of International Regimes', *International Organization*, 41 (Summer 1987), 513–14. See also Robert O. Keohane and Joseph S. Nye, Jr., 'Power and Interdependence Revisited', *International Organization*, 41 (Autumn 1987), 742; Robert O. Keohane, *After Hegemony: Cooperation and Discord in the World Political Economy* (Princeton, NJ: Princeton University Press, 1984), 85–109.

Second, regimes can alter a state's perception of how issues affect their national interests.[2] They can do so by redefining the paradigms through which policy-makers conceptualize their national interests. These redefinitions may occur when states involved in the regime learn the benefits of co-operating on certain issues or when formal institutions, if they exist within the regime, present policy alternatives that shape debates and decisions within national bureaucracies. In the inter-war years the international refugee regime influenced the way states treated refugees by enhancing co-operation between governments and by changing the perceptions of those same governments.

Making Co-operation More Likely

There is an abundance of examples in Part II that suggest that the international refugee regime facilitated co-operation between states on refugee issues. To begin with, the regime reduced the costs of making agreements between states through the institutional mechanism of the League of Nations. The forum provided by the political bodies of the League helped identify the sources of the refugee problems and served as a place for the discussion of solutions. In the Council, representatives of the Great Powers met on a regular basis and discussed refugee issues. Without the Council, the Greek, Bulgarian, and Armenian refugee settlement schemes probably never would have been undertaken. The Council also gave its members, especially the Great Powers, the opportunity to raise refugee issues of particular concern to them. France, for instance, championed the case of the Armenian and Saar refugees. Acting jointly, the British and French governments proposed that the Council approve assistance for Austrian and Czech refugees.

In the Assembly, delegates from virtually all of the then independent states met to debate refugee issues. Over time, these

[2] This insight about international regimes has been developed by cognitive theorists, who emphasize the importance of knowledge and learning in explaining regimes. On the cognitive approach to regimes, see Ernst Haas, 'Words Can Hurt You; or, Who Said What to Whom about Regimes', in Stephen D. Krasner (ed.), *International Regimes*, (Ithaca, NY: Cornell University Press, 1983), 23–60; id., 'Is There a Hole in the Whole? Knowledge, Technology, Interdependence and the Construction of International Regimes', *International Organization*, 29 (Summer 1975), 827–76.

annual meetings helped to create common rules governing the treatment of refugees and establish mutually acceptable standards for national governments, particularly in regard to the prohibition of expulsion. In addition, the Assembly sessions contributed to the emergence of transnational coalitions on refugee issues, a necessary step if the emerging international norms were to be translated into concrete assistance projects.[3] The Assembly also enabled host countries to internationalize their own refugee problems. Throughout the 1920s and 1930s the countries of eastern and central Europe that hosted large numbers of Russian refugees depended on the Assembly for support. At the 1933 Assembly the Dutch Foreign Minister brought the issue of refugees from Germany before the League and asked for the aid of other countries in assisting them. Under Nansen's leadership the Assembly even spearheaded international co-operative efforts to provide emergency relief to refugees in the Near East following the conclusion of the 1922 Graeco-Turkish war.

The intergovernmental conferences on refugees, held under the auspices of the League of Nations, also helped to make co-operation on refugee issues easier. Unlike the Assembly sessions, the special intergovernmental conferences brought together bureaucrats from the government departments concerned with refugees.[4] These conferences resulted in numerous international agreements on the treatment of refugees and the development of the first international refugee law. The Nansen passport system and the first comprehensive refugee convention can be counted among their outstanding accomplishments. Though these rules were not always adhered to, they still gave states a mutually agreed upon standard by which their behaviour could be judged. The rejection by a number of western European countries of the practice of expulsion can to a large extent be attributed to the creation of the rule of non-*refoulement* as expressed in the 1933 and 1938 Refugee Conventions.

When facilitating government co-operation, the political bodies

---

[3] This point has been made about the Assembly in general. See Martin David Dubin, 'Transgovernmental Processes in the League of Nations', *International Organization*, 37 (Summer 1983), 491; and Major-General A. C. Temperly, *The Whispering Gallery of Europe* (London: Collins, 1938), 109.

[4] The IGCR differed in this regard. It was made up of non-refugee experts. Even the Chair, Myron Taylor, was considered a novice in the field.

of the League of Nations received support services from the Secretariat. Beginning with the very first initiative to help Russian refugees, the Secretary-General and his staff provided technical and administrative expertise to both the Council and Assembly. They consulted with governments on their positions and often wrote reports for government delegates. In other words, the Secretariat assumed responsibility for the 'paperwork' of decision-making. Secretariat officials also fostered communication between governments by collecting information and then circulating it to all concerned parties. In addition, the Secretariat served as a source of unbiased information. Governments widely respected the technical sections of the League as a source of sound advice and fair evaluations. In the cases of Greek and Bulgarian refugee settlement, the approval of the Economic and Financial Section proved to be crucial in convincing governments that the schemes were workable.

Although the Secretariat played an important role in encouraging international co-operation on refugee issues, primary credit for this task must be given to the refugee agencies of the League of Nations. These agencies encouraged co-operation in a variety of ways. The refugee agencies, particularly under Nansen's leadership, acted as a liaison between refugee host countries and other members of the international refugee regime. This greatly increased the chances that governments would reach an agreement on a refugee assistance project. In addition, the refugee agencies brought state and non-state actors together, which was beneficial because of the important role private organizations played in financing refugee assistance. In the case of Armenian refugee settlement in Syria, close collaboration between the Refugee Section of the ILO, the Advisory Committee of Private Organizations, and the French government proved to be crucial. High Commissioner McDonald also acted as a liaison between governments and private organizations assisting refugees from Germany. Most importantly, the refugee agencies acted as a catalyst to international co-operation because they developed ideas on refugee assistance and helped to implement projects.

The refugee agencies of the League of Nations also made international co-operation easier by providing governments with more information than would have been available otherwise. In general, this information was perceived as being unbiased and non-political.[5] The High Commissioner for Refugees, in conjunction with the ILO, conducted the very first official census of a refugee population in 1922. Afterwards the refugee agencies of the League of Nations and ILO collected statistics on the number, location, and employment status of refugees. The Refugee Section of the ILO, for instance, acted as a clearing-house for information on employment opportunities for refugees, matching prospective employers in one country with prospective employees in another. Although the statistical data on refugees collected by the League were not always accurate, they still served to give governments and relief organizations a basis for making decisions about refugees.

The international refugee regime also promoted co-operation by providing linkages among the international efforts to assist different refugee groups. Arrangements created to deal with Russian refugees were later applied to Armenians and several other refugee groups. Similarly, the Greek refugee settlement scheme proved to be the model for refugee settlement in Bulgaria. In addition, the regime resulted in the integration of different types of refugee services, such as the provision of legal protection and durable solutions. While the international refugee regime seemed to aid intergovernmental co-operation on refugee matters, its success was not repeated in regard to related issues. For example, proposals to extend international assistance to disaster victims, the unemployed, the stateless, and persecuted peoples still within their own country failed.[6]

Changing the Preferences of Governments

From the above discussion it is clear that the existence of the international refugee regime facilitated co-operation on refugee

---

[5] Although the refugee agencies generally maintained a reputation for being non-political, this does not mean they were always uncontroversial. The Soviet Union, for instance, accused the Nansen Office of engaging in anti-Soviet propaganda. See above, Ch. 7.

[6] Keohane predicts that the creation of an international regime will enable governments to create economies of scale by linking issues. Consequently, regimes will be 'nested' in a series of regimes. In the case of the international refugee regime of the Inter-war Period, this appears not to have been the case. In the post-1945 era, however, the international refugee regime centred on the United Nations has come to be nested in a wider human-rights regime. Keohane, *After Hegemony*, 90.

issues in a number of ways. Perhaps more importantly, the international refugee regime also influenced the preferences and interests of governments by helping to define the 'refugee problem'.
As a result of the regime, this concept constantly evolved during
the inter-war years. In 1921 the 'refugee problem' only referred
to the plight of Russian refugees. At the time, the over one million
Russian refugees composed only a fraction of the total refugee
population. From this small beginning, the scope and functions of
the international refugee regime grew. In 1938 the Royal Institute
of International Affairs in London conducted a massive survey
of the 'refugee problem' to be used as a discussion piece on the
reorganization of refugee work at the Nineteenth Assembly of
the League of Nations. This report contains information on over
ten refugee groups making up virtually the entire European refugee population. It also includes information on many aspects of
refugee life, including legal protection, settlement, repatriation,
employment, and immigration.[7]

By defining the content of the 'refugee problem', the international refugee regime established a framework within which
governments made decisions about refugees. Even if the decision-
making process took place entirely at the national level, the regime still shaped government policy because it set the parameters
for discussions on refugees. One example of this is the ongoing
discussions held within governments about solutions to this or
that refugee crisis. Within the context of the regime, a 'refugee
problem' was 'solved' when a refugee or group of refugees returned to their home country or became self-sufficient citizens in
a new one. These solutions reflect a government's point of view,
not those of the refugees. For the refugees, naturalization was
not necessarily a total solution if their attachments to their home
countries continued. From a psychological point of view, a person
remains a refugee as long as he or she hopes to return home
when circumstances permit. Even then, refugees carry the scars
of their experience in flight and exile.[8] Similarly, from a refugee's

---

[7] Sir John Hope Simpson, *Refugees: Preliminary Report of a Survey* (London: Royal
Institute of International Affairs, 1938). The information in this report was expanded in *The Refugee Problem: Report of a Survey* (London: Oxford University Press,
1939).

[8] Paul Tabori, *The Anatomy of Exile* (London: Harrap, 1972), 34; Barbara E.
Harrell-Bond, 'Repatriation: Under What Conditions is it the most Desirable
Solution for Refugees? An Agenda for Research', *African Studies Review*, 32/1
(1989), 62.

point of view, taking a job might be only the beginning of a new way of life, and not an end in itself.[9] If a group harbours hopes of returning, refugee status may continue beyond the first generation: both the Greek refugees from the 1922 Graeco-Turkish conflict[10] and the Palestinian refugees from the 1948 Arab–Israeli War passed on their status to their children and grandchildren.[11] In the international refugee regime, however, the solutions discussed and eventually implemented reflected the desire of governments to fit refugees back into the normal parameters of the state system. Other types of solutions were essentially excluded from the public debate about refugees of the inter-war years.

Another example of how the international refugee regime helped to define the refugee problem concerns the connotation of the word 'refugee'. Implied in this word is the notion that refugees are needy people, and somehow different from other types of migrants, especially those who leave their home countries primarily for economic reasons. Within government circles, discussions on refugees were treated as a separate issue different from disaster relief or unemployment. Eventually this categorization had a profound effect on government behaviour towards refugees, including immigration policy. As shown in Chapter 6, in the late 1930s several countries began to amend their immigration laws to include preferential measures in favour of refugees. These policy initiatives reflected the belief that refugees should be treated as a category of migrant deserving special assistance.

On some occasions the international refugee regime directly affected the interests and preferences of governments by influencing the domestic policy-making process. This occurred primarily because the formal institutions associated with the regime provided governments with policy alternatives they would not have thought of otherwise. For instance, High Commissioner Nansen and the Refugee Section of the ILO developed many project proposals relating to refugees, including plans for refugee settlement in Greece, Bulgaria, Erivan, and Syria. When the British

[9] On this theme see Eduard Heimann, 'The Refugee Speaks', *Annals*, 203 (May 1939), 106–13.

[10] Renée Hirschon, *Heirs of the Greek Catastrophe: The Social Life of Asia Minor Refugees in Piraeus* (Oxford: Clarendon Press, 1989).

[11] Ilan Peleg, 'The Palestinian Refugees: A Political Perspective', in Elizabeth Ferris (ed.), *Refugees and World Politics* (New York: Praeger, 1985), 158.

government supported the Greek and Bulgarian refugee loans, and the French government advocated Armenian refugee settlement in Syria, they did so out of a combination of humanitarian and security concerns. But, without the existence of the regime, it is likely that the governments would have found other, less humanitarian ways of achieving their goals. Although the proposal for Armenian refugee settlement in Erivan did not come to fruition, the intense debate it provoked within the British government demonstrates the influence of the regime on the policy-making process within countries.

WHY WAS THE IMPACT OF THE INTERNATIONAL REFUGEE REGIME UNEVEN?

Despite the many areas in which the international refugee regime had a significant influence on state behaviour, the information given in Part II also shows that the regime's impact was uneven. For one thing, the regime seemed to have a greater impact in the 1920s than in the 1930s. In addition, its immediate impact on the treatment of Jewish refugees in the late 1930s appears to have been minimal. Also, while the regime significantly affected the treatment of refugees within host countries, its influence on governmental decisions about immigration policy or repatriation was much less. Thus, the impact of the regime varied over time, both among different refugee groups and by issue. The reasons for the divergence between the humanitarian ideals of the regime and actual state behaviour towards refugees can be explained with reference to factors both internal and external to the regime itself.

Differences over Time

One of the primary reasons for differences in the international refugee regime's impact over time has to do with factors external to the regime itself, especially the health of the world economy. The creation and initial development of the regime took place during the relatively prosperous 1920s. Then, in the 1930s, an unprecedented depression shook the global economy. As a result of high unemployment, a business recession, and bank failures, governments were less willing to admit refugees and had less funds available to donate to international refugee assistance projects. Consequently, countries increasingly ignored the regime's assistance and burden-sharing norms and the rules governing the treatment of refugees. Perhaps more importantly, the governmental actors in the regime increasingly opted for unilateral solutions to their refugee problems. Hence, the international refugee regime became less relevant to refugee crises of the later 1930s.

In addition to the health of the world economy, the political structure of the international system also affected the international refugee regime's influence. In the 1920s the regime operated in a climate favourable to international co-operation which coincided with the founding of the League of Nations. It is worth noting that other regimes were established during this period, most notably in the areas of health and labour.[12] After 1933 a resurgent Germany mounted a serious challenge both to the League of Nations and to the Treaty of Versailles, the punitive peace treaty imposed on it by the victors of the Great War. The Nazi doctrine of racial supremacy and anti-Semitism launched an ideological challenge to the humanitarian principle of the regime. With its quest for empire, the Third Reich also rejected the sovereignty principle, a belief which underpinned not just the international refugee regime but the entire international system. In other words, the challenge from Germany and its allies represented an attack on the existing world order, not just on the international refugee regime. Despite these attacks, the international refugee regime strove to maintain itself throughout the 1930s. This struggle, however, was in the end hopeless. The regime ceased to function altogether once the Second World War began in Europe.

Given the dependence of the international refugee regime on broader structural factors, one might be tempted to conclude that the regime did not affect the behaviour of states when it conflicted with their short-term interests. This conclusion, however, does not explain why some governments still acted according to the norms and rules of the regime when it might have been more politically expedient to ignore them. For instance, governments continued to assist refugees, albeit on a reduced scale, even during the

---

[12] On the international human-rights regime centred on the ILO, see Jack Donnelly, 'International Human Rights: A Regime Analysis', *International Organization*, 40 (Summer 1986), 628–31.

economic crisis of the 1930s when so many nationals went without jobs. In fact, the legal status of many refugees actually improved during this period because of the creation of formal refugee conventions. Moreover, the governments of France, Czechoslovakia, and other host countries continued to aid Russian refugees even at a time when these same countries wanted to establish closer ties with the Soviet Union because of the growing German threat.[13] In addition, Jewish and political refugees from the Third Reich did receive some international aid in spite of strong opposition from the German government and the desire of Great Britain and France to appease Hitler. These are but a few examples of times when the norms and rules of the international refugee regime were partially upheld even though they conflicted with the short-term interest of member states.

Differences among Refugee Groups

At first glance, the explanation for variations in the regime's impact on different refugee groups seems obvious: prejudice. This explanation most commonly emerges in comparisons between the treatment of Jewish refugees and other refugee groups. In the inter-war years, prejudice, racism, and xenophobia inspired immigration restrictions and influenced refugee assistance programmes. But prejudice alone does not explain uneven responses to different refugee groups. For instance, the Jewish refugees from the Saar found asylum easily and received aid not available to Jews fleeing from Nazi persecution in Germany itself. In order to explain why some groups received more aid than others, we need to understand how the major actors in the international refugee regime applied the humanitarian principle and assistance norm.

It is important to realize that sometimes the principles and norms of a regime are really 'collective aspirations' and are not meant to be rigorously enforced.[14] This is especially common in human-rights regimes because governments want to appear to be moral even if

---

[13] For a brief overview of how changing attitudes towards the Soviet Union affected the policies of France and other host countries towards the Russian refugees, see Mark Raeff, *Russia Abroad: A Cultural History of the Russian Emigration, 1919–1939* (New York: Oxford University Press, 1990), 38–40.

[14] Haggard and Simmons, 'Theories of International Regimes', 514.

they have no intention of completely meeting the standards of the regime. In the international refugee regime, the humanitarian principle had an aspirational quality and the assistance norm set a very high standard—assistance for all refugees without discrimination on the basis of race, religion, nationality, creed, strategic importance, or any other factor not directly relevant to the needs of the refugees. And this standard had to be implemented in a world characterized by conflict among minority and majority ethnic groups, those espousing competing ideologies, and powerful states striving for military and strategic advantage. In the inter-war years the refugee assistance record of each of the major actors in the international refugee regime fell short of its standards. This was true largely because each actor balanced the humanitarian principle against other considerations.

To begin with, governments were more generous in aiding refugees when it coincided with broader foreign or domestic policy objectives.[15] They provided more aid to refugees fleeing their enemies than to those fleeing their friends, as the countries of eastern Europe did when they helped refugees from the Soviet Union but not those from Germany. They were also likely to aid host countries which were their allies or of strategic importance; British support for both Greece and Bulgaria fits this pattern. Or governments helped refugees when they had an additional political responsibility, as the French and Italians did for the Saar refugees. Moreover, governments welcomed refugees with a similar ethnic background to that of the majority of the population within their territories, while discouraging those who were different. Also, all governments proved more willing to admit or assist refugee groups at times when they needed immigrant labour, or when prosperity reigned, than in times of unemployment and recession.

It would be a mistake, however, to conclude that governments used humanitarian rhetoric simply as a cloak for self-interest. To

---

[15] This pattern continued in the Cold War period. In a study of American refugee policy since 1945, Loescher and Scanlan emphasize the importance of foreign policy considerations in shaping US refugee policy. In a study of Canada's refugee policy, Dirks concludes that economic and political factors have been the most important in determining whether Canada accepts refugees. See Gil Loescher and John A. Scanlan, *Calculated Kindness: Refugees and America's Half-Open Door, 1945 to the Present* (New York: Free Press, 1986); Gerald E. Dirks, *Canada's Refugee Policy: Indifference or Opportunism?* (Montreal: McGill-Queen's University Press, 1977).

do so is to ignore the often deep divergences in the opinions of government officials about the importance of humanitarian concerns in refugee policies. Some officials quickly placed humanitarian concerns behind those of military strategy or fiscal stringency, while others urged that they should be given a more prominent place. This same conflict also took place within the minds of individual leaders. Hence, Roosevelt called the Evian conference partly as a humanitarian response and partly to ward off his political critics. Similarly, Australian Prime Minister Bruce's proposal to admit refugees from Germany under a special quota was motivated by a combination of humanitarian concern for the refugees, pressure from Great Britain and the United States, and a desire to be seen as being humanitarian.

In addition, domestic political constraints sometimes prevented leaders from meeting the regime's standards. The clearest example of this happened in regard to the Erivan settlement scheme. Despite Austen Chamberlain's sincere promise to Nansen, he was unable to secure a British donation for Armenian refugee settlement in the Soviet Union. Chamberlain and the Foreign Office lost to Churchill and the Treasury in a bureaucratic battle, though not for lack of trying. Similar misfortune befell American leaders. After March 1938 the Roosevelt administration desired to do more to assist refugees but found itself tightly constrained by restrictionist forces within Congress and by an isolationist public. In both these cases, domestic political considerations dominated decisions on refugee assistance and state behaviour fell short of humanitarian aspirations.

The attitude of intergovernmental organizations towards refugees also reflected a mixture of humanitarianism and other concerns. This was especially evident in the League of Nations, the intergovernmental organization which figured most prominently in the international refugee regime. Its major political organs, the Council and Assembly, were composed of representatives appointed by governments, so they could not be free from national concerns. But decision-making within the League was not simply the sum total of government positions; it had its own dynamics. Within the League, a struggle about the place of refugee assistance continually took place. Some delegates clearly wanted to subvert refugee assistance to wider political goals, such as keeping Germany in the League or placating the Soviets after they had jointed the Assembly. Other delegates argued that humanitarian concerns should be given priority over political ones. Still others seemed to be motivated primarily by a desire to limit the financial commitments of the League.

As a result of these conflicting goals, refugee assistance by the League of Nations, an organization which made decisions on the basis of consensus, was the product of compromise. Assistance was to be temporary and limited to certain groups. Its programmes dealt with refugees in Europe or in the nearby Middle East, not those in what was perceived to be far-off Africa or Asia. The delegates also expressed more humanitarian concern on behalf of Christian refugees, and to a lesser extent towards Jewish ones, than they did for those of Muslim origin. On some occasions, especially in regard to the treatment of Russian refugees in China, League members displayed a bias in favour of whites. In 1934 the Nansen Office reported on the occupations common to Russian refugee women in China: prostitute, professional dancing partner, restaurant waitress, and 'what are perhaps the most ignoble cases of all, exhibition of unfortunate white Russian women to coolies who pay a few cents for the spectacle'. In response to the report, a Chinese newspaper commented that 'it is shocking that such sympathy should be shown with Russian women in Shanghai when none is shown with Chinese women here, most of whom are in far worse straits than most Russian women', and asked: 'is it that the League is simply a League of *White* Nations, interested only in white women . . . ?'[16]

The League also went out of its way to make sure that its refugee assistance programmes did not seriously offend any member. This was especially important because all members, even refugee-producing ones, had a veto over League activities. One of the most difficult decisions on refugees ever made within the League demonstrates this point. In September 1937 the Soviet delegate to the Assembly asked that the Nansen Office be dissolved because his government considered it to be a propaganda tool of the White

---

[16] At the Fifteenth Assembly, delegates, especially the females ones, were stunned by the report and organized a coalition to discuss it, giving more attention to women refugees than at any other time in the history of the League of Nations. League of Nations, Nansen International Office for Refugees, 'Report of the Governing Body' (20 Aug. 1934) [A.12.1934], 20; *Official Journal*, Special Supplement no. 130, Fifteenth Assembly, Sixth Committee (Geneva, 1934), 12–16; *The People's Tribune*, 7 (1 Oct. 1934), 306, 308. LNA C1530.

Russians. Halvdan Koht, the Norwegian delegate, urged the Eighteenth Assembly to continue refugee assistance because of the great needs of the refugees due to both the depression and the creation of new refugees. In the Sixth Committee, the French delegate correctly couched the conflict as one between a state acting within its sovereign rights and humanitarianism. In an effort to break the deadlock, the Assembly reached a compromise. The Soviets agreed to support the continuation of assistance to Russian refugees under the direction of a new High Commissioner for Refugees but only under the condition that no refugees be employed by this agency. As a result, the staff members who were refugees lost their jobs.[17] For the Assembly, it was a painful compromise but one which allowed refugee assistance to continue.

Even the private voluntary organizations participating in the international refugee regime were unable to live up to the humanitarian principle. These organizations seemed to unleash their humanitarian passions on behalf of refugees with whom they shared a common religion and culture more often than they did for refugees who were noticeably different. British and American philanthropic groups, for instance, primarily helped Christian refugees living in the Muslim Middle East. In response to the German refugee crisis, sectarianism was even more pronounced: Jewish organizations helped Jewish refugees, Catholic organizations helped Catholic refugees, Socialist organizations helped Socialist refugees, and Communist organizations helped Communist refugees. In this environment of selective humanitarianism, the Quakers stand out as one of the few organizations (possibly the only) which helped all types of refugees, be they Christian, Jew, Socialist, or Communist.

In making decisions about refugee assistance, each of the actors in the international refugee regime acted under resource constraints. Because of a scarcity of time, money, and energy, each of the actors had to make choices about which refugees to assist. By setting priorities, each fell short of meeting the humanitarian standard of helping refugees without regard to race, religion, creed, or strategic importance. In choosing to help some refugees, they neglected others, and indirectly practised a form of discrimination. By linking refugee assistance to wider foreign policy

---

[17] *Official Journal*, Special Supplement no. 175, Eighteenth Assembly, Sixth Committee (Geneva, 1937), 76–7.

goals, they injected a political element into refugee assistance programmes. Consequently, none of the actors completely met the high standards of the humanitarian principle.

Differences By Issue

The international refugee regime's influence also varied according to the type of issue concerned. The regime had the most impact on the legal protection and provision of durable solutions for refugees already hosted by governments. This was evidenced by the creation of the Nansen passport system and other legal rules about the treatment of refugees, and by the provision of consular services for refugees by the High Commissioner's delegates within host countries. It was also shown by the successful completion of settlement projects for Greek, Bulgar, and Armenian refugees, and by the provision of small loans and help in finding employment for Russian and other refugees. The regime had less impact on decisions by governments about admitting refugees. While Nansen was able to convince Serbia and other countries to accept Russian refugees in the aftermath of the First World War, this type of operation was rarely repeated. Despite much fanfare, the Evian Conference did not result in dramatic changes in the immigration policies of the countries in attendance. Similarly, the failure of the Nansen–Soviet repatriation plan shows the inability of the international refugee regime to affect decisions by governments about allowing refugees to return to their home countries. Finally, the regime had virtually no impact on the conditions within countries which create refugees in the first place; the failure of High Commissioner James G. McDonald's attempt to stop the Nazis' abuse of the Jewish population within Germany is the best example of this.

The difference in the international refugee regime's influence by issue can largely be explained by the degree to which a particular proposal affected national sovereignty. At one extreme, the intervention in Germany's domestic affairs urged by James G. McDonald would have been a fundamental challenge to a government's exclusive right to decide how to treat people within its borders. In an era before widespread recognition of protection of human rights as a legitimate international concern, McDonald's appeal fell on deaf ears. At the other extreme, efforts aimed at the provision of durable solutions for refugees already granted asylum actually reinforced state sovereignty. In the case of Greek refugee settlement, for instance, international programmes contributed to the government's goal of creating a more ethnically homogeneous state. Consequently, efforts along this line met with greater success than those that would have restricted national sovereignty.

Most issues fell between the two extremes: that is, they challenged some aspect of national sovereignty but potentially reinforced others. In regard to legal protection, for instance, the High Commissioner's delegates in host countries represented an international authority within a sovereign state. But these same delegates enhanced the host government's control over its population by providing resources and order to a potentially destabilizing group. Similarly, the Nansen passport system gave refugees an internationally recognized legal status independent of a particular state. At the same time, the system increased state sovereignty by giving governments more control over the refugees because it clearly identified them. In contrast, most efforts to modify asylum practices challenged a key feature of national sovereignty without strongly reinforcing other aspects. Consequently, only marginal changes in government policies took place in the 1920s and 1930s in this area. For example, despite the absence of any obvious strengthening of their sovereignty, the United States, Great Britain, Australia, and several other countries accepted small numbers of additional refugees after the Evian conference. Governments were more likely to amend their immigration policies in those instances where some offsetting enhancement occurred. Some governments, for instance, increased the number of refugees admitted to their countries because the Refugee Section of the ILO found them jobs and facilitated their relocation. Even in this case, the refugees involved were few. In making their decisions, these governments did not violate the asylum norm of the international refugee regime because it gave states the right to grant or deny asylum to refugees.

Because most of the international efforts to assist refugees compromised some aspect of national sovereignty, it was never guaranteed that the states would support them. They had to believe either that their national sovereignty would be enhanced in other ways or that humanitarian concerns were more important. But they did not reach these conclusions automatically. In the case of the regime's formation, leadership was necessary to convince governments that they could fulfil a humanitarian purpose and benefit from co-operation on refugee issues. By the same token, leadership continued to be vital to the international refugee regime after its inception.

WHAT WERE THE SOURCES OF LEADERSHIP FOR THE INTERNATIONAL REFUGEE REGIME?

The international refugee regime can be best characterized as a negotiated, rather than a hegemonic, regime. In other words, the creation, development, and operation of the regime did not depend on the influence of a dominant power. Instead, it resulted from a complex bargaining process which required the consent of each of the participants in it.[18] In a negotiated regime, an actor exercises leadership when it takes the initiative on a particular problem and attempts to create a consensus around a solution. In the international refugee regime, several states, private organizations, inter-governmental organizations, and individuals had the opportunity to play significant roles in its operations. While all these actors formed an important component of the regime, the primary source of leadership came from the refugee agencies of the League of Nations and from particular individuals.

States: A Source of Support and the Holders of Veto Power

Taken as a whole, states play a crucial role in negotiated regimes because they create their rules and institutions. They also retain ultimate responsibility for policy-making and implementation on an ongoing basis. Taken individually, or in blocs, states have the potential to exercise leadership within a regime. In the case of the international refugee regime, France and Britain were the two countries that seemed to have the most influence on international efforts towards refugees. These two Great Powers played a crucial role in providing financial support for refugee assistance because

[18] Oran Young developed a typology of negotiated, imposed, and spontaneous regimes now commonly used by others: 'Regime Dynamics: The Rise and Fall of International Regimes', *International Organization*, 36 (Spring 1982), 277–97.

only they had significant surplus capital which could be spent on refugees outside their own countries. The British government, for instance, supported loans to finance refugee settlement in Greece and Bulgaria while the French funded housing for Armenians in Syria. Their decisions also paved the way for donations by other countries and private organizations to international projects.

The Great Powers also played an important political role in the international refugee regime because they could effectively veto projects. The British government, for instance, helped to kill the Erivan settlement scheme by refusing to contribute to it. Acting together, the British and French governments effectively opposed a proposal before the League Assembly in 1935 which would have resulted in the creation of one agency to deal with all refugees. These two countries, however, did not have a monopoly on veto power. Any member of the international refugee regime could prevent efforts to aid refugees within its borders. In 1928, for instance, the Austrian government successfully opposed a proposal to extend legal protection to Ruthenians and Hungarians within Austria. Moreover, if a state belonged to the League of Nations, it could veto or severely hamper any refugee assistance efforts. The German opposition to aid to refugees fleeing the Reich is the best example of this.

Although the Great Powers exercised a powerful negative influence on any attempts to change the rules and institutions of the international refugee regime, they did not often exercise leadership in the positive sense. Only rarely did France or Britain urge that protection be extended to an additional refugee group or develop an innovative proposal concerning refugees. Most proposals for refugee assistance either came from officials of the League of Nations, representatives from smaller countries, or staff of private organizations. The ICRC, for instance, made the initial proposal to help Russian refugees. In addition, High Commissioner Nansen, in collaboration with other officials of the League of Nations, first developed the idea of travel and identity documents and the first refugee settlement scheme. In the 1930s the Dutch government made the initial proposal to help refugees from Germany, and the Norwegian government spearheaded efforts to reorganize refugee assistance provided by the League of Nations.

The failure of either France or Britain to play a leadership role in refugee affairs was due, in part, to the fact that neither government made refugees its top priority. Throughout the inter-war era the leaders of these two countries were preoccupied with unemployment and other domestic political issues. In the foreign policy arena they focused on maintaining and adapting the post-war settlement. Even if the leaders of these countries had made refugees a higher priority, any proposal closely associated with one of them would have been politically suspect. Both the British and French governments distrusted one another, and other countries did not trust them. Consequently, it would have been difficult to win international support for any proposal directly associated with either one. In the case of the Evian Conference, a major power, the United States, did take the initiative. At the time, however, the USA was not a superpower but rather a neutral country considered to be outside European politics.

PVOs: A Valuable Source of Funding and Information

In the international refugee regime, private, voluntary organizations also played an important role, primarily because they were a major source of funding for refugee aid. A group of British and American private organizations, for instance, contributed half the funds towards Armenian refugee settlement in Syria. In the case of Jewish refugees, assistance from PVOs was even more essential. Private organizations also provided a great deal of information about the conditions of refugees. For instance, reports from the ICRC first brought the attention of policy-makers to the health conditions facing Armenian refugees in Syria, and the Save the Children Fund exposed the plight of Russian refugees subject to the French practice of expulsion. Moreover, governments and the League of Nations officially relied on private organizations, especially those associated with a refugee group, to inform them of the desires of refugees who lived far from the capitals of Europe. The Armenian and Russian refugee organizations were especially important in this regard.

Despite their many valuable functions, significant constraints existed on the ability of private organizations to provide leadership for the international refugee regime. The most important constraint was that they lacked the authority necessary to deal with governments.[19] Representatives from private organizations had to rely on the Dutch government in 1933 and the Norwegian government in 1935 to champion their proposals because they could not address delegates of the League of Nations directly. In addition, all PVOs depended to some extent on the support of governments. The American Red Cross, an organization which had played such an important relief role in the First World War and after the Graeco-Turkish War, worked closely with the United States government. Consequently, when the USA retreated into isolationism, the Red Cross went with it. Similarly, the British PVOs would not agree to finance any refugee projects for Armenians in the Middle East without the express permission of the Foreign Office. In the 1930s American Jewish organizations concerned about their co-religionists from Nazi Germany received pressure from the Roosevelt administration to accept the Rublee plan. Although in theory the private organizations could have acted independently, in fact they both depended on and were influenced by governments.

The League of Nations: A Forum for Co-operation and a Source of Innovation

Given the unwillingness or inability of particular states and private organizations to provide leadership for the international refugee regime, it is worth considering whether the League of Nations filled this void. As shown above, the Council and Assembly of the League provided a valuable forum for intergovernmental co-operation on refugee issues. But did the refugee agencies exercise direct leadership? According to conventional accounts of the refugee work of the League of Nations, the answer is 'no'. Since the demise of the League, much of the scholarship on this subject has been critical. A case in point is the evaluation given by F. P. Walters in his comprehensive history of the League. Walters points out that the League made an early decision not to accept responsibility for the relief, maintenance, or settlement of refugees. This left these functions in the domain of governments and private organizations, and condemned the League's endeavours 'to be

---

[19] Arieh Tartakower and Kurt R. Grossman make this point in their evaluation of private organizations in *The Jewish Refugee* (New York: Institute of Jewish Affairs of the American Jewish Congress and World Jewish Congress, 1944), 498.

always a palliative, never a cure'. In addition, Walters contends that the refugee agencies were an 'unpopular institution' with most governments and that 'no efficient and well-defined organization was ever built up'. In his final assessment, Walters concludes that 'the League's record [on refugees] was regrettably inadequate and confused'.[20]

Contrary to the position put forward by Walters and others, the League of Nations played a valuable part in refugee assistance in inter-war Europe, as shown throughout this book. Furthermore, Walters' claim that the League never built up a well-defined organization in the field of refugee assistance is inaccurate. While it is true that the refugee agencies went through no less than six reorganizations, their internal structure remained remarkably untouched. For the first decade, Nansen himself directed the League's refugee work. Thomas Frank Johnson, Nansen's assistant, had a fifteen-year career in refugee work, serving first with the High Commissioner, then as Director of the Refugee Service of the ILO, and finally as Managing Director of the Nansen Office. In addition, the local level staff of the refugee agencies also provided a source of permanence. Many of the chief delegates served at their posts for the most of the inter-war years.[21]

Though the refugee agencies of the League of Nations generally did not employ large numbers of personnel, this often was a strength rather than a weakness.[22] High Commissioners Nansen and McDonald both worked with a small staff of personally chosen

[20] F. P. Walters, *A History of the League of Nations* (London: Oxford University Press, 1960), 187–9. Michael Marrus essentially adopts Walter's interpretation of the League's refugee work in *The Unwanted: European Refugees in the Twentieth Century* (New York: Oxford University Press, 1985), 90. For other critical evaluations, see Tartakower and Grossman, *The Jewish Refugee*, 426–8; John G. Stoessinger, *The Refugee and the World Community* (Minneapolis: University of Minnesota Press, 1956), 8.

[21] Some of the long-standing representatives of the refugee agencies include the following: A. Masaryk (Czech) in Prague, 1922–38; B. Serafimov (Russian refugee) in Sofia, 1925–38; A. Kotelnikov (Russian refugee) in Athens, 1925–38; G. Burnier (Swiss) in Constantinople and Beirut, 1922–38; S. Yourieff (Russian refugee) in Belgrade, 1927–38; M. Schlesinger (German) in Berlin, 1922–30; E. Gallati (Swiss) in Riga, Warsaw, and Paris, 1922–1936. See reports of refugee agencies to the Council and Assembly of the League of Nations: e.g. 'Representatives of the High Commissioner in Various Countries', *Official Journal* (May 1922), 395; Nansen International Office for Refugees, 'Report of the Governing Body' (10 Aug. 1938) [A.21.1938.XII], 19–20.

[22] Keohane and Nye point out that 'often the most effective international organizations are surprisingly small', in 'Two Cheers for Multilateralism', *Foreign Policy*, 60 (Fall 1985), 156.

colleagues. As a result, their organizations maintained a flexibility and creativity not generally found in well-established bureaucracies. In addition, the small size of the agencies kept the League in close contact with refugees and their problems, rather than accentuating the distance between them.

Walters correctly points out that the refugee agencies of the League of Nations operated under tight budget constraints. Throughout the Inter-war Period, the refugee agencies ran on tiny budgets, put together on a piecemeal basis without the benefit of long-term financial planning.[23] Nansen started his work with a grant of £5,500 for 1921–2. Then, from 1923 until 1931, the various refugee organs operated on a League grant of £10,000–£15,000 per year. From 1932 until 1938 the Nansen Office used a planned budget, guaranteeing about £12,000 a year from the League.[24] In addition, the League only provided tiny sums for the assistance of refugees from Germany. From 1936 until 1938 the League granted the High Commissioner less than £4,000 a year, not even enough to maintain local representatives.[25]

Nevertheless, the refugee agencies successfully developed other sources of funds. From 1923 until 1931 the sale of Nansen stamps (£16,000) and special government contributions (£240,000) supplemented the basic grant to the High Commissioner and Refugee Section.[26] During the lifetime of the Nansen Office the humanitarian fund had grown to £40,000 a year. Though this sum was far too small to finance major settlement projects, it provided the Office with a nest-egg for grants to individuals and refugee organizations. In addition, the close co-operation between

[23] Louise Holborn makes this point in 'The League of Nations and the Refugee Problem', *Annals*, 203 (May 1939), 134.

[24] Budget information is contained in the annual reports of the Refugee Section of the ILO and of the Nansen Office to the Assembly over the period 1925–38. A summary of these data is given in Simpson, *The Refugee Problem*, 195. (All conversions made at the rate of £1 = 25 Swiss francs.)

[25] The 1937 budget of the High Commissioner was £3,750, and in 1938 it dropped to £3,400. About half the budget went to Malcolm's salary and travel expenses. League of Nations, 'Refugees Coming from Germany: Report Submitted to the Eighteenth Assembly by High Commissioner, Sir Neill Malcolm' (1 Sept. 1937) [A.17.1937.XII], 5.

[26] League of Nations, 'Russian, Armenian, Assyrian, Assyro-Chaldean and Turkish Refugees: Report by the Secretary-General on the Future Organisation of Refugee Work' (30 Aug. 1930) [A.28.1930.XIII], 8; Simpson, *The Refugee Problem*, 206; League of Nations, Committee on International Assistance to Refugees, 'Report by the Committee Submitted to the Council of the League of Nations' (3 Jan. 1936) [C.2.M.2.1936.XII], 7.

private organizations and the League, especially in regard to Armenian and Jewish refugees, helped to compensate for the lack of funding. The work of the League of Nations in the field of refugee assistance also benefited from the large number of refugees who participated in it. Without refugee staff members, the local offices of the High Commissioner would never have been able to operate. They often accepted lower wages, spoke the language of the refugees, and were familiar with their customs and culture. In regard to Greek refugee settlement, the major construction projects never would have been possible without the human capital of refugee staff members, labourers, and agriculturalists. In the Inter-war Period, the Nansen Office even included two refugees on its Governing Body, assuring that refugees would have a direct input to decision-making at a high level. In addition, refugees helped to develop the international arrangements and conventions developed by the League. In particular, the Russian refugee legal scholar J. L. Rubinstein is credited with drafting the 1933 Refugee Convention. Of course, the League of Nations did not always work closely with refugees in devising projects. The unsuccessful Latin American settlement scheme for Russian refugees is one example of this. The paltry results of this project further demonstrate that the involvement of refugees in the planning and implementation of any project is essential for success.

Walters' characterization of the refugee work of the League as unpopular with its members is overstated. Popular or not, the fact remains that a strong pro-refugee coalition existed within the League Assembly. The countries of eastern Europe consistently supported funds for refugee assistance, as did France and the Scandinavian countries. Though Walters correctly notes that opposition from the German government severely hindered the League's response to German refugees, this was not true in the case of Russian refugees. Although the Soviet government hampered increases in assistance to Russian refugees from 1934 until 1939, and pressed for the removal of all White Russians from the staff of the Nansen Office, it never vetoed aid entirely, despite its ability to do so.[27] This allowed the Nansen Office to continue its

[27] On the Soviet position on refugee assistance by the League, ILO, and UN, see Harold Jacobson, *The USSR and the UN's Economic and Social Activities* (Notre Dame, Ind.: University of Notre Dame Press, 1967), 59–60.

protection of Russian and other refugees during the 1930s, and even to expand them in the area of legal protection.

In addition, Walters' interpretation of the British position is especially misleading. Over the twenty-year history of the League, the British attitude towards refugee assistance went through several swings. Initially the British government strongly supported aid for the Greek refugees. By the mid-1920s, however, British enthusiasm for refugee assistance had waned. This trend culminated at the 1928 Assembly when Austen Chamberlain called for an end to all aid to refugees.[28] In keeping with this policy Chamberlain refused to allow a British delegate to participate in the proceedings of the Intergovernmental Advisory Commission for Refugees.[29] The following year, however, the British government reversed its direction after being pressured by the League of Nations Union, and specifically asked to be placed on the Commission.[30] By the end of the 1930s Britain once again became one of the strongest supporters of refugee assistance.

Overall, the refugee agencies of the League clearly had the ability to play a leadership role independent of the wishes of any one member state. In the 1920s they exercised this leadership by winning support for programmes which they innovated. While these efforts did not meet the needs of the entire refugee population, they helped some of the neediest refugees. The Greek Refugee Settlement Commission, for instance, was not only the first major internationally sponsored refugee settlement project but also was a pioneering venture in economic development. As pointed out in the Introduction, the value of combining refugee and development aid was only rediscovered by United Nations agencies in the 1980s. The Nansen Office's small-scale loan programme was valuable because it made capital directly available to refugees so that they could start their own businesses. This approach was also revived by the United Nations in the 1980s with great success.[31]

---

[28] *Official Journal*, Special Supplement no. 69, Ninth Assembly, Fifth Committee (Geneva, 1928), 51.

[29] T. F. Johnson to Nansen, 19 Dec. 1928, *re* Council meeting on Chamberlain. LNA C1406.

[30] *Official Journal* (Nov. 1929), annex 1159, p. 1642. The League of Nations Union was instrumental in convincing the British government to take a greater interest in refugees. See letter from G. Murray to Sir Austen Chamberlain, 26 Feb. 1929. LNA C1406.   [31] 'Patching up Poverty', *The Economist* (20 Aug. 1988).

The refugee agencies were able to play a successful leadership role for several reasons. In contrast to states, they were primarily concerned with refugee issues. Unlike private organizations, their association with the League of Nations gave them the authority to negotiate with governments directly. Because their proposals were generally perceived as being non-partisan, they were also more likely than those from the Great Powers to win a consensus. Of course, the ability of the refugee agencies to exercise leadership ultimately depended on the overall stature of the League of Nations. Consequently, the decline in the League's prestige after the failure of the Council and Assembly to stop the Italian invasion of Ethiopia severely hampered the effectiveness of the refugee agencies. When created, the IGCR was expected to be a more forceful agency because it would be independent of the League. In fact, the IGCR's autonomy deprived it of the prestige and authority that the League's refugee agencies derived from their association with a universal organization. Nor did the IGCR ever benefit from outstanding leadership such as that provided by key individuals to the League's agencies.

The Role of Individuals

During the Inter-war Period a number of individuals played a decisive role in marshalling the resources necessary for refugee assistance projects. In the League of Nations' initial decision to assist Russian refugees, for instance, Philip Noel-Baker helped to get the project going. Although many great names are associated with the League's refugee work,[32] Fridtjof Nansen's strong and creative leadership left a mark on refugee assistance which is still evident today. Louise Holborn describes him as 'a man of great vision, humanity, and warmth of heart' and 'the great organizer of

---

[32] Grahl-Madsen presents a list of the individuals from six countries who made the greatest contribution to refugee assistance during the Inter-war Period. They include Gustave Ador, Max Huber, and Georges Werner from Switzerland; Fridtjof Nansen and Michael Hansson from Norway; Lord Robert Cecil, Gilbert Murray, Philip Noel-Baker, Sir Samuel Hoare, Thomas Frank Johnson, Sir Neill Malcolm, and Sir Herbert Emerson from Great Britain; Albert Thomas from France; Paul Hymans from Belgium; and James G. McDonald, Myron Taylor, George Rublee, and Franklin Roosevelt from the United States. See Atle Grahl-Madsen, 'The League of Nations and the Refugees', in United Nations Library, *The League of Nations in Retrospect: Proceedings of the Symposium* (New York: Walter de Gruyter, 1983), 366.

refugee work and the conscience of the League of Nations and the international world'.[33] Elmer Bendiner characterizes Nansen more simply, calling him 'the League's private saint and conscience'.[34] Like other idealists, he was profoundly affected by the Great War: 'To him it was the greatest confession of defeat of humanity, a degradation, devoid of meaning, an orgy of self-destruction in which nothing flourished but the lust for power, hatred, and stupidity— the bitter fruits of which mankind must eat for a generation.'[35] Nansen saw in the League of Nations a hope for a better world. In 1919 he became president of the Norwegian League of Nations Society and strongly advocated that his government should join the League. He remained a devoted supporter of the League and served as the Norwegian delegate to the Assembly until his death in 1930.

As High Commissioner, Nansen personally embodied the humanitarian principle of the international refugee regime. His exploits as an Arctic explorer had made him a hero, but his work for refugees won him the hearts of the world. High Commissioner Nansen set a moral example above and beyond what is normally expected of international civil servants. He lived in a Spartan manner, eating the simplest food, and was described as always wearing the same worn jacket. On refugee-related work, he rode third class on the trains. Moreover, he never accepted any salary for his refugee work. These qualities more than made up for his lack of training as a politician or diplomat and helped him to win a reputation as being 'above politics'. Nansen also believed that the High Commissioner should carry out refugee assistance in a non-political, humanitarian way, and conducted himself accordingly.

Ironically, Nansen initially refused to become High Commissioner. Secretariat officials wanted him as a candidate because he could combine refugee activities with those for the Russian famine, get support from voluntary organizations, negotiate with

[33] Louise W. Holborn, *Refugees: A Problem of our Time: The Work of the United Nations High Commissioner for Refugees, 1951–1972* (Metuchen, NJ: Scarecrow Press, 1975), 19–20; David Wyman concurs in *Paper Walls* (New York: Pantheon Books, 1985), 30. See also Grahl-Madsen, 'The League of Nations and the Refugees', 359–60.

[34] Elmer Bendiner, *A Time for Angels: The Tragicomic History of the League of Nations* (New York: Alfred A. Knopf, 1975), 187.

[35] J. Sorensen, *The Saga of Fridtjof Nansen* (London: Allen & Unwin, 1932), 270.

the Soviets, and work for free.[36] But, when Nansen was first approached by the Secretariat in June 1921, he rebuffed their appeal. Always a perfectionist, Nansen doubted what he alone could do: 'I could not do anything useful without going thoroughly into the whole question,... it requires a man, who would be able to take up this great work with his whole soul and, though tempting it is, it is absolutely impossible for me to take it upon myself.' Nansen, then in his sixtieth year, had already had a long career of service to his country and hoped to return to his first career: 'I am now buried in work here, have three big scientific works that have been waiting and waiting, and now must be finished, and this is after all my real work . . .'.[37]

Nansen might never have become High Commissioner at all if the League of Nations' search for a candidate had been more successful. In the early summer of 1921, Secretariat officials had hopes of getting a prominent American to take the job, but both official and personal diplomatic efforts failed.[38] Suggestions for the appointment of a High Commissioner from one of the Great Powers met with strong opposition. Sir Eric Drummond's candidate, Turati, the leader of the Italian Socialist party, was dropped after it became clear that the Yugoslav government, a great supporter of the Russian refugees, would object if a man who was both Socialist and Italian took the job.[39] Jean Monnet's candidates, Mr Hoare of Great Britain and M. Clémentel of France, were disqualified because of their nationality. One critic pointed out that, if a British or French High Commissioner was appointed, it would appear that the 'League is an Anglo French or a francoEnglish concern'.[40] Ultimately, it was the continued prodding of Nansen's

[36] Philip [Noel-]Baker(?), 'Advantages of Having Nansen', Secretariat note, undated. NBKR 4/450a.

[37] Letter from Nansen to Frick, 24 June 1921. NP, MS fo. 1988.K.10.C.

[38] When official negotiations with the US government failed, Jean Monnet pursued personal diplomacy with Dwight Morrow, an associate of the Morgan bank and a friend of the then Vice-President, Calvin Coolidge, but these negotiations failed as well. See 'Réfugiés russes', Secretariat note of 21 July 1921; telegram from Jean Monnet to Dwight Morrow of 22 July 1921, care of Morgan, New York; Jean Monnet to Lamont, care of Morgan, New York, undated; Lamont to Monnet of 10 August 1921. LNA C1405.

[39] Telephone message from Drummond to Monnet of 3 August 1921; 'Note pour le Secrétaire Général', 4 August 1921. LNA C1405.

[40] 'Réfugiés russes', Secretariat note by M. [Jean Monnet] of 22 July; untitled note by B. Attslory of 28 July 1921, with comment by F. P. Walters of 1 August 1921. LNA C1405.

friend Philip [Noel-]Baker and his own sense of humanitarian duty that eventually influenced him to accept the nomination.[41] He would later write that 'When, however, I understood that it was my duty to do what I could for the Russian famine, I thought I could as well take over the work for the Russian refugees.'[42]

Shortly after his appointment, Nansen set up the office of the High Commissioner. In doing so, he established the basic institutions of the international refugee regime. His appointment of delegates and the acceptance of them by host governments is especially remarkable. Though widely accepted today as an integral part of international refugee assistance programmes, this was not the case in 1921.[43] Beyond creating the institutions at the centre of the international refugee regime, Nansen helped to translate the regime's norms into concrete rules. Because of his initiative, governments gathered together and created the first internationally recognized identity certificate for refugees, commonly called 'Nansen passports'. Though many other people participated in the development of international refugee law, Nansen rightly deserves credit for this first important step.[44]

Nansen, who was the first European to cross Greenland from east to west, who proved his theory of Arctic drift by lodging his ship in the polar ice cap for three years, and who travelled further north than any explorer before him, brought this spirit of adventure to his refugee work. He was responsible for many 'firsts', including crisis management at Constantinople and Greece, interventions on behalf of refugees in Poland and Romania, and refugee settlement projects in Greece and Bulgaria. In delivering the Nansen Memorial Lecture in 1961, Philip Noel-Baker pointed out that Nansen pioneered the development work that the World Bank does now.[45] It is also important to note that systemic factors, especially the advent of an international crisis, provided Nansen with the opportunity for expanding the scope and func-

[41] Baker to Nansen, 26 June 1921. NBKR 4/450b.

[42] Letter from Nansen to Hebe Spaull, Lysaker of 23 October 1924, in Jacob Worm-Müller (ed.), *Fridtjof Nansen Brev* (Osloi Universitetsforlaget, 1966), iv, no. 929.

[43] Atle Grahl-Madsen, *The Status of Refugees in International Law*, i (Leyden: A. W. Sijthoff, 1966), 55–6.

[44] Grahl-Madsen, 'The League of Nations and the Refugees', 360.

[45] P. J. Noel-Baker, 'Addresses on Nansen (iv)', in J. H. Whitehouse (ed.), *Nansen: A Book of Homage* (London: Hodder & Stoughton, 1930), 17.

tions of the international refugee regime.[46] The mass exodus of
refugees from Asia Minor is a case in point.

After Nansen's death in 1930 the refugee work of the League of
Nations suffered a tremendous loss. In the words of Robert Cecil,
'it was a bad day for Peace, Humanity and the League when he
died at a comparatively early age. He has left no successor.'[47] But
the institutions and rules which Nansen helped to create continued to function. They weathered the political and economic storms
of the 1930s and continue to this day in the form of the United
Nations High Commissioner for Refugees.

So successful was Nansen's work in the 1920s that many won-
dered if he would have been able to solve the German refugee
crisis. In the midst of the refugee crisis of the late 1930s, journalist
Dorothy Thompson wrote that 'what the whole refugee problem
needs today, more than anything else, is another Nansen'.[48] Given
the prevailing circumstances at the end of the 1930s, it is unlikely
that even Nansen could have solved the refugee problem. In
the 1920s he had operated in an environment conducive to co-
operation between states and expansion of international institutions
and law. In addition, no major power strongly objected to refugee
assistance: indeed, the Great Powers proved to be strong supporters of it on occasion. And, in the case of the Erivan scheme, even
Nansen's most persuasive speech could not convince the British
government to act against its perceived national interests. In the
1930s, in contrast, Hitler's Germany actively challenged both the
principles of the international refugee regime and the entire world
order. Governments also retreated into an economic and political
nationalism resulting in greater immigration restrictions than those
which had existed soon after the First World War. In addition, the
appointments of High Commissioners Malcolm and Emerson indicate that the British and French governments did not want a
forceful advocate for refugees in an official position. Given this

---

[46] Michael G. Schechter reaches a similar conclusion about other executive
heads: 'Leadership in International Organizations: Systemic, Organizational and
Personality Factors', *Review of International Studies*, 13 (1987), 197–221; id., 'Directors-General of the International Atomic Energy Agency: Locating the Place of
Executive Heads in Regime Theory', unpub. paper (1988), 34–5.

[47] Lord Robert Cecil, *A Great Experiment: An Autobiography* (London: Jonathan
Cape, 1941), 131.

[48] Dorothy Thompson, *Refugees: Anarchy or Organization?* (New York: Random
House, 1938), 17.

inhospitable atmosphere, Nansen, or a person like him, would only have been able to act as the regime's conscience, not ensure adherence to its norms. Nevertheless, the important role that Nansen and others played in the League of Nations indicates that individuals can be a significant source of leadership for international organizations and for the development of the institutions, scope, and functions of international regimes.[49]

LOOKING AT REFUGEES IN A NEW LIGHT

At the beginning of Part II, international regime theory was offered as a tool for studying the familiar topic of refugees in a new light. Regime theory has proved its usefulness by revealing several interesting points about international efforts to assist refugees. As stated above, most conventional accounts of refugee assistance in the inter-war years focus on its inadequacies. The primary insight of the regime approach is that it helps us to see how internationally agreed upon standards and rules affected the way in which states treated refugees. The international refugee regime facilitated co-operation between governments which resulted in the provision of legal protection and durable solutions for more than one million refugees. Over time the regime also influenced how governments perceived the 'refugee problem'. While one can rightly criticize the actors in the regime for not doing more to help refugees, this evaluation should be tempered with the knowledge that they engaged in a pioneering effort to assist refugees on an international scale. What is really remarkable is that they accomplished so much with so few resources.

A secondary insight of a regime approach to inter-war refugee issues is that it reveals the interactions between humanitarianism and other motivations for the provision of refugee aid. This is important because refugee assistance is generally thought of as a purely humanitarian endeavour. In the case of the international refugee regime, the underlying motivation for refugee aid was humanitarianism. But this alone rarely provided sufficient

---

[49] The need for strong leadership in the development of an international organization has been pointed out by Robert W. Cox in 'The Executive Head: An Essay on Leadership in International Organizations', *International Organization*, 23 (Spring 1969), 205.

incentives for action. In most cases, each of the members of the regime balanced humanitarianism against other objectives, such as a desire to protect national sovereignty, promote foreign policy goals, or provide economic growth. As a result, none of them perfectly lived up to their expressed humanitarian principles. This result, however, was to be expected from a regime which embodied both humanitarian aspirations and respect for state sovereignty.

Although the major beliefs underpinning the international refugee regime were potentially contradictory, they were not necessarily so in practice for two reasons. One reason was that a myriad of both state and non-state actors participated in the regime. Although individually each of the actors in the regime only partially fulfilled the humanitarian principle, taken as a whole their activities provided a much closer approximation to it. Added together, their efforts amounted to a virtual universalization of refugee assistance, even though no one actor took responsibility for all refugees. The participation of both state and non-state actors in the regime facilitated the development of coalitions on behalf of different refugee groups which could advocate their cause in diverse forums. This co-operation also brought a form of outside scrutiny to governmental decision-making about refugees. The participation of many actors did not guarantee a perfectly humanitarian outcome, but it did make such an outcome more likely. The second reason was that forceful leadership helped to channel diverse interests into concrete policies that incorporated the humanitarian ideals of the regime as much as possible. In the inter-war years, leadership primarily came from the refugee agencies of the League of Nations and from key individuals working within them. They exercised leadership by developing innovative solutions to refugee problems and by convincing governments that they would benefit from adopting them.

THE LEGACY OF THE INTERNATIONAL REFUGEE REGIME

Using a regime approach also helps us to assess the long-term impact of organized international co-operation on refugee issues in the Inter-war Period. If one evaluated the lasting legacy of these efforts merely by assessing the fate of formal institutions, one would have to conclude that there was little. Of all the institutions associated with the League of Nations, only the ILO found a place in the United Nations system. But a regime consists not only of formal institutions, but also of internationally agreed upon principles, norms, rules, and decision-making procedures; these could potentially survive the demise of formal institutions. If we look at the contemporary refugee regime, we find that it differs significantly from its inter-war counterpart in that it is more global: the majority of its members are countries located in Africa, Asia, and Latin America rather than Europe, and its scope includes the millions of refugees in the developing world. Beyond this expansion, however, there are important similarities between the two regimes.[50]

Both the inter-war and contemporary refugee regimes embody the sometimes conflicting principles of humanitarianism and state sovereignty and also norms establishing standards for asylum, assistance, and burden-sharing.[51] Of these, it is the asylum norm which continues to generate the most controversy. It is often labelled 'state-centric' because it affirms the right of states to grant asylum rather than the right of individuals to be granted asylum. States used this norm to justify preventing the entry of refugees, including Jews fleeing Nazi Germany, in the inter-war years. Since then, Western leaders and publics have almost universally expressed regret for virtually closing their borders in the late 1930s because this indirectly increased the number of Holocaust victims. But this regret has not brought about a change in the asylum norm. After the conclusion of the Second World War, an attempt was made to incorporate in international law a 'right to asylum' for individuals. In 1948, at the international conference charged with preparing the United Nations Declaration of Human

---

[50] For a comparison of the two regimes, see Claudena M. Skran, 'The International Refugee Regime: The Historical and Contemporary Context of International Responses to Asylum Problems,' in Gil Loescher (ed.), *Refugees and the Asylum Dilemma in the West* (University Park, Penn.: Penn. State University Press, 1993), 8–35.

[51] For thought-provoking examinations and criticisms of the basic premises of the contemporary international refugee regime, see James C. Hathaway, 'A Reconsideration of the Underlying Premise of Refugee Law', *Harvard International Law Journal*, 31/1 (Winter 1990), 129–83; Jack I. Garvey, 'Towards a Reformulation of International Refugee Law', *Harvard International Law Journal*, 26/2 (Spring 1985), 483–500.

Rights, considerable debate took place about whether individuals should be granted the right of asylum. Despite support for recognizing such a right, the conference embraced the traditional position on asylum and adopted article 14 (1), which states that 'everyone has the right to seek and to enjoy in other countries asylum from persecution'. In using this wording, the conference deliberately rejected a proposal which included the words 'to be granted' asylum. The gathered governments also turned down a second proposal giving the United Nations the power to secure asylum for refugees. In 1968, at an international conference on territorial asylum, governments once more failed to agree on a right of asylum for the individual.[52] This defeat signalled the continued unwillingness of governments to change fundamentally the premises on which international refugee assistance efforts are carried out. Until such a change is made, only the rule of non-*refoulement* will temper the asylum norm and guarantee an individual a right to temporary asylum.

While the principles and norms of both the inter-war and contemporary refugee regimes are quite similar, the rules have changed considerably. Under the terms of the 1951 Refugee Convention, a refugee is defined as a person who has left his home country because of a 'well-founded fear' of persecution for reasons of race, religion, nationality, membership of a particular social group or political opinion. This definition of a refugee differs from those used in the League of Nations era in that it applies to individuals rather than to groups, and it uses persecution as the litmus-test for refugeehood. But the definitions used in both the inter-war and contemporary regimes have more in common than is immediately obvious. Both definitions place refugees in a special category. The importance of this should not be underestimated, in as much as the categorization is incorporated into immigration policy, where the United States and other countries have preferential quotas for refugees that are not available to those immigrating for economic reasons. It also affects the provision of legal protection and material assistance. Intergovernmental agencies and most countries provide aid to refugees separately from that given to victims of famine, natural disasters, and poverty. The practice of

---

[52] Guy S. Goodwin-Gill, *The Refugee in International Law* (Oxford: Clarendon Press, 1983), 104–14; Atle Grahl-Madsen, *The Status of Refugees in International Law*, ii (Leyden: A. W. Sijthoff, 1972), 6–11. See also Atle Grahl-Madsen, *Territorial Asylum* (London: Oceana Publications, 1980).

treating refugees separately from broader social and economic issues is perhaps the most important legacy of the international refugee regime.[53]

Even if we look at the now defunct refugee agencies of the League of Nations, we find that they established precedents that have been adopted by their successors. When the United Nations created the office of High Commisioner for Refugees in 1951 it essentially followed the Nansen model. Following this model, the office was organized as 'a man and his staff', until the appointment of Sadako Ogata in 1991 made it the office of 'a woman and her staff'. The UNHCR has also adopted Nansen's practices of having protection officers in major host countries and working closely with representatives of private organizations. In addition, the UNHCR's statutes define the work of the High Commissioner to be 'of an entirely non-political character'.[54] In so doing, they are accepting Nansen's conviction that the High Commissioner must be politically neutral if he is to be effective in providing humanitarian assistance to refugees. Thus, the refugee regime centred on the UNHCR owes much to the first international efforts on behalf of refugees begun by Fridtjof Nansen and the League of Nations in the early 1920s.

[53] This separation also remains controversial. See e.g. Roxanne Dunbar-Ortiz and Barbara E. Harrell-Bond, 'Who Protects the Human Rights of Refugees?', *African Affairs* (1st/2nd Quarters 1987), 110–13; Charles Keely, *Global Refugee Policy: The Case for a Development-Oriented Strategy* (New York: The Population Council, 1981).   [54] UNHCR Statutes, art. 2.

BIBLIOGRAPHY

1. PRIMARY SOURCES

1.1. *Archives and Paper Collections*

Bodleian Library, Oxford, Sir Alfred Zimmern Papers.
British Library, Lord Robert Cecil Papers.
British Library Newspaper Library, League of Nations Union Collection of Press Clippings.
Churchill College, Cambridge, Philip Noel-Baker Papers.
Columbia University Library, James G. McDonald Papers.
Public Record Office, Kew, British Foreign Office Archives.
Royal Institute of International Affairs, London, *Refugee Survey Special Reports 1937–8*, vols. i–xi.
United Nations Library, Geneva, League of Nations Archives.
National Library, Oslo, Fridtjof Nansen Papers.

1.2. *League of Nations Documents*

Official Records

Monthly Summary of the League of Nations (1921–39).
Records of the Second Assembly: Plenary Meetings (Geneva: League of Nations, 1921).
Records of the Third Assembly: Plenary Meetings (Geneva: League of Nations, 1922).
League of Nations Treaty Series (1922–39).
Official Journal (1922–39).

Reports by the High Commissioner for Refugees, 1921–1930

'Russian Refugees', 1 Aug. 1921. [C.126(a).M.72(a).1921.VII]
'Conference on the Russian Refugee Question: Resolutions', 26 Aug. 1921. [C.277.M.203.1921.VII]
'Russian Refugees: Report to the Council on March 24th, 1922 by Dr. Nansen', *Official Journal* (May 1922), 385–95.
'Russian Refugees: Report to the Council by Dr. Nansen of 13 May 1922', *Official Journal* (June 1922), 612–16. [C.280.M.152.1922]
'Russian Refugees: Report by Dr. Nansen to the Council of 20 July 1922', *Official Journal* (Aug. 1922), 923–8. [C.472.M.297.1922]

'Russian Refugees: Report by Dr. Nansen to the Council of 1 September 1922', *Official Journal* (Nov. 1922), 1125–7. [C.602.M.360.1922]

'Russian Refugees: Report by Dr. Nansen to the Fifth Committee of the Assembly of 15 September 1922', *Official Journal* (Nov. 1922), 1134–41.

'Reciprocal Exchange of Racial Minorities Between Greece and Turkey: Report by Dr. Nansen of 15 November 1922', *Official Journal* (Jan. 1923), 126–9. [C.736.M.447.1922]

'Relief Measures for Refugees in Greece and Asia Minor: Report by Dr. Nansen of 18 November 1922', *Official Journal* (Jan. 1923), 133–6. [C.736(a).M.447(a).1922]

'Refugees in the Near East: Report by Dr. Nansen to the Council of 2 February 1923', *Official Journal* (Mar. 1923), 383–6.

'Russian Refugees: Report by Dr. Nansen to the Council of 2 February 1923', *Official Journal* (Mar. 1923), 387–93.

'Russian Refugees: Report by Dr. Nansen, Submitted to the Council of 7 July 1923', *Official Journal* (Aug. 1923), 1040–5. [C.473.1923]

'Report on the Work of the High Commission for Refugees Presented by Dr. Fridtjof Nansen to the Fourth Assembly' (4 Sept. 1923). [A.30.1923.XII]

'Near East Refugees: Report by the High Commissioner to the Council of 11 March 1924', *Official Journal* (Apr. 1924), 591–4. [C.103(b).1924]

'Russian Refugees: Report by Dr. Nansen to the Council of 12 June 1924', *Official Journal* (July 1924), 958–63. [C.249.1924]

'Report by Dr. Nansen, President of the Commission Appointed to Study the Question of the Settlement of Armenian Refugees of 28 July 1925', *Official Journal, Special Supplement no. 38, Sixth Assembly, Fifth Committee* (1925), 88–92.

'Conference on Russian and Armenian Refugee Questions: Report by Dr. Nansen to the Council of 10 June 1926', *Official Journal* (July 1926), 983–6. [C.327.1926]

'Legal Status of Refugees: Report by Dr. Nansen on the Inter-Governmental Conference on the Status of Refugees (Geneva, June 1928) of 15 August 1928', *Official Journal* (Mar. 1929), 483–8. [C.392.M.183.1928.VIII]

'Russian, Armenian, Assyrian, Assyro-Chaldean and Turkish Refugees: Report to the Tenth Assembly' (15 Aug. 1929), pt. III. [A.23.1929.VII]

Reports by the High Commissioner for Refugees and the Refugee Section of the ILO, 1925–1928

'Russian and Armenian Refugees: Report to the Sixth Assembly', *Official Journal, Special Supplement no. 38, Sixth Assembly, Fifth Committee* (1925), 115–24.

'Armenian and Russian Refugees: Report to the Seventh Assembly' (3 Sept. 1926). [A.44.1926]

'Russian and Armenian Refugees: Report to the Eighth Assembly' (1927). [A.48.1927.XIII]

'Measures in Favour of Russian, Armenian, Assyrian, Assyro-Chaldean and Turkish Refugees: Report to the Ninth Assembly' (1928). [A.33.1928.VIII]

Reports by the Nansen International Office for Refugees, 1932–1938

'Report of the Governing Body' (16 Aug. 1932). [A.24.1932]

'Report of the Governing Body' (30 Aug. 1933). [A.19.1933]

'Report of the Governing Body' (20 Aug. 1934). [A.12.1934]

'Report of the Governing Body' (29 Aug. 1935). [A.22.1935.XII]

'Report of the Governing Body' (3 Sept. 1936). [A.23.1936.XII]

'Special Report Submitted to the 17th Assembly by M. Michael Hansson, Acting President of the Governing Body' (7 Sept. 1936). [A.27.1936.XII]

'Report on the Liquidation of the Office by Judge Hansson, President of the Governing Body' (14 June 1937). [C.226.1937.XII]

'Report of the Governing Body' (20 Aug. 1937). [A.21.1937.XII]

'Report of the Governing Body' (10 Aug. 1938). [A.21.1938.XII]

'Report by M. Michael Hansson, Former President of the Governing Body' (1939). [1939.XII.B.2]

Reports by the High Commissioner for Refugees coming from Germany, 1936–1938

'Refugees Coming from Germany: Report to the Seventeenth Assembly by Sir Neill Malcolm' (1 Sept. 1936). [A.19.1936.XII]

'Report Submitted to the Eighteenth Assembly by . . . Sir Neill Malcolm' (1 Sept. 1937). [A.17.1937.XII]

'Report to the Nineteenth Assembly by Sir Neill Malcolm' (22 Aug. 1938). [A.25.1938.XII]

Reports by the High Commissioner for Refugees, 1938–1939

'International Assistance to Refugees: Report by Sir Herbert Emerson' (24 July 1939). [A.18.1939.XII]

'International Assistance to Refugees: Supplementary Report to the Twentieth Assembly by Sir Herbert Emerson' (20 Oct. 1939). [A.18(a).1939.XII]

Special Reports by the Secretariat and Other League of Nations Bodies

'The Settlement of Greek Refugees', *Monthly Summary of the League of Nations: Supplement* (Nov. 1924).

Greek Refugee Settlement Commission, 'Report to the Council' (1924–31).
Economic and Financial Committee, *Greek Refugee Settlement* (Geneva: League of Nations, 1926).
Second Committee, Assembly, 'Settlement of Bulgarian Refugees' (21 Sept. 1926). [A.84.1926.II]
International Relief Union, 'Draft Statutes and Statement drawn up by the Preparatory Committee for the Ciraolo Scheme', Nov. 1926 [C.618.M.240.1926.II].
Commissioner for the Settlement of Bulgarian Refugees, 'Report to the Council' (1926–32).
Intergovernmental Advisory Commission for Refugees, 'Russian, Armenian, Assyrian, Assyro-Chaldean and Turkish Refugees: Report to the Tenth Assembly' (15 Aug. 1929), pt. I. [A.23.1929.VII]
Secretary-General, 'Russian, Armenian, Assyrian, Assyro-Chaldea and Turkish Refugees: Report on the Future Organisation of Refugee Work' (30 Aug. 1930). [A.28.1930.XIII]
—— 'Report on the Future Organization of Refugee Work', 30 Aug. 1930. [A.28.1930.XII]
Information Section, *The Settlement of the Assyrians: A Work of Humanity and Appeasement*, League of Nations Questions, pamphlet no. 5 (Geneva, 1935).
Committee on International Assistance to Refugees, 'Report by the Committee Submitted to the Council of the League of Nations' (3 Jan. 1936). [C.2.M.2.1936.XII]
International Relief Union, 'Convention and Statutes', July 1927 [C.364.M.137.1927].
Council Committee, 'International Assistance to Refugees' (25 Aug. 1938). [A.27.1938.XII]
Information Section, *The Refugees*, League of Nations Questions, pamphlet no. 9 (Geneva, 1938).

1.3. *Other Official Sources*

Houses of Parliament, Great Britain, *Parliamentary Papers* (1923–39).
International Labour Office, *Refugee and Labour Conditions in Bulgaria*, Studies and Reports, ser. B (Economic Conditions), no. 15 (London: P. S. King & Son, 1926).
—— *Annual Review* (Geneva: Alfred Kundig, 1931).
—— *The I.L.O. Year-Book* (Geneva: Alfred Kundig, 1931–40).
—— *International Labour Conference: Conventions and Recommendations, 1919–1937* (Geneva: International Labour Office, 1937).
Intergovernmental Committee for Refugees, *Proceedings of the Intergovernmental Committee, Evian, July 6th to 15th 1938: Verbatim Record of the Plenary Meetings of the Committee and Resolutions* (July 1938).

1.4. *Newspapers and Periodicals*

Cleveland Plain Dealer
Daily News
Daily Telegraph
Die Zeit
Le Monde
Manchester Guardian
Morning Post
New York Times
Ottawa Citizen
Roul
The Economist
The Times
Washington Post

1.5. *Contemporary Publications*

ADAMS, WALTER, 'The Extent and Nature of the World Refugee Problem', *Annals of the American Academy of Political and Social Science*, 203 (May 1939), 26–36.

—— 'Refugees in Europe', *Annals of the American Academy of Political and Social Science*, 203 (May 1939), 37–44.

Archbishop of Canterbury, *The Assyrian Settlement National Appeal* (London, 1936). Pamphlet.

BARTON, JAMES L., *Story of Near East Relief (1915–1930): An Interpretation* (New York: Macmillan, 1930).

BENTWICH, NORMAN DE MATTOS, *The Refugees from Germany, April 1933 to December 1935* (London: Allen & Unwin, 1936).

Board of Deputies of British Jews and Council of the Anglo-Jewish Association, 'The Jewish Minority in Roumania', unpub. paper (Apr. 1928).

BURNIER, GEORGES, 'Les secours en Syrie', *Revue Internationale de la Croix-Rouge* (Feb. 1926), 94–104.

BURTT, JOSEPH, 'Report on Armenian Refugees in the Near East' (Society of Friends, 1925).

BUXTON, DOROTHY FRANCIS, *The Economics of the Refugee Problem* (London: Focus Publishing, 1939). Pamphlet.

CARR, E. H., *The Twenty Years' Crisis, 1919–1939* (London: Macmillan, 1939).

CECIL, Lord ROBERT, *A Great Experiment: An Autobiography* (London: Jonathan Cape, 1941).

DAVIS, HARRIET EAGER (ed.), *Pioneers in World Order: An American Appraisal of the League of Nations* (New York: Columbia University Press, 1944).

DEAN, VERA MICHELES, 'European Power Politics and the Refugee Problem',

302   BIBLIOGRAPHY

Annals of the American Academy of Political and Social Science, 203 (May 1939), 18–25.

EDDY, CHARLES B., *Greece and the Greek Refugees* (London: Allen & Unwin, 1931).

EMERSON, Sir HERBERT, 'Postwar Problems of Refugees', *Foreign Affairs* (Jan. 1943), 211–20.

ESTORIK, ERIC, 'The Evian Conference and the Intergovernmental Committee', *Annals of the American Academy of Political and Social Science*, 203 (May 1939), 136–42.

—— and ERIKA MANN, 'Private and Governmental Aid of Refugees', *Annals of the American Academy of Political and Social Science*, 203 (May 1939), 142–54.

Friends' Council for International Service, *Report of the Delegation to Bulgaria* (17 Nov. 1925).

GRACEY, Captain G. F., 'The Truth about the Assyrians: Their Appeal to the Conscience and Sympathy of Christendom', *Evangelical Christendom: Organ of the World's Evangelical Alliance (British Organisations)* (Nov.–Dec. 1934), 205–8.

GRATTAN, C. HARTLEY, 'Refugees and an Underdeveloped Economy', *Annals of the American Academy of Political and Social Science*, 203 (May 1939), 177–82.

HANSSON, MICHAEL, *The Refugee Problem* (Granchamp: Annemasse, 1936). Pamphlet.

—— 'The Refugee Problem in the Near East', *Journal of the Royal Central Asian Society* (1937), 397–410.

—— *The Refugee Problem and the League of Nations* (Geneva, 1938). Pamphlet.

—— *Address delivered at the Nobel Institute, Oslo, on the occasion of awarding the Peace Prize of 1938 to the Nansen International Office* (10 Dec. 1938). Pamphlet.

HEIMANN, EDUARD, 'The Refugee Speaks', *Annals of the American Academy of Political and Social Science*, 203 (May 1939), 106–13.

HOLBORN, LOUISE W., 'The Legal Status of Political Refugees, 1920–1938', *American Journal of International Law*, 32 (1938), 680–703.

—— 'The League of Nations and the Refugee Problem', *Annals of the American Academy of Political and Social Science*, 203 (May 1939), 124–35.

INMAN, SAMUEL GUY, 'Refugee Settlement in Latin America', *Annals of the American Academy of Political and Social Science*, 203 (May 1939), 183–93.

Institut de Droit International, *Annuaire* (1936).

JANOWSKY, OSCAR I., and FAGEN, MELVIN M., *International Aspects of German Racial Policies* (New York, 1937).

JASZI, OSCAR, 'Political Refugees', *Annals of the American Academy of Political and Social Science*, 203 (May 1939), 83–93.

JENNINGS, R. YEWDALL, 'Some International Law Aspects of the Refugee Question', *British Yearbook of International Law* (1939), 98–114.

JOHNSON, T. F., *International Tramps: From Chaos to Permanent World Peace* (London: Hutchinson, 1938).

LADAS, STEPHEN P., *The Exchange of Minorities: Bulgaria, Greece, and Turkey* (New York: Macmillan, 1932).

League of Nations Union, *Refugees and the League* (London: League of Nations Union, 1935).

LEWIS, READ, and SCHIBSBY, MARION, 'Status of the Refugee under American Immigration Laws', *Annals of the American Academy of Political and Social Science*, 203 (May 1939), 74–82.

MCDONALD, JAMES G., *Christian Responsibility toward German Refugees* (Jan. 1934). Pamphlet.

—— *Letter of Resignation . . . Addressed to the Secretary-General of the League of Nations. With an Annex* (London, 1935).

—— 'Refugees', in Harriet Eager Davis (ed.), *Pioneers in World Order*, 208–28.

MAUCO, GEORGES, *Les Etrangers en France* (Paris: A. Colim, 1932).

MEARS, ELIOT GRINNEL, *Greece Today: The Aftermath of the Refugee Impact* (Stanford, Calif.: Stanford University Press, 1929).

MILLER, WILLIAM, *The Ottoman Empire and its Successors: 1801–1927* (Cambridge: Cambridge University Press, 1936).

MORGENTHAU, HENRY, *I was Sent to Athens* (New York: Doubleday, Doran, 1929).

—— *An International Drama* (London: Jarrolds, 1930).

MORLEY, FELIX, *The Society of Nations: Its Organization and Constitutional Development* (London: Faber & Faber, 1932).

NANSEN, FRIDTJOF, *The First Crossing of Greenland*, tr. H. M. Gepp (London: Longmans, 1923).

—— *Russia & Peace* (London: Allen & Unwin, 1923).

—— *Adventure and Other Papers* (London: Hogarth Press, 1927).

—— *Episodes from Farthest North* (London, 1927).

—— *Armenia and the Near East* (London: Allen & Unwin, 1928).

—— 'Refugees', *Encyclopaedia Britannica*, 14th edn. (1939).

NOEL-BAKER, PHILIP J., *Disarmament* (London: Hogarth Press, 1926).

—— *The League of Nations at Work* (London: Nisbet, 1926).

OSTROLENK, BERNARD, 'The Economics of an Imprisoned World—A Brief for the Removal of Immigration Restrictions', *Annals of the American Academy of Political and Social Science*, 203 (May 1939), 194–201.

PALENCIA, ISABEL DE, *Smouldering Freedom: The Story of the Spanish Republicans in Exile* (New York: Longmans, 1945).

PEAKE, CYRUS H., 'Refugees in the Far East', *Annals of the American Academy of Political and Social Science*, 203 (May 1939), 55–62.

PHELAN, E. J., *Yes and Albert Thomas* (London: Cresset Press, 1936).

POPPER, DAVID H., 'A Homeland for Refugees', *Annals of the American Academy of Political and Social Science*, 203 (May 1939), 168–76.

'Refugees', *Annals of the American Academy of Political and Social Science*, Special Issue, 203 (May 1939).

REYNOLDS, E. E., *Nansen* (London: Geoffrey Bles., 1932).

ROUCEK, JOSEPH S., 'Minorities: A Basis of the Refugee Problem', *Annals of the American Academy of Political and Social Science*, 203 (May 1939), 1–16.

RUBINSTEIN, J. L., 'The Refugee Problem', *International Affairs* (Summer 1936), 716–34.

SARGENT, BETTY, 'Done up in Mothballs . . .', *Southern California Alumni Review* (Nov. 1941), 14–15.

Save the Children Fund, *Report on Russian, Armenian, German, and Saar Refugees in France* (London: Save the Children Fund, 1935).

SCHAUFUSS, TATIANA, 'The White Russian Refugees', *Annals of the American Academy of Political and Social Science*, 203 (May 1939), 45–54.

SCHLEMMER, RAYMOND, 'Mission en Syrie', *Revue Internationale de la Croix-Rouge* (Jan. 1926), 1–15.

SHOTWELL, JAMES, *War and its Renunciation as an Instrument of Policy in the Pact of Paris, 1929* (New York: Harcourt and Brace, 1929).

SIMPSON, Sir JOHN HOPE, 'The Work of the Greek Refugee Settlement Commission', *International Affairs*, 8 (Nov. 1929).

—— *Refugees: Preliminary Report of a Survey* (London: Royal Institute of International Affairs, 1938).

—— 'The Refugee Problem', *International Affairs*, 17 (Sept.–Oct. 1938), 607–20.

—— *The Refugee Problem: Report of a Survey* (London: Oxford University Press, 1939).

—— *The Refugee Question*, Oxford Pamphlets on World Affairs, no. 13 (Oxford: Clarendon Press, 1939).

—— *Refugees: A Review of the Situation since September 1938* (London: Oxford University Press, 1939).

SORENSEN, J., *The Saga of Fridtjof Nansen* (London: Allen & Unwin, 1932).

STAFFORD, R. S., 'Iraq and the Problem of the Assyrians', *International Affairs*, 13 (Mar. 1934), 159–82.

—— *The Tragedy of the Assyrians* (London: Allen & Unwin, 1935).

TARTAKOWER, ARIEH, and GROSSMAN, KURT R., *The Jewish Refugee* (New York: Institute of Jewish Affairs of the American Jewish Congress and World Jewish Congress, 1944).

TEMPERLY, Major-General A. C., *The Whispering Gallery of Europe* (London: Collins, 1938).

THOMPSON, DOROTHY, *Refugees: Anarchy or Organization?* (New York: Random House, 1938).

TOYNBEE, ARNOLD J., and KIRKWOOD, KENNETH P., *Turkey* (London: Ernest Benn, 1926).

WHITE, F., *Geneva: 1935* (London: League of Nations Union, 1935).

—— *Geneva: 1937* (London: League of Nations Union, 1937).

—— *Geneva: 1938* (London: League of Nations Union, 1938).

WHITEHOUSE, J. HOWARD (ed.), *Nansen: A Book of Homage* (London: Hodder & Stoughton, 1930).

WILLIAMS, Sir JOHN FISCHER, 'Denationalization', *British Yearbook of International Law*, 8 (1927), 45–61.

ZIMMERN, ALFRED, *The League of Nations and the Rule of Law: 1918–1935* (London: Macmillan, 1936).

2. SECONDARY SOURCES

ARENDT, HANNAH, *The Origins of Totalitarianism* (New York: Harcourt, Brace, 1951).

ARMSTRONG, DAVID, *The Rise of the International Organisation* (London: Macmillan, 1982).

AUFRICT, HANS, *Guide to League of Nations Publications, 1920–1947* (New York: Columbia University Press, 1951).

BADEAU, JOHN S., and STEVENS, GEORGIANA G. (eds.), *Bread from Stones: Fifty Years of Technical Assistance* (Englewood Cliffs, NJ: Prentice-Hall, 1966).

BARROS, JAMES, *Betrayal from Within: Joseph Avenol, Secretary-General of the League of Nations, 1933–1940* (New Haven, Conn.: Yale University Press, 1969).

—— *The League of Nations and the Great Powers: The Greek–Bulgarian Incident, 1925* (Oxford: Clarendon Press, 1970).

—— *Office Without Power: Secretary-General Sir Eric Drummond, 1919–1933* (Oxford: Clarendon Press, 1979).

BAUER, YEHUDA, *My Brother's Keeper: A History of the American Jewish Joint Distribution Committee, 1929–1939* (Philadelphia: Jewish Publication Society of America, 1974).

—— *American Jewry and the Holocaust: The American Jewish Joint Distribution Committee, 1939–1945* (Detroit: Wayne State University Press, 1981).

—— *A History of the Holocaust* (New York: Franklin Watts, 1982).

BENDINER, ELMER, *A Time for Angels: The Tragicomic History of the League of Nations* (New York: Alfred A. Knopf, 1975).

BENTWICH, NORMAN, *The Rescue and Achievement of Refugee Scholars: The Story of Displaced Scholars and Scientists, 1933–1952* (The Hague: Martinus Nijhoff, 1953).

—— *They Found Refuge* (London, 1956).

BERNARD, WILLIAM S. (ed.), *American Immigration Policy: A Reappraisal* (New York: Harper & Brothers, 1950).

BLAKENEY, MICHAEL, *Australia and the Jewish Refugees, 1933–1948* (Australia: Croom Helm, 1985).

BRAMWELL, ANNA C. (ed.), *Refugees in the Age of Total War* (London: Unwin Hyman, 1988).

BREITMAN, RICHARD, and KRAUT, ALAN M., *American Refugee Policy and European Jewry, 1933–1945* (Bloomington, Ind.: Indiana University Press, 1987).

BRIGGS, VERNON M., JR., *Immigration Policy and the American Labor Force* (Baltimore: Johns Hopkins University Press, 1984).

BROOK-SHEPHERD, GORDON, *The Storm Petrels: The Flight of the First Soviet Defectors* (New York: Harcourt Brace Jovanovich, 1977).

BULL, HEDLEY, *The Anarchical Society* (London: Macmillan, 1977).

CANTRIL, HADLEY (ed.), *Public Opinion 1935–1946* (Princeton, NJ: Princeton University Press, 1951).

CLAUDE, INIS, *Swords into Plowshares* (New York: Random House, 1984).

CLAY, Sir HENRY, *Lord Norman* (London: Macmillan, 1957).

CLOGG, RICHARD, *A Short History of Modern Greece* (Cambridge: Cambridge University Press, 1979).

COBBAN, ALFRED, *The Nation State and National Self-Determination* (New York: Thomas Y. Crowell, 1969).

CONOT, ROBERT E., *Justice at Nuremberg* (New York: Harper & Row, 1983).

CONQUEST, ROBERT, *The Harvest of Sorrow: Soviet Collectivization and the Terror-Famine* (New York: Oxford University Press, 1986).

—— *The Great Terror: A Reassessment* (New York: Oxford University Press, 1990).

COOPER, ROBERT, *The Economics of Interdependence* (New York: McGraw-Hill, 1968).

COX, ROBERT W., 'The Executive Head: An Essay on Leadership in International Organizations', *International Organization*, 23 (Spring 1969), 205–30.

CRAMPTON, R. J., *A Short History of Modern Bulgaria* (Cambridge: Cambridge University Press, 1987).

CRISP, JEFF, 'The Challenge of Protection', *Refugees*, 46 (Oct. 1987).

CROSS, GARY S., *Immigrant Workers in Industrial France* (Philadelphia: Temple University Press, 1983).

DAWIDOWICZ, LUCY, *The War Against the Jews: 1933–45* (Harmondsworth: Penguin, 1975).

DELLIN, L. A. D. (ed.), *Bulgaria* (New York: Frederick A. Praeger for Mid-European Studies Center of the Free Europe Committee, 1957).

DIRKS, GERALD E., *Canada's Refugee Policy: Indifference or Opportunism?* (Montreal: McGill-Queen's University Press, 1977).

DIVINE, ROBERT A., *American Immigration Policy, 1924–1952* (London: Oxford University Press, 1957).

DONNELLY, JACK, 'International Human Rights: A Regime Analysis', *International Organization*, 40 (Summer 1986), 599–642.

DOWTY, ALAN, *Closed Borders: The Contemporary Assault on Freedom of Movement* (New Haven, Conn.: Yale University Press, 1987).

DUBIN, MARTIN DAVID, 'Transgovernmental Processes in the League of Nations', *International Organization*, 37 (Summer 1983), 469–93.

DUNBAR-ORTIZ, ROXANNE, and HARRELL-BOND, BARBARA E., 'Who Protects the Human Rights of Refugees?' *African Affairs* (1st/2nd Quarters 1987), 105–25.

FEINGOLD, HENRY L., *The Politics of Rescue* (New Brunswick, NJ: Rutgers University Press, 1970).

FELSHTINSKY, YURI, 'The Legal Foundations of the Immigration and Emigration Policy of the USSR, 1917–27', *Soviet Studies*, 34 (July 1982), 327–48.

FERRIS, ELIZABETH G. (ed.), *Refugees and World Politics* (New York: Praeger, 1985).

FLORA, PETER, and HEIDENHEIMER, ARNOLD J. (eds.), *The Development of Welfare States in Europe and America* (New Brunswick, NJ: Transaction Books, 1981).

FORSYTHE, DAVID P., *Humanitarian Politics: The International Committee of the Red Cross* (Baltimore: Johns Hopkins University Press, 1977).
—— *The Internationalization of Human Rights* (Lexington, Mass.: Lexington Books, 1991).

FRENCH, DAVID, 'Spy Fever In Britain, 1900–1915', *The Historical Journal*, 21/2 (1978), 355–70.

GARVEY, JACK I., 'Towards a Reformulation of International Refugee Law', *Harvard International Law Journal*, 26/2 (Spring 1985), 483–500.

GENIZI, HAIM, *American Apathy: The Plight of Christian Refugees from Nazism* (Jerusalem: Bar-Ilan Press, 1983).

GOODWIN-GILL, GUY S., *The Refugee in International Law* (Oxford: Clarendon Press, 1983).

GORDENKER, LEON, *Refugees in International Politics* (New York: Columbia University Press, 1987).

GORMAN, ROBERT F., *Coping with Africa's Refugee Burden: A Time for Solutions* (Dordrecht: Martinus Nijhoff, 1987).

GRAHL-MADSEN, ATLE, *The Status of Refugees in International Law*, i–ii (Leyden: A. W. Sijthoff, 1966, 1972).
—— *Territorial Asylum* (London: Oceana Publications, 1980).
GROTIUS, HUGO, *De jure belli ac pacis libri tres*, tr. Francis W. Kelsey (Oxford: Clarendon Press, 1925).
HAAS, ERNST, 'Is There a Hole in the Whole? Knowledge, Technology, Interdependence, and the Construction of International Regimes', *International Organization*, 29 (Summer 1975), 827–76.
—— 'Words Can Hurt You; or, Who Said What to Whom about Regimes', in Krasner (ed.), *International Regimes*, 23–60.
HAGGARD, STEPHAN, and SIMMONS, BETH A., 'Theories of International Regimes', *International Organization*, 41 (Summer 1987), 491–517.
HARRELL-BOND, BARBARA E., 'Repatriation: Under What Conditions is it the most Desirable Solution for Refugees? An Agenda for Research', *African Studies Review*, 32 (Apr. 1989), 41–69.
HATHAWAY, JAMES C., 'A Reconsideration of the Underlying Premise of Refugee Law', *Harvard International Law Journal*, 31/1 (Winter 1990), 129–83.
—— *The Law of Refugee Status* (Toronto: Butterworths, 1991).
HELLER, MIKHAIL, and NEKRICH, ALEKSANDR, *Utopia in Power: The History of the Soviet Union from 1917 to the Present* (New York: Summit Books, 1986).
HIGHAM, JOHN, *Strangers in the Land: Patterns of American Nativism 1860–1925* (New Brunswick, NJ: Rutgers University Press, 1955).
HIRSCHFELD, GERHARD (ed.), *Exile in Great Britain* (Leamington Spa: Berg Publishers, 1984).
—— 'German Refugee Scholars in Great Britain, 1933–1945', in Bramwell (ed.), *Refugees in the Age of Total War*, 152–63.
HIRSCHON, RENÉE, *Heirs of the Greek Catastrophe: The Social Life of Asia Minor Refugees in Piraeus* (Oxford: Clarendon Press, 1989).
HOCKÉ, JEAN-PIERRE, *Beyond Humanitarianism: The Need for Political Will to Resolve Today's Refugee Problem*, Inaugural Joyce Pearce Memorial Lecture, Oxford University, 29 Oct. 1986 (Oxford: Refugee Studies Programme with the Ockenden Venture, 1986).
HOLBORN, LOUISE W., *The International Refugee Organization, a Specialized Agency of the United Nations: Its History and Work, 1946–1952* (London: Oxford University Press, 1956).
—— *Refugees: A Problem of our Time: The Work of the United Nations High Commissioner for Refugees, 1951–1972* (Metuchen, NJ: Scarecrow Press, 1975).
HØYER, LIV NANSEN, *Nansen: A Family Portrait*, tr. Maurice Michael (London: Longmans, Green, 1957).
HURD, CHARLES, *The Compact History of the American Red Cross* (New York: Hawthorn, 1959).

International Organization, 36 (Spring 1982). Special issue on international regimes.

—— 46 (Winter 1992). Special issue on knowledge, power, and international policy coordination.

JACKSON, GEORGE, and DEVLIN, ROBERT (eds.), *Dictionary of the Russian Revolution* (New York: Greenwood Press, 1989).

JACOBSON, HAROLD KARAN, *The USSR and the UN's Economic and Social Activities* (Notre Dame, Ind.: University of Notre Dame Press, 1967).

JACOBSON, JODI L., *Environmental Refugees: A Yardstick of Habitability*, Worldwatch Paper no. 86 (Nov. 1988).

JOHANSEN, ROBERT C., *The National Interest and the Human Interest: An Analysis of U.S. Foreign Policy* (Princeton, NJ: Princeton University Press, 1980).

JOHNSON, CRYSTAL D., 'Refugee Law Reform in Europe: The Belgian Example', *Columbia Journal of Transnational Law*, 27/3 (1989).

JOHNSTON, G. A., *The International Labour Organisation: Its Work for Social and Economic Progress* (London: Europa Publications, 1970).

JOHNSTON, ROBERT H., *New Mecca, New Babylon: Paris and the Russian Exiles, 1920–1945* (Kingston, Ontario: McGill-Queen's University Press, 1988).

JOYCE, JAMES AVERY, *Red Cross International and the Strategy for Peace* (New York: Oceana Publications, 1959).

—— *Broken Star: The Story of the League of Nations (1919–1939)* (Swansea: C. Davies, 1978).

KEELY, CHARLES, *Global Refugee Policy: The Case for a Development-Oriented Strategy* (New York: The Population Council, 1981).

KEMP, TOM, *The French Economy, 1913–39: The History of a Decline* (London: Longmans, 1972).

KEOHANE, ROBERT O., 'The Demand for International Regimes', in Krasner (ed.), *International Regimes*, 141–172.

—— *After Hegemony: Cooperation and Discord in the World Political Economy* (Princeton, NJ: Princeton University Press, 1984).

—— and NYE, JOSEPH S., *Power and Interdependence: World Politics in Transition* (Boston: Little, Brown, 1977).

—— and NYE, JOSEPH S., JR., 'Two Cheers For Multilateralism', *Foreign Policy*, 60 (Fall 1985), 148–67.

—— —— 'Power and Interdependence Revisited', *International Organization*, 41 (Autumn 1987), 725–53.

KHOURI, FRED J., *The Arab-Israeli Dilemma* (Syracuse, NY: Syracuse University Press, 1976).

KITAGAWA, JOSEPH M. (ed.), *American Refugee Policy: Ethical and Religious Reflections* (New York: Presiding Bishops Fund for World Relief, The Episcopal Church with Winston Press, 1984).

KRASNER, STEPHEN D., 'Structural Causes and Regime Consequences:

Regimes as Intervening Variables', *International Organization*, 36 (Spring 1982), 185–205.

KRASNER, STEPHEN D., (ed.), *International Regimes* (Ithaca, NY: Cornell University Press, 1983).

KULISCHER, EUGENE M., *Europe on the Move* (New York: Columbia University Press, 1948).

KUPER, LEO, *Genocide: Its Political Use in the Twentieth Century* (New Haven, Conn.: Yale University Press, 1982).

LANG, DAVID MARSHALL, *Armenia: Cradle of Civilization* (London: Allen & Unwin, 1970).

LEAVITT, MOSES A., *The JDC Story: Highlights of JDC Activities, 1914–1952* (New York: American Jewish Joint Distribution Committee, 1953).

LEWIS, BERNARD, *The Emergence of Modern Turkey* (London: Oxford University Press, 1968).

LOESCHER, GIL, and SCANLAN, JOHN A., *Calculated Kindness: Refugees and America's Half-Open Door, 1945 to the Present* (New York: Free Press, 1986).

LYTTLETON, ADRIAN, *The Seizure of Power: Fascism in Italy 1919–1929* (Princeton, NJ: Princeton University Press, 1987).

MACARTNEY, C. A., *Hungary: A Short History* (Edinburgh: Edinburgh University Press, 1962).

—— *National States and National Minorities* (New York: Russell and Russell, 1968).

—— and PALMER, A. W., *Independent Eastern Europe* (London: Macmillan, 1962).

MAGA, TIMOTHY P., 'Closing the Door: The French Government and Refugee Policy, 1933–1939', *French Historical Studies*, 12 (Spring 1982), 424–42.

—— *America, France, and the European Refugee Problem, 1933–1947* (New York: Garland, 1985).

MARKWELL, D. J., 'Sir Alfred Zimmern Revisited: Fifty Years On', *Review of International Studies*, 12 (1986), 279–92.

MARRUS, MICHAEL R., *The Unwanted: European Refugees in the Twentieth Century* (New York: Oxford University Press, 1985).

MAWDSLEY, EVAN, *The Russian Civil War* (Boston: Allen & Unwin, 1987).

MENDELSOHN, EZRA, *The Jews of East Central Europe between the World Wars* (Bloomington, Indiana: Indiana University Press, 1983).

MICHAELIS, MEIR, *Mussolini and the Jews: German–Italian Relations and the Jewish Question in Italy 1922–1945* (Oxford: Clarendon Press, 1978).

MÓCSY, ISTVÁN A., *The Effects of World War I—The Uprooted: Hungarian Refugees and Their Impact on Hungary's Domestic Politics, 1918–1921* (New York: Columbia University Press, 1983).

MOORE, BOB, *Refugees from Nazi Germany in the Netherlands 1933–1940* (Dordrecht: Martinus Nijhoff, 1986).

MORGENTHAU, HANS J., *Politics Among Nations: The Struggle for Power and Peace* (New York: Knopf, 1949).

MORSE, ARTHUR D., *While Six Million Died: A Chronicle of American Apathy* (New York: Random House, 1968).

NICHOLS, BRUCE, 'Rubberband Humanitarianism', *Ethics and International Affairs*, 1 (1987), 191–210.

—— and LOESCHER, GIL (eds.) *The Moral Nation: Humanitarianism and U.S. Foreign Policy Today* (Notre Dame, Ind.: University of Notre Dame Press, 1989).

NICOLSON, HAROLD, *Peacemaking 1919* (London: Constable, 1964).

NOEL-BAKER, PHILIP J., *Nansen's Place in History*, Nansen Memorial Lecture, 11 October 1961, Norwegian Academy of Science and Letters (Oslo: Universitetsforlaget, 1962).

NORWOOD, FREDERICK A., *Strangers and Exiles: A History of Religious Refugees*, i–ii (Nashville: Abingdon Press, 1969).

OGATA, SADAKO, 'A Safer World', *Refugees* (Mar. 1991).

OPPENHEIM, L., *International Law: A Treatise*, i–ii (London: Longmans, Green, 1905, 1906).

PEARSON, RAYMOND, *National Minorities in Eastern Europe, 1848–1945* (London: Macmillan, 1983).

PELEG, ILAN, 'The Palestinian Refugees: A Political Perspective', in Ferris (ed.), *Refugees and World Politics*.

PENTZOPOULUS, DIMITRI, *The Balkan Exchange of Minorities and its Impact upon Greece* (Paris: Mouton, 1962).

PROUDFOOT, MALCOLM J., *European Refugees: 1939–52. A Study in Forced Population Movement* (London: Faber & Faber, 1957).

PULZER, P. G. J., *The Rise of Political Anti-Semitism in Germany and Austria* (New York: John Wiley and Sons, 1964).

RAEFF, MARC, *Russia Abroad: A Cultural History of the Russian Emigration, 1919–1939* (New York: Oxford University Press, 1990).

REMEC, PETER PAVEL, *The Position of the Individual in International Law according to Grotius and Vattel* (The Hague: Martinus Nijhoff, 1960).

ROJER, OLGA ELAINE, *Exile in Argentina, 1933–1945: A Historical and Literary Introduction* (New York: Peter Lang, 1989).

ROSE, KENNETH, *The Later Cecils* (London: Weidenfeld and Nicolson, 1975).

ROTHSCHILD, JOSEPH, *East Central Europe between the Two World Wars* (Seattle: University of Washington Press, 1974).

ROVINE, ARTHUR W., *The First Fifty Years: The Secretary-General in World Politics, 1920–1970* (Leyden: A. W. Sijthoff, 1970).

RUGGIE, JOHN GERARD, 'Human Rights and the Future International Community', *Daedalus*, 112/4 (1983), 93–110.

SALOMON, KIM, *Refugees in the Cold War: Toward a New International*

Refugee Regime in the Early Postwar Era (Lund, Sweden: Lund University Press, 1991).

SANDERS, RONALD, *Shores of Refuge: A Hundred Years of Jewish Emigration* (New York: Schocken Books, 1988).

SCHECHTER, MICHAEL, 'Leadership in International Organizations: Systemic, Organizational and Personality Factors', *Review of International Studies*, 13 (1987), 197–221.

—— 'Directors-General of the International Atomic Energy Agency: Locating the Place of Executive Heads in Regime Theory', unpub. paper (1 Apr. 1988).

SCOTT, GEORGE, *The Rise and Fall of the League of Nations* (London: Hutchinson, 1973).

SELINCOURT, AUBREY DE, *Nansen* (London: Oxford University Press, 1957).

SETON-WATSON, HUGH, *Nations and States: An Enquiry into the Origins of Nations and the Politics of Nationalism* (London: Methuen, 1982).

SHACKLETON, EDWARD, *Nansen: The Explorer* (London: H. F. & G. Witherby, 1959).

SHACKNOVE, ANDREW E., 'Who is a Refugee?', *Ethics*, 95 (Jan. 1985), 274–84.

SHERMAN, A. J., *Island Refuge: Britain and Refugees from the Third Reich: 1933–1939* (London: Paul Elek, 1973).

SJÖBERG, TOMMIE, *The Powers and the Persecuted: The Refugee Problem and the Intergovernmental Committee on Refugees (IGCR), 1938–1947* (Lund, Sweden: Lund University Press, 1991).

SKRAN, CLAUDENA M., 'Profiles of the First Two High Commissioners', *Journal of Refugee Studies*, 1 (1988), 277–96.

—— 'The International Refugee Regime: The Historical and Contemporary Context of International Responses to Asylum Problems' in Gil Loescher (ed.), *Refugees and the Asylum Dilemma in the West* (University Park, Penn.: Penn. State University Press, 1992), 8–35.

SLATTER, JOHN (ed.), *From the Other Shore: Russian Political Emigrants in Britain, 1880–1917* (London: Frank Cass, 1984).

SMITH, ROGER K., 'Explaining the Non-Proliferation Regime: Anomalies for Contemporary International Relations Theory', *International Organization*, 41 (Spring 1987), 251–81.

SMYSER, W. R., 'Refugees: A Never-Ending Story', *Foreign Affairs*, 64 (Fall 1985), 154–68.

—— *Refugees: Extended Exile*, The Washington Papers 129 (Washington, DC: Praeger Publishers/Center for Strategic and International Studies, 1987).

SNIDAL, DUNCAN, 'The Limits of Hegemonic Stability Theory', *International Organization*, 39 (Autumn 1985), 579–614.

STEIN, ARTHUR A., 'Coordination and Collaboration: Regimes in an Anarchic World', in Krasner (ed.), *International Regimes*, 115–40.

STEIN, LOUIS, *Beyond Death and Exile: The Spanish Republicans in France, 1939–55* (Cambridge, Mass.: Harvard University Press, 1979).

STEWART, BARBARA MCDONALD, *United States Government Policy on Refugees from Nazism, 1933–1940* (New York: Garland Press, 1982).

STOESSINGER, JOHN G., *The Refugee and the World Community* (Minneapolis: University of Minnesota Press, 1956).

SUHRKE, ASTRI, 'Indochinese Refugees: The Law and Politics of First Asylum', *Annals of the American Academy of Political and Social Science*, 467 (May 1983), 102–15.

TABORI, PAUL, *The Anatomy of Exile* (London: Harrap, 1972).

TEITELBAUM, MICHAEL S., 'Immigration, Refugees, and Foreign Policy', *International Organization*, 38 (Summer 1984), 429–50.

United Nations Library, *The League of Nations in Retrospect: Proceedings of the Symposium* (New York: Walter de Gruyter, 1983).

United States Committee for Refugees, *World Refugee Survey* (Washington, DC: United States Committee for Refugees, 1980–92).

VATTEL, EMER DE, *Le Droit des gens ou principes de la loi naturelle appliqués à la conduite et aux affaires des nations et des souverains* (Geneva: Slatkine Reprints, 1983). Photographic repr. of the 1758 edn.

VERNANT, JACQUES, *The Refugee in the Post-War World* (London: Allen & Unwin, 1953).

VINCENT, R. J., *Human Rights and International Relations* (Cambridge: Cambridge University Press and the Royal Institute of International Affairs, 1986).

WALTERS, F. P., *A History of the League of Nations* (London: Oxford University Press, 1960).

WASSERSTEIN, BERNARD, *Britain and the Jews of Europe 1939–1945* (Oxford: Clarendon Press, 1979).

—— 'The British Government and the German Immigration 1933–1945', in Hirschfeld (ed.), *Exile in Great Britain*.

WEBSTER, DONALD EVERETT, *The Turkey of Atatürk: Social Process in the Turkish Reformation* (Philadelphia: American Academy of Political and Social Science, 1939).

WIDGREN, JONAS, 'International Migration and Regional Stability', *International Affairs*, 66 (Oct. 1990), 749–66.

WIECZYNSKI, JOSEPH L. (ed.), *The Modern Encyclopedia of Russian and Soviet History* (Gulf Breeze, Fla.: Academic International Press, 1978).

WILLIAMS, ROBERT CHADWELL, *Culture in Exile: Russian Emigres in Germany, 1881–1941* (Ithaca, NY: Cornell University Press, 1972).

WISTRICH, ROBERT, *Who's Who in Nazi Germany* (New York: Macmillan, 1982).

WORM-MÜLLER, JACOB S. (ed.), *Fridtjof Nansen Brev*, 5 vols. (Oslo: Universitetsforlaget, 1966).

WYMAN, DAVID S., *Paper Walls: America and the Refugee Crisis, 1938-1941* (New York: Pantheon Books, 1985).

YOUNG, ORAN R., 'Regime Dynamics: The Rise and Fall of International Regimes', in Krasner (ed.), *International Regimes*, 93-114.

—— 'The Politics of International Regime Formation', *International Organization*, 43 (Summer 1989), 349-75.

ZOLBERG, ARISTIDE R., 'The Formation of New States as a Refugee-Generating Process', *Annals*, 467 (May 1983), 24-38.

—— and SUHRKE, ASTRI, and AGUAIO, SERGIO, *Escape from Violence: Conflict and the Refugee Crisis in the Developing World* (New York: Oxford University Press, 1989).

ZUCCOTTI, SUSAN, *The Italians and the Holocaust: Persecution, Rescue, and Survival* (New York: Basic Books, 1987).

INDEX

Academic Assistance Council
(Britain) 200
Ador, Gustave 84, 104, 146, 151
Afghanistan 6
AFL-CIO 219–20
Africa 4, 7, 57, 73, 190, 212, 217, 224,
225, 294
Albania 153, 167
American Legion 220
American Relief Administration 187
American Jewish Congress 253
American Jewish Joint Distribution
Committee (JDC) 202, 253, 254
American Red Cross (ARC) 81, 207,
282
and Greek refugees 81, 160, 282
and Russian refugees 81, 186–8
Americas 26, 73, 200, 225
North 192, 208
South 192, 208, 213, 220, 224
Anglo-American Jewish Communities
202
Angola 217
Anti-Semitism 27, 48, 51, 56–7, 194,
216, 246, 271
Anschluss 49, 52, 206, 207, 221, 246
Arendt, Hannah 27, 29
Argentina 23, 24–5, 27, 191, 192, 217
and Jews 54, 217, 220
Armenia 42, 171
Soviet 45, 171, 173–6, 183
Armenian Benevolent Union 83
Armenian Fund (Lord Mayor's) 82–3
Armenians 19, 123
and Erivan settlement scheme
170–7, 179, 180, 262, 270, 291
genocide of 44–5, 82, 171
and Ottoman Empire/Turkey 41–6,
47, 148, 158, 171
and phil-Armenian PVOs 82, 172,
177–81, 281
and refugee organizations of 83, 134,
171–2, 176, 178, 180, 181, 281
as refugees 4, 9, 14, 28, 43, 44, 45,
47, 60, 72, 82–3, 85, 99, 105, 109,

113, 114, 116, 121, 123–4, 133,
144, 148, 157–8, 167, 168, 170–82,
192, 194, 223, 224, 229, 241, 264,
267, 277, 281
and settlement in Lebanon and
Syria 171, 177–82, 183, 270
Arrangement of 1926: 108, 109
Arrangement of 1928: 108, 124, 133
Arrangement of 1936: 113, 120, 142
Asia Minor 148, 165
Asia 4, 7, 73, 225, 294
Asquith, Herbert Henry 173
Assyrians, as refugees 72, 113, 114,
116, 144, 204, 224
Assyro-Chaldeans, as refugees 72,
114–16, 144
Asylum 6, 68–70, 101, 121, 128, 130,
138, 185, 195, 223, 255, 294–5
Atatürk, Mustafa Kemal 43, 158
Australia 26, 73, 131–2, 190, 194, 274
and immigration 22, 24, 220–1, 278
Austria 26, 31, 78, 189–90, 206
and Germany 52, 133, 206, 207
and Jews 52, 54, 206, 207
and legal protection 114, 120, 144
and refugees 52, 206, 280
Austrians, as refugees 54, 114, 144, 211
Austro-Hungarian Empire 18, 19, 31,
55
Avenol, Joseph 77, 142, 198, 238

Baldwin, Stanley 173–4
Balfour, Arthur James 88, 158
Balkans 41, 47, 168, 241
Baltic States 31
Barbados 217
Bauer, Yehuda 252–3
Bendiner, Elmer 288
Belgium 26, 135–6, 178, 189–90, 208,
213
and League 86, 125, 129–30, 136
and refugee protection 108, 114,
117, 144
and refugees 123, 206, 216, 218–19,
223

Intergovernmental Committee for
Refugees (IGCR) 78, 147,
214–15, 218, 224, 251, 253, 287
and asylum 217, 224, 248
and German refugees 215
and League of Nations 214, 287
and Rublee Plan 214–15, 248, 253
International Near East Association
178
International Committee of the Red
Cross 79, 84, 98, 168, 181, 228
and Bulgarians 165
and Armenians 177, 178, 281
and Russians 90, 92, 97, 187, 280
International refugee regime:
and assistance norm 70–1, 147, 157,
185, 222, 223, 294
and asylum norm 68–70, 101, 121,
138, 185, 223, 294–5
and burden-sharing norm 71, 147,
157, 180, 294
collapse of 85, 271
functions of 102, 138, 142, 143–4,
226, 292
and Great Powers 87–8, 264,
279–81
and humanitarianism 68, 85, 86,
212, 224, 229, 273, 294
impact of 144–5, 182–4, 223–5,
261–70, 271–2, 272–9, 293–6
leadership of 95–100, 207, 279–93
and League of Nations 7, 74–8,
207, 264, 282–7, 296
membership of 73–4
origins of 84–90, 92–100
and PVOs 78–83, 281–2
and refugee participation 83–4, 87,
156, 165, 192, 257
and rules 71–3, 101–2, 104–5,
108–9, 113–16, 122, 124–5,
128–9, 133–8, 144–5, 295–6
scope of 85, 226, 292
and state sovereignty 67, 121, 130,
156, 212, 229, 278–9, 294
theory of 7–9, 65–6, 263–4, 279,
292
and UNHCR 7, 184, 296
International Relief Organization
(IRO) 6, 184
International Christian Committee for
German Refugees 204
International Relief Union (IRU) 98,
99

Iraq 1, 132, 204
Ireland 15, 132, 189–90
Istanbul see Constantinople
Italian–Ethiopian Conflict 73, 143,
209
Italians:
as refugees 4, 14, 15, 55–7, 60, 143
as immigrants 23, 25, 55–6
Italy 26, 42, 56, 57, 158, 208–9
and Armenians 172, 174, 178
and anti-semitism 56–7, 209
and Fascism 55
and France 55, 123
and League of Nations 73, 76, 94,
116, 161, 189–90, 207, 209
and refugees 17, 196, 209, 273
and 1933 Convention 125, 129–30,
136

Jamaica 217
Janowsky, Oscar 234
Japan 34, 76, 207
Jennings, R. Yewdall 102
Jewish Agency for Palestine 82, 203,
245
Jewish Colonization Association
115–87
Jewish Labor Committee 253
Jews see also Holocaust and under
specific countries and Jews 15, 19,
25, 41, 138, 199, 209, 212, 213,
228, 231, 239, 257
and anti-Semitism 27, 48, 51, 56–7,
194, 216, 246
explusions of 28, 133, 137–9, 253
and Germany/Third Reich 48–54,
194–202, 215, 217, 223, 230, 234,
245–8, 250–7, 272
and Nazism 17, 20, 27, 48, 49, 133,
137, 206, 215, 219, 224, 234–5,
250, 252, 253, 254, 272, 277
and private organizations of 82,
139, 187, 198, 202–5, 214, 222,
248, 253, 276, 282
as refugees 4, 6, 9, 14, 17, 28, 33–4,
36, 40, 48–54, 109, 113, 121, 182,
194–202, 202–5, 205–9, 215–24,
232, 234, 246–8, 251–3, 270, 272,
276, 294
and Russian Empire 32–4, 138
and Statelessness 32, 48, 94, 113,
114–15, 200
and Zionism 56, 218, 222